D0088023

FOURTH EDITION

BUSINESS COMMUNICATIONS

With Writing Improvement Exercises

Phyllis Davis Hemphill, M.S.
Rio Hondo College

With
Donald W. McCormick, Ph.D.
Antioch University, Los Angeles

Prentice Hall
Englewood Cliffs, N.J. 07632

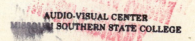

Library of Congress Cataloging-in-Publication Data

Hemphill, Phyllis D. [date]
    Business communications with writing improvement exercises. -- 4th
  ed. / Phyllis Davis Hemphill with Donald W. McCormick.
        p.   cm.
    Includes index.
    ISBN 0-13-092255-2
    1. Commercial correspondence. 2. Business communication.
  3. Business writing. I. McCormick, Donald W.   II. Title.
  HF5721.H46 1991
  651.7'4--dc20
                                                            90-21941
                                                               CIP

Editorial/production supervision and
    interior design: Fred Dahl, Inkwell
Cover design: Mariane Frasco
Prepress buyer: Ilene Levy
Manufacturing buyer: Edward O'Dougherty

 © 1991, 1986, 1981, 1976 by Prentice-Hall, Inc.
A Simon & Schuster Company
Englewood Cliffs, New Jersey 07632

Printed in the United States of America

10 9 8 7 6 5 4 3 2 1

ISBN 0-13-092255-2

Prentice-Hall International (UK) Limited, London
Prentice-Hall of Australia Pty. Limited, Sydney
Prentice-Hall Canada Inc., Toronto
Prentice-Hall Hispanoamericana, S.A., Mexico
Prentice-Hall of India Private Limited, New Delhi
Prentice-Hall of Japan, Inc., Tokyo
Simon & Schuster Asia Pte. Ltd., Singapore
Editora Prentice-Hall do Brasil, Ltda., Rio de Janeiro

To Charles
and
Anita

Contents

v

CHAPTER 8 Sales Letters and Persuasive Requests, 153

CHAPTER 9 Credit Letters and Collection Letters, 179

CHAPTER 10 **Memorandums,** 205

CHAPTER 11 **Oral Communications,** 223

CHAPTER 12 **Employment Guides: Finding a Job;**
Holding a Job; Earning a Promotion;
Changing Jobs, 245

Preface

This book has been used successfully in college classrooms since 1976. It explains basic business communication principles and then gives students practice in applying them. Students are shown how to organize and express ideas in preparing letters, memorandums, reports, proposals and oral communications.

Features of the Fourth Edition:

- New developments in word processing, computers and other electronic media such as fax machines, electronic mail, desktop publishing
- Student guidelines for writing specific types of communications, which become instructor guidelines for grading
- Simple patterns for communications that might be prepared in early years of employment
- Written in readable, understandable and entertaining style with humor and lively anecdotes used when appropriate for illustrating ideas
- Chapter review questions carefully correlated with text
- Valuable tips on finding, keeping and leaving a job; employment resumes, application letters, other employment letters and employment interviews
- More examples of specific types of communication
- More workbook Writing Improvement Exercises which give students immediate opportunity to review and apply what they have learned
- Assignments matching experience level of early college students
- Strong visual impact with more than letters, forms, pictures, drawings, diagrams
- Quick references: "80 Questions Frequently Asked in Employment Interviews," condensed punctuation rules, commonly misspelled words, encouragement in mastering a word processor, desktop publishing vocabulary and an extensive index
- Planned for teaching and self-study

Organization of the Book

Chapter 1 explains the theory of communication and the advantages of studying business communication. Chapters 2, 3 and 4 discuss the three basic qualities used in preparing effective communications: attractive appearance, good will tone and clear and complete message. Then in an easy-to-follow format, the balance of the book applies these three qualities to preparing specific types of communications.

Acknowledgments

I am truly grateful to a number of people for their encouragement, inspiration, information, example communications and special help in completing this and other editions.

Naming individuals, I first thank Pam Wilder, production editor who steered my last three text editions to completion. She was always cheerful, professional and patient. May she have many pleasant years in her new Florida home.

Next, I thank Hal Balmer, still a Prentice Hall stalwart, who initially prodded me to "try" to write the first workbook textbook in college business communication.

Special thanks to my family members for sharing time and expertise in their fields: my husband Charles F. Hemphill, legal matters; sons Robert D. Hemphill, information and communication technology; and Tom Hemphill, special editing.

Finally, I am deeply grateful to those fine Prentice Hall men and women in the field who help improve education by putting up-to-date texts in the hands of teachers and students.

PDH

I would like to thank my wife Anita for her support and feedback. There is nothing quite so helpful for improving one's writing as marrying a teacher of composition and literature.

D W McC

BUSINESS COMMUNICATIONS
With Writing Improvement Exercises

CHAPTER 1
You and Business Communications:
The Communication Theory

Why Study Business Communications?

Basically, there are two reasons for learning to prepare good business communications: (1) to benefit you, the student, and (2) to benefit business and industry.

Benefit to Student

In a *Harvard Business Review* article that has become a classic, Peter Drucker, highly respected business management consultant and educator, asks what is taught in college to help a person in future employment and then gives this answer:

> ...they teach the one thing that is perhaps the most valuable for the future employee to know. But very few students bother to learn it.
>
> This one basic skill is the ability to organize and express ideas in writing and in speaking.... The letter, the report or memorandum, the ten-minute "presentation" to a committee are basic tools of the employee.

Two thousand business executives from all levels of management supported this statement when asked which factors lead to promotion of employees. These people listed ability to communicate as the most important factor, above such other qualities as ambition, drive, education, experience, self-confidence, and good appearance.

Information from many other sources also supports this attitude. For example, a survey of former university business students asked if they had observed people having problems in written communication in their work. The response: 77 percent, "yes"; 14 percent, "no."

Of those answering yes, the following are some of the troubles that were reported:

> Given that the individual knows his business, the difference between a shot at the top job and being buried someplace lower is the ability to communicate that knowledge.
>
> I feel that not enough emphasis is being placed on written communication in our colleges. Although most individuals are able to compose a letter of sorts, they are totally lost, particularly in ability to organize anything of substantial length.

1

I would never wish to sell drive, ambition, and technical expertise short. But, in order to succeed, the ability to communicate properly is more important.

The largest portion [of CPA work] is for record purposes only and is not reviewed or edited for construction, grammar, etc., but only for content . . . . A prerequisite for advancement to higher levels is ability to write properly. Poor writing catches up with one eventually.

My business communication course was one of the most useful of my undergraduate courses.[1]

Benefit to Business

Many industry leaders believe so strongly in the importance of business communication training that their firms offer their own courses or pay employees' tuition for private college classes in the subject. Among such firms are the American Institute of Banking, the American Savings and Loan Institute, Bell & Howell, Control Data Corporation, New York Life Insurance Company, Sears, and General Electric. When such emphasis is given, a student who has already studied college level courses in business communication will have a potential employment advantage over those who have not, and eventually should have a better chance of promotion.

Whenever representatives of business and industry meet with college educators to determine what courses are most needed by students entering the job market, these business leaders overwhelmingly put "need for communication skills" at the top or near the top of their lists of priorities.

Studies show that those at management or executive level spend at least 25 percent of their time on the job writing or dictating and about the same amount of time speaking. It must be acknowledged that the volume of writing must be kept in check so that the paper work does not bury business. Yet at the same time, we must understand why it is often necessary to write letters and other business messages.

A century ago, communication in business was simple because much work was done by hand, and customers were usually personal acquaintances of the craftsman or business person who was selling a product or performing a service. Also, people performed most of their own work and often prepared in their own homes many materials that are commonly bought today. When society and business became more complex, face to face contact between customers and suppliers became more difficult and time consuming. Writing business letters, reports, and memorandums was a natural development. And communicating by telephone eventually became routine in business.

Industrial Age → Information Age

Today's world has developed rapidly from an **Industrial Age** to an **Information Age.** In and out of business, computers obviously help lead this enriching — but jarring — revolution. Not long ago the multimillion dollar Media Center at Massachusetts Institute of Technology was founded on the concept that all communication methods will eventually combine into one extensive field of interrelated computerized media. This shows the trend of the future.

Business letters, memorandums, and reports will join books, newspapers, movies, television, music, telephones and so forth, forming small or giant networks. Networks can connect and interact locally or internationally on signal.

[1]Homer Cox, "The Voices of Experience: The Business Communication Alumnus Reports," *The Journal of Business Communication,* Summer 1976, p. 35ff.

Communication networks focus beyond the individual's desktop. Given the necessary electronic equipment and networking capabilities, workers can send computer data, hold video conferences at their desks, send copies of charts, graphs and pictures, and even transfer funds. Further technological advances are coming.

The vice president of Information Systems of a major corporation recently said that people in the computer industry are convinced the automobile industry has not concentrated on the working efficiency of their machines the way the computer industry has. According to this charge, if those automotive giants had made the same improvements as the computer industry in the last 20 years, we would all be driving cars that cost less than $1000 and getting more than 200 miles per gallon.

What Next?

A major Washington newsletter reports that fiber optic telephone lines with high clarity and reliability are replacing copper wire for sending information all over the world. Satellites will fill in where fiber optics will not go.

More and more, compatibility standards are making it possible for computers to talk to each other. Pocket-size computers with the power of current desktop personal computers will be hooked up to phones, bringing your office with you anywhere you go. Voice activated computers should once again free both hands for driving while still making it possible to communicate from your car. Laptop computers that cost $3000 in 1990 will cost about $600 by the mid-90s.

Business Communication Classes = Prestige Courses

In a business communication journal, Joel Bowman of Western Michigan University stated, "Good language skills are no longer sufficient for success in communication...graduating seniors need to know how to use computers to solve communication problems."[2]

As employers continue to demand that employees write better, business communication classes have become prestige courses on the job market. Completion of college business communication classes is a plus on any employment resumé. If you can write clearly in an organized manner, your work will stand out because of the obvious general lack of such talent. To people upstairs, organized writing means organized thinking. With today's information boom, there is always room at the top for people who can write.

Because of the new easy operation and efficiency of desktop computers and word processors, increasing numbers of people at management and other executive levels are writing, composing, and creating sophisticated communications at their own desktop computers. They made diagrams, charts and electronic spreadsheets—much more than writing simple memos.

Communication Channels

To learn to communicate effectively, it is helpful to understand something about the various communication methods or **channels,** and also the ideas behind the communica-

---

[2]Joel Bowman, "And Not a Shot Was Fired...," *Bulletin of the Association for Business Communication,* December 1987, p. 33.

tion theory. The following channels will be studied: nonverbal, oral, written, combining oral and written, and newer communication methods.

Nonverbal Communication

Nonverbal communication—that is, communication without words—is frequently more effective than any spoken or written message. (The word *verb* originally meant *word;* therefore, *nonverbal* means *without words*.) Nonverbal forms of sending messages include such things as red and green traffic lights, road pictographs directing traffic around the world, police and fire sirens, the telephone ring, and the telephone busy signal. Although no words are used, each provides a clear message.

Another extremely effective means of nonverbal communication is the use of **body language**, which was originally given the scientific name *kinesics*. Body language is used in many forms, such as nodding or shaking the head, raising eyebrows, pointing thumbs down, pointing a finger, raising a fist, winking, smiling, frowning, glaring, kissing, clapping, or shaking hands. In fact, body language can often transmit a stronger message than verbal language. For example, if a man is asked if he likes another man, he might say, "Of course I like him." But if he should at the same time use a "thumbs down" gesture, or make a motion with his forefinger as if to slit his own throat, this would totally contradict the spoken verbal message.

Sign language such as that used for communicating with the deaf is considered a means of verbal communication because, although signs are used, communication is taking place by means of words.

Oral Communication

The chief advantage of **oral** (spoken) **communication** is that it furnishes an opportunity for a speedy and complete exchange of ideas—in other words, immediate feedback. This gives an opportunity to clarify any matters that may be questionable.

The first and highest level communication channel is speaking in person, face to face. This channel rates high because, besides exchanging words, we can see all signs of body language. Also, when we hear another person speak, we can get additional information from noticing vocal cues of tone, loudness, pronunciation, emphasis, grammar usage, and so forth.

Telephoning, the second level communication channel, is not always as completely effective as face to face because of the absence of body language. But the telephone does furnish vocal cues and an opportunity for immediate feedback. Use of the telephone for business communication continues to grow because of the telephone's convenience and its real or imagined economy.

Written Communications

Written or printed communication such as letters, memorandums and reports, are generally considered the third level communication channel. Some of these communications are prepared on paper (hard copy), and others are stored on computer disks or displayed on computer terminals. Although these visual communications lack some advantages of personal oral messages, written ones are frequently preferred.

A business communication is often too important not to be put in writing. Correspondence within a company, contacts between customers and clients, monthly statements, credit and collection matters, and appointment confirmations are just a few examples where records might be needed.

As business grows, it becomes apparent that the chief advantages of having a copy of a communication are these:

1. Saving time and money. In business, saving time *is* saving money. Salaries and wages are often the biggest expense of a business. Going across town to carry a message can be far too expensive because of the time it takes. Telephone calls, although immediate and effective, may interrupt the receiver at the wrong time and may also limit the time when the caller is able to reach the other person.

2. Having a written record. A major advantage of written communications is that the writer and receiver may each have a copy for immediate and future reference. Letters, memorandums, and reports, written properly, can save hours that could be wasted in looking for facts and figures. Attempting to recall all details of a face to face interview or a telephone call often produces incomplete or inaccurate information.

3. Working when convenient to writer and receiver. Another major advantage of written communication is convenience. One writer may be able to handle the bulk of preparing correspondence and reports at a regular time each day. Another might snatch a few minutes periodically throughout the day, thereby leaving time free for other pressing matters. Similarly, the person who receives the message can read it more leisurely at a convenient time.

4. Preventing "Telephone Tag." Written communication also prevents the problem called "**telephone tag.**" In this frustrating game, you call busy Mr. Jones but reach only his answering machine or a secretary. When Mr. Jones returns your call, he gets your answering machine or secretary because you are likewise busy. You get the message and try to contact him, and so on. This back-and-forth game can go on for a long time before you actually reach the person you want.

The chief thrust of this text will be to teach the various types of written communications for these two reasons:

• A high percentage of traditional and electronic communication is done by the written word.

• The need for training in business writing is obvious.

Combining Oral and Written Communication

As noted earlier, some advantages of person to person meetings and telephone calls can be offset by the loss or confusion of actual details. Participants might remember (or forget) different parts of the spoken messages. As we will see later, surveys of all business communications show that a high percentage are unclear and completely misleading.

Therefore, a combination of oral and written message channels, combining the advantages of both, can be extremely effective to help clarify the information exchanged. Notes written before, during and/or after interviews, speeches, conferences, telephone calls, and so on can refresh memories of participants. At times, such notes have even held up as evidence in court.

However, taking and retaining too many unnecessary notes can create a glut of paper garbage in office files. (See Chapter 11, "Oral Communications.")

Newer Communication Channels

Speed and efficiency of **computers** and **word processors** enable more managers and higher executives to compose communications at their desks, freeing secretaries for tasks other than dictation. Even small businesses are benefitting from such use of these machines.

Figure 1.1 illustrates an office similar to offices of many administrators and executives today. The individual's computer would be placed conveniently on a work table at the back or side of the desk.

Computer + Telephone

By combining the electronic power of the computer with the convenience of the telephone, many different channels of communication develop. Here are some comparatively new examples:

- **Electronic mail** sends and receives printed words and pictures through computers connected by phone lines.

- **Electronic chatting** permits live printed conversation between persons operating computers at different locations. When wanted, a hard copy printout can be made.

- **Voice mailboxes** store spoken messages that can be retrieved on another phone by furnishing the right code.

FIGURE 1.1
In Today's Office.

- **Electronic bulletin boards** hold diverse types of messages that can be called up by using a computer, a code, and phone lines. There are electronic bulletin board want ads.
- **Conference telephone calls** connect any number of people at diverse locations.
- **Teleconferences** combine two-way video with sound, allowing widely separated individuals or groups to see and hear each other.

Multiple Mailings by Mail Merge

Applying mail merge is an example of using electronic equipment to save time and money. This method results in easy reproduction of typed documents that are basically similar but contain different specific sections for different readers.

By using mail merge, a main letter is composed that can be sent to many readers. But there are blanks in the main letter where specific information for each reader can be merged into the letter, making it appear that the total letter was composed specifically for that one person. With the word processor or computer properly programmed, the main letter is run off, stopping at each blank to merge individual information, then continuing with the basic document to the next blank where specific information is inserted, and so on.

Savings from using mail merge for business, professional, technical, and scientific mailings are immense. Just think of the legal documents that are being programmed into mail merge systems, saving hours of tedious typing of each original document.

Someone must know how to write or prepare mail merge communications. Also, someone has to know how to update them continually both for changes in facts and for changes in policy of an organization.

Fax Machines

With lowered prices, **fax machines** have become indispensable in traditional and home offices. Over telephone lines they can send and receive letters, memos, reports, graphics, hand-written or scribbled notes and diagrams, photos, etc. A fax machine can reduce materials automatically, store your list of fax numbers, and delay transmission of your message until a more convenient time. If desired, you can have your speech synthesized to greet the fax caller in your voice.

The Communication Theory

Today, scientific researchers are studying the **communication theory** to help us improve our methods of communicating effectively with each other. This research helps us formulate and send messages that are complete and clear—in other words, received with the same meaning that was intended by the sender. Studies show there are innumerable causes of misunderstandings, beginning with the formation of the message in the mind of the sender. Going through various stages where meaning might become unclear, it is recognized that the understanding and effect of a message can even be changed drastically by the mood of the person receiving it.

Input, Message, Channel, Output, Feedback

Figure 1.2 shows the communication cycle. This cycle is the communication theory in action. It shows the ideas of the *sender* being transmitted to the *receiver,* with the receiver's resulting *feedback* or reaction to the message.

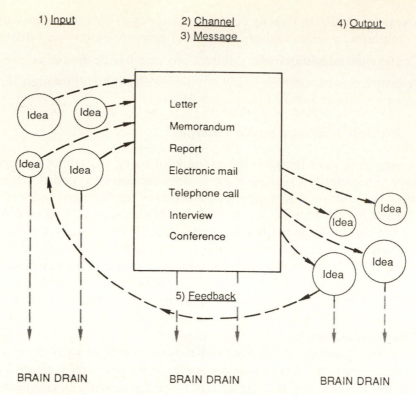

FIGURE 1.2
Communication theory in action, showing ideas being transmitted from sender to receiver.

The communication theory centers on a study of sending and receiving messages. The main steps of the process are as follows:

1. **Input:** information or ideas sender plans to give receiver
2. **Channel:** the selected type of message: letter, memorandum, electronic mail, report, telephone call, conference, etc.
3. **Message:** the actual message that is sent
4. **Output:** information the receiver gets
5. **Feedback:** receiver's response or nonresponse to the message

Figure 1.2 also shows *feedback,* or reception of the message, as the dotted lines going from *output ideas* back to *input ideas.* Improper feedback can occur at any step in the communication process because of messages being sent or received poorly. This lack of understanding is called *entropy* by scientists. However, in this text the term **brain drain** is used for such confusion between sender and receiver. This usage is a new and different application of the term. Vertical arrows labeled "brain drain" are placed to indicate that misunderstandings can occur at any stage: input, selection of channel, preparation of message, output, or feedback.

Obviously, innumerable barriers can block immediate understanding of a message. It pays to write clearly so a message can be understood on the first reading.

"Closing the Loop" of Communication

In communication research, the proper feedback of information from receiver to sender is called **"closing the loop"** of communications.

Following is a simplified example of the communication theory in action, showing *input, message, output,* and *feedback,* closing the loop of communication.

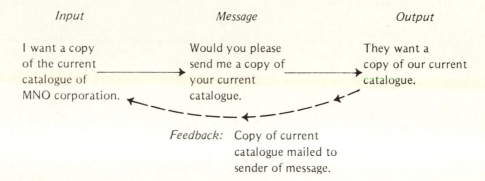

Input	*Message*	*Output*
I want a copy of the current catalogue of MNO corporation.	Would you please send me a copy of your current catalogue.	They want a copy of our current catalogue.

Feedback: Copy of current catalogue mailed to sender of message.

"Brain Drain"

Not all messages are as simple as the foregoing request for a copy of a company catalogue, and "brain drain," a breakdown in the communication cycle, frequently occurs. This breakdown means the communication loop has not been closed properly. Such breakdowns result in all those unclear messages and can be due to one or more of the following:

Improper formulation of the message in the mind of the sender

Improper statement of the information in the message

Improper reception of the information by the receiver

The common occurrence of **brain drain** in all communications indicates an emphatic need for study in the field of planning and preparing better communications.

Communication Barriers that Damage or Destroy the Receiver's Understanding

Even when a message is planned and prepared well, it may not be received and understood properly. Poor understanding might be caused by **barriers** that can exist between the parties sending and receiving.

To help us communicate clearly, we must be aware that such potential problems increase the need for writing clearly and concisely. For examples, here are a few barriers that can block the receiver's understanding:

• Emotional status—pressures of receiver's job and personal life

• Differences in age, cultural background, sex, economic status or education between sender and receiver

• Time pressures on the receiver

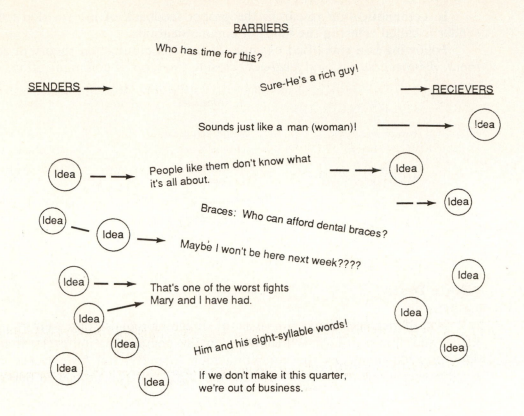

Figure 1.3
Examples of barriers between individuals that might
cause the receiver to misunderstand a message.

Figure 1.3 pictures the process of trying to send a message of various ideas through a maze of potential mental and emotional blocks or barriers. Count the number of ideas being sent and the number of ideas being received.

Uses of Business Communications—External and Internal

Business communications perform many functions both inside and outside an organization. Inside a business, the chief **functions of communications** are these:

To inform management about operations to enable the business to continue successfully

To inform workers of job requirements—those that remain the same and those that change

To improve morale by keeping employees informed of overall business operations and personnel matters

The major uses of communications outside an organization are as follows:

To receive goods and services

To sell goods and services

To make necessary reports to owners/stockholders

To make necessary reports to the government

To create and maintain good will for the business

How you express yourself not only affects your readers' confidence in you, it also affects your ability to influence your readers.

Figure 1.4 is a humorous example of a typical communications **brain drain** that can occur when a new product is developed.

FIGURE 1.4
A communications brain drain.

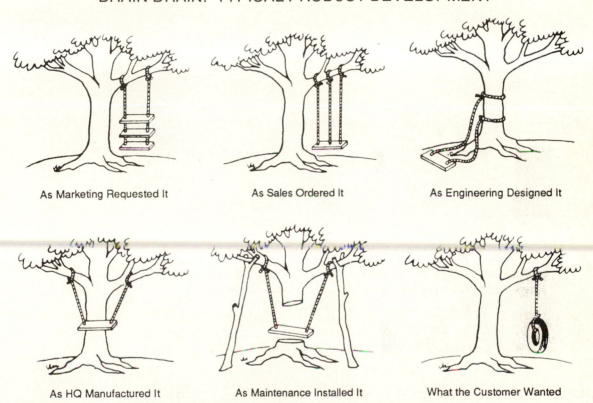

BRAIN DRAIN: TYPICAL PRODUCT DEVELOPMENT

As Marketing Requested It　　　As Sales Ordered It　　　As Engineering Designed It

As HQ Manufactured It　　　As Maintenance Installed It　　　What the Customer Wanted

REVIEW AND DISCUSSION

Chapter 1 *You and Business Communications: The Communication Theory*

In answering the following questions, *keep replies brief.*

1. Name two basic reasons for studying business communications.

   _____

   _____

2. Business management consultant Peter Drucker states that _____

   _____

   is the one thing that is most valuable for an employee to know.

3. The book says that _____ have helped lead the revolution from an industrial age to an information age.

4. Name three different types of communication that can be conducted with similar equipment at the stations of sender and receiver.

   _____

   _____

5. Do people in the computer industry feel that the automobile industry is putting their best efforts into improving the efficiency of their cars?   Yes   No

6. A professor at Western Michigan State University has written that students not only need good language skills but also need to know _____

   _____

   to solve today's communication problems.

7. Give four examples of non-verbal communication. _____

   _____

8. In two words, what is the biggest advantage of oral or spoken communication channels?

   _____

9. Name three advantages of having communications in written form.

   _____

   _____

   _____

Chapter 1   You and Business Communications: The Communication Theory *(Continued)*

10. What are two disadvantages of spoken communication? _____
_____
_____

11. How can we help offset these disadvantages? _____
_____

12. From the text or from other sources name and explain three recently developed channels of communicating electronically. _____
_____
_____
_____
_____

13. Name some conditions that could be barriers to effective communication between individuals. _____
_____

14. What are some uses of business communications within a business? _____
_____
_____
_____

Vocabulary: Give business communication definitions of the following terms:
15. body language _____
16. mail merge _____
17. channel _____
18. feedback _____
19. brain drain _____
20. closing the loop of communication _____
_____

CHAPTER 2
Qualities of a Good Business Communication:
Attractive Appearance

> *The neater the document, the more competent the sender seems to be. Other factors being equal, readers pay closer attention to — take more seriously — the document with the better appearance.[1]*

Are you insulting your readers?

Do you turn people off before your letter even gets started?

Unknowingly, many business people are approving and signing letters that mark themselves and their businesses as outdated. Or, undoubtedly worse, some are insulting their readers by approving letters that are unsightly because of poor preparation, or smudges caused by cheap paper, careless handling, or unsatisfactory correction of typing errors.

When a shoddy, unattractive letter is received, the reader may not bother to pinpoint any reason for an initial negative reaction to the entire letter. But there may be an immediate mental response like this: "Well, if their way of doing business is like their letters, let's find someone else for our business!"

Most of this book covers the *content* of business communications—how to write them. But this one early chapter covers the appearance of written communications because of the recognized importance of this element. Of course, not all information relating to the appearance of letters can be covered completely in one chapter. For greater detail, see an up-to-date secretarial manual.

Much responsibility for the appearance of a good letter should rest in the hands of someone at the management or executive level. Company letterhead, quality of paper, style of type, and other such matters should be studied thoroughly. Secretaries and typists are responsible for the production phase of letter appearance, but the total appearance is important enough for the attention of top-level officials, who should understand the reasons for careful decisions on these matters.

[1]Joel P. Bowman and Debbie A. Renshaw, "Desktop Publishing: Things Gutenberg Never Taught You," *The Journal of Business Communication,* Winter 1989, p. 60.

Stationery

Stationery is one of the first things that the reader of a business letter notices. The three chief matters that must be settled before the decision is made about what type of stationery will be selected for office correspondence are (1) size, (2) quality, and (3) color.

Stationery Size

Most business stationery is the standard 8 1/2-by-11 inches. This size paper fits in standard office file drawers. Even legal offices and courts are changing from the traditional 8 1/2-by-14-inch "legal size" paper to the 8 1/2-by-11-inch size.

Sometimes a special size of paper is used for executive prestige correspondence or for other special mailings. For the sake of appearance, this paper, usually 7 1/2-by-10 1/2 or 6-by-9 inches, may have a high rag-fiber content. However, a disadvantage of the smaller sheets is that they tend to become lost in file drawers built to accommodate standard-size stationery.

Stationery Quality

The most common business **stationery quality** is 16– to 20–pound weight, which is the weight used on most word processing printers.[2] Lighter weight paper usually is not opaque, showing the printing of the sheet underneath. Heavier paper resists wear; therefore, 20–pound bond, even though more expensive, might be preferred to 16–pound. Also, heavier paper gives the reader the impression of quality. On 20–pound continuous fold bond paper, edges are not rough where perforated margins have been torn off. Rough margins are more apt to show on lighter paper.

Paper that has 25 percent **rag content** might be used for more important communications. (Rag content refers to the percentage of cotton fiber contained in the paper—the more rag fiber, the better the quality.) Some better-quality papers may have 50 to 100 percent rag content. To check the cotton fiber amount, hold it up to the light and you will see a watermark showing the percentage of cotton used. Rag paper is selected because it looks and feels attractive, is durable, and resists yellowing.

With today's growing international business activity and the sharply increased rates for foreign mail, many businesses stock a good quality onionskin paper for that mail. Letterheads, second sheets, and envelopes are all stocked in this lighter weight paper.

Stationery Color

While most business letters are written on standard white paper with black print, use of color is a growing tendency. Probably the greatest advantage of using colored stationery is that it reduces glare.

Black ink on white paper gives off a great amount of glare and is therefore hardest on the eyes. Accountants have long used accounting papers in soft yellows and greens. Given the number of hours all office people spend reading various communications, we must give more attention to adopting any practice, such as use of color, that spares eyestrain. Good quality copying machines copy print on light tints as clearly as white.

---

[2]Weight of paper is determined by weighing 500 sheets of the paper, each measuring 17 by 22 inches (four times the size of a standard 8 1/2 by 11-inch sheet). Thus, one 500-page ream of standard 8 1/2 by 11-inch paper weighs one-fourth the amount of paper weight given. For example, one ream of 20-weight bond paper weighs five pounds.

Continuous fold computer paper comes in light gray and blue shades, and additional colors may soon be available. Single sheets of stationery in many acceptable colors can be purchased through stationers and office supply firms. Matching envelopes can also be ordered.

Two other advantages of using tinted stationery are color coding and psychological effect. For some time, color coding various papers has been used for making papers stand out. Having your own letters and reports on stationery of a distinctive color makes them easier to find. And, in effect, you are also color coding your correspondence in other offices.

Colors have a psychological effect. In selecting stationery, you might consider the image a business is trying to project. Many businesses adopt colors that correspond with their logos or trademarks and advertising. A limited amount of color might also be used on the letterhead. Following is a list of some color associations:

Blue	Sincerity, harmony
Green	Life, restfulness, coolness
Buff	Conservatism, dignity
Gray	Confidence, wisdom
Pink	Femininity, daintiness
Yellow	Cheerfulness, vigor
Purple	Tradition, high rank
Brown	Strength, usefulness
Red	Excitement, danger

Care must be taken when using colored paper. Be sure to select tones that reproduce as clearly as white on copying machines.

Multiple Page Letters

The second and any following pages of a letter should be of the same quality paper as the letterhead paper. Otherwise, it may appear that you are putting on a false front by having only the first page of top quality. Pages after the first should be numbered, and many businesses also have the date and the name of the addressee on these subsequent headings. This information should begin on the seventh line (leaving a one-inch top margin), and should be followed by a triple space (two blank lines) before the body of the letter is continued. To save space, this information can be shown horizontally on one line:

Dr. S. I. Yoshiro   2   September 1, 19XX

Methods of Preparing Communications

Automation and computerization speed composing and final typing of all kinds of business writing. As a matter of fact, many **word processing machines** are being replaced by more flexible **microcomputers** with word processing capabilities. Many of these computers are less expensive than many word processors, in addition to having more uses.

Computers can be used solely for their word processing capabilities as sophisticated typewriters. Of course, the microcomputers are stand alone machines, not dependent upon the availability of time on a larger mainframe computer, making them totally independent. With each year, computers are becoming more user oriented; that is, they are becoming simpler to master. At the same time they are becoming competitively priced.

Typing errors can be completely removed from word processing or computer print-outs, with no evidence of the error's having been made. A poorly made correction of a typing error can stand out so badly that it offends any reader. Self-correcting typewriters on today's market have technically advanced methods of removing errors totally and replacing them with corrected copy. There may always be a place for typewriters in offices. But, as one newspaper columnist observed, "... computers do word work infinitely better than typewriters."[3]

Letter Placement

The two most popular forms for **letter placement** on a page today are the standard length line and the picture frame. With the memory capabilities of word processing, letters can be reformatted, even after typing. Any letter placement pattern can be stored in the machine memory for future use.

Standard Length Line Placement

For the **standard length line placement,** side margins for all letters are set for approximately 1 1/4-inch width. The space between date and address can be varied according to the length of the letter, leaving more space for a short letter, less space for a longer one. Space variation can also be made between the closing parts of the letter, such as the complimentary closing, signature lines, and typist's initials.

The standard length line form of placement is generally preferred because it saves time and therefore money. Also, this form has gained popularity because, with increased use of machines for dictation and transcription, the transcriber cannot always estimate in advance the length of a letter, as can be done from dictated notes. The standard length line relieves the typist from having to reset margin stops for each paper typed.

Picture Frame Placement

The **picture frame** pattern of placing a letter on a page has become less popular. In the picture frame form, the letter appears on the page with side margins nearly equal and top and bottom margins nearly equal, framing the letter as if it were a picture. This placement is sometimes used for executive level correspondence, where more time and attention can be given to special appearance.

The following chart is a good rule of thumb for placing letters under the picture frame plan:

Words in Body of Letter	Side Margins
up to 100	2 inches
101–300	1½ inches
over 300	1¼ inches

The inside address of the letter should begin from four to thirteen lines below the date line, with six to eight lines the most common space. Shorter letters will have wider top and bottom margins as well as wider side margins; longer ones will have narrower margins.

[3]Joe Morgenstern, "Be It Ever So Humble, There's Nothing Like an Old Typewriter," *Los Angeles Herald Examiner,* July 24, 1984, p. A3.

Simplified Placement; Memorandum Form

A different pattern is **simplified placement.** For efficiency and brevity, this form follows standard placement but leaves out the salutation and the complimentary closing. Many people like this style. Perhaps the lack of general acceptance, however, is a reaction against omitting the traditional personal touches of salutation and closing.

A natural development is that instead of using the simplified form, some firms use the memorandum form for routine communications not only inside an organization but also for outside mailings. Evidently this form is accepted because of its efficiency and also because of people's familiarity with it for in-house communicating. Also, it has no obvious omission of personal touches. The memorandum form usually has the following headings:

To:	Date
From:	Subject:

Memorandums are studied in more detail in Chapter 10.

Upper Placement

Another letter placement form, **upper placement,** is not yet accepted by many letter-writing purists. This form has the standard length line with the letter written in the upper portion of the page, leaving room for the return message to be typed at the bottom. The upper placement form originally came into use in letters and memorandums between individuals in or branches of the same business.

With routine messages, this placement form can also be used outside a business. If the entire message with reply is needed for the files, a print can be made on a copy machine. Frequently, no copy of this type of message is made, and the answered original is simply returned to the sender, requiring no unnecessary typing and filing. Or, a fax copy of the answered original can be sent.

Letter Styles

In studying business correspondence, we soon learn that every year, one or more new ideas will be adopted that previously would have been considered unthinkable. With office costs spiraling upward, most of today's changes have resulted from an interest in economy. One factor that changes from time to time is letter style. Currently, the two most popular letter styles in American business correspondence are block and modified block.

Block and Modified Block Letters

In the **block letter style,** shown in Figure 2.1, all lines, including those of new paragraphs, start at the left margin. This saves the typist the time of setting the machine for various indentions and reduces the chance of error in doing so.

Computers and most word processors can also make the right margin blocked by justifying the right margin—that is, setting the machine to make all lines space out to finish at the right margin. However, some people object to the streams of space that sometimes flow down through papers because of adding extra spaces to many lines. Detailed research

---

BUSINESS WRITING CONSULTANTS, INC.   **Letterhead**
77 Wilshire Boulevard, Suite 1101
Los Angeles, California 90030
Telephone:
(213) 234-5678

October 15, 19XX   **Date line**

Mr. Peter R. Graham   **Inside address**
6902 Interregional Highway
Austin, Texas 78752

Dear Mr. Graham   **Salutation**

This letter is written in the form that is known as block style. You will notice   **Body of letter**
that all parts of the letter, including date, inside address, salutation, paragraphs,
complimentary closing, and signature lines, begin at the left margin. Also, there
are no punctuation marks such as a colon or comma after the salutation (Dear
Mr. Graham) or after the closing (Sincerely yours).

The block letter style shown here with unpunctuated salutation and closing is one
of the preferred styles of letters because of its efficiency in minimizing the amount
of time it takes for typing.

This example uses picture frame placement; that is, the left and right margins are
approximately equal, and the top and bottom margins are also nearly equal.

Please let me know if you would like any other information on appearance of
business communications.

Sincerely yours   **Complimentary
                                                           closing**

Roger K. Nelson, Ph.D.   **Signature lines**
Writing Consultant

mam   **Reference initials**

FIGURE 2.1
Example of block style letter with no punctuation after salutation and
complimentary closing. Letter also shows picture frame placement.

by a United States government agency shows that such letters are more difficult to read
than letters with the traditional, uneven ragged margins.[4]

[4]*Guidelines for Document Designers,* American Institutes for Research, 1055 Thomas Jefferson Street,
N.W., Washington, D.C.

October 15, 19XX

Mr. Peter R. Graham
6902 Interregional Highway
Austin, Texas 78752

Dear Mr. Graham

This letter is written in the form known as block style. You will notice that all parts of the letter, including date, inside address, salutation, paragraphs, complimentary closing and signature lines, begin at the left margin. Also, there are no punctuation marks such as a colon or comma after the salutation (Dear Mr. Graham) or after the closing (Sincerely yours).

The block letter style shown here with unpunctuated salutation and closing and all parts starting at the left margin is one of the preferred styles of letters because of its efficiency in minimizing the amount of time it takes for typing.

FIGURE 2.2
First two paragraphs of block letter in Figure 2.1 written with right margin justified.

Figure 2.2 shows the first two paragraphs of the letter in Figure 2.1 written with justified right margins. Choice of right margin form is a matter of personal taste, but most people choose not to justify the right margin.

Still the most popular business letter style is the **modified block.** Most parts of this letter (Figure 2.3) begin at the left margin; the paragraphs may or may not be indented five, seven, or ten spaces. The date might be centered at the top, started at the center of the page, or placed so that it ends at the right margin. Then the complimentary closing and signature lines would start vertically in line with the starting position of the date line. Figure 2.3 also shows the proper notation for enclosures. If you have more than one enclosure, the number could be shown as "Enc. (3)" or "Enclosures (3)."

Choice of Letter Styles

Often, a particular letter style is selected for all correspondence of a firm. Such information is circulated by interoffice memorandum or through a correspondence manual that contains materials relating to proper form for preparing company communications.

Personal Business Letter

Figure 2.4 is a good example of a form for a personal/business letter. This form is used for handling your own business or personal affairs when you do not have a letterhead with address information. Your return address and phone number must be shown either above the dateline or below the signature with or without your telephone number. If you do not include this information, people will not know where to contact you. Figure 2.4 is prepared in modified block style with indented paragraphs. (It is completely improper to appropriate your employer's stationery for your own use.)

BUSINESS WRITING CONSULTANTS, INC.
77 Wilshire Boulevard, Suite 1101
Los Angeles, California 90030

                                       Telephone:
                                  (213) 234-5678

Letterhead

                              October 15, 19XX   **Date line**

Mr. Peter R. Graham   **Inside address**
6902 Interregional Highway
Austin, Texas 78752

Dear Mr. Graham   **Salutation**

This letter is written in modified block style with salutation and closing not punctuated. You can see that like the block letter in Figure 2.1, most of the parts of this letter start at the left margin, including the paragraphs. You will notice that the date in this letter begins at the center of the page, as do the complimentary closing and the signature lines.   **Body of letter**

In the modified block letter the date line is sometimes written as this is, beginning at the center of the line, but in this style of letter the date is sometimes centered under the letterhead or typed so that it ends at the righthand margin.

Many people like the appearance of this letter style, as it is felt that having parts of the letter begin on the right side balances the page.

In this style of letter picture frame placement is often used, and the margins of the letter should balance, top to bottom and side to side.

You will notice that the notation "Enc." for "Enclosures" is typed a double space below the typist's intitials. I am enclosing copies of other styles of letters.

                                  Sincerely yours   **Complimentary**
                                                      closing

                                  Roger K. Nelson, Ph.D.   **Signature lines**
                                  Writing Consultant

mam   **Reference**
                                                      initials

Enc.   **Enclosure**
                                                      notation

---

FIGURE 2.3
Example of modified block style letter with no punctuation after salutation and complimentary closing.

483 Sunset Boulevard
Beverly Hills, California 90212
October 15, 19XX

Mr. Peter R. Graham
6902 Interregional Highway
Austin, Texas 78752

Dear Mr. Graham:

     This letter, called the personal business letter, has the return address written above the date line. It is important that you include the return address as part of the heading of this letter, because this information is not shown in a letterhead. This letter form would be proper for use in any business matters that an individual might have.

     In this example the modified block style is followed. There is a colon after the salutation and a comma after the complimentary closing. You might choose to use block style with or without these marks of punctuation. Any such choices would be acceptable.

     Many people prefer indented paragraphs and the inclusion of punctuation marks after the salutation and closing. Therefore, this letter style is used a great deal.

     Picture frame placement is used in this letter, and in all it makes a very attractive communication.

              Cordially yours,

              Roger K. Nelson, Ph.D.
              Management Consultant

mam

Labels (right margin): Return address · Date line · Inside address · Salutation · Body of letter · Complimentary closing · Signature lines · Reference initials

FIGURE 2.4
Personal business letter in modified block style, punctuated after salutation and complimentary closing. Letter shows placement of return address when none is shown on a letterhead. Also, this is an example of picture frame letter placement.

Parts of the Business Letter

     Major and minor parts of a business letter are shown in Figures 2.1, 2.2, 2.3, and 2.4. A blank line should be left between all parts. To help make a short letter fill a page, extra blank lines can be left between the date line and the first line of the address, and an extra blank line can be left between paragraphs. The complimentary close (when used) and signature can also be used as **elevator lines,** that is, extra blank lines can be left between these parts to further balance a page.

The standard order of letter parts is set out here. In this list, minor parts, those parts that may or may not be used, are set out in italics.

1. Letterhead
2. Date (at left margin or centered under letterhead)
3. *Special mailing instructions (in all capital letters)*
4. *File number*
5. *Personal or Confidential*
6. Mailing address
7. *Attention line*
8. *Salutation*
9. *Reference (RE) or subject line (when used)*
10. Body of letter
11. *Complimentary close*
12. Signature
13. *Reference initials*
14. *Enclosures*
15. *Copies*
16. *Postscripts*

The following information about some specific letter parts may be helpful.

Letterhead

Assistance in designing a **letterhead** can be obtained from stationery supply firms, printers, letter writing consultants, and advertising agencies. Many catalogues with letterhead examples are available, and from these an original style can be made. The trend today is toward simple design with a minimum of printing and little contrasting color, although some sales letters are vividly illustrated. Letterheads should show business name, complete address including ZIP code, telephone number including area code, cable address and overseas telephone number where applicable, and fax number.

Some letterheads also show the business trademark or emblem, trade name of products or services, names of officers and/or board members, and date the business started. Figure 2.5 is an illustration of some typical business letterheads.

An innovation in this trend toward simpler letterheads is the use of what might be termed a **letterfoot.** Some businesses place only part of the traditional letterhead data, such as the company name, at the top of the page, placing all other pertinent information across the lower margin of the letterhead page. The bottom of Figure 2.5 shows the letterhead and letterfoot of General Motors Corporation.

Date Line

Unless there is a specific reason for doing otherwise, the **date line** typed on the letter should be the date the letter was dictated, not the date it was transcribed. The receiver of the letter may need to know at what point in communications it was composed.

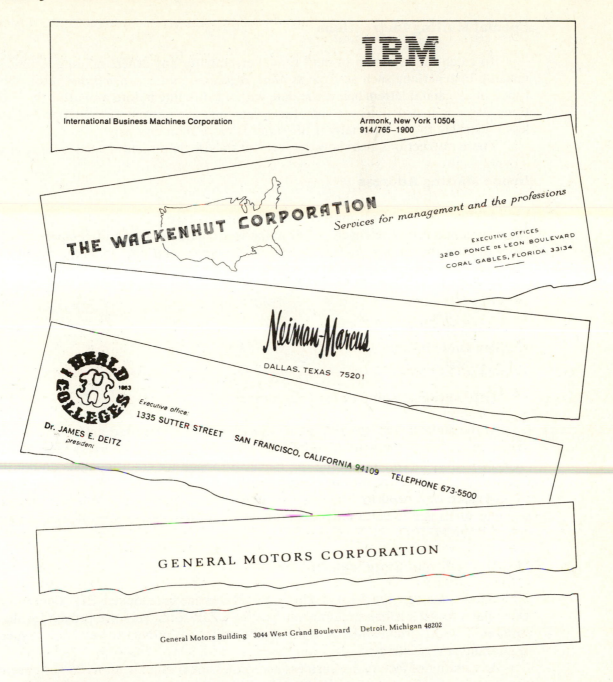

FIGURE 2.5
Examples of letterheads of some of today's businesses. One letterhead with letterfoot is shown.

In block style letters, all lines, including the date line, begin at the left margin. In modified block style letters, the design of the letterhead often determines the placement of the date. In these letters, the date can be centered, it can be started at the center of the line directly aligned with the signature lines, or it an be typed so that it ends at the right margin of the page.

A space of at least three lines should be left between the date and the inside address. As stated, this space can be varied to balance placement, according to the length of the letter, leaving more blank lines for a short letter, fewer blank lines for a longer one.

Special Mailing Instructions

To catch the attention of mail room personnel or any others mailing letters, **special mailing instructions** such as *Express Mail, registered mail, certified mail* etc., should be typed in all capital letters below the date with a blank line before and after these instructions. Mailing instructions are sometimes shown at the bottom of the letter, but they are less noticeable there, especially if the letter is more than one page.

These instructions also show the receiver that the letter had special mailing attention.

Inside Mailing Address

All lines of the **inside mailing address** should start even with the left margin. (The *outside address* is on the envelope.) If a line is exceptionally long in comparison with the other lines of the address, it can be continued on a second line, indented a few spaces:

Mr. Charles Rosselli
Vice President and
      General Manager
Sunshine Markets
Post Office Box 100
City, State 00000

Title Accompanying Name in Address

In the address line, the first name or initials should be used before the surname of the person to whom the letter is addressed, and the appropriate courtesy title, such as *Mr., Miss, Ms., Mrs.,* or *Dr.,* preceding the name. Although we traditionalists do not like the trend, courtesy titles seem to be disappearing.

Because of a need for economy in addressing volume mail, *Occupant* and *Resident* mailings often ignore rules for proper addressing of letters, conforming only to minimal postal requirements.

ZIP Code and State Identification

Some years ago the United States Postal Service introduced **ZIP Codes** and **two-letter state identifications** simultaneously. While ZIP Numbers have proven invaluable in rapid mail sorting, the two-letter state identification has proven somewhat less successful in guaranteeing accuracy.

As a matter of fact, many business and professional organizations do not use the two-letter state identification. Instead, their mail must be addressed with full state name, or the more identifiable standard state abbreviation, such as *Mich., Conn., Ariz., Fla.* Litton Industries and Fluor Corporation are examples of major organizations that follow this policy. Such clearer identification of state names helps assure that mail will be delivered correctly.

The *United States Post Office Domestic Mail Manual* gives three different recommended styles for showing state names in addresses: one with the full state name, one with the standard state abbreviation, and one with the two-letter state identification:

Chicago, Illinois 60652

Bloomington, Ind. 47405

Toledo, OH 43603

Postal employees working in mail sorting areas regularly confirm the wisdom of avoiding the use of two-letter state identification. Optical character reading machines that operate in large cities are designed to read ZIP Code numbers. But humans sort mail by state name, and human error can occur in the rapid handling of the mail. Further, a typist might have made a simple one-letter mistake—for example, changing MI (Michigan) to MO (Missouri), MN (Minnesota), MA (Massachusetts), ME (Maine), MD (Maryland), or MT (Montana).

For heavy mailings, use of the more recent **9-digit (ZIP + 4)** code should be investigated. The post office will furnish printed copies of the pamphlet "New Postal Rates and Fees," which is updated frequently. If rates are discounted enough, this 9-digit ZIP system could save money.

All lines of the address must be checked carefully for absolute accuracy, particularly numbers, the spelling of names, and any words written in a foreign language.

Later chapters will show how word processors and computers can merge different addresses and salutations with copies of the same letter to make multiple copies.

For classroom exercise letters that will not be mailed, **nonsense ZIP Code** numbers of *00000* or *12345* can be used. This prevents looking up each ZIP Code unnecessarily or using incorrect ZIP Codes.

The inside mailing address of the letter and the outside address on the envelope should be identical because the internal copy of the letter will be used for future reference in addressing communications or locating people.

Figure 2.6 is an alphabetical list of states with standard abbreviations and two-letter abbreviations. For speedy, accurate distribution of mail, ZIP Codes must always be used.[5]

Two-letter abbreviations and standard abbreviations
of state names

Alabama	AL	Ala.	Missouri	MO	Mo.
Alaska	AK	. . .	Montana	MT	Mont.
Arizona	AZ	Ariz.	Nebraska	NE	Nebr.
Arkansas	AR	Ark.	Nevada	NV	Nev.
California	CA	Calif.	New Hamp-		
Canal Zone	CZ	C.Z.	shire	NH	N.H.
Colorado	CO	Colo.	New Jersey	NJ	N.J.
Connecticut	CT	Conn.	New Mexico	NM	N. Mex.
Delaware	DE	Del.	New York	NY	N.Y.
District of			North Carolina	NC	N.C.
Columbia	DC	D.C.	North Dakota	ND	N. Dak.
Florida	FL	Fla.	Ohio	OH	. . .
Georgia	GA	Ga.	Oklahoma	OK	Okla.
Guam	GU	. . . .	Oregon	OR	Oreg.
Hawaii	HI	. . .	Pennsylvania	PA	Pa.
Idaho	ID	. . .	Puerto Rico	PR	P.R.
Illinois	IL	Ill.	Rhode Island	RI	R.I.
Indiana	IN	Ind.	South Carolina	SC	S.C.
Iowa	IA	. . .	South Dakota	SD	S. Dak.
Kansas	KS	Kans.	Tennessee	TN	Tenn.
Kentucky	KY	Ky.	Texas	TX	Tex.
Louisiana	LA	La.	Utah	UT	. . .
Maine	ME	. . .	Vermont	VT	Vt.
Maryland	MD	Md.	Virgin Islands	VI	V.I.
Massachu-			Virginia	VA	Va.
setts	MA	Mass.	Washington	WA	Wash.
Michigan	MI	Mich.	West Virginia	WV	W. Va.
Minnesota	MN	Minn.	Wisconsin	WI	Wis.
Mississippi	MS	Miss.	Wyoming	WY	Wyo.

FIGURE 2.6
Alphabetical list of state names with standard abbreviations and two-letter abbreviations.

[5]The first digit of the zip code identifies the general geographic area, consisting of three or more states; the second digit designates a state within that geographic area. The third digit pinpoints a large city or postal area, and the last two digits indicate a specific delivery zone, such as part of a heavily populated city or an entire smaller town.

Salutation

Titles in Salutation.

The invention of the typewriter first brought women into the business office. In 1884, the "Remington Type-Writer" became the first mass-produced machine of its kind. Seven years later, the New York City YWCA trained eight young women as experts on these typewriters. (At this time, people were trained to use two fingers of each hand for all typing. The choice of which keys were struck with which fingers was a matter of personal choice.)

The entry of these eight women—themselves called "typewriters"—seemed revolutionary in the business world. There were dire predictions of the dreadful social consequences of having men and women mingling in offices. Also, there was great fear that the delicate physiques of these gentlewomen could not take the rigors of such work.

But times, scenes and attitudes change. Everyone today knows of the steady increase of women into all levels of business. So what do we do about the traditionally established business letter **salutations** of *Gentlemen* and *Dear Sir?* In general, when addressing a business or another organization, instead of using *Gentlemen,* we are instructed to use *Ladies and Gentlemen.* After all, the letter may be answered by a woman. Better still may be the use of appropriate titles: *Dear Supervisors, Dear Board Members, Dear Department Heads,* and so forth.

When addressing a person whose name is not known to us, instead of *Dear Sir,* we can use the title of the unknown person, such as *Dear Credit Manager, Dear Customer, Dear Subscriber,* and so forth. Checking our own correspondence, we might find *Dear Sir or Madam.* Does that sound awkward?

When a person's name is known, we can use the acceptable title with the surname or use the full name. In salutations, capitalize all titles, names, and nouns.

Dear Ms. Bracken   My dear Mr. Brown   Dear Joseph Brewerton

Punctuation and format of salutation.

A noticeable trend is to have **open punctuation** in letters, that is, no punctuation after the salutation and complimentary closing. If punctuation is used after the salutation, it should be a colon in a business letter or a comma in a friendly letter. The comma can be used in a business letter when the sender and receiver are well acquainted.

To conform with accepted letter styles, if the letter has a colon or a comma after the salutation, it should also have a comma after the complimentary closing at the end of the letter, to make these two parts match. Figures 2.1, 2.2 and 2.3 show letters without punctuation after the salutation and complimentary closing. Figure 2.4 shows punctuation after these two letter parts. As just noted, either form is acceptable, but the trend is away from the unnecessary use of these marks.

Dear Mr. Bracken	or	Dear Mr. Bracken:
Dear Dr. Wright	or	Dear Dr. Wright:
Dear Carol	or	Dear Carol,

There should be at least a double space—in other words, one blank line—between the last line of the address and the salutation. There should also be at least one blank line between the salutation and the body of the letter. The salutation should name the person or persons shown on the first line of the address. If a person's name is used in the address, be sure to use the name in the salutation, since it gives the letter a more personalized touch. If there is an attention line in the address, the salutation should be for the first line of the address, *not for the name or title in the attention line*. In the letter, the attention line would be set out beneath the inside address with a blank line separating it from the address and another blank line before the salutation.

These examples show how the salutation agrees with the first line of the address. The last example shows the proper format for a letter with an attention line.

Mr. Charles Rosselli
Vice-President and
 General Manager
Sunshine Markets
Post Office Box 100
City, State 00000

Dear Mr. Rosselli *or*
Dear Charles Rosselli

Vice-President
Sunshine Markets
Post Office Box 100
City, State 00000

Dear Vice-President

Sunshine Markets
Post Office Box 100
City, State 00000

Ladies and Gentlemen

Sunshine Markets
Post Office Box 100
City, State 00000

Attention: Mr. Charles Rosselli

Ladies and Gentlemen

To conform with Postal Service instructions, the **attention line** on the envelope should be placed in the upper left corner below the return address or below the first line of the address. This will not interfere with the read zone of an optical scanner.

Subject Line or Reference

If there is a **subject line** or **reference,** it is typed a double space below the salutation. This line may start at the left margin, or it may be centered if the letter is a modification of the block style:

Mr. Charles Rosselli
President and
 General Manager
Sunshine Markets
Post Office Box 100
City, State 00000

Dear Mr. Rosselli

Re: Your Invoice #12310

There should also be a blank line between the reference line and the body of the letter.

Body of the Letter

The **body of the letter** is the main section of the letter and contains the message. Most of this text deals with the writing of the body of a letter, memorandum, or report.

Almost all business letters today, even short ones, are typed single spaced with one blank line between paragraphs. If the letter is double spaced, leave an extra blank line between paragraphs. In the modified block style, paragraphs indentions of five, seven, or ten spaces are commonly used.

Complimentary Closing

There should be at least one blank line between the body of the letter and the **complimentary closing.** In the block letter style, the closing begins at the left margin; in the modified block letter, it will usually line up vertically with the date line. Common complimentary closes of business letters today are *Sincerely, Sincerely yours, Very truly yours, Yours very truly, Cordially, Cordially yours.* Notice that only the first letter of the closing is capitalized.

As mentioned earlier, there should be a comma after the complimentary closing if there is a colon or comma after the salutation at the beginning of the letter.

Signature Lines

Leave at least three blank lines between the complimentary closing and the typed **signature** of the sender, making room for the signature, which should always be written in ink. Three lines is generally enough space, but sometimes more space is needed for a particular signature. The position of the sender, such as *President, General Manager,* or *Supervisor,* if included, is typed immediately below the name. If a person's name and title are shown on the letterhead, the title is usually not typed below the signature, since this is unnecessary repetition.

In signing a letter, a person should normally not give himself or herself a title. An exception to this rule is for the person who has a given name suitable for either a man or woman, such as *Cary, Carol, Leslie, Terry, Shawn,* and so forth. In these cases, when desired, it is acceptable to show a title. Also, women frequently indicate which title— *Miss, Ms.,* or *Mrs.*—they prefer. When such a title is shown, it should be typed with the name below the signature rather than having the sender of the letter sign the title with the signature:

Cordially,

Leslie Taylor

Mr. Leslie Taylor

Cordially,

Nancy H Angelo

Ms. Nancy H. Angelo

On legal papers such as business correspondence, checks, and other legal documents, a married woman should not sign her name with her husband's given name, such as *Mrs. Charles F. Stevens,* but should always sign her own given name, such as *Jane M. Stevens,* because this is her legal name. She should do this because there may have been or there may be in the future another person using her husband's name—for instance, another *Mrs. Charles F. Stevens.* To indicate that she wishes return mail addressed to her by her social name (her husband's name) she would have that name typed below her signature or written in parentheses below her signature:

Jane M Stevens　　　　　　　　　*Jane M Stevens*

Mrs. Charles F. Stevens　　　　*(Mrs Charles F. Stevens)*

Reference Initials

Reference initials identifying the person who typed the letter are placed at the left margin a double space below the signature line. These initials often show on internal office copies only and not on outgoing copies.

Enclosure Notation

If an enclosure is being sent with the letter, an **enclosure notation** is placed at the bottom of the letter at the left margin, a double space below the typist's reference initials, to remind the person mailing the letter that one or more enclosures are to be sent. The enclosure notation also reminds the receiver to look for enclosures. If more than one enclosure is being sent, the number can be shown in parentheses after the word *Enclosures* or the abbreviation *Enc.*

Enclosure   *or*   Enc.
Enclosures (3) *or*   Enc. (3)

Copy Distribution

Copy distribution should be shown at the left margin, a double space below all other information. (One "c" stands for "copy" or "copies;" "cc" stands for the old "carbon copy" or "carbon copies." Today few "carbon copies" are made.)

c: James Finley

If you are sending copies to two or more people, list their names alphabetically, unless an executive is listed first.

Copies are often distributed without showing this information on the original outgoing communication. If this is done, the abbreviation *bc* for *blind copy* and the alphabetic list of recipients are typed on internal copies only.

Postscripts

If there is a **postscript,** it should start a double space beneath all other information and can be preceded by the initials *PS* or *PPS* (postscript, second postscript). However, the current trend is to omit these initials. The postscript may be signed or initialed.

A postscript is not necessarily an afterthought. The value of occasionally using one intentionally should not be overlooked. A busy person reading mail will often read the postscript while noticing very little else, knowing that here may be found the most interesting tidbits of the letter. Many business people write postscripts for emphasis rather than as afterthoughts.

Addressing Envelopes

Identification of Sender

In addressing a business envelope, first type the sender's name above the firm's name in the upper left-hand corner. Better still, have a supply of envelopes ready with the name of the individual sender printed or typed above the return address. Figure 2.7 shows the name of the dictator or writer above the return address for possible quick reference.

```
        Carol L. Lindstrom

  BUSINESS WRITING CONSULTANTS, INC.
    77 Wilshire Boulevard, Suite 1101
     Los Angeles, California 90030                                REGISTERED MAIL

  PERSONAL AND CONFIDENTIAL


                              Mr. Jefferson T. Whiteley
                              40 West Eighth Avenue
                              Oshkosh, Wisconsin 54906
```

FIGURE 2.7
Name of individual sender above the firm's return address; preferred
placement of special addressee notations beneath the return address; special
mailing notations beneath the stamp position.

Placing the name of the specific person who sent the letter above the return address is important because a great deal of mail is returned to the sender. Much time is wasted by mail room or other personnel trying to route returned letters to the right people. Records show that one-fifth of the American populace move each year. Also, people die, are transferred, or are simply replaced.

The Outside Address

The **outside address** on the envelope should be in the same form as the inside mailing address of the letter and should contain the same information. If there is an attention line, it should be typed as the second line of the envelope outgoing address. Or it should be placed a triple space below the return address. For machine or manual reading, the Postal Service requests that the **attention line** not be placed below the outgoing address. Figure 2.7 shows how special **addressee notations** such as *Personal, Confidential, Hold for Arrival, Please Forward,* and so forth, should be typed in all capital letters and placed a triple space below the return address.

Figure 2.7 also shows that **special mailing notations** such as **Registered Mail, Certified Mail, Airmail** (for foreign destinations) should be typed in all capital letters below the stamp position.

The post office has special requirements for the machine reading of envelopes: The outgoing address should be placed in the lower 2 1/2 inches of the envelope, at least one-half inch above the bottom, with at least a one-inch margin on the left side. For better appearance, most envelopes are addressed in the lower right quarter section of the envelope. On smaller envelopes, the lines may start one-half inch left of center of the envelope and one-half inch higher than the middle, leaving more room for the address. For better machine reading, there must always be at least one-half inch of blank space between the right edge of the address and the right edge of the envelope.

If a **window envelope** is used, with the address typed on an insert, the insert should be of a size that prevents it from moving beyond the window.

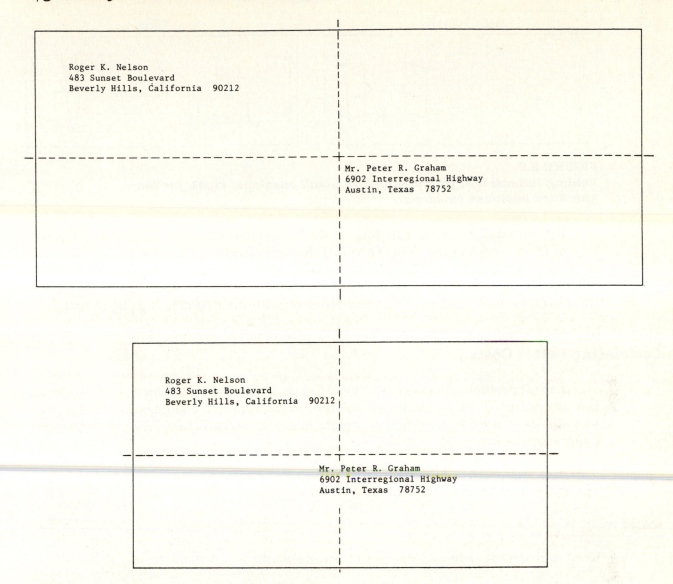

FIGURE 2.8
Large business envelope and small envelope, showing placement style of outgoing and return addresses. The dotted lines have been added to show vertical and horizontal centers of the envelopes. [Reduced in size.]

If you use **pull-out flaps,** put them on the right or postage side of the envelopes so they do not blow open while passing through machines.

Figure 2.8 shows **placement of addresses** on large and small envelopes addressed for personal business usage—that is, when there is no printed return address. Dotted lines have been drawn in to show the vertical and horizontal centers of the envelopes.

Folding Letters

If a letter is prepared carefully, it should not be stuffed randomly into an envelope. Rather, it should be folded to fit neatly inside the size envelope that will carry it. Figure 2.9 shows how to fold standard size stationery into standard size small and business envelopes.

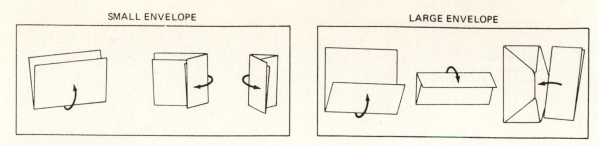

FIGURE 2.9
*Folding letters: left, for the standard small envelope; right, for the
standard business envelope.*

For the small envelope, first fold up the bottom half of the page to within one-half inch of the top edge of the page. Then fold the right-hand third toward the left; fold the left-hand third toward the right. Insert into envelope.

For the large envelope, first fold up the bottom third of the paper. Then fold the top third over the bottom third. Insert into envelope with the first crease going in first.

Estimating Letter Costs

The preparation of letters costs more than most people realize, when you consider all factors involved. With rising costs of salaries, wages, supplies, equipment, buildings, and so forth, an average letter would cost more than $10 today. Figure 2.10 shows how this figure was attained.

Chapter 2 *Writing Improvement Exercise*

Wasted Words

Keep your writing tight and sharp. Don't waste words.

> *We beg to advise you and wish to state*
> *That yours has arrived of recent date.*
> *We have it before us; its contents noted.*
> *Herewith enclosed are the prices we quoted.*
> *Attached you will find, as per your request,*
> *The forms you wanted, and we would suggest,*
> *Regarding the matter and due to the fact*
> *That up to this moment your order we've lacked,*
> *We hope that you will not delay it unduly.*
> *We beg to remain, yours very truly.*

Why do phrases like these in this old rhyme appear in today's business letters? Undoubtedly, someone with little writing or dictating experience, confronted with preparing his or her first business correspondence, looked into the files to see how someone else composed a letter. And there was a letter dictated by someone else who similarly had had no business writing experience and also had checked into old correspondence files... *ad infinitum.*

Make your writing concise—don't waste words!

FIGURE 2.10
Costs of preparing a letter: More than $10. a) fixed charges, such as office space, furniture, and equipment, b) dictating or composing time; c) secretarial time; d) materials; e) nonproductive time; f) filing costs; g) mailing procedures and stamps.

Knowing that a reader's time is valuable, eliminate all unnecessary words in business writing. Concise writing benefits the writer as well as the reader, because the brief, clear message costs less to produce and will probably be read more quickly and acted upon more promptly.

The following list contains stereotyped, outdated, or simply wordy expressions that can be shortened or altogether eliminated to make writing more concise and therefore clearer. Almost all writing can be improved by similar paring down.

Wasted Words

Wordy	Concise
1. a large number of	1. many, several
2. absolutely complete	2. complete
3. period of one week (day, month)	3. one week (day, month)
4. are of the opinion that	4. believe
5. at a distance of 50 feet	5. at 50 feet
6. at a later date	6. later
7. at all times	7. always
8. at an early date	8. soon; at once; immediately
9. attached please find	9. attached is; here is
10. at the present time	10. now
11. beg to remain	11. (omit)
12. circular in shape	12. circular; round
13. consensus of opinion	13. consensus *or* opinion (*consensus* cannot be anything but opinion)
14. costly from a money standpoint	14. costly; expensive
15. costs the sum of	15. costs
16. despite the fact that	16. although
17. due to the fact that	17. since; because
18. during the year of 1980	18. during 1980
19. during the course of	19. during
20. enclosed herewith is	20. enclosed is
21. first of all	21. first
22. for the purpose of	22. to; for
23. for the reason that	23. since; because
24. in a satisfactory manner	24. satisfactorily
25. in addition	25. also; further
26. in order to; in order that	26. so; to
27. in regard to	27. regarding; about
28. in the amount of	28. for
29. in the event that	29. if
30. in the meantime	30. meantime
31. in the near future	31. soon
32. in the normal course of events	32. normally
33. in this day and age	33. now; today
34. in view of the fact that	34. since; because
35. information which we have in our files	35. our information
36. inquired as to	36. asked
37. is at this time	37. is
38. kindly be advised that	38. (omit)
39. long period of time	39. long time
40. made the announcement that	40. announced
41. my personal opinion	41. my opinion (it can't be anything but *personal*)

Wasted Words (continued)

Wordy	Concise
42. not in a position	42. cannot
43. please do not hesitate to write	43. please write
44. pursuant to our agreement	44. as we agreed
45. reached the conclusion	45. concluded
46. seldom ever	46. seldom
47. sign your name	47. sign
48. sometime in the early part of next month	48. early next month
49. the thing is... the thing is	49. (omit)
50. this is to inform you	50. (omit)
51. trusting you will...; trusting this is...	51. (omit)
52. under separate cover	52. separately
53. until such time as	53. when; until
54. we are in the process of	54. we are
55. we ask your kind permission	55. may we
56. we wish to acknowledge	56. we acknowledge
57. we would like to ask	57. please; would you
58. will you be kind enough	58. please
59. you know...you know...	59. (omit)
60. your letter under date of...	60. your letter of

Chapter 2 *Writing Improvement Worksheet*

Wasted Words

Rewrite the following sentences, deleting unnecessary words. (Acceptable answers may vary.)

1. You know, one of our major problems is a low inventory. → _____
   _____

2. As per your suggestion, attached hereto are the samples you requested. → _____
   _____

3. Due to the fact that the supply shortage is past, we will ship your order in the very
   near future. → _____
   _____

4. The computer was installed during the time that our workload was heaviest, for the
   reason that it was the only time that delivery could be made. → _____
   _____
   _____

5. In reply to your letter I wish to state that we are also sending the wall braces. → ____
   _____

6. Could you supply us with details of Order #10017 until such time as the auditors arrive?
   → _____
   _____

7. Our bank is not in a position to furnish that information to the press. → _____
   _____
   _____

8. This is the information we have in our files. → _____
   _____

9. Mr. Frost said that in the event you were absent again, you should complete this form.
   → _____
   _____

Chapter 2   Writing Improvement Worksheet (*Continued*)

10. Could we make up the vacation schedule sometime during the month of April? → ___
_____

_____

11. It is our consensus of opinion that completion of the project will take a period of about one year. → _____

_____

12. The thing is, our opponents had the ball more of the playing time than we did. → ___
_____

13. In the meantime, please be advised that we are in the process of clarifying the supervisor's opinion. → _____

_____

14. Kindly be advised that we seldom ever ask for additional details. → _____

_____

15. Would you be kind enough to fill in the enclosed form and return it immediately. →
_____

_____

16. You should take into consideration rising interest rates. → _____

_____

17. Permit me to take this opportunity to thank you for your help in preparing the new work schedule. → _____

_____

18. The welding process ended being of an unsatisfactory nature. → _____

_____

19. A check for the amount of of $1000 was deposited in your account on the date of January 1. → _____

20. Please be so kind as to furnish us the name of your bank. → _____

_____

REVIEW AND DISCUSSION

Chapter 2 *Qualities of a Good Business Communication: Attractive Appearance*

Please make answers brief.

1. Why is the appearance of a business communication important?
   _____
   _____

2. True or False: The appearance of business communications should be the responsibility solely of the secretarial and word processing staffs. Explain. _____
   _____

3. Name three major factors that must be decided concerning stationery.
   _____

4. What are the advantages of using paper with rag fiber content? _____
   _____
   _____

5. Standard size paper measures ____ by ____ inches.

6. Give three advantages of using tinted stationery. _____
   _____
   _____

7. Name two advantages of using automation and computers in preparing business communications. _____
   _____

8. Describe standard length line letter placement. _____
   _____
   _____

9. Describe picture frame letter placement. _____
   _____
   _____

Chapter 2   Qualities of a Good Business Communication: Attractive Appearance (*Continued*)

10. What is upper placement style? _____

    _____

    _____

11. In a block style letter, all lines begin _____

    _____

12. The most popular business letter style is _____

    _____

13. In a personal business letter, what information should be included at the top or bottom
    of the letter that is not needed on a business letter that has a printed letterhead? ___

    _____

14. The trend today is for (simpler, fancier) letterheads. _____

15. The salutation should be directed to the person or persons on which line of the inside
    address? _____

16. What would be a good salutation for a letter addressed to Second Security Bank?

    _____

17. Should all offices use the two-letter state abbreviations? Why or why not? _____

    _____

18. What would be a good salutation for a letter addressed to Personnel Director, Federal
    Savings and Loan Association? _____

    _____

19. If a letter is addressed to Mr. John J. Sims, Personnel Director, Second Security Bank,
    the salutation should read: _____

    _____

20. A woman whose maiden name was Ann Marie Carter and whose husband's name is
    Peter B. Steele should sign her name (Mrs. Peter B. Steele, Ann C. Steele). _____

    _____

21. How can postscripts be used in letters? _____

    _____

    _____

22. The outside envelope address should be copied from _____

    _____

23. What information should be placed above the firm's return address on an outgoing en-
    velope? _____

Chapter 2   Qualities of a Good Business Communication: Attractive Appearance (*Continued*)

    24. Why should we try to eliminate all unnecessary words in all our business writing?

    _____

    _____

    25. Make this sentence shorter and clearer. I beg to inform you that it is the consensus of opinion of the committee that much of the eyestrain could be eliminated by studying the causes. _____

    _____

CHAPTER 3
Qualities of a Good Business Communication:
Good Will Tone

The **tone** of a message profoundly influences the effect that message will have upon the person to whom you are speaking or writing. When you write, it is essential that you keep in mind the person or people who will be reading what you have to say. The written message should in no way offend its audience. Rather, it should have a good will tone that creates a favorable impression.

Remember: *Your letter is you and whomever you represent.*

There is an Oriental expression, "between the leaves," which is a somewhat poetic way of expressing our **"between the lines"**—the unwritten or unspoken message that comes across in communications. Broadly, this might be considered the tone of the communication.

The sender of a message—spoken or written—might think that snide remarks slipped "between the lines" will scarcely be noticed. But actually, such comments usually jump out and are exaggerated in the mind of the listener or reader, damaging the effect of the total message.

Most businesses do not have to place a price tag on the value of their good will, but a business stays in business because it creates and maintains good will. To do this, its people hold current customers, bring back old customers, and bring in new ones. Business **good will** is defined as the value of the business in excess of its tangible assets.

For instance, if you were offered $250,000 for your small business and the tangible assets of that business amounted to only $200,000, you would be getting paid $50,000 for your business' good will. This good will would come from your relations with customers, high reputation, location, new approach(es) to old problems, and so on.

Good will tone, then, is the overall unspoken courteous message that comes across in a communication that promotes friendly relations with customers and suppliers.

Also, any business has an investment in the training and experience of its employees. It is advantageous to consciously apply the theories of good will in communications circulated within a company—its memorandums, reports, and various other announcements to employees.

Creating a Good Will Tone

Identify Reader; Write at Reader's Level

Before starting to write, identify the person or persons to whom you are writing so that you can set the right tone. One of the best ways to create a good will tone is to pretend you are sitting across the desk from a person to whom you are writing. Create a mental image of the reader; try to imagine what you would say and how you would say it. Try to imagine what the other person's reaction would be if you were speaking in person. Then let your letter have a tone of writing to that one person, not to a crowd.

For instance, you might consider the following aspects of the reader or readers:

Background on the subject

Education

Relationship to you or your organization

Depth of information desired

Personality traits

Pompous writing by an ego-inflated person usually repels the reader. But the writer should beware of the other end of the scale—becoming too humble.

The business writer should avoid writing either up to a reader or down, attempting instead to reach the reader at a neutral level. Writing naturally can help direct business writing to the proper level for the reader.

In order to find the neutral level of writing that should be used, try to employ **empathy.** That is, as the Indians say, you should try to "walk in the moccasins" of the other person, saying, "How would I feel if I were the person receiving this message?"

Frequently, business or technical writing must be adapted to the understanding of a lay person. Usually, long words and difficult terms should be replaced by shorter, more common usages. If a difficult term must be used, it should be explained in understandable language.

Of course, if a letter is intended for a highly educated, professional person, it might be written at a higher level than that written for the very young or for the person of limited education. But keep in mind that even a pompous person rarely cares to receive pompous communications. A worker who receives a condescending memo might become resentful, thinking, "What do they think I am—stupid?" And the work might suffer. Business writing that is obviously written down to such groups as youths and housewives is apt to miss its target or offend its audience. Today's general market is better educated, accustomed to more serious thinking, and more sophisticated than was the market of past generations. Consumer protection movements are undoubtedly part of a people's rebellion against being underrated.

For many reasons, the best level of most business communications is a straightforward, eyeball to eyeball exchange of ideas.

Figure 3.1 is a summary of recommended tones for neutral, upward, and downward communications.

Use Good Grammar

Use of poor grammar gives others a negative impression. Nonstandard or inaccurate English marks a person as uneducated or careless. On the other hand, use of standard

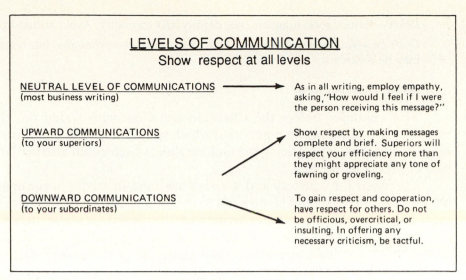

FIGURE 3.1
Summary of recommended attitudes for various levels
of writing.

English makes a good impression, giving people confidence in you. Also, good grammar helps make what you say and write clearer, so people need not unscramble a message that might be clouded through the use of poor English.

Next: Set Good Will Tone

Here are the chief ways of setting a **good will tone:**

Write naturally.

Write courteously.

Be sincere.

Use a positive mental attitude.

Write from the "you viewpoint."

Write at the reader's level—not up or down.

Watch word connotations.

Be careful with humor and sarcasm.

Hold your temper.

Close in a good will tone.

Write Naturally

A. R. Russon, author, lecturer, and business communications professor, says that before you can effectively write business communications, you must be in the proper frame of mind. Dr. Russon gives the following advice on how this can be achieved by writing naturally:

Let your reader understand that you are the sort of person who would be liked and trusted.

Talk—don't write. Let your reader hear the voice of a considerate person.

Relax—reflect good manners, not dignity and formality. Avoid stilted expressions.

Don't be afraid to use I and me. Don't overuse these pronouns, but constantly avoiding them may be awkward.

Write Courteously

Five centuries before the Christian era, Confucius stated the **Golden Rule** in this manner: "Do not do unto others that which you do not wish done to yourself." **Courtesy,** or good manners, is practicing the Golden Rule, which could also be defined as "consideration of others before self."

The need for courtesy and a courteous tone in business communications seems so obvious that there should be no need to mention it. But studies of actual business communications show that many letter writers need to give this matter more thought.

In seeking the proper tone, writers must avoid making accusations, asking awkward questions, or casting aspersions on the character of the reader. Here are some negative examples that would surely arouse an undesired response in the reader:

You neglected to . . .

Why haven't you given us all the necessary details?

You should have realized what you were doing.

What's wrong with your outfit, anyway?

You claim . . .

Each of these expressions could be restated more courteously or could be eliminated altogether. The *Writing Improvement Exercise* at the end of this chapter gives practice in changing some discourteous statements to more courteous forms.

Be Ethical

You are practicing good **ethics** when you are conscientiously honest, combining honesty with a sincere desire to meet the needs of others.

To be ethical, try to maintain that attitude of sitting across from the reader face to face. It is difficult for a conscientiously honest person to look someone in the eye and be dishonest or insincere. Phoniness usually comes through between the lines of a communication more clearly than much of the specific written message. When you have judged that the message is suitable to the people involved and the purpose that prompts it, and that you are being honest, then you can proceed with a straightforward letter, memorandum, or other communication.

In the extremes, if you are unethical you may find yourself in trouble with the law along with the person or people who ordered you to be dishonest. Words to live by can be taken from this old rhyme:

I have to live with myself and so
I want to be fit for myself to know. . . .

Emphasize the Positive

BE POSITIVE!
This is a must in business correspondence, as it is in business. Psychologists tell us that the person who works with a **positive attitude** will probably get results that match this attitude.

This positive approach is shown in the letters a person writes. A conscious, continuing effort must be made to achieve a good attitude, but once this is practiced, it can become routine. You should avoid reference to any potentially negative situation, trying instead to better the situation by providing information about what can be done to remedy it.

To write with a positive attitude, choose a positive statement over the negative one, avoiding, if at all possible, any negative reference. The following positive and negative words are helpful to keep in mind:

Negative (People Don't Like)	*Positive* (People Like)
neglect	please
sorry	thank you
anxious	welcome
fear	happy
mistake	enjoy
you claim	like
damage	appreciate
late	pleasure
rotten	you're right
overdue	generous
unhappy	free
wrong	praise
died, death	agree
negligent	benefit
disagreement	commendable
unpleasant	courtesy
unwelcome	cheerful
difficult	satisfactory

Practice in changing negative statements to positive ones with the same basic message is given in the *Writing Improvement Exercise* at the end of Chapter 7.

Write from the "You Viewpoint"

Letter writers will profit from noticing how frequently the words, *you, your,* and *yours* are used in headlines of today's advertisements. Advertisers have learned that they benefit from talking directly to individuals, bringing them immediately into the picture. Here are some headlines from current ads:

Hanging basket—Holds your favorite fruit, flowers, potted plant, or what-have-you.

Nothing can convey your feelings better than a colorful scarf—the proper adornment for your casual or dressy outfit.

Your new Honda Accord will get you there.

Gives you twice as much of the best-known pain reliever.

Now—yours at truly great savings—any 4 stereo tapes for only $5.99.

Dry Yogurt Nuggets—Carry a Packet in Your Purse or Pocket.

Writers can adopt this "**you viewpoint**" in their correspondence, giving letters the personal touch. In business letters, we do this by phrasing our communications, when possible, in terms of the advantage to the reader and his or her interests. This is more advantageous than phrasing them in terms of the writer's interests. You get the reader's attention and you hold it by playing up to those matters that concern that reader. The business person who does not keep customer and client interests uppermost in mind will find bumps in the road to success.

Practice in changing letters from the writer's viewpoint—"we viewpoint"—to the "you viewpoint" is given in the *Writing Improvement Exercise* at the end of Chapter 8.

Watch Your Word Connotations

Not only must we be sure we use words that give the correct specific meaning we desire, we must also be careful of word associations, or word **connotations.** This means that we must be concerned with various associations and unspoken meanings particular words might bring to another person's mind.

Euphemisms are sometimes employed to avoid unpleasant word connotations. A euphemism is the substitution of an acceptable word or term for a blunt expression that may be objectionable. An example of a euphemism is given in the story of the young executive who drove up in a new car and parked next to his rather mature secretary. She complimented him, "I like the color of your car, Mr. Hempstead—bottle green," "Thank you," he beamed, "uh—but the dealer calls it 'British racing green.'"

Study the meanings of the following terms and consider the advantage of using the second form of each:

Original *(Possibly Negative)*	*Euphemism* *(Positive Connotation)*
complaint department	customer service department
down payment	initial investment
pilferage	shrinkage
janitor	custodian
cheap	economical
poor	disadvantaged
affair	alternate life style
died	passed away
bossed	managed; supervised
stupid, ignorant	unsophisticated
dean of student affairs	dean of students
waiter/waitress	server
funeral	services
you're lying	your memory is playing tricks on you; aren't you going past the truth?
room deodorant	air freshener
cubes of jello	jeweled dessert

Although appropriate use of euphemisms is advisable, this trend can lead to obscure writing that repels people. These terms can also be confusing. Consider another young man who was an assistant city administrator and accustomed to the gobbledygook of many government offices. Having been asked to find the names of some garbage collectors, he attacked the Yellow Pages of the local telephone directory. First he looked under *refuse collectors*—negative; then *sanitary engineers*—negative; *trash collectors*—negative. Finally, he found the desired listings—under *garbage collectors*.

Here is an example of an exaggerated euphemism. The late U.S. Senator Everett Dirksen, known for his mellifluous tones and his mastery of the language, was once asked to define a euphemism. "Well," he answered, "*you* might say that your father was hanged. *I* would say that he died at a large public gathering when the platform collapsed."

Be Careful with Humor and Sarcasm

Humor, when used acceptably, can be a very effective tool in any communicating process. But heavy humor, which becomes **sarcasm,** can be hazardous, and should be used only under limited circumstances between people well acquainted with each other.

The story is told that George Bernard Shaw sent tickets for his latest play to an old friend, Winston Churchill, with the note:

Here are two tickets to the opening of my new play—one for you, and one for a friend—if any.

Churchill returned the tickets with this note:

Sorry, am unable to attend opening night. Please send me tickets for second performance—if any.

Use of the appropriate light touch in even routine correspondence is often recommended. Business people state that they will shuffle through a stack of letters and reports and give immediate attention to something written by a person who has a reputation for adding a little humor to everyday business matters. They claim they welcome such a break in routine because it is so unusual.

It often challenges a writer's imagination to find a way to use humor appropriately. But this light touch has a reciprocal advantage—it also gives the writer a lift.

Hold Your Temper

"Cool down before you crack down" is the advice professionals give to letter writers.

Occasionally, almost anyone feels prompted to write a letter really "telling off" somebody. Perhaps it is a supplier who frequently misreads an order, or a purchasing agent who regularly fails to include all the information for filling an order. Or it may be someone with a frequently overdue account.

No matter what the justification may seem to be, there is rarely, if ever, a time when losing your **temper** is justified. These are the reasons why:

Point one   Time often quenches or diminishes anger.

Point two   When we think more calmly about it, we realize that we really don't want to have anyone know us at our worst.

Point three Old matters can come back to haunt us, and someone whose opinion does not seem to matter at one time may be in a different position at some later date.

Point four   If threats are made, which might be done when a person is angered, there might be cause for legal action.

Point five   Passionately unloading your anger on another person is rarely the best way to get the response you want from that person.

Point six   Temper flareups can damage your health.

If you are angry and all the will power you possess cannot stifle the luxury of blowing off, go ahead and write the letter. Then—destroy it immediately!

In business and in personal life, a flare of temper is an extravagance you cannot afford. The great hazard of temper explosions is that they can become a pattern, and the symptoms may get worse each time. The phrase, "Cool down before you crack down!" might be changed to: "Cool down before you CRACK UP!"

Some people believe that loudly expressing anger toward others is good because it "gets it off your chest" and makes you feel calmer afterwards. However, psychological research has shown that people who lose their temper and express it are angrier after a period of time than people who do not express anger.

The basis of showing good will in writing business communications is to present ourselves and our business at our very best.

Close with a Positive Statement

We are constantly cautioned to make our letters as brief as possible. But you can always add the extra word or sentence to close with a positive statement. For instance, saying "thank you" doesn't cost anything, but it can pay high dividends.

Prompt Answers

How do you feel when you do not receive an answer to a letter within a reasonable time? There is that nagging conviction that you and your concerns are not important to the person who should be replying to your letter. Similarly, it is advantageous to you and your business to keep matters as current as possible.

Recognizing this, many firms establish a rule that letters must be answered within a given short period, sometimes 24 or 48 hours. To outsiders, immediate attention to correspondence is sometimes seen as a picture of the competence of an entire business enterprise.

Sometimes there may be an understandable reason for delaying an answer. If so, it frequently pays to send a brief note explaining the delay, such as:

Thank you for your inquiry regarding specifications of our new rotary widget engine. Our engineering department is preparing a paper containing detailed information, accompanied by diagrams, and we will send you a copy as soon as it is available.

Or, when the person to whom a business letter is addressed is out of town for an extended period of time:

Mr. Baker is on vacation, but I am sure he will be able to give you full details when he returns next week.

Knowledge of Company Policy

Frequently questions come up concerning procedures to be followed to maintain a company's good will with customers, such as printed materials to be circulated free of charge, or the type of adjustments to be made on returned merchandise. Most firms have established policies relating to questionable situations, but borderline cases must sometimes be handled. For questions on procedures, you should be well acquainted with established **company policy** and should get proper authorization for any variance from it. Your job could depend on this knowledge.

Resale in Business Letters

Resale in business letters is anything that reinforces a customer's decision to do business with you and encourages them to continue to do so. One type of resale is to reassure the customer of the wisdom of having made a purchase: "I am sure you will get several seasons' wear from your new suede jacket," or "Your new Bennox air conditioning unit should bring you many summers of unbelievable comfort."

Resale can also be used at any time by including promotional materials on items other than the specific ones purchased. Or, you might add information about other materials or services available through your firm: "You would probably also like to drop in and look over our new selection of suede slacks and skirts."

Names

You know that you are particular about the correct spelling and pronunciation of your **name.** If your name is misspelled, you may even wonder if a letter is actually intended for you. Everyone, foreign or American, feels the same about the treatment of his or her name. Because we are usually not familiar with the spelling and markings of **foreign names,** it is easy for us to make errors. Therefore, we must be especially careful to check spelling, capitalization, and markings of each foreign name every time we use it.

For some time, businesses that operate internationally have learned to investigate foreign interpretations of coined names and slogans. Until it was changed, the Flemish translation of General Motors' "Body by Fisher" was "Corpse by Fisher." Then, there seemed to be no explanation for the fact that the Chevrolet Nova did not sell in Puerto Rico. Translated literally, *no va* in Spanish means "doesn't go," or, "It doesn't run." When the car was renamed "Caribe" for that market, it sold well.

Good Will = Courtesy = Good Manners

An article in *The Royal Bank Letter* in Canada summarizes a discussion of **courtesy,** which is the basis of good will, as follows:

> Courtesy is the lubricant that eases the friction arising from differences among human beings.... Concern about people is what courtesy is all about ... if there is courtesy, manners will look after themselves.[1]

Chapter 3 *Writing Improvement Exercise*

Discourteous → Courteous

"Your manners are always under examination, and by committees little suspected, awarding or denying you very high prizes when you least think of it." This is a quotation from Ralph Waldo Emerson, nineteenth-century American writer and philosopher.

Carrying on Emerson's philosophy, in both personal and business contacts, courtesy is the basis of smooth relationships. The good will tone comes through if the writer or speaker is courteous and respectful in dealing with others. Use empathy, that is, say, "How would I feel if someone else wrote (or said) this to me?" That is a good test of good will tone.

A few generations ago, most business was conducted on a face to face basis, frequently between friends. Under these circumstances, pleasant relationships were naturally the general rule of business conduct. However, as business and industry have grown and the need of doing business with others has increased, it has become necessary to conduct much of today's business by other means of communication—by telephone, which is two-way but sometimes not as effective as face to face communications, and through letters and reports, which can be less effective one-way communications.

When methods of communication become less personal, it becomes easier to overlook courtesies that would be routine if people were meeting in person. A written discourteous tone is often exaggerated in the mind of the receiver. Further, we know that a message can convey a discourteous tone even when that tone is unintentional.

It is important that a business letter contain no statement that might be interpreted as discourteous, because in today's business there is always someone else eager to take over an account that is being lost because of a writer's bad manners. Similarly, poor spoken communications can be costly. There is always time for courtesy.

To improve the tone of communications, you should avoid writing or saying anything that could be interpreted as the following:

Accusations: "You claim," "you neglected," "you must think," etc.

Negative overtones—negative connotations

Anger

Ultimatums: "Do this or else...."

Unflattering or insulting implications

---

[1]"The State of Courtesy," *The Royal Bank Letter,* Royal Bank of Canada, March/April 1981.

Following are a few examples of discourteous statements that have been restated in more acceptable forms. Perhaps you have other suggestions for improving them.

1. You'll have to wait. I have a call on the other line. → Please excuse me; I'll be right back. I have to answer another call.

2. You neglected to tell us the time your plane arrives. → Could you tell us when your plane arrives?

3. We expected you to read the instructions before assembling Model #1009. → Enclosed is a copy of instructions for assembling Model #1009.

4. Here is the repair kit for your waterbed. We hope it comes in handy. → Here is the repair kit for your waterbed—which you probably will not need.

5. The employees therefore request that you give us a 10 percent hourly increase in wages *or nothing.* → We therefore ask that you give us a 10 percent hourly increase in wages.

6. We cannot grant you credit until you complete the enclosed forms. → We should be able to grant you credit as soon as you complete the enclosed forms.

Chapter 3 *Writing Improvement Worksheet*

Discourteous → Courteous

Rewrite the following statements, making them more courteous. Answers, of course, will vary. (Use your imagination).

1. Your letter did not state clearly what your problem is. → _____

_____

_____

2. We are surprised that you expect a refund when you did not fill in the necessary form. → _____

_____

3. Although you claim that the order was mailed three weeks ago, we have not yet received it. → _____

_____

_____

4. Now that you are getting older, we would like to help you make plans for retirement.

→ _____

_____

5. Why didn't you enclose your check with your order and get the 5 percent discount? → _____

_____

_____

6. Bank employees must limit personal telephone calls to five minutes. → _____

_____

_____

7. Although you didn't attend the meeting, it doesn't matter. The rest of us had a good time. → _____

_____

_____

Chapter 3   Writing Improvement Worksheet (*Continued*)

8. Why don't you study the directions folder that we furnished with the sink disposer unit? → _____

   _____

   _____

9. Your assumption that defective merchandise was shipped to you is entirely wrong, and we are surprised that a man in your position would not realize that damage might have occurred in shipment. → _____

   _____

   _____

10. In the case of a new business with as little capital behind it as yours, we can do business only by cash or c.o.d. orders. → _____

    _____

    _____

11. Does your insurance protect you from the potential loss caused by a devastating fire? →

    _____

    _____

12. We hope you won't find any lawn fertilizer better than ours. → _____

    _____

    _____

13. We trust this lease is not filled with unclear legal phrases. → _____

    _____

    _____

14. Avoid the fear of spending your later years with inadequate income. → _____

    _____

    _____

15. I hope I have not called at a bad time. → _____

    _____

    _____

REVIEW AND DISCUSSION

Chapter 3 *Qualities of a Good Business Communication: Good Will Tone*

Make your answers to the following questions as brief as possible.

1. Define *good will* as used in a business sense. _____

_____

_____

2. Name three advantages of using good grammar. _____

_____

_____

3. Give at least five ways of setting a proper good will tone in business communications.

_____

_____

_____

4. How can we put the "you viewpoint" into our letters? _____

_____

5. What is "word connotation"? _____

_____

6. Name three words or terms not listed in the book that have negative connotations to
you. _____

_____

7. Name three words or terms not listed in the book that have positive connotations to
you. _____

_____

8. Define *euphemism* and give an example not shown in the book. _____

_____

_____

_____

Chapter 3   Qualities of a Good Business Communication: Good Will Tone (*Continued*)

9. Tell when humor might be used appropriately in business communications. _____

_____

_____

_____

10. True or False: A flareup of temper is frequently a good manner of treating a difficult business or personal situation. _____

11. Give three reasons for "cooling off before cracking down." _____

_____

_____

_____

12. Name two advantages of answering correspondence promptly. _____

_____

_____

_____

13. What is "company policy"? _____

_____

14. Define "resale in business letters," and tell how it is used. _____

_____

_____

_____

15. Why is it important to spell names correctly? _____

_____

_____

16. Is your name ever misspelled? ____ If so, how? _____

_____

17. Give your personal definition of *courtesy*. _____

_____

_____

18. It does not matter if you offend your readers in your business communications as long as what you say is true. True or False? _____

19. We can be excused for being rude when we are in a hurry. True or False? _____

Rewrite the following sentences in a more courteous tone:

Chapter 3   Qualities of a Good Business Communication: Good Will Tone (*Continued*)

20. You should have kept the instructions booklet that came with the printer. → _____
_____

_____

21. Sometimes you lie when you are tryng to convince us. → _____

_____

22. You failed to tell us which paint color you chose. → _____

_____

23. What are you birds up to? → _____

_____

24. We will take care of your problem when your number comes up on our list. → _____
_____

_____

25. We can't expect people with your background to understand these matters. → _____
_____

_____

CHAPTER 4
Qualities of a Good Business Communication:
Clear and Complete Message—The Letter as a Whole

> The first thing necessary in writing letters of business is extreme clearness...every paragraph should be so clear and unambiguous, that the dullest fellow in the world may not be able to mistake it, nor obliged to read it twice in order to understand it.
>
> Lord Chesterfield, English diplomat and writer, in Letters to His Son, classic eighteenth-century literature

Once, a young lady—we'll call her Ann—decided to accept her sister's invitation to spend a vacation in California. Although Ann had written her sister planning to say when her train would get in, there was no one to meet her when she arrived. After waiting a few minutes, she called her sister's home. "Ann," she heard, "I'm so glad you called. I'll be right down. I have your letter, and I know you meant to say when you would arrive. But you didn't. I'll bring the letter to show you."

Do business letters always clearly contain the planned message? Or do some of them leave the reader "waiting at the station," wondering what, if any, message was intended?

Some time ago, a survey produced the startling fact that a full one-fourth of all business letters were so unclear that the reader could not understand them. Further, the findings showed that 15 percent of the letters studied were written to clarify previously written unclear letters. Approximately 10 percent were so tactless or unclear that they got no answer at all or brought complaints. According to numerous studies of today's business letters, if these percentages have changed since that report, they have only worsened.

Evidently, unclear writing is common in fields other than business. The former dean of the School of Law of Columbia University once said of law students, "Even the most tolerant of critics will concede that whatever be the arts of which the students are bachelors, writing is not one of them."

Drs. Lois and Selma DeBakey spent years teaching scientific communication to doctors. They said their goal was to help eliminate "Pompous, confusing, vague, monotonous, and ambiguous medicalese" in medical journals and conversations of physicians. Further, recent entrants into the arena of unclear writing seem to be the writers of many computer manuals, prompting a *Time* magazine writer to conclude, "But for now, at least, many consumers are likely to continue to find [computer] operating booklets more frustrating than enlightening. Indeed, some may feel like twisting the famous bromide 'If all else fails, consult the manual' into a new admonition: 'No matter what happens, do not look at the manual!' "[1]

In the effort to write letters that bring about the desired feedback, a major concern must be the elimination of brain drain, so that each letter contains the message intended. Letters must be written clearly and concisely, inviting easy reading. Such letter writing will eliminate the need for any follow-up letters or conversations to clarify the meaning. Clear letters, further, will help end the confusion that results from misunderstanding instructions.

Classifying The Letter

Most letters that a person contemplates writing can be classified under one of four categories:

The nonletter: no letter to be written
The "A" letter: routine information letter or the "yes" letter
The "B" letter: "no" letter
The "C" letter: sales letter or the persuasive request

George Eliot (pseudonym of Mary Ann Evans), nineteenth century English novelist, once wrote, "Blessed is the man who having nothing to say, abstains from giving us wordy evidence of the fact."

Including a **nonletter** category in a book on business communications may seem questionable. However, businesses and industries are struggling to reduce today's avalanches of unnecessary paperwork. An unwarranted amount of money goes for time spent preparing, composing, typing, and filing such correspondence. Storage costs also become unreasonable. Further, as the volume of mail we send continually increases, problems for the mail services naturally increase. Business and industry need to eliminate any unnecessary correspondence.

A Denver architect stated that members of his firm never write letters. "When I have a question, I pick up a phone or hop in a car and drive over to speak to the person I want to contact. Face to face we clear up everything right on the spot."

This of course, is an idyllic situation, but a rare one. Limits of time and travel usually do not permit this type of communication.

As illustrated in Figure 2.10 (page 35), preparing a letter is more costly than most people realize. **Costs** entail not only stationery and postage, but also a considerable expenditure of time for both the originator and the secretary or typist, plus other general office expenses. Estimates place the cost of preparing the average business letter at more than $10. With current rates for toll and long-distance calls, a telephone call frequently costs less.

However, written communications are basic in business. Communication by mail and fax is a multibillion-dollar business, which grows even while we know the growth should be curbed.

Harold Koontz, authority on business management, reports that most of a manager's day may be spent communicating—reading, writing, speaking, and listening. "Under these circumstances," Koontz says, "unnecessary messages are clearly costly."[2]

---

[1]John Greenwald, "How Does This #%@! Thing Work?" *Time,* June 18, 1984, p. 64.
[2]Harold Koontz, *Essentials of Management,* 2nd ed. (New York: McGraw-Hill, 1978), p. 405.

Establishing a category of nonletters emphasizes the fact that there are letters you don't have to write and shouldn't. There is, of course, another category of letters you don't have to write, *but should.* These include various types of courtesy letters that are advantageous to others and ourselves. Courtesy letters are discussed more fully in Chapter 14.

The "A" Letter—The Routine Information Letter or the "Yes" Letter

The **"A" letter,** the **routine information** letter, is sometimes called the **"yes" letter.** It is a letter or memorandum that asks for or gives routine information or **good news.** Of the "A," "B," and "C" letters, this first one, the routine information letter, is the easiest to write. Fortunately, most business communications fall into this category. The chief caution here is to follow notes to be sure that all necessary information is included.

Figure 4.1 is a pattern for the "A" letter. As shown in the pattern, the main message is stated at the beginning of the letter, and any additional information simply follows in order of importance. The "lift" at the end is usually a pleasant sign-off, looking to the future. Chapter 6 covers this type of letter in more detail.

The "B" Letter—The "No" or Bad News Letter

The "B" letter is the **"no" letter,** which carries a disappointing or **bad news message,** such as a refusal. As noted previously, business letters should carry the good will of the sender. Therefore, it takes more care to plan a negative letter, in the hope that it will be accepted by the reader without offense.

FIGURE 4.1
Pattern for the "A" letter, the routine information letter, sometimes called the "yes" letter.

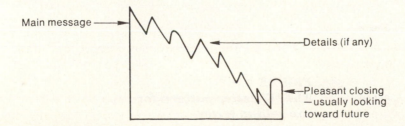

Main message →

Details (if any)

Pleasant closing
—usually looking
toward future

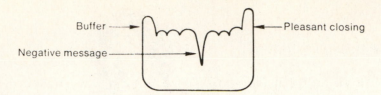

FIGURE 4.2
The "B" letter pattern for the "no" message or the
bad news letter.

Generally, the best plan for this letter, is to (1) start with an idea with which the reader will agree in order to put the reader in a frame of mind to accept the negative message; (2) give the negative message quickly and clearly; and (3) end on a pleasant tone. This letter is diagrammed in Figure 4.2. Chapter 7 is a study of writing these more difficult letters.

The "C" Letter—The Sales Letter or the Persuasive Request

Much business revolves around the effective writing of the "C" letter, the sales letter or the persuasive request. The sales-type letter is not always designed to sell a product or service. Sometimes it is planned more as a persuasive request, to sell or promote an idea. Even the job application letter with a resumé can be considered a type of sales letter, since it is written to "sell" the applicant to a potential employer.

The "C" letter might be diagrammed as pictured in Figure 4.3. The star at the top of the diagram represents the attention getter of the sales letter. To get the attention of the reader, it is generally necessary to have some distinguishing feature at the beginning of the message to prevent this letter from becoming lost among the rest of the incoming mail or being filed in the circular file (trash can).

Under the star, the circles resting on each other represent the ideas planned to build up the reader's interest in doing what the letter asks and also to build up the desire to follow through.

The last feature of this outline is a hook—like a fishhook—planned to grab the reader and move him or her to the desired action. Chapter 8 is a study of sales letters, and Chapters 12 and 13 cover employment guides and employment letters.

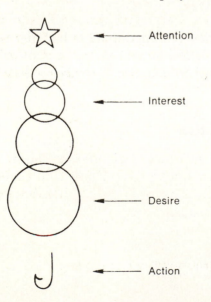

FIGURE 4.3
The "C" letter pattern for
the selling letter.

Planning the Letter

Make Notes or Outline

To write clearly, you must organize your thoughts logically. An old slogan states, "Disorganized, illogical writing reflects a disorganized, illogical mind." Undoubtedly, one of the problems of letter writing is that too much preparation is done from mental **notes.** Even those who are practiced in dictation find that their communications benefit from written notes or **outlines.**

If you are writing in reply to another letter, you must read thoroughly the letter you are answering. Underline each statement that requires a comment, whether the comment is specifically requested or the request is merely implied. Then, in the margin of the letter, between the lines or on a note pad, you can list each underlined item and number it in the order it will be covered in your letter.

If you are not writing in reply to another letter, simply make a brief list of all information to be included. Usually, all that is needed is a word or phrase to remind you of each topic. A memo pad, possibly of a distinctive color, used solely for the purpose of outlining letters, will prove invaluable. The next step is to identify by number the order in which each item could logically be covered. Notes or an outline might include such notations as the following:

2. How will prefab cabin be shipped?

3. Delivery when?

1. $ estimate

How often have you said, "I know what it is. I just don't know how to explain it"? Go back and think it over. If you can't explain something, you simply do not understand it well yourself.

So it is in letter writing, and this is the "input" stage of planning a communication. When you have all the information necessary, you yourself must understand exactly what you want to say. Then the ideas begin to fall into place easily and quickly. Each time you write from an outline or list, it becomes easier. Soon, well planned, clear, and concise letters become almost automatic. The letter should make itself.

That is the best type of writing—when it sounds so simple that it seems to have written itself. Study your favorite author and see how uncomplicated truly good writing is. What is clearly understood by the writer is more readily transmitted to the reader.

Figure 4.4 is an example of a bank letter with the notations alongside that tell what is to be covered in the answer letter.

Arrange Ideas in Logical Order

In a recent survey, graduates of business communications courses at Southern Illinois University said that **"arrangement of ideas"** came first as the training most needed to improve the writing of people they work with. Various types of writing training were given the following order of importance:

1. Arrangement of ideas

2. Practice in solving problems and explaining the solutions in writing

3. Sentence construction

THE THIRD NATIONAL BANK OF BANKTOWN
BANKTOWN, MINNESOTA 12345
(612) 654-3210

October 30, 19XX

The First National Bank of Weston
Weston, Minnesota 00000

Gentlemen:

We shall appreciate it if you could tell us of the financial responsibility, the credit standing, and the management characteristics of:

Phoenix Auto Supply
301 Main Street
Weston, Minnesota 00000

based on your dealings with this company.

This inquiry is made to enable us to get information to help us furnish banking services to this company, and should not be construed as being in any way unfavorable to this company.

Please consider this request as confidential, and you are assured that any information you may furnish to us will be treated in a similar manner.

We appreciate your cooperation and will of course be willing to be of similar service to you at any time.

Sincerely,

Juan Perez
Vice President

1. **Glad to furnish info.**
2. **Financial**
3. **Credit**
4. **Mgmt.**
5. **Confidentiality**
6. **Reciprocate**

FIGURE 4.4
Bank letter simulation showing underlining of items to be covered in reply and numbered notations in margin for assistance in dictating.

4. Selection of ideas

5. Spelling

6. Grammar

7. Punctuation

Other: Conciseness, practice in dictating, handwriting, reducing arguments to writing

Figure 4.5 illustrates this information.

1.	Arrangement of ideas
2.	Practice in solving problems; explaining solutions in writing
3.	Sentence construction
4.	Selection of ideas
5.	Spelling
6.	Grammar
7.	Punctuation
8. etc.	Conciseness, practice in dictating, handwriting, reducing arguments to writing, basic organization, exact expression

FIGURE 4.5
Chart showing that arrangement of ideas has top priority of factors most needed to improve writing, according to Southern Illinois University survey of business people all over the United States. [Source: Homer Cox, "The Voices of Experience." The Journal of Business Communication, Summer 1976, p. 35ff.]

Make Message Clear

In identifying problems in today's business correspondence, business writing consultants agree that vague or murky messages lead to many costly consequences. One type of costly consequence is that an unclear letter can require the writing of still another letter to clarify the first two letters. And obviously, there are countless hazardous consequences of those letters that are misunderstood.

When we write a letter or report, we sometimes like to picture the person who receives it as saying, "Well! Here is that letter (or paper) from Smith. Don't disturb me with any phone calls, messages, or callers. I want to read this without interruptions." Actually, there may be many matters calling for the attention of the person to whom you are writing. As your letter is being read, there may be business or personal interruptions, as well as a waiting stack of correspondence that sometimes overflows onto a table.

When we think about the attention that our written material receives, we might keep in mind the picture of the man in Figure 4.6 who is going through his daily mail.

Writing the Letter

Check Information for Accuracy

Gather all your information, then, before you start to write or dictate, check all that information for **accuracy.**

Occasionally, checking for accuracy can take more time than writing. When all facts are in, you may even find no need for the communication. If something you want to say is

FIGURE 4.6
Going through the daily mail.
[Source: "Do They Really Read
Your Letters?" (Hartford,
Conn.: Connecticut Mutual Life
Insurance Co.), p. 18.]

doubtful, do not report it; or report it as being doubtful and explain why you have some question. Otherwise, any matter you recount then or in different circumstances might be suspect to others. Making sure your information is honest and correct helps give validity to the rest of what you say and do. Suspicion can damage your reputation in many ways.

One author who conducts grammar and writing seminars for editors regularly emphasizes the need for accuracy. He leaves his audiences with this quote: "Suspect everything. If your mother tells you she loves you, check it out."

Speak Directly to the Reader

In business, you should try to write as if you are sitting across from the other person **speaking directly** to that person. If you are writing to more than one person, pretend you are speaking to just one of them. This one-to-one communication process is a strong force to help make your writing clear. The executive director of the Association for Business Communication, Robert Gieselman, says, "In the triangle in which the three bases are the reader, the writer, and the text, we contend that in business communications the **reader** is the most important of the three."[3]

Words, Sentences and Paragraphs

Words

In general, short words are easier to understand than long ones. Top government officials frequently try to institute drives to make government writing more clear—to eliminate **gobbledygook.** According to the dictionary, *gobbledygook* is talk or writing, especially of officialdom, that is pompous, involved, and full of jargon and long words. Following are examples of gobbledygook rewritten to improve clarity.

[3]Therese R. Welter, "Overwhelmed by Info?" *Industry Week,* November 2, 1987, p. 30.

Gobbledygook	*Improved*
As a general rule, and certainly not applicable in all situations, the briefing memoranda forwarded to the secretary have been loaded with an excessive amount of verbiage.	Most of the briefing memoranda forwarded to the secretary have been too wordy.
The airplane engine experienced high temperature distress.	The airplane engine overheated.
It is envisioned that this sort of writing will not require more than a page and a half to two pages at the most.	No more than two pages should be required.
Loose aggregate could be ingested into the engine.	Gravel could be drawn into the engine.
Due to metabolic inability to cope with a recent shift change, I did not respond to external stimuli, thereby remaining in a comatose condition.	I overslept.
motorized attendance modules	school buses
interior intrusion detection systems	burglar alarms
acoustical attenuation for ball activity area	soundproofing of the gym

Another example of the need for clear writing is that jargonistic, long-winded writing frequently keeps business and professional people from reading technical and professional papers they should read.

Because business and professional writing by its nature must often use technical and specific terms, you should increase your vocabulary in order to use these terms when necessary. But you should discipline yourself to use long words only when necessary, when they cannot be replaced by shorter ones.

Vocabulary Improvement

A dictionary. Instructors who succeed in getting students to buy a good desk-size **dictionary** as a supplemental text regularly receive reports of the continuing advantage such a volume is to the students and their families.

Owning a good, reliable, current dictionary is extremely helpful to students in any field. Educated people constantly improve their vocabularies and knowledge by reading the dictionary and checking it for meaning, pronunciation and spelling of unfamiliar words. The advice "Never use a long word when a short one will do," is valid. But an enlarged vocabulary enables a person to use clearer, more specific language in both speaking and writing. Any business, professional, or technical field has its own vocabulary, and learning new terms quickly is a job asset.

Also, authorities claim that 50 percent of any college course is learning the vocabulary of that course. When you learn the new terms, you have the major grasp of the subject.

A thesaurus. A **thesaurus** is a reference book containing word synonyms and antonyms, and using one will broaden your vocabulary. A thesaurus gives you a wide choice of words with similar meanings so you can select the best word for your purpose.

References to a thesaurus also provides all writers with new words and phrases to substitute for overused ones, as well as giving more specific terms for a given meaning. Probably the best and most popular book of this kind is *Roget's International Thesaurus,* published by Thomas Y. Crowell Company, New York. People typing on lapboard computers on planes are seen using a pocket-size thesaurus, a handy jewel. Students may prefer a small paperback thesaurus, but any office should have a hardback copy.

Other helps. Since you are studying business, a good business dictionary can prove very helpful. The author's recent review of current business dictionaries showed that these two are probably the most understandable and authoritative: *Webster's New World Dictionary of Business Terms,* (Simon & Schuster, New York), and *Dictionary of Business and Management,* (John Wiley & Sons, New York).

To gain a better education you will benefit from word study with a standard dictionary, a thesaurus, a specialized business dictionary, textbooks, general news and business periodicals, and other worthwhile publications.

Sentences

There is no specific rule about the best length of either **sentences** or paragraphs. But there is no doubt that short ones are usually clearer, and therefore better. People who make their living by teaching others how to write effective business communications state that 15– to 20–word sentences are easily understandable. Therefore, it is recommended that most sentences not be longer than that.

Also, sentences written in active form are more readily understood than sentences written in passive form. This means simply:

Active   *More effective*—subject performs action.

Subject   Object

The committee prepared the report.

Passive   *Less effective*—subject receives action.

Subject

The report was prepared by the committee.

The *Writing Improvement Exercise* at the end of this chapter shows how to change passive sentences to active sentences. It must be pointed out that both passive and active sentences are good grammar forms. However, a good writer uses the direct statement, the active sentence, more than the passive, thereby making the writing move along more clearly.

Paragraphs

William Caxton, known as the father of English printing, was a writer and scholar who brought printing to England in the fifteenth century. At this time, printing was done in large solid blocks of type, uninterrupted by **paragraphs.** But Caxton decided this style of printing tired the eyes, making reading difficult. Therefore, he began to mark resting places with the paragraph mark (¶). Later, this mark was used as a signal to indent the first line of the next unit of print.

In preparing letters, memorandums, and reports, a good writer follows the English grammar teaching that a paragraph should contain a unified idea. Yet there is often valid disagreement about where one idea ends and another begins. We can still go back to the fifteenth-century ruling for paragraphs. That is, they can still be used for giving the eyes a welcome rest. Many business letters have been rewritten solely for the purpose of breaking large black paragraph blocks into shorter, more digestible units. One writing authority recommends that long thoughts be broken down into "thoughtlets" because short paragraphs are easier to read.

It is suggested that the beginning paragraph of the standard business letter be short and inviting, two to five lines. The other paragraphs should usually be four to ten lines long.

Transition

In writing classes we are taught to eliminate unnecessary words that clutter the clarity of our writing. Adding **transition** words might seem to contradict this principle. But it is not a contradiction—rather, adding these words and phrases aids continuity and clarity within and between sentences and paragraphs. Transition words tie ideas together or smooth changes, helping the other person understand what you have said. You might say they help take your readers/listeners by the hand and lead them more easily through what you are saying.

Here the idea of transition is explained in a classic text about bank communications:

A series of sentences is similar to a string of freight cars. Both need couplings. When a train is made up, unless the couplings between cars are made secure, part of the train may become disconnected. The couplings between sentences are those words and phrases that refer to preceding ideas or look forward to coming ideas.[4]

The chief transition devices are *repetition of key words and phrases* and *linking words and phrases.*

Repetition of Key Words and Phrases

Any reader understands written material better if **key words and phrases** are repeated. Intentionally repeating parts is especially valuable in complicated business, technical, or professional writing. In the following examples, key words have been highlighted to demonstrate how repetition helps the reader follow the ideas:

Our committee has prepared a report that includes several suggestions for **cost cutting** in the production and computing departments of all manufacturing branches. These **cost cutting** suggestions can be implemented immediately.

Air travelers using Los Angeles International Airport found their trip hampered by a mammoth traffic **crunch,** which began Thursday. To avoid this **crunch,** an airport official had suggested that passengers park in perimeter lots and ride the airport shuttle buses.

Solar energy is designed at **three levels** of complexity. The **simplest level** relies on architectural design to permit passive solar heating. Structures are designed to absorb maximum sunlight, such as having south-facing windows to allow the sun to come in during cold months.

[4]W. George Crouch, *Bank Letters and Reports* (New York: American Institute of Banking, 1961) p. 104.

At a **more complex level** are active heating systems, such as flat-plate collectors mounted on rooftops. These are more advanced methods of collecting heat and sending it to protected storage units.

At the **top level** of complexity are different systems for focusing sunlight optically for high temperature heat needed for heavy industrial usage or for turning sunlight directly into electric current.

Linking Words and Phrases

The most common types of **linking words and phrases** used for transition are those that:

follow a time sequence
support what is being said
oppose what is being said
make conditions to what is being said

Following a Time Sequence

now	while	soon
then	earlier	later
during	meanwhile	before
after	concurrently	when
finally	next	first, second, etc.
last	previously	formerly
meantime	by that time	at last
in conclusion	to conclude	again

Examples

At the monthly board meeting, the chairman droned on and on. **At last,** a door opened and a cart carrying refreshments appeared.

We had waited for our ride in the dark, deserted parking area for an hour. **Meanwhile,** our company dinner party was going full swing.

Supporting What Is Being Said

and	furthermore	to show
therefore	consequently	as a result
accordingly	so	thus
in addition	moreover	because
in view of	for example	again
also	too	likewise
similarly	in other words	for example
stated another way	to illustrate	further

Examples

I am last on the list of eight executives who have access to the corporate jet. **Accordingly,** I make plans around travel of higher ranking executives.

Headquarters has cut our budget 15 percent. **As a result,** we must find ways to trim waste.

Opposing What Is Being Said

but	conversely	on the other hand
however	yet	in contrast
nevertheless	notwithstanding	on the contrary
still	despite	even so
in spite of	otherwise	

Examples

Other corporate vice presidents outrank me. **On the other hand,** what if my trip is more urgent than theirs?

In spite of the tightened budget, we cannot bypass safety rules.

Making a Condition to What Is Being Said

if	supposing	assuming
provided	in case	unless
however	even though	although
naturally	unless	as a result
under such circumstances		

Examples

If the airport is fogged in, we must postpone the conference.

Assuming our competition made a lower bid, what do we do?

Many other terms can be used for transition to help guide readers and listeners through your message. The preceding lists and examples, however, should give you some good suggestions.

Grammar

Use of Good English

For both white collar and blue collar jobs, better positions can depend on a person's ability to use **good English.** When more than one person's job performance is expected to be satisfactory, the one selected for hiring or promotion will often be one who makes a good impression on others by using good English. Besides earning that person respect, he/she will communicate more clearly and accurately on the job.

People using poor English will not always follow job instructions correctly or give orders to others clearly.

Some native Americans and many foreigners are crippling their chances of success because they fail to make the effort—and it certainly takes effort—to improve their English. Regardless of their intelligence and ability, if they are hired, they are assigned to low-paying, low prestige positions with little or no chance of advancing.

An officer of the B.F. Goodrich Company once stated:

> The improper use of grammar, including punctuation and spelling, is one of the biggest headaches in today's business world. We have entry level employees who have completed sec-

condary school education, and some who have even completed work for degrees at colleges and universities, who have no idea how to put a sentence together.[5]

To prepare effective business communications, a person should have a reasonable command of the English language. Here are three basic reasons for learning to use **good grammar** in these communications:

1. To make messages clear
2. To earn respect of your listeners and readers
3. To get ahead in your career

A Bank of America official who regularly hires college graduates consistently evaluates each applicant's writing ability and experience. His major concern about classroom training in English grammar is, "Do they teach agreement of subject and verb? Applicants seem to think that the verb should agree with whatever word is nearest." He also questions students' ability to use pronouns properly. Exercises on pronoun usage follow Chapters 11 and 12.

With the passing of time, some rules of acceptable grammar, spelling, and punctuation usage gradually change. General reading magazines such as *Time, Newsweek, U.S. News & World Report,* and *Business Week* are frequent innovators in language usage. Their new usages are sometimes adopted in the classroom and in business writing. However, business should be slow to adopt language innovations and should follow changes only when they are widely accepted.

For any questions of proper language usage, a good current dictionary should be the final source of authority. Small paperback editions do not have sufficient detail, but larger, unabridged dictionaries are excellent sources. Current editions of the following intermediate-size dictionaries are recommended by the National Council of Teachers of English. These are all desk-size or collegiate editions:

Webster's New World Dictionary of the American Language

Webster's New Collegiate Dictionary

The American Heritage Dictionary of the English Language

Funk and Wagnall's Standard Desk Dictionary

The American College Dictionary

Punctuation

Why study punctuation?

Some people may think that **punctuation** is scattered around a page only to make it look better. Others may even think that the main use for studying punctuation is to keep English teachers employed. But actually, punctuation is used only to make meaning clearer. Punctuation is the only difference in each of the following couplets:

Woman without her man is a savage.
Woman! Without her, man is a savage.

---

[5]Robert E. Swindle, *The Business Communicator* (Englewood Cliffs, N.J.: Prentice-Hall, 1980), p. 31.

Carter acted fairly honestly and conscientiously.
Carter acted fairly, honestly, and conscientiously.

The professors said the students are stupid.
The professors, said the students, are stupid.

Punctuation Rules

Authorities on punctuation agree that the sole purpose of punctuation is to make writing clear and recommend that we drop punctuation marks if the meaning is clear. However, some authorities disagree on a few specific rules. For instance:
Some say to use commas in a series but not before the conjunction:

red, white, green and blue; 1, 2 or 3

Others who recommend using this particular comma before the conjunction add that it can be omitted, but should be used if needed for clarity. See Appendix A, "Punctuation."

Appendix A contains condensed rules for correct use of punctuation marks. Also, grammar texts and some dictionaries contain more thorough studies of these rules.

Spelling

In a survey of 150 business executives, written use of the English language was rated as the skill most lacking in their high school graduate employees, and "blistering comments" were made regarding **spelling.** Why is correct spelling in our business letters important?

Correct spelling does help make our meaning clear and specific. But it does more than that. Whether the attitude is right or wrong, errors in spelling have come to identify the writer as being ignorant, uneducated, careless, lazy, or any combination of these. You may think this is unreasonable, but spelling errors are considered gross. We cannot overemphasize the need to check the spelling of any questionable words in all internal and external business communications.

One executive, knowing her own weakness, claims she owes part of her success to the fact that she regularly carries a small speller's dictionary in her purse or pocket.

Appendix B contains a list of words that are useful for the business writer to learn to spell correctly. To check spelling, word usage, punctuation and reference in other writing mechanics, every office should have an up-to-date unabridged dictionary or a reliable desk-size or collegiate dictionary, as suggested previously.

If you use a computer to create business communications, you should use software that finds misspelled words. These computer programs, called "spelling checkers" are generally inexpensive and easy to use.

Those of you with a love for both computers and writing may be interested in "style checking" computer programs that find and help you correct grammar errors, punctuation errors and instances where you have used passive verbs.

Summarizing and Listing

Summarizing and **listing** items can be genuine timesavers to the reader. In many instances, they can also save time and money for the writer who is giving a list of information, making a number of requests, or asking a number of questions. When the writer summarizes each statement and puts it in a list at the end of the letter or memorandum, the reader should understand the message more clearly. For instance, at the end of a letter that asks several questions, it is worthwhile to restate each question in a summary form and number the questions in the order in which they appeared in the earlier part of the letter. Then the receiver can simply check each item to see if all the necessary information has been given. If more information on any item is needed, additional details can be learned from the preceding sections of the letter.

Figure 4.7 is a good example of a letter that effectively summarizes information already given. The fifth paragraph summarizes information given in detail in paragraphs 2, 3, and 4.

FIGURE 4.7
Letter in which paragraph 5 summarizes information
contained in paragraphs 2, 3, and 4.

Chapter 4 *Writing Improvement Exercise*

Passive Sentences → Active Sentences

Active Sentences Are Usually Preferred

Why are some writers good and some just so-so? If we analyze their writing, we can pinpoint some patterns of the better writers.

Most good writers help make their writing clearer by using the **active** sentence form more than the **passive** sentence form. In the **active** sentence, the **subject performs the action.** In the **passive** sentence, the **subject receives the action.** Somehow, our minds follow the active sentence more quickly: Subject–Verb–Direct Object.

Subject   Verb
Active   Mr. James <u>dictated</u> the letter.

Subject   Verb
Passive   The letter <u>was dictated</u> by Mr. James.

Passive sentences lend variety to our writing and can be used in good writing. However, if a piece of your writing somehow does not seem to be as clear as it should be, you will probably find that direct statements are not being used enough—that the passive sentence form is used too frequently. Then, if you follow the type of editing that has been done with the following sentences, your writing will be more alive and clear.

S   V
Passive   Many <u>orders</u> <u>have been taken</u> by Mr. Thompson.

S   V
Active   Mr. <u>Thompson</u> <u>took</u> many orders.

S   V   V
Passive   The <u>markups</u> <u>have</u> not <u>been received</u> from this manager.

S   V   V
Active   This <u>manager</u> <u>has</u> not <u>sent</u> in her markups.

S   V
Passive   The <u>error</u> in the computer printout <u>was found</u> by Mr. Horn.

S   V
Active   <u>Mr. Horn</u> <u>found</u> the error in the computer printout.

Check the works of the best writers, such as Ernest Hemingway, William Shakespeare, Winston Churchill, and the King James version of the Bible. You will see that clarity comes from much use of the active sentence form.

Passive Sentences Are Occasionally Preferred

Passive sentences are good grammar and should be used occasionally to give variety to sentence forms so that all sentences do not run in the same pattern. Also, this type of sentence can be used intentionally to avoid giving criticism or reprimand:

Active   You made two mistakes in this report.
Passive Two mistakes were made in this report.

Active   Did you send that letter to Omaha?
Passive Was that letter sent to Omaha?

Chapter 4 *Writing Improvement Worksheet*

Passive Sentences → Active Sentences

Change the following sentences from the passive to the active form. Answers may vary in some details. In some sentences, you may have to supply your own subject.

1. The sentences were revised by the students. → _____

_____

2. The cabin was built by Mr. Swallow. → _____

_____

3. The records were brought to the office by Mr. Stone. → _____

_____

4. Last month's meeting was attended by only fourteen members. → _____

_____

5. Copies of the report were sent to all board members from the chairman of the board.

→ _____

_____

6. Between 10:00 last night and 6:00 this morning, our store was burglarized. → _____

_____

7. This letter was received by our office today. → _____

_____

8. The invoice was placed on my desk by the mail clerk. → _____

_____

9. A request for his or her desired vacation period should be turned in by each employee.

→ _____

10. Praise from the office manager was often received by the secretarial staff. → _____

_____

_____

_____

Chapter 4   Writing Improvement Worksheet (*Continued*)

11. Agenda items will be submitted by Board members. → _____

_____

12. In the entryway a temporary ramp was installed by carpenters. → _____

_____

_____

13. During the meeting several questions were asked by stockholders. → _____

_____

_____

14. Each fall, a schedule of insurance options is prepared by the Personnel Department.
→ _____

_____

15. At the meeting, the financial report is read by the treasurer. → _____

_____

_____

16. The message was handed to me by the secretary. → _____

_____

17. A high-quality computer paper was ordered by the purchasing agent. → _____

_____

_____

18. Our meeting was interrupted by a loud noise. → _____

_____

To avoid a tone of criticism, change the following sentences from active to passive.

19. Did you contact all the branch offices on the trip to the Midwest? → _____

_____

20. You ordered the wrong type of paper for these reports. → _____

_____

REVIEW AND DISCUSSION

Chapter 4 *Qualities of a Good Business Communication: Clear and Complete Message*

Complete the following exercises. Make your answers brief.

1. Give three basic reasons why business letters or other letters should contain clear, complete messages. _____

_____

_____

2. Give an example of "brain drain" that happened because of an unclear written or spoken message in a personal or business situation of your own experience. _____

_____

_____

_____

_____

3. This book suggests that there are many planned letters that should not be written. Explain. _____

_____

4. Any letter you plan to write could be placed in one of four categories. Name and describe each.
(1) Nonletter.

_____

_____

_____

5. Complete this old statement: "Disorganized, illogical writing reflects a _____

_____

6. A Southern Illinois University survey revealed that American business people consider _____

to be the quality that needs most improvement in business writing.

7. In general, _____ words are easier to understand than _____ ones.

8. *Gobbledygook* means _____

_____

Chapter 4   Qualities of a Good Business Communication: Clear and Complete Message
(*Continued*)

9. How can a thesaurus help educate you? _____
_____

10. Authorities claim that ____ percent of any college course is learning the vocabulary of that course.

11. In general _____ sentences are clearer than _____ ones.

12. William Caxton, the father of English printing, first devised the paragraph mark (¶) as
_____

13. How does transition help make your writing clear? _____
_____
_____

14. Give two valid reasons for using good English grammar in business communications.
_____

15. Why study punctuation? _____

16. Give two reasons for using correct spelling in all communications. _____
_____
_____

17, 18, 19, 20. Change the following sentences to active form. That is, make the subject perform the action.

17. All office vents were cleaned by a chimney sweep. _____
_____

18. Copies of new work assignments were posted by the supervisors. _____
_____

19. The electricians' work was completed ahead of schedule. _____
_____

20. The report was improved by your editing. _____
_____

CHAPTER 5
Qualities of a Good Business Communication:
Clear and Complete Message—The Letter and Its Parts

Watch Your Language

Today much business, even with some smaller organizations, is being conducted with individuals or firms in foreign countries. We must take special care to avoid potential language difficulties.

"Watch your language" here means to be careful which language is used in your communications. Use English unless you are certain that your use of another language is exceptionally good.

English is becoming the global language. While exploring, trading and establishing settlements during the eighteenth and nineteenth centuries, passengers and crews of English sailing vessels spread their language around the world. The common phrase, "The sun never sets on the British Empire," was certainly not an exaggeration. Today, worldwide radio and television English language broadcasts make it the most commonly known and studied language on earth. English is the acknowledged universal language of business, science and aviation in most places.

For clearer understanding it is far wiser to write well in English than poorly in another language. Many foreign firms have their own English translators; many foreign people doing business with American firms will know English or have access to translators. English is the second language of millions of people around the world and is a mandatory foreign language requirement in many schools in other countries. Japanese students must study English beginning in the seventh grade.

Because of growing international traffic in business, bilingual or multilingual ability is a great asset on the job market. Job seekers are encouraged to learn to speak and understand other languages. But you should write your letters in a foreign language only if you are absolutely certain of your competence. Otherwise, use the talents of a person with full competence in that language.

The following letter demonstrates how people in one French firm would have preferred receiving a letter written in good English instead of bad French:

We have received your letter, translated into "French" (???). We haven't the slightest idea what the translator was trying to say, but we do thank him for the best laughs we have had since the last Fernandel film. Please write us again—in English, this time—and we shall try to take immediately the action you desire.[1]

Be Careful with Foreign Correspondence

Tips for Writing to Foreigners

For **corresponding with foreigners,** Patricia S. Beagle gives the following guidelines. Ms. Beagle has translated engineering and general business documents from French to English and English to French.

1. Do not use abbreviations. Write out words to avoid errors in translation.
2. Use simple words and simple sentences. No sentence should be too long.
3. Avoid slang and colloquialisms. They do not translate well.
4. Write out months in dates; 4-5-90 means April 5 in the United States and May 4 in France.
5. Courtesy is exceptionally important in some countries. Be particularly careful to be courteous.[2]

Slang

In our contacts with foreigners, we will notice that even those who have studied our language well will be puzzled at many of our **colloquial** or **slang** expressions. Therefore, we should always check any mail going outside this country and eliminate such terms. Colloquial words and phrases that are accepted as standard to native-born speakers of American English might pose problems to those who have learned the language in foreign classrooms.

For example, think of the picture a foreigner might get in trying to give a literal translation to any of the following: *hang in there, shipshape, stuffed shirt, haywire, easy mark, cold feet, highbrow, brainchild.*

When translated literally, English can come out quite strangely: Various translations of the advertisement, "Come Alive with Pepsi," came out as, "Pepsi Brings Your Ancestors Back from the Grave," or "Come out of the Grave."

A newly appointed United States Ambassador to Japan had just arrived in Tokyo. Trying to be relaxed and friendly at his first press conference, he said, "Ladies and gentlemen, I'm the new boy on the block. Shoot!" His stunned interpreter hesitated and finally translated "new boy" as *kozokko,* meaning junior apprentice. "Shoot" was just ignored. For some time, puzzled Japanese reporters were questioning U.S. embassy officials, trying to learn what the esteemed gentleman had said.

Avoid "Buzz Words"

A new type of colloquial term seems to be creeping into our language by leaps and bounds. These terms are classified as **buzz words,** which are defined as words or

---

[1]Leslie Llewellyn Lewis, *The Dartnell Business-Letter Deskbook* (Chicago: The Dartnell Corporation, 1969), p. 154.

[2]With special permission.

phrases used by members of some in-group, having imprecise meaning but sounding impressive to outsiders.

Buzz words seem to fit into business interchange. Such business terms might not be clearly understood by people in other fields, of course, but actually they come from spontaneous origin and are often regional.

Some of these terms will spread from their places and fields of origin, but it is predicted that, like slang, most will disappear from the language entirely. Therefore, they should not be used in standard business communications until and unless they become adopted into standard language. Also, slang and buzz words can give writing a tone that is too casual for business usage.

Here are some buzz words with their current regional definitions:

Buzz Words	*Current Definitions*
run it up the flagpole	to give something a tryout
fiscally impacted	financially ruined
reinventing the wheel	thinking you are doing something new when in fact it has been done before
back to square one	to go back where you started
GIGO	Garbage In, Garbage Out; originated with computer operations
ballpark figure	a roughly estimated general figure
paid my dues	to have done one's share
comes with the territory	anything that can be expected as part of an assignment; as part of a promotion; as part of any activity
old boy (girl) network	a system whereby men of a specific common background help each other; where women who are part of a network (system) help out other women
loose cannon	anything that cannot be controlled and might cause considerable damage (has nothing to do with ballistics)
neat freak	one who is exceptionally tidy
culture shock	a shock or disturbance caused from moving in an environment different from one's own
bottom line	the basic element
MBO	management by objective

Profanity Is Out of Place

Casual language creeps into usage, but **profanity** in business communications can leave a negative impression. It is very difficult to tell when others will become offended and see you as crude and uneducated. This, of course, occurs in situations other than business. A judge once cautioned attorneys and clients against using "expletives" in the courtroom, saying, "When a person has to resort to foul language it's because he isn't able to come up with more articulate and meaningful words."

Further, with increased international activity, businesses must be aware that profanity can deeply offend peoples of other cultures who are accustomed to using formal language in business dealings.

Avoid Computerese

We have cautioned against using technical terms to the point they are not understandable. Now we have a new concern—translation by computer. Because the saying, "If the mind can conceive, man can achieve," doesn't yet seem to hold with computer translation, we must avoid using **computerese.**

For example, the phrase "out of sight, out of mind," when translated by computer into Russian and then back into English came out "invisible maniac."

Write Concisely

Advantages of Being Concise

Vigorous writing is **concise.** A sentence should contain no unnecessary words, a paragraph no unnecessary sentences, for the same reason that a drawing should have no unnecessary lines and a machine no unnecessary parts. This requires not that the writer make all his sentences short, or that he avoid all detail and treat his subjects in outline, but that every word tell.[3]

William Strunk, Jr.

The clearest, most effective business writing does not contain words or phrases that could be eliminated or stated in simpler language. You owe it to your readers to write not only in a manner they will understand but in a manner they will understand as easily and quickly as possible. This does not mean all communications must be short; some require several pages. But we should remember how busy most readers are. When we make our letters brief, we are not only saving our own time and money; we are being considerate of the reader.

Business writing consultants firmly believe that 50 percent of business writing could be eliminated if material were written more carefully. A typical editing of one business report planned for wide distribution changed the original 50-page report to 20 pages. Everyone agreed the shortened report was much clearer. Undoubtedly, more of the people who received it read it.

Elimination of Unnecessary Words—Wasted Words

Examples of editing that can be done to improve most writing are shown here:

at ~~the hour of~~ one o'clock   during ~~the year of~~ 1985

~~in the~~ meantime   enclosed ~~herewith~~

if ~~it is at all~~ possible   ~~at a~~ later ~~date~~

---

[3]William Strunk, Jr. and E. B. White, *The Elements of Style,* 3rd ed. (New York: Macmillan Publishing Company, Inc., 1979), p. 23.

because ~~of the fact that~~	~~absolutely~~ complete
~~in order~~ to	after ~~the time of~~
on ~~the~~ average	in ~~the~~ future

Long Version	*Concise Version*
at this point in time	now; at this time; at this point
under separate cover	separately
during the time	while
at all times	always
we are not in a position to	we cannot
under date of	on
in the normal course of events	normally

A *Writing Improvement Exercise* on eliminating "wasted words" is at the end of Chapter 2.

Concise: To Be or Not to Be

You can improve your writing by checking carefully for words, phrases, sentences, and even paragraphs that can be omitted. In general, the shorter your message, the clearer it will be. The remaining message is cut to its essentials.

However, when you are working with complicated business or technical material, you might make improvements by certain rewriting that makes the writing somewhat longer. In many places you should probably use a few short words to replace a difficult long one.

Also, *do not progress too speedily through difficult material*. To smooth the flow of the writing, back up and use some of the transition devices. These steps tie ideas together or smooth abrupt changes. For instance, repeat the cores of some ideas: restate an idea to help the reader understand for sure what you are talking about. Then, try adding other transition words and phrases (*next, therefore, also, consequently, nevertheless, unless,* and so on). These words bridge the gaps, helping you grasp the reader by the hand so you both glide along more easily. (See "Transition.")

Look for a place to break up any sentence longer than 20–23 words. Doing this smoothly may mean you must repeat some words or add others. Then, read what you have written in these shorter sentences and you will see that your writing is clearer. With **shorter sentences,** more people will read it. More people will understand it.

Business and technical writers sometimes try to impress audiences by displaying their "mastery" of writing by using **overlong words** and sentences. So do some doctors, lawyers—even college professors—and others. Their writing is often not understood even by people in their own fields. The best writing is readily understood on the first reading.

So what about impressing your readers? If you write concisely and clearly they will respect and envy you for your writing style. And, as said, they will understand you.

In striving for conciseness, however, you can be so brief that you become ambiguous. A good example of this is the story of the Hollywood reporter who wanted some personal details about a movie star. He wired the star's agent:

HOW OLD PAUL NEWMAN?

The reply came back:

PAUL NEWMAN FINE. HOW YOU?

Is the Message Clear and Complete?

Check Notes

Surely checking a letter or other communication for clarity and completeness is as important as any other part of its preparation. By referring to your earlier **notes,** you can see if all planned points were covered.

Check for Legality

Occasionally, contents of a business letter come under **legal examination.** Courts generally hold that when a person signs a letter about company business on company stationery, that person is acting as an agent for the business. Since the dictator or originator is a legal agent, the business is responsible for the letter contents. Of course, few letters will come under such scrutiny, but mistakes can be perilous.

Check all statements that could be interpreted as defamation of character, invasion of privacy, fraud, or implied contracts. Also look for statements related to laws regarding employment, credit and collections. Later chapters covering specific types of communications will refer to their legal aspects.

Proofread

Before sending your communication, **proofread** it for major and minor errors. Nobody is perfect, not even you or your secretary. Besides checking the general content of the letter, both typist and dictator should check technical details such as money amounts and other figures, verifying them carefully for complete accuracy.

Proofread carefully. Even after careful proofreading, errors can slip through. The *Prentice-Hall Author's Guide* cautions:

> It is not enough to read only for sense and accuracy of facts, dates, and statistics. Each word and each mark of punctuation should be examined. The eye has a way of seeing what it wants and expects to see, and it is very easy to skip over misspellings and even omissions.[4]

Form Letters and Guide Letters

Businesses turn to the use of **form and guide letters** for many reasons—saving time and money, having recurring need of the same type of letter, and making the largest mailings possible for a given situation. Another reason is the creation of better letters: By a reduction in the amount of time and talent needed when all letters are individually prepared, more time and better talent are available to prepare form letters, as well as those that require individual preparation.

If the form and guide letters are well planned, they reduce the office work load and help ensure that all correspondence coming from the firm will be of better quality than it would be if each piece were individually dictated and produced. Care must be taken, however, because sending poorly prepared letters can damage a firm's reputation. And, ill will can result if form letters are used when individually planned letters would produce better results at a reasonable cost. Finally, form letters should not be used excessively, because they can be dehumanizing to their readers.

[4]*Prentice-Hall Author's Guide,* 5th ed. (Englewood Cliffs, N.J.: Prentice-Hall, 1978), p. 75.

Saving Money by Using Form Letters

When a firm sets out to achieve economies in preparation of written communications, one of the first plans adopted is to set up a form and guide letter system. If such a system is already in operation, it is given a thorough review and overhaul.

A recent government survey revealed that on the average, form letters cost 90 percent less than individually prepared letters. This survey also showed that guide letters cost less than half what individually dictated and typed letters cost.

Electronic Text-Editing Machines

Today's electronic equipment—computers, word processors, memory typewriters—greatly simplifies the preparation of form and guide letters. These machines can be programmed to run off any number of copies of a complete letter without anyone in attendance at the machine, similar to printing. Further, they can also be programmed to insert automatically any individual information at specific places within a communication.

For instance, they can be programmed to insert specific addresses and salutations, then print general information that is included in all copies, inserting specific information for each individual copy at any position. Many direct mail advertising pieces show effective use of these machine capabilities.

Types of Form and Guide Letters

There are three basic types of form and guide letters: the standard form letter, the paragraph form letter, and the guide letter.

Standard Form Letter

The **standard form letter** is the most common form or guide letter. This letter is prepared in advance, and all copies of the body of the letter are exactly alike. Some mailings have individual names and addresses inserted at the top of the letter; many do not. The sales letter that might be sent to hundreds, thousands, or tens of thousands of people is an example of this type of form letter. However, the standard form letter is used for many other business communications, such as orders, acknowledgments, credit notices, and collections.

Paragraph Form Letter

Paragraph form letters are used when situations are the same but details vary. Therefore, different paragraphs are composed for differing information, and the dictator simply indicates each paragraph to be used. This is done by identifying each paragraph with a letter, a number, or a combination of letter and number. As an example, the following form paragraphs might be set up for collection letters to ensure that not all delinquent accounts receive the same letter, or that the holder of an account does not receive the same letter each time that account becomes delinquent.

Paragraph Forms: Overdue Invoice Balance

Form paragraph A-1

May we remind you of the overdue balance of your account in the amount indicated above.

Form paragraph A-2

Have you forgotten payment of the amount above on your account?

Form paragraph A-3

Here we are again to remind you that the payment of your account is past due.

Form paragraph B-1

If there is a specific reason for this delinquency, would you please let us try to help you rearrange the terms of your payments.

Form paragraph B-2

We are aware of the general slowdown of work in your area and would like to offer to help set up an easier schedule of payments.

Form paragraph B-3

Is there any reason you can give us to explain why you have not paid this account?

Form paragraph B-4

As you once previously had a delinquent account that you did pay in full, can we expect the same treatment of your account this time?

Form paragraph C-1

If your check is not received by _____, we will be forced to turn your account over to a collection agency.

Form paragraph C-2

If your payment is not received by _____, we will put this matter in the hands of a collection agency.

Form paragraph C-3

We will have no choice but to turn to your account over to a collection agency if payment is not received by _____.

The person planning a particular letter might indicate the choice of message by listing:

A-2

B-3

C-1

Then, when the letter is sent, instead of a copy of it being filed in the account file, it would be possible to simply give the date of the letter and list on the account the identification of paragraphs sent.

Guide Letter

The **guide letter** is prepared in advance with blanks left in certain areas where specific details will be included for each person receiving the letter. It is called a *guide* because the basic information is the same for all letters, and the dictator need only furnish details to be inserted in each blank of the basic letter, which is thus used as a guide for several letters:

Letter 1

Because we are sure you do not want to be without insurance coverage, we would be glad to reinstate your policy # _____ immediately if you will send us your check for the amount of $ _____ not later than _____ .

If there is some unusual situation that makes it impossible for you to pay at this time, please contact us, and we believe we will be able to help you work it out.

Letter 2

The records show you own title to a tract of land located in Section _____ Range _____ Township _____ Arizona. Parcel # _____ .

We specialize in land and acreage sales. If you are interested in selling, please complete the enclosed forms and return the original to us.

We prefer an exclusive listing, which permits us to give it the broadest exposure before the public through varied means of advertising.

We offer courtesy to other realtors.

Using Postal Cards or Postcards

Many routine form and guide messages can be sent by post office **postal cards** or by **postcards** made up especially by the company itself. For small or large mailings when the information is routine and open to public scrutiny, cards save money because they cost less to send than letters and they save the extra preparation of envelopes. The following information was printed on the message side of a postal card:

Thank you for your inquiry about our Twin-Pack tape cartridge. Although it is identical in size and appearance to a single cassette tape, the playing time is approximately doubled.

We have welcomed this opportunity to explain.

Uses for Form and Guide Letters

Besides being used for the familiar sales letter, form and guide letters can be used for almost every type of business communication. Here is a list of some of the types of letters and memorandums for which they can be planned:

Sales letters	Reporting out-of-stock items
Order acknowledgments	Collection letters
Payment acknowledgments	Routine claims
Routine inquiries	Routine adjustments
Routine answers to inquiries	Announcements
Routine announcements to employees	Welcome to new customers
Routine employee information	Inquiries of job seekers
Routine requests of employees	Price change lists
News release cover letters	Introduction of new products
Letters to revive old accounts	

Setting up a Form and Guide Letter System

It may seem that there is no need for form and guide letters when an office operation is small. However, even the smallest operation will have frequently recurring situations for which the same or similar letters will suffice.

To set up a system of form and guide letters for any size office operation, an extra copy of all letters should be kept for a period of time—such as one month for a large office, two months for a smaller one. These letters should be classified by subject matter. In any office, even a large number of letters will fall into a small number of categories. In one study, 1,200 letters were classified under 23 subject headings.

Starting with the category that has the largest number of letters, make up a letter that includes all essential information. Continue this procedure for all frequently recurring types of letters. To give outgoing letters some variety, more than one letter can be prepared for the largest categories. However, strictly routine matters may be stated succinctly with no variation. Some letters will convert to standard form letter format; that is, no blanks will be left for including specific data. Others will fit better into the paragraph form letter pattern, and still others can follow the guide letter format with blanks indicated. Because of the number of times they will be copied, letters must be edited thoroughly to see that they contain all necessary information and are concise, grammatically correct, and courteous.

Forms and guides should not be composed for letters that are not written frequently or for letters that should show clearly that they are intended for one person.

Who Should Write Form and Guide Letters?

Because form and guide letters sometimes represent the activities of many people, several people are frequently involved in their preparation. Large nationwide mailings of direct mail sales letters are sometimes composed by a committee of writers, whose product is then edited by other people in top-level positions. However, in small mailings, the preparation of the letters can be assigned in each department to a person who has exhibited interest and ability in preparing good business correspondence. Care must be taken in this selection. Outside business writing consultants and advertising agencies earn handsome fees for performing this type of specialized service when it is impossible to find in-house correspondence talent.

The Format of Form Letters

Because a form letter is frequently fighting the reader's decision to discard it without a thorough reading, it pays to give particular attention to matters of format.

Quality Paper

Good quality paper should be used to give the letter an appearance of importance.

Color

Sometimes **colored stationery** is appropriate. Even wild, vivid colors can be effective in certain types of mailings. Colored printing, such as blue, red, or brown, can catch the reader's eye. Combinations of colored paper and colored print might be considered such as: deep blue on pastel blue; deep green or pastel green; brown on buff; or various combinations of the same or different colors.

Using two colors of ink within the body of a letter also is effective—perhaps one for primary use and one for highlighting statements and underlining.

First-Class Mail

If the additional cost can be justified, **first-class mail** should be used, because this helps take the communication out of the junk mail category.

Signatures

An original **signature** should be used on form and guide letters when possible, unless the information is obviously of a common, routine nature. Even on printed letters, however, it often pays to use a different ink for the signature to give it the appearance of having been done by hand. Or it may be worthwhile to actually sign them personally. Have you ever scrutinized a letter to see if it actually has a *personal* signature?

Reproducing Form Letters

Any office can justify the expense of purchasing electronic equipment. As noted earlier, these machines simplify the preparation and typing of any letter, memorandum, or report. Also, the time of the clerical staff that is saved justifies such expenses. Further, almost any office can save money by preparing frequent-use forms and letters, for which these machines are invaluable.

Bulk mailings of thousands of letters are usually printed. Various types of professional printing processes are available; and the quality of the finished product depends upon the paper used, the printing process employed, and the care taken in preparation. Sales letters are generally printed.

If copies of printed form letters are desired, these can be prepared in sets by the printer. Specific information for each letter can be typed in and copies rapidly separated for distribution.

Retrieving Copies of Form and Guide Letters

After form and guide letters are prepared, they can, of course, be stored in the memory of electronic equipment and can be called up on command for any hard copy (paper) printout. Naturally, several copies of a computer master file can be made for the use of several people.

Or printed copies can be gathered together in file folders or portfolios to show what types of communications are available. These copies should be readily accessible to everyone who might use them. If several people are using the same sets of letters and there is a chance that they might not be replaced properly, the letters can be placed in a master book in inexpensive permanent binding. Several copies of a portfolio can be made and distributed.

In the portfolio, divider sheets should separate types of communications, and an index should be on each divider sheet or immediately following it listing all styles of the letters in that section.

Enclosures with Form Letters

As postal rates increase, it becomes imperative that we get full value of postage on each piece of mail. Frequently, sales promotion materials, good will items, or other materials can be sent at no extra cost. Also, many questions can be answered most effectively by pictures or diagrams that might accompany the form or guide letter.

Caution in the Use of Form Letters

We acknowledge the advantages of using form and guide letters when they are appropriate to the occasion and are prepared properly. On the other hand, we must use **caution** and be fully aware of their potential for offending people. Therefore, when preparing and sending these letters, we should constantly review the basic principles of good letter writing: attractive appearance, good will tone, and clear and complete message.

Surveys show that excessive use of form letters damages relationships with customers. Such damage is done from hastily written letters that carry a tone showing that they were machine-prepared. In addition, people frequently receive form letters that are not completely appropriate to the occasion.

A firm's **present and former customer list** is the best and easiest market to maintain. Also, new customers are not often easy to find. Great effort should be spent in preparing form letters that go out to old and new customers and clients.

Attractive Appearance

Sometimes, in the process of rapid reproduction of form and guide letters by individual typing, automatic typing, or some method of printing, the end product has a less-than-appealing appearance. Although the letter as planned may have been satisfactory, such things as cheap paper, poor typing or printing processes, poor reproduction of illustrations, or obviously careless handling can hurt the reputation of the company and result in a negative reaction to the letter. Rereading Chapter 2 for information on **attractive appearance** of communications would be helpful in preparing multiple communications.

Good Will

People prefer receiving and reading letters addressed solely to them, and the character of form letters can easily fail to convey **good will** because they are prepared for so many people. Although the many advantages of form letters are acknowledged in business, every effort must be made to offset, as much as possible, their disadvantages. In many instances, it will be advantageous to write an individual letter instead of a form letter to a particular person, with statements obviously made just for that person. The letter might refer to past business dealings, details of the current business matter, or other material making it clear that no one else is to receive that particular letter.

Form and guide letters must have the **tone** of a letter that is directed to one person, even though the information is made applicable to many. Although the writer is aware of the vast audience to which the letter is directed, the letter should be written in a personal manner, the way the writer would talk if the reader were sitting across the desk. This style of writing is stripped of the stiffness and impersonality that are found in too many form letters.

Further, the original writer or writers of the form letter must reread it slowly and carefully to see that it conveys the intended message. It should also be read and edited by others not directly involved in the original preparation, who may read from it some messages of connotation, euphemism, or regionalism not obvious to the original writers.

Clear and Complete Message

In trying to economize by putting messages in form letter style, planners sometimes become overzealous with the savings they can foresee and try to use form letters when individual letters should be written. This may result in false economy, because letters might be sent out that are incomplete and unclear. Extra money should be spent on preparing individually dictated and typed letters when situations warrant them.

Another Hazard: Outdated Information and Outmoded Terminology

Because form and guide letters can be so readily adapted to business situations, it is easy to forget to give them the care and attention they need—to review them regularly and bring them up to date. Form and guide letters can get out of date for many reasons. They may have **outdated information** because no one took the time to change the affected letters. Also, business terminology may become outmoded or trite, and colloquialisms and clichés follow fashions of usage. New terms can often be more expressive than older ones. Don't let form letters get stale!

Additional Hazard: Updating Names and Addresses for Form Letters

Statistics show that at least one-fifth of the people on a mailing list move each year, and in some areas and businesses, the rate of address change is far higher. Therefore, every effort must be made to **update names and addresses.** Because the best mailing list is that of current customers, this data should be protected by adding and deleting names and changing addresses when such information is available. Many firms include prestamped, self-addressed postcards for customers to fill in with new addresses so that records can be kept current. Most firms that send out monthly or quarterly statements leave a box on the statement that asks for changes in address.

Mastering the Word Processor

There it sits. Your new word processor or computer—the new mass of electronics that you are going to master in order to make your writing easier. Easier?? Lucky you if you were in on the selection and were able to sway the choice to a machine described as "user friendly"—computer language for "easy to learn."

So it sits there in your office. You may be eager to get to it. Or you may be a person who lets a day or two—or three—go by before you decide that maybe, perhaps, the two of you can learn to speak to each other.

William Zinsser, former professor of nonfiction writing at Yale University and successful author and editor, acknowledged that he was a confirmed nonmechanical person. But he became a convert and said:

> . . . with a word processor you can play with your writing on the screen until you get it right, and the paragraphs will keep rearranging themselves, no matter how many words you change or add or cut, and you don't have to print it until it's just the way you want it. The printer will print exactly what's on the screen—word for word, line for line.[5]

Easy to Learn?

First, you will need someone you can contact who is familiar with that machine model and its software for any problem that might develop. *Might* develop? Your machine presents strange operations to any first user. You soon discover that before you can master your machine, you need to learn the language it brought with it. But you cannot understand the language in the manual until you learn to use the machine. Some place someone cries: "NEVER consult the manual." For instance, in some manuals, upper and lower margins are listed as "header" and "footer." And that cute little TV is not really a TV, but is a "screen" or "monitor" or maybe something else. "Window" takes on a new meaning.

Speaking of that word processing or computer manual: At first it really is easy to follow—up to the point where you don't understand it. So call that reference person. Actually, you will be surprised how simple most solutions prove to be. Early on you might find it helpful to keep your own little personal "manual" where you note instruction interpretations briefly in terms you understand. Take heart that for some time you probably will have little use for many of the machine operations.

BUT YOU WILL MASTER IT AS FAR AS YOU NEED IT. AND YOU WILL LEARN TO LOVE IT.

[5]William Zinsser, *On Writing Well,* 3rd ed. (New York: Harper & Row, Publishers, 1985), p. 209.

"The Blind Men and the Elephant"

When figures show that a high percentage of our writing and speaking is not clearly understood, we must look for all methods to help us communicate more clearly. It is a sad fact that, given the same information, different people will sometimes report it differently. We must always be aware that such a situation can occur. The classic parable of "The Blind Men and the Elephant"[6] represents this situation graphically:

It was six men of Indostan / To learning much inclined,
Who went to see the Elephant / (Though all of them were blind),
That each by observation / Might satisfy his mind.

The First approached the Elephant, / And happening to fall
Against his broad and study side, / At once began to bawl:
"God bless me! but the Elephant / Is very like a wall!"

The Second, feeling of the tusk / Cried, "Ho! what have we here
So very round and smooth and sharp? / To me 'tis very clear
This wonder of an Elephant / Is very like a spear!"

The Third approached the animal / And happening to take
The squirming trunk within his hands / Thus boldly up he spake:
"I see," quoth he, "the Elephant / Is very like a snake!"

The Fourth reached out an eager hand, / And felt about the knee:
"What most this wondrous beast is like / Is very plain," quoth he;
"'Tis clear enough the Elephant / Is very like a tree!"

The Fifth, who chanced to touch the ear / Said: "E'en the blindest man
Can tell what this resembles most; / Deny the fact who can,
This marvel of an Elephant / Is very like a fan!"

The Sixth no sooner had begun / About the beast to grope
Than, seizing on the swinging tail / That fell within his scope,
"I see," quoth he, "the Elephant / Is very like a rope!

"And so these men of Indostan /
Disputed loud and long,
Each in his own opinion /
Exceeding stiff and strong.
Though each
was partly in the right, /
They all were in the wrong!

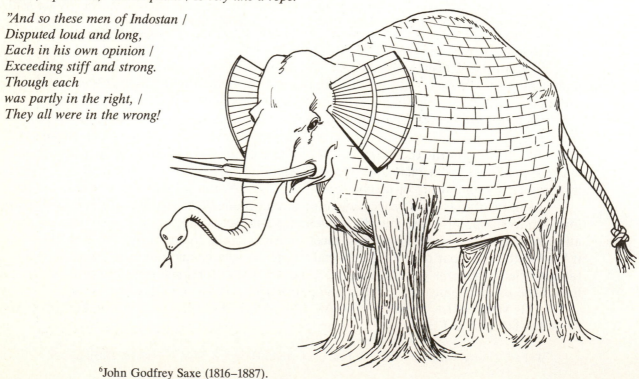

[6]John Godfrey Saxe (1816–1887).

Chapter 5 *Writing Improvement Exercise*

Proofreaders' Marks

    Proofreaders' marks are useful in making corrections on copy that is to be retyped or printed. These marks are useful in working with all types of written business communications, but especially when working with reports.

    Proofreaders' marks are made on handwritten, typed, or printed materials to indicate changes, deletions, or additions. These marks are universally recognized and used. Once you learn them you can use them all over the world.

Proofreaders' Marks

⊙	Insert period
∧	Insert word(s) (in the ∧ event)
+ #	Add space
− #	Less space
eq. #	Equalize spacing
⌢	Close up space (han⌢d)
[	Move to left
]	Move to right
⌐¬	Move up
⌊_⌋	Move down
e	Delete (now)
∽	Transpose (Ju e n)
. . . . *stet*	Let it stand. (Write *stet* in margin and make dots beneath words that had been crossed out.)
¶	Paragraph
no ¶	No paragraph
l.c.	Lower case (or draw diagonal line through capital letter: Lower ₵ase.)
___ *ital.*	Italics (Draw line under word(s) and write *ital* in margin.)
Caps	Capitals: c̲a̲pitals
‖	Straighten vertically
=	Straighten horizontally
[ ]	Make brackets
( )	Make parentheses
∿ *b.f.*	Boldface type (Write *b.f.* in margin and draw zig-zag line under word.)
◯	Spell out in full (Ave.)

Chapter 5 *Writing Improvement Worksheet*

Proofreaders' Marks

In the column at the right, indicate the meaning of the symbol at the left.

	Symbol	*What It Means*
1.	⊄	_____
2.	+ #	_____
3.	Apr**il**	_____
4.	jack	_____
5.	ℓ	_____
6.	b.f̶ Examples	_____
7.	⌐‾‾‾⌐	_____
8.	— #	_____
9.	way, go	_____
10.	stet do not know	_____
11.	Main St.	_____
12.	⌐	_____
13.	‖	_____
14.	══	_____
15.	⊙	_____

REVIEW AND DISCUSSION

Chapter 5 *Qualities of a Good Business Communication:*

Clear and Complete Message

Make answers to the following questions as concise as possible.

1. English is becoming the universal language of business, _____ ,

   and _____ .

2. Foreigners like us to write our business communications in their languages rather than English, even if our use of their language is poor. True or False?

3. In writing to foreigners in English why should we avoid using slang? _____

   _____

4. On the subject of courtesy, what is Ms. Beagle's experienced suggestion for communicating with foreigners? _____

5. What is computerese? _____

6. Give three reasons for making our communications as short as possible. _____

   _____

   _____

7. When is it advisable to lengthen our communications to make them more understandable to the reader/listener? _____

   _____

8. How do you check to see if all the points you planned to cover in a message have been covered? _____

9. Which kinds of statements could be interpreted as being illegal? _____

   _____

   _____

10. If you have written or typed a document that you feel sure has no typing or spelling mistakes, should you read it for possible errors? ____Why or why not? _____

    _____

Chapter 5 Qualities of a Good Business Communication: (*Continued*)

11. In the *Prentice-Hall Author's Guide,* authors are cautioned to proofread carefully because "The eye has a way of seeing _____
_____

12. Briefly, name three reasons businesses use form and guide letters. _____
_____

13. A test made by the United States government shows that use of form letters can save up to ____ percent of the cost of producing individually dictated letters.

14. Why are postcards or postal cards sometimes used for form and guide messages?
_____
_____

15. List ten types of letters for which form or guide letters might be sent. _____
_____
_____

16. Who should write form or guide letters? _____
_____

17. Why must we be especially critical of the content of form and guide letters? _____
_____

18. Why are enclosures often included with routine form letters? _____
_____

19. Name five potential hazards of using form letters.

    a. _____
    b. _____
    c. _____
    d. _____
    e. _____

20. What is the moral of "The Blind Men and the Elephant?"_____
_____

CHAPTER 6
The Routine Information Letter:
The "Yes" Letter

> *If any man wishes to write in a clear style, let him first be clear in his thoughts.*
>
> Johann Wolfgang von Goethe (1749-1832), German poet and dramatist

Of the three basic letter forms—the "yes" letter, the "no" letter, and the selling or persuasive request letter—the form that is used most is the first, the **"yes" letter,** the **routine information letter.** This type of letter simply sends information or makes a request that will automatically be granted, or it announces good news. More than 80 percent of business letters are of this type. This situation is fortunate, because these letters are by far the easiest to write.

The person receiving a negative letter or a selling letter might not be expected to be receptive to the ideas in it. Therefore, it is usually beneficial for these letters to be written with a special psychological treatment so that the negative message or the sales presentation will be accepted more readily. But the person who gets the routine information letter is usually in a more receptive frame of mind. Preparing this type of letter should take less writing talent and experience. Basically, all that is required is a direct statement of facts.

Of course, all the elements of a good letter or memorandum are necessary here: satisfactory appearance, a tone of good will, and a clear and complete message. A pattern for the "yes" letter, the routine information letter, is shown in Figure 6.1 as the "A" letter.

FIGURE 6.1
Pattern for the "A" letter, the routine information letter.

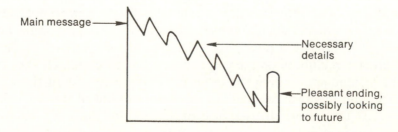

Main message → | Necessary details | Pleasant ending, possibly looking to future

The Routine Information "Yes" Letter Plan

The writing plan for the "A" letter, routine information letter, is as follows:

1. State the main idea of the message.

2. Give all details that are necessary to support the main idea.

3. End pleasantly—generally looking to the future.

State the Main Idea of the Message First

The routine information message begins immediately with the **main idea.** This is what the reader wants to know and what you want the reader to know. Further, no purpose is served by delaying the main impact of the letter.

Give All Details Necessary to Support the Main Idea

The middle section of the letter may be short or long, depending upon the nature of the information being sent. To make sure that the message is **clear and complete,** check it for the following points:

Does it leave out any essential information?

Does it include more information than necessary?

Does it leave out any essential information? To be sure that a letter includes all essential information, the writer should make notes of everything that should be included in each letter. If the letter is outlined well, however briefly, it will pass this first point.

Does it include more information than necessary? Conciseness in writing will be emphasized throughout this text. Wasted words are a constant expense of any organization. Wasted words can also be the downfall of any writer. Anyone who is involved in writing will benefit from checking for all words, phrases, sentences, and paragraphs that can be omitted.

However, this idea should not be carried to the other extreme. Sometimes two people have done business together for some time. Under these circumstances, a personal business relationship may have developed, and pleasant personal comments are proper even in routine correspondence. Business by its nature is often too impersonal. As long as business is being conducted among human beings, such personal comments will usually be welcomed in the multitude of necessarily impersonal mail. Further, if people doing business together are well acquainted, it would be a discourtesy to neglect to make an appropriate personal comment. Such comments can be made in the main body of the letter or in a typed or handwritten postscript. They might refer to such matters as past meetings at a conference or club, or on the golf course or tennis court. Or they might refer to some news heard or read concerning the other person or members of the family.

Should mention be made in the letter outline of the intention to include something personal? Of course. In the rush of getting out the day's mail, you might easily forget to make a planned personal comment in one of the day's letters. Such an oversight might cause the receiver to say, "Well, he surely forgot me in a hurry.... He's only out to make a buck!"

End Pleasantly, Possibly Looking to the Future

The routine information letter should end quickly, and it usually has a slight upswing at the end, generally looking toward the future. You might make a statement like one of these:

I hope this meets with your approval.

Let us know if we can be of further help.

I will appreciate receiving this information as soon as possible.

Form Letters and Cards for Routine Messages

Form letters are not always welcomed by those who receive them. However, people are learning to accept them for many routine messages. As stated in Chapter 5, businesses have form letters already prepared, enabling them to save money by not having to compose individual letters for all correspondence. Then more time and money can be spent preparing letters of a less routine nature that require individual attention.

Correspondence should be reviewed constantly to see if additional form letters should be planned for new types of messages that are becoming routine.

A form letter can be prepared to appear the same as an individually prepared letter. We have many situations, however, in which a preprinted form letter or memorandum obviously prepared for many mailings may be used.

Figure 6.2 shows a few sample form letters or memorandums.

Postal Cards for Routine Messages

Using **postal cards** for brief, routine messages saves time, paper and postage. The standard 3 1/2 by 5 1/2 inch cards, the size purchased at the post office, are completely acceptable when mailings are extremely common and open to public scrutiny.

However, a card measuring up to 4 1/2 by 6 inches can also be sent for the same amount of postage as the smaller card. The larger card has other advantages: It is more distinctive; it is more easily located in the mails; and more information can be included. Postal regulations forbid mailing cards or letters smaller than 3 by 5 inches.

Figure 6.3 illustrates the actual size of a larger postal card, 4 by 6 inches, printed with the appropriate return address of the sender.

When using postal cards, the complete return address should be on the address side of the card. It is not necessary to include this information again on the message side. In this manner, more room is available for date, salutation, message, and signature.

Types of Routine Information Messages

There are many different **types of routine information letters.** The ones listed here are the most common and will be covered in this chapter. Other routine messages could follow these same patterns.

Orders

Acknowledgements of orders

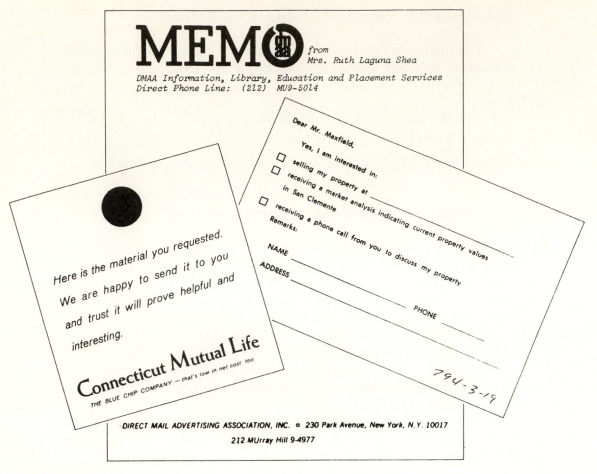

FIGURE 6.2
Sample of business form letters or memorandums.

Transmittal of information; announcements

Routine inquiries or requests

Replies to routine inquiries or requests

Letters sending materials

Routine claim letters

Routine claim adjustments

Orders

Businesses regularly order supplies and equipment by mail. Many of them also receive **orders** for their merchandise by mail—from individuals and from other firms. Orders and acknowledgements of orders are the heart of any business operation. A business cannot survive unless they are handled properly.

Orders from customers and orders to suppliers are the most common type of business communication and the most important. They are also the easiest type of message to send. To save time and money and ensure accuracy, most people order merchandise by filling in either mail order blanks or purchase order forms. First-time customers or buyers making nonroutine purchases may need to send an order letter, which is a simple "A" type information letter.

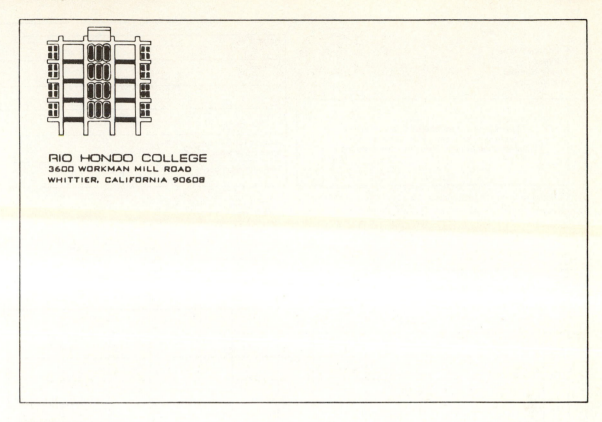

RIO HONDO COLLEGE
3600 WORKMAN MILL ROAD
WHITTIER, CALIFORNIA 90608

FIGURE 6.3
Postal card measuring 4 by 6 inches, printed with complete return address.

Sears, Spiegel, and J.C. Penney are three of the best known mail order firms, but other retailers in various parts of the country also prepare catalogues that include mail order forms for the convenience of customers. Macy's of New York City, Marshall Field's of Chicago, and Nieman-Marcus of Dallas have large mail order operations. Many other large and small firms help meet the continuing demand for this type of purchasing and selling. Ordering by mail is a necessity and convenience to businesses, institutions, invalid or incapacitated individuals, and other people who cannot do all their shopping in person. The working woman has become a major mail order buyer.

The **mail order blank,** the **purchase order form,** or the **order letter** is the first step of a legal contract to buy, so it must be specific. Proper completion of the order is vital to both the buyer and seller, and all information, especially numbers, must be proofread carefully on the form or in the letter. Attention to details will eliminate the necessity of additional phoning or writing to get needed facts. Figure 6.4 is a standard retail customer order blank with necessary information indicated.

An order letter must be checked carefully to see that it contains all information necessary on an order blank for that particular merchandise. Following the "A" letter outline for the routine information letter, the order letter should give the most important information first, followed by needed details and a brief closing:

1. The first sentence should state clearly that this is an order, so that it will get the attention it deserves—an order is a most welcome communication. Say something like, "Please ship me . . . ," "Please send me . . . ," or "Attached is my order for . . . ."

	Name			

Company Name
Address
Phone Number
Fax Number

Name

Address

City   State   ZIP

Place peel-off address label from back cover here. If address is incorrect, please provide correct information at right (including code from top of label).

Address Label Code (from top of label) **5R** _ _ _ _ – _ _ _ _ _ – _ _ _

Telephone Number(s)

☐ Check or money order enclosed

Charge: ☐ MasterCard   ☐ Visa   ☐ American Express

Account Number | | | | | | | | | | | | | | | | |

Expiration date _____   Signature _____

Please have catalog and credit card handy.

Page	Description of Item	Item Number	Size	Initials/ Monogram	Qty.	Item Price	Packing/ Shipping/ Insurance	Gift Wrap (add $2.00)	Item Total

✱ Please add packing, shipping, and insurance charges as shown in parentheses following item price.

Georgia residents add sales tax:

Total Order _____

FIGURE 6.4
Example of a standard retail customer order blank.

2. The next section should contain all needed details, such as:
   a. Number of units, description of merchandise and/or catalogue number, size, color, weight, special features, unit price, total price, tax (where applicable).
   b. How payment will be made: personal check, money order, C.O.D., charge card, open account, bank draft, certified or cashier's check.
   c. Method of shipment, if necessary. For instance, "f.o.b." (free on board) indicates that shipping charges are paid by the seller.
3. This letter closes briefly, perhaps referring to the expected arrival time of the merchandise.

Following is a typical order letter:

**Makes clear
this is
an order** ⟶ This order is from your Spring-Summer 19XX catalogue, page 570.

Necessary details	⟶	Please send me one metal file cabinet catalogue number AH 195-0624 A, shipping weight 48 pounds, price $159.99.
		I am enclosing a check for $165.00, which includes $5.01 shipping charges, figured from the chart on page 7.
Closing	⟶	Please send this item as soon as possible. We are ready to use it immediately.

If several items are being ordered by letter, details for each item should be set out in a separate paragraph, so that items will not be confused. Or columns similar to those on a catalogue order form can be used. The columns will result in better accuracy in setting out the orders, and it will be simpler for the supplier to follow details. A longer order could be set out in the middle of the letter in columns, as follows:

1 screen porch tent	AH 195-6852A		$159.99	48.00 pounds
1 Coleman 2-burner gas stove	AH 195-6824A		29.99	11.00
1 Coleman gas lantern	AH 195-1325A		22.99	5.00
2 Sof-Puff sleeping bags	AH 195-0756A	$39.99 ea.	79.98	11.00
2 foam pads	AH 195-1770A	9.99 ea.	19.98	3.80

Acknowledgments of Orders

Letters of acknowledgment for orders are sent for two reasons: (1) to assure the purchaser that the order was received and is being handled promptly and properly, and (2) to promote good will toward the company filling the order.

Routine Order Acknowledgments

Acknowledgment communications are "A" type routine information letters; that is, they should state the message in the first sentence and end quickly. When merchandise is to be shipped promptly, a preprinted postcard or letter to this effect can be sent to the purchaser in frequently occurring matters. If there is a short delay, you might send a form letter or postcard with blanks filled in showing the disposition of the order. A postcard acknowledgment form might read:

Thank you for your order for _____.
The order will be shipped by _____.
We hope you will remember us when making future orders.

Sometimes, to acknowledge first orders, custom orders, or exceptionally large orders, a letter should be sent that is individually prepared, or appears to have been individually prepared. Purchases that might be routine to the seller are often not routine to the buyer, who likes to know that patronage is appreciated. This letter follows the "A" letter outline:

1. The first sentence should state that the order has been received; it is common courtesy to thank the customer for it.

2. The next part of the letter should state what is being done with the order.

3. The next part, the closing, can contain a "you attitude" reference to the use of the merchandise and it can use resale material promoting the firm or its products. It can

close with a service attitude, offering help or information. At any rate, it should indicate pleasure in doing buiness with the customer. An order blank can be enclosed for future use.

This letter can be very brief, according to the nature of the transaction. An individually prepared acknowledgment letter might read:

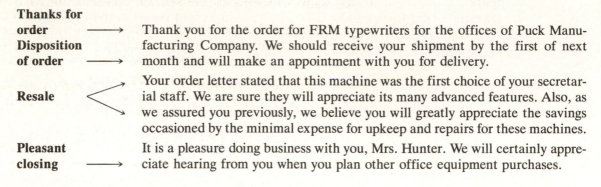

Thanks for order	Thank you for the order for FRM typewriters for the offices of Puck Manufacturing Company. We should receive your shipment by the first of next month and will make an appointment with you for delivery.
Disposition of order	
Resale	Your order letter stated that this machine was the first choice of your secretarial staff. We are sure they will appreciate its many advanced features. Also, as we assured you previously, we believe you will greatly appreciate the savings occasioned by the minimal expense for upkeep and repairs for these machines.
Pleasant closing	It is a pleasure doing business with you, Mrs. Hunter. We will certainly appreciate hearing from you when you plan other office equipment purchases.

Cordially,

Here is a routine acknowledgment of a reservation for a hotel in Canada. Notice the British spelling of *cheque*.

Thank you	Thank you for your letter and cheque confirming your reservation of an upper apartment for the period 16th to 17th July, inclusive.
Disposition of order	Please find enclosed our receipt No. 1458 for your deposit of $40, which is refundable upon two weeks' notice of cancellation, or if we are able to rerent the apartment for the full period.
Pleasant closing	We look forward to meeting you and to welcoming you to the King's Domain later this month.

Yours truly,

Nonroutine Order Acknowledgments

Quite often it is necessary to make a nonroutine response to an order when there must be a long delay in shipment or when it is impossible to make shipment at all. These letters contain a negative message, or a modified negative message, and will be covered in Chapter 7, "The Negative Communication: The 'No' Letter."

Sending Information; Making Announcements

Many routine memorandums and letters are simply **transmitting information** or **making announcements.** Quite often, this type of information can be posted on a bulletin board where several people may read it. Or individual copies may be mailed to people concerned. For information of considerable importance, in addition to being posted on bulletin boards, individual copies may be mailed to people concerned.

As far as possible, such information and announcements should be stated in positive terms. That is, if a negative subject is being handled, rather than saying what cannot be done or what should not be done, the message should be what *can* or *should* be done:

| Original | Employees should not use the administrative and customer parking lot. |
| **Improved** | A special parking lot for employees is provided at the east wing of the administration building. |

| Original | The newsstand is closed from 10 p.m. to 7 a.m. |
| **Improved** | The newsstand is open from 7 a.m. to 10 p.m. |

Many types of routine information communications are sent to employees, stockholders, customers, clients, and the like. Following are announcement letters that should be good news to people who receive them.

Letter 1

Dear Orange Shareholder

Main message ——→ I'm very pleased to enclose with this letter your first dividend check from Orange Computer, Inc.

Necessary details ——→ On April 23 your Board of Directors declared Orange's first quarterly cash dividend. It is for the quarter ended March 27, 199X, and the cash amount is $.06 per share for any shareholder on the date of record, May 15, 199X.

We believe that declaration of this dividend demonstrates our high level of confidence in Orange Computer, and we're happy to be in a position to benefit our shareholders. If you have questions, please contact our Shareholder Relations office at (592) 000-0000.

Sincerely,

Address update ——→ P. S. If your address on this check is not correct, please help us update our records by following instructions printed on the check.

Letter 2

Main message ——→ We were pleased to receive your recent letter concerning traffic patterns in your neighborhood, Mrs. Davis. Partly because of your excellent suggestion, we will incorporate a left-turn lane at the intersection of Firestone Boulevard and Palm Avenue.

Details ——→ Yes, we certainly are concerned about the safety of children traveling to and from the new city park. This new left-turn lane should divert some traffic away from roadways adjoining the park.

Closing ——→ We are glad you took the time to write us, Mrs. Davis. We welcome suggestions from you and other citizens.

Routine Inquiries and Requests

Businesses are glad to receive letters requesting information about their products and services. When you write to ask for material or information that you can automatically expect to receive, this can be considered a routine request or inquiry. If you can expect resistance to your letter, this type of letter would be classified not as routine, but instead as a persuasive request, a type of selling letter.

The **routine request or inquiry** should be written in this order:

1. Make the request or inquiry in the first sentence.

2. If necessary, clarify or justify the request.

3. If possible, close with a positive statement looking toward the future.

When your routine letter is a request that you expect to be granted without question, you should close the letter with some word expressing your appreciation for the favor that is being done for you. A phrase like "Thanking you in advance," or "Hoping to hear from you soon" should not be used. These are outdated ways of ending a letter with a dangling verbal phrase.

Following are some examples of routine requests and inquiries:

Letter 1

Would you please send me a copy of your free brochure showing T-shirts, jackets, emblems, and sweatshirts, as advertsed in the August issue of *Car Craft*.

I would like to have this brochure immediately, as I am eager to order identical jackets or sweatshirts for employees at our car dealership.

I would appreciate hearing from you soon.

Letter 2

Please reserve me a single room for the nights of July 14, 15, and 16. I will be attending the convention of the Electronic Data Processing Programmers at your hotel on those dates.

A check for the first night is enclosed. Will you please send me a confirmation.

Letter 3

GENERAL UNITED CORPORATION WOULD LIKE TO PARTICIPATE IN YOUR CONTRACT 1-72-91-1 FOR THE PURCHASE OF GASOLINE ON CREDIT CARDS.

ARE WE TO CONTACT STANDARD OIL COMPANY DIRECTLY AND REQUEST CARDS FROM THEM FOR PREMIUM GAS? DO YOU NEED ANY ADDITIONAL FORMS COMPLETED BY US FOR YOUR RECORDS?

I WOULD APPRECIATE RECEIVING THIS INFORMATION AS SOON AS POSSIBLE AS I FEEL CERTAIN WE CAN BENEFIT FROM THE USE OF THIS CONTRACT.

Replies to Routine Inquiries and Requests

Form letters or cards are frequently used for **replies to routine requests and inquiries.** Although the memorandum form is generally used only for interoffice and intraoffice communications, in many routine matters it also serves for outside business correspondence. Figure 6.2 showed memorandum forms sent outside the firms.

The basic information in the routine reply letter or memorandum would do the following:

1. Answer the question clearly

2. Supply any further information necessary

3. End with a good will closing

Following are examples of replies to routine requests:

Letter 1

We are happy to reserve a room for you for the nights of July 14, 15, and 16. Your check will be applied to special rates for members of the EDP Programmers Association.

Let us know what we can do to help you enjoy your stay with us.

Letter 2

In response to your inquiry, we are sending you a catalogue listing specifications and prices of our line of Wodget Womplies.

May we suggest that you place your order soon, as our supplies are limited.

Letter Sending Materials (Letters of Transmittal)

A **letter sending materials,** sometimes called a **letter of transmittal,** should do the following:

1. State specifically what is being sent
2. Tell how it is being sent, and any other important details:
   a. Enclosed, or
   b. Separately—mail, truck, air, etc.
3. Close with a positive statement

Here is a welcome letter of transmittal sent to stockholders:

Enclosed is your 100 percent stock distribution on the common stock of the Company, declared by the Board of Directors on June 1, 19XX, and payable to holders of common stock of record July 1, 19XX.

The purpose of the 100 percent stock distribution is to increase the potential number of owners of the Company. It also reflects the Board's confidence in the Company's future growth.

Another welcome letter:

Enclosed is a copy of the ad on your book we have scheduled to run in *The Wall Street Journal* during the week of September 6.

Hope you like it!

Routine Claim Letters

Occasionally it is necessary to make a **routine claim** against a business for money, materials, or service that the company can be expected to agree to automatically. This is an "A" type routine information letter, where the request is made early in the letter, with any necessary supporting facts following immediately. The letter can end with a statement of what is wanted. Here is an example of such letters:

I am sending separately with a copy of this letter my Bestclox watch, which I purchased under a one year warranty. As the watch consistently loses about twenty minutes a day, I would like it repaired or replaced according to your company warranty. Manual adjustments I can make with the lever on the back of the watch do not help.

The warranty on this watch was mailed to you on November 5, 19XX, the date of purchase. I would like very much to have this watch in working condition as soon as possible.

Very truly yours,

Routine Claim Adjustments

A **routine claim adjustment** letter is a good news letter, an "A" letter, and states very simply that the claim or request has been satisfied. This letter should be brief. Resale material might be used here, because you have shown that your firm treats customers fairly.

The best way to write this letter is to avoid the use of negative words like *problem, trouble, damage,* and so forth. Instead, refer to the fact that the product is now in good condition and can be expected to operate properly:

We are returning in today's mail your Bestclox watch, which has been completely repaired by our service department, according to our guarantee. This watch will now give you satisfactory performance because it has also been checked by our testing department.

We hope you will keep Bestclox in mind in future purchases of watches and clocks. We make every effort to satisfy our worldwide number of customers.

Notice that the closing section of this letter makes no reference to the previous unsatisfactory condition of the watch. Neither does it suggest that more trouble might occur. In this manner, the letter ends on a positive tone rather than a negative.

Nonroutine claim adjustments, negative communications, are covered in Chapter 7.

News Releases

In a small firm, a new employee may sometimes be assigned the task of preparing **news releases.** This often happens because no one else on the present staff has shown talent for writing news stories. In more established organizations, news releases are usually prepared by the marketing or customer relations staffs. Either way, people writing news releases must work closely with top management to make certain that information presented is accurate and is being handled in accordance with company policy at the time.

Any news release is distributed to print and/or broadcast media with hope of obtaining free publicity. Frequently, the same article is distributed to several different media. You should know that it is in stiff competition with other articles, and the better it conforms to regular news writing standards, the better its chances for publication. If the article is written acceptably and is used, the news outlet benefits in getting a story already written by outsiders.

Also, you might have more success getting your news release accepted by small, local, or trade publications than by major newspapers, wire services, radio stations, or TV networks.

Small News Outlets

Don't discount **small news outlets.** Small outlets are hungrier for news, and even if your news releases don't get published in *The Los Angeles Times,* the article that was published in the *Beverly Hills Weekly* might land on the doorstep of an executive who reads it and becomes interested in doing business with you.

If you are going to write news releases on a regular basis, keep a list of newspapers, magazines, radio, and TV stations that might be interested in your firm's stories.

Typical Items for News Releases

Below are some typical topics for **business news releases:**

New products or services	Special support of community interests
New plants or facilities	Number of new employees to be hired
Election of new officers	Contests
Appointments of top personnel	Environmental concerns and activities
Promotion of personnel	Prominent visitors
Mergers and acquisitions	Research breakthroughs

Grants to community, arts, or other organizations

Community work done by employees

New contracts

Employee activities

Your Story

A Catchy Story

The editor who decides if your article will be published is looking for something to **catch the reader's eye.** Try to find an interesting twist—some novel angle—on which to hang your story. Ask yourself, "What is the most interesting, exciting, or unusual aspect of this story?" But stay within reason. Don't go too far out. If you find and use such an acceptable twist, your story will probably get earlier attention than 50 percent of competing stories.

Your Audience

Always, always consider your audience just as you do in writing letters or reports, and write to that audience. Newspaper readers and broadcast audiences are part of a general population, so do not use in-house or trade jargon not understandable to outsiders. Also, avoid overlong words. They won't impress the editor or your audience. You can consider using these terms for other announcements to groups who will follow what you are talking about.

Who? What? When? Where? Why?

Editors recognize the work of professionals, and the more professional the wording and format of your release, the less rewriting needs to be done by the editorial staff. And the better are the chances for survival of your article under the editor's scissors.

A regular news staff member is trained to include in the lead of the story—the first one or two paragraphs—the answers to as many of these **"5 W's"** as are pertinent to the story:

Who?   Names make news: Name the people involved.

What?   Say what happened that is newsworthy.

When?   Say when it occurred. Remember: old news is usually not news. Timing is important.

Where?   Location is usually of great importance.

Why?   You often don't have information for this W. Yet, when it is part of a story, it can be the heart of the story.

With the "5 W's" in front of you, you can see that your job will be easier than you thought. These will be the notes you can follow to write the news release.
Make it catch the reader's attention!

Writing the News Release

Like a good news story, a good news release will generally follow a modified "A" letter outline. The most important news must come early. Additional information should be included in decreasing order of importance, leaving the least important to last.

The modified "A" letter outline that can be followed for a press release is shown in Figure 6.5, together with an illustration of a long article being clipped shorter. To fit available space, when brevity is needed, editors almost always clip the article from the bottom up.

Now follow these writing guidelines:

1. Make the story sound important—without false puffery.

2. Write in third person, not in first:
   This:
   Leo's Video store will give free Leo's T-shirts to *its* first 100 customers at *its* store opening. . . .
   Not this:
   We will give free Leo's Video T-shirts to the first 100 customers at *our* store opening. . . .

3. Follow the rules for being clear, complete, and concise. Use good grammar, spelling, and punctuation. Less rewriting will be needed, making your article more appealing to the editor, the person with the scissors.

Format of News Releases

Most news releases are typed *double spaced* on plain white paper. At the top of the page in all capital letters, blocked against the left margin, type *FOR IMMEDIATE RELEASE* or *NEWS*. Above or below this heading, type the name, address, and telephone number of your company, together with the name of the person releasing the news. Also, the editor will appreciate your furnishing the approximate number of words in the article. Mark the end of the article by typing the journalistic symbol for the end (# # #) at the center of the line below the copy. Figure 6.6 is an outline for a news release.

Checkpoints for Routine Information or "Yes" Messages

1. Identify your reader(s) and write at that level.

2. Is the appearance satisfactory?

FIGURE 6.5
Modified "A" letter outline for a press release, showing effect cutting might have.

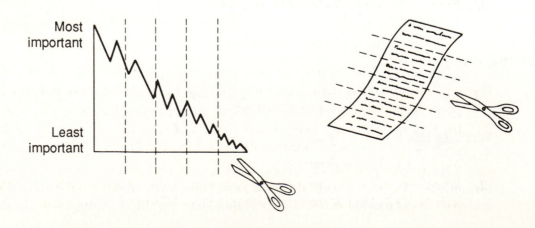

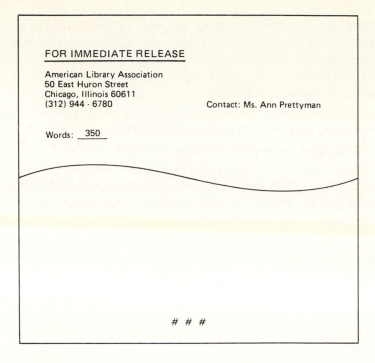

FIGURE 6.6
Format for news release.

3. Is it courteous?

4. Is the message clear and complete? Check your letter outline or notes.

5. Is the main information given early in the first paragraph?

6. Have you included all necessary details? Have you eliminated unnecessary information?

7. Does the letter end pleasantly?

8. Eliminate wasted words and sentences.

9. Could any sentence be interpreted as discourteous?

10. Check to see that you have few, if any, passive sentences.

11. For variety in sentence form, some sentences should start with descriptive words, phrases, or clauses. (See exercise page 123.)

12. Recheck for correct grammar and spelling.

Writing Assignments

1. Send a letter to Mr. Clarence C. Brook, Bud's Flower Shop, 122 Colorado and Ocean Blvd., Santa Monica, California 90401, welcoming him as a new customer and thanking him for his order. Suggest other items of stationery you might send him, and enclose a copy of your latest catalogue. Sign the letter with your name as General Manager of Dallas Stationers.

2. Write a personal-business letter with your home return address to Cable Car Clothiers, No. 150 Post Street, San Francisco, California 94108. Order the following mer-

chandise: a man's sleeveless sweater, catalogue #28C3, size 38, price $29.95, red; swim trunks, catalogue #27H3, size 32, blue-red combination, price $50.00; casual Knockaround Keds, catalogue #49AC, white, price $40.00. Enclose a personal check for the order, adding sales tax if you are a resident of California. Be sure to include your full name and address.

3. In response to the letter in assignment 3, write a letter to yourself signed by A. B. See, Manager, Customer Accounts, thanking you for your order and asking the desired size of the Knockaround Keds, catalogue #49AC.

4. From Tiffany & Company, Fifth Avenue and 57th Street, New York, N.Y. 10022, order one bracelet of 18-karat gold, set with diamonds and emeralds, catalogue #A-65, price $1,950. Also, order earrings to match, catalogue #C-65, price $1,290. Ask that the merchandise be billed to your regular account and delivered to you by bonded messenger. Include your complete address.

5. Write a letter to yourself thanking you for the order of bracelet and matching earrings in assignment 4. Sign the letter "Gott Roks, Director of Customer Relations."

6. Send an order to the University Shop, 3900 Jackson Road, Ann Arbor, Michigan 48103. You would like them to select for you a gift for your niece, Miss Priscilla Winslow, a student at the University of Michigan, and ask to have it delivered to her at her college address, 2901 Wagoner Road, Apt. 201, Ann Arbor. You may make a suggestion, noting that you are not sure of her dress size so you cannot suggest specific wearing apparel. Ask them to charge it to your MasterCard Account #SZ31-00012-27AC. Specify a limit of $50.

7. Write a letter to Miss Carol Newman, Customer Service Representative, Sheraton-Tampa Motor Hotel, Cass and Morgan Streets, Tampa, Florida 33602, telling her that your firm no longer carries the cotton-linen banquet cloths and napkins she had ordered, but carries only a new line of a combination of linen-polyester banquet cloths, which have proved more satisfactory for appearance and long-wearing qualities. You have substituted these cloths for the order from the Sheraton-Tampa at the price of the cloths ordered, although the regular price of the new line of linens is approximately 10 percent higher than the cotton-linen cloths. Sign your name to the letter, giving yourself the title of Manager, New Products Division.

8. You are employed by the Aspen Ski Hut and have received a letter from a new customer, Miss Terri Fick, saying that when she received her new short skis, the ski poles recommended were not included, although they were on the bill she received. Write a letter to Miss Fick saying that you are sending the ski poles and she will receive them by special delivery. Assure her that this will not happen again.

9. Write a letter that will be sent to all members of the Lakeside Junior Chamber of Commerce, of which you are program chairman. The next meeting will be held at the Lakeside Country Club at 12 noon, Monday, September 9, 19XX, in the Lakeview room. The speaker will be Fred Snyder, director of community relations of the local college. Lunch, including gratuities, will cost $10. Give details of the meeting and ask the members to inform you whether or not they will attend. Make up the name and address of one person to whom you are writing this letter.

10. You are the owner of a new business, Cyd's Cycle Shop, and are interested in participating in the local Thanksgiving Day parade either by preparing a float or by assisting a volunteer group in the preparation of its float. Write a letter to the head of the Thanksgiving Day Parade Committee, Ms. Lucia Stark, 4500 Nema Road, Tucson, Arizona 85034.

11. Write a letter to a large corporation asking for a copy of its annual report. If you wish to state a reason, say that (1) you are interested in investing in the company, (2) you are thinking of seeking employment with the company, or (3) you need a copy of the report for work in a business writing class at your college. Consider actually mailing this letter to get a report for use later in the course during the study of business report writing.

12. You recently sent in a mail order for $175.62 for four items of clothing from Country Squire Clothiers, South Hero, Vermont 05486. The merchandise you received was what you ordered except for a man's leather belt, catalogue number 10608S. You ordered size 32 and you received size 42. Write a letter informing Country Squire that you are returning the belt with a copy of your letter, and you would like the belt in the correct size.

13. As program chairman of the Lakeside Junior Chamber of Commerce, write Mr. Fred Snyder a letter thanking him for speaking at the event noted in assignment 9.

14. As publicity chairman of the Lakeside Junior Chamber of Commerce, write a news release about what took place at the September 9 meeting. You will have to make up the subject of Mr. Snyder's speech and any possible details.

15. As a member of the consumer relations department of a business, make up a news release about a recent development of the firm. You might look at pages 116-117 for the topic that you report.

Chapter 6   *Writing Improvement Exercise*

Variety in Sentence Forms

The mail clerk made several errors in the dim light.
In the dim light, the mail clerk made several errors.

Several overdue orders were on his desk.
On his desk were several overdue orders.

The announcement came as a surprise to all of us.
To all of us, the announcement came as a surprise.

We can start the celebration as soon as the election returns are in.
As soon as the election returns are in, we can start the celebration.

Of all the exercises for improving writing, this one on using **variety in sentence forms** may prove most helpful.

In each of the sentences that introduce this exercise, the first sentence follows the traditional pattern of the English language: *Subject–Verb,* followed by modifiers. Continual use of this pattern leads to extremely monotonous, unprofessional, singsong writing. The suggested improvement of each of these examples places modifying words, phrases, or clauses before the subject.

When a person's writing is not smooth—the kind sometimes described as *choppy*—it can usually be improved tremendously by simply applying the principles of writing given here and changing the order of some of the sentences. Frequently, amateurish writing becomes professional just through the use of such changes as these. You must be cautious, however. Moving an element to the beginning of a sentence tends to emphasize it. Do not emphasize negative information unnecessarily.

Here are some suggestions for varying the form of the traditional sentence.

1. Start with a descriptive word or phrase:
   a. These exercises can frequently be applied to my own writing. → Frequently, these exercises can be applied to my own writing.
   b. The jury brought in a verdict of guilty after deliberating four hours. → After deliberating four hours, the jury brought in a verdict of guilty.
   c. The tired and hungry board members ended their negotiations at 3 a.m. → At 3 a.m., the tired and hungry board members ended their negotiations.
   d. He finished his work, not complaining even though he was tired. → Not complaining even though he was tired, he finished his work.
   e. Her opportunity to accept the job offer is gone. → Gone is her opportunity to accept the job offer.
   f. We received the news of the accident early that evening. → Early that evening, we received the news of the accident.

2. Start with a subordinate clause:
   a. They can participate in the discussion if they desire to do so. → If they desire to do so, they can participate in the discussion.
   b. We can try this method when all else fails. → When all else fails, we can try this method.
   c. We can be satisfied that we were honest, whatever else happens. → Whatever else happens, we can be satisfied that we were honest.
   d. You may use our reception area if the weather turns bad. → If the weather turns bad, you may use our reception area.

Chapter 6 *Writing Improvement Worksheet*

Variety in Sentence Forms

Rewrite the following sentences by placing something other than the subject at the beginning of the sentence. Acceptable answers may vary.

1. Tellers must count the cash twice for each customer.→_____

_____

_____

2. Mr. Bernie left the meeting in a flurry of excitement.→_____

_____

_____

3. Replies to the mail order letter came in from all over the country.→_____

_____

_____

4. The exasperated bank manager called her staff together.→_____

_____

_____

5. The record of the committee's work is somehow lost.→_____

_____

6. Construction can start after the next meeting of the city council.→_____

_____

7. We will open another branch store if this one proves to be a success.→_____

_____

8. Many people will want to buy the stock when the market settles.→_____

_____

_____

9. One of the members of the board of trustees was absent at the last meeting, owing to a family emergency.→_____

Chapter 6   Writing Improvement Worksheet *(Continued)*

10. You may have to establish an educational trust fund, since you have small children.→

_____

_____

_____

11. The announcements of the store opening will be mailed at the end of the month.→

_____

_____

12. The crew chief handed out assignments as each person arrived.→_____

_____

_____

13. We will have to work overtime because of the coming bank holiday.→_____

_____

_____

14. We should never throw shredded confidential papers during a ticker tape parade.→

_____

_____

15. They found the key to the coded message under his lunch.→_____

_____

_____

REVIEW AND DISCUSSION

Chapter 6 *The Routine Information Letter: The "Yes" Letter*

Complete the following exercises. Be concise.

1. What is the most common type of business letter and the easiest to write? _____

   _____

2. Name the three basic qualities of a good business communication. _____

   _____

   _____

3. Draw a diagram of an "A" letter pattern and identify the information that should be contained in the beginning, middle, and closing.

4. What two questions can you ask to check if a letter or memorandum is clear and complete? _____

   _____

5. How should the routine information letter end? _____

   _____

6. Why are form letters and postal cards sometimes used for routine mailings?

   _____

   _____

7. Name five types of communications that can be written following the "A" letter pattern. _____

   _____

   _____

Chapter 6   The Routine Information Letter: The "Yes" Letter (*Continued*)

8. Give three reasons why an order must be clear and specific. _____

_____

_____

9. What information should be in the three sections of an order letter?
   a. Beginning: _____
   b. Middle: _____
   c. Closing: _____

10. What information should be included in the letter that acknowledges an order?
    a. Beginning: _____
    b. Middle: _____

    _____

    c. Closing: _____

11. List the order of information that should be included in a routine request or inquiry.

_____

12. List the information that should be included in a reply to a routine request or inquiry.

_____

_____

13. List information that should be in a letter of transmittal.

_____

_____

_____

14. What information should the first part of a routine claim letter give?

_____

_____

15. Why is it especially appropriate to enclose resale materials or messages in a routine claim adjustment? _____

_____

16. What are the five W's that should be included in the lead section of most news releases? _____

17, 18, 19, 20. To give variety to these sentences, rewrite them so something besides the subject starts the sentence:

17. Applause broke out loudly when the new bank hours were announced.→_____

_____

18. The managers were making the choice of microcomputers without consulting with the clerical staff.→_____

_____

19. Wage adjustments will be made for late night and early morning shifts.→_____

_____

20. Management frequently made adjustments on indoor and outdoor assignments.→

_____

_____

CHAPTER 7
The Negative Communication:
The "No" Letter

> *I try to think of things very positive and nothing negative. Instead of saying, "Don't sit back," I say, "Always stay forward." Instead of saying, "Don't hang behind," I say, "Always attack." Instead of saying, "Don't be tense," I say, "Hang loose." Believe me, I think that is the difference.*
>
> Gold medal champion slalom skier
> when asked how he managed to win

The champion skier quoted above believes that a **positive mental attitude** pays off. This optimistic viewpoint can also pay off in other experiences—especially in writing letters and other communications.

As emphasized earlier, business writers must be concerned with three basic qualities of their written communications: attractive appearance, good will tone, and clear and complete message. Of the three types of letters—the "A" or routine information letter, the "B" or negative message, and the "C" sales letter or persuasive message—it is the negative communication that presents the greatest challenge in the area of good will. This is because you are sending a **disappointing or "bad news" message** that probably will not be welcome. Your aim in writing this message is to say the negative briefly in a manner that is acceptable, paying special attention to retaining the reader's good will.

Writing this type of letter requires considerable talent and attention. Studies show that too many business letters and memorandums contain statements that are unnecessarily offensive to the readers—statements that might make readers take their business elsewhere. Intentionally, or frequently unintentionally, negative ideas are too often sent that do not help your purpose. In fact, a negative tone can completely cancel an otherwise clear message. We must prepare negative communications with an ear that is sensitive to the other person's feelings. If we approach negatives with a positive attitude, we can be more successful in making the unwelcome message sound acceptable.

Patterns for the "No" Letter

A simple pattern that can be used for most negative messages, such as refusals, partial adjustment replies, and complaints, is shown in Figure 7.1. The negative communica-

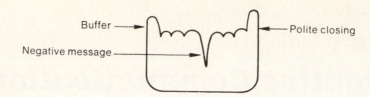

FIGURE 7.1
Pattern for a "B" letter, the "no" or negative communication.

tion, the "no" letter, contains three elements: (1) the buffer, (2) the negative message, and (3) a polite closing.

Another pattern to use for giving bad news would be to borrow from the entertainment industry and follow the format of a director giving actors suggestions after a rehearsal. This format also has buffer, negative message and pleasant closing. Called a "praise sandwich," it consists of two slices of praise wrapped around a chunk of criticism. Figure 7.2 is an illustration of this concept.

The Buffer

A very effective way to start a letter with a negative message is to open with a **buffer.** A buffer is used for the same purpose that a bumper was originally designed for on an automobile—that is, to cushion a blow. If you give the "no" reply at the beginning of a letter, you will probably turn away the reader, who will lose interest in the rest of the message where the reasons for the "no" are given. Instead, first make some pleasant statement with which the reader will agree. Next, lead to the negative part of the message, generally giving the reason or some of the reasons for the coming negative. This plan is all part of the buffer leading to the main message.

The buffer should not sound so pleasant that the reader expects a "yes" or favorable communication, because it would then be far more difficult to accept the "no" when it does come. You might actually have given false hope.

FIGURE 7.2
Pattern for a "praise sandwich."

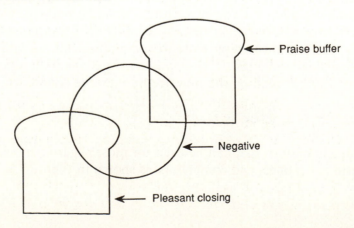

The Negative Message

Make the negative brief.

After the buffer opening and some explanation of the reasons behind the negative message, the **"no" message** should be given very clearly and *as briefly as possible.* This section should not be labored with negative-sounding statements. Good will is best served by saying it as pleasantly as possible and getting on with the closing.

Whenever possible, avoid reciting here any of the negative aspects of your communication, such as repeating the details of a complaint. Repetition only serves to etch these details into the reader's mind.

Not this:

> We do not understand why you have had so much trouble with our watch for so long and why it does not keep good time for you. [This statement could be left out entirely.]

Not this:

> I am sorry that I cannot speak to your group, as I have a previous speaking engagement for that night. I know it will be difficult for you to try to find another speaker at this date, and I hope that you won't have further problems with the rest of the program . . . [This paragraph could close with the first sentence.]

Do not "talk down."

Regardless of how provoked you are, do not talk down to people. Don't "slap their wrists." They might respond behind your back, doing the opposite of what you have ordered—or worse. (See Chapter 3 on "Good Will Tone," and particularly the section on "Write Courteously.")

The Polite Closing

After the tone of the letter drops down for the "no" message, as shown in the diagram, the tone should come back up, closing on a positive note. When appropriate, the closing can contain additional reasons for the negative message. If possible, try to show that a reason behind the refusal might be of potential advantage to the reader. This is done in the following credit refusal:

> We are able to offer merchandise at these low prices only because of our credit policies.

A furniture store explained the policy of not delivering furniture in this manner:

> The costs of maintaining regular furniture delivery routes in a widespread area like the Los Angeles valley are tremendous, and these costs would have to be passed on to our customers. We have discovered that customers are able to arrange far more economical deliveries on their own, often carrying their purchases in their own vehicles.

Skillfully done, this closing section can often make a counterproposal and/or contain resale material encouraging further business.

In the closing, care must be taken not to pretend to have done something you haven't done. Don't say:

> We hope we can be of help to you again. [You weren't this time.]

> We are sure this will meet with your approval. [It might not.]

Tone in Negative Communications

As contradictory as it seems, in negative messages we should avoid using negative words and phrases as much as possible. Letters set out in this chapter will demonstrate how this can often be accomplished. The German philosopher Friedrich Nietzsche said, "We often dispute an opinion when what we really object to is the tone in which the opinion was uttered." Somebody else said, "It isn't what you say, it's the way that you say it!"

We want to give others a favorable picture of ourselves and our organization. Therefore, we should choose words for their connotations or potential associations as well as for their specific meanings. (See the discussion of words and their meanings in Chapter 3.) Avoid using words that have particularly unpleasant negative associations, and if necessary, go to a dictionary or a thesaurus for an acceptable euphemism.

Here are four columns of words showing how much more pleasant the positive words are than the negative ones.

Negative		*Positive*	
shut up	never	yes	gift
no	inferior	please	delighted
can't	careless	fortunately	admire
don't	terrible	happy	easy
won't	damage	special	winner
regret	error	vacation	wonderful
unsatisfactory	complain	free	superb
bad	problem	good	superior
failed	insult	fair	bargain
difficult	sorry	correct	achievement
late	dissatisfied	efficient	enthusiastic
wrong	neglect	satisfactory	thank you
ignorant	inefficient	excellent	honor
criticism	lying	appreciate	admire
complicated	incorrect	agree	praise
annoy	stupid	success	can
idiot	grouch	glad	grateful
forgot	illogical	welcome	like
big mouth	demand	love	pleasure
wrong	sarcastic	enjoy	you
disagree	insinuate	positive	cheerful
sad	overdue	courtesy	

The following lists show how certain common phrases should be avoided because of their unflattering connotations.

Words and Phrases with Critical
Between-the-Lines Overtones

When You Say	They Hear
Apparently you are not aware...	Stupid!
I question what you say...	Lying?
Our unassailable position...	We're always right.
We are not inclined to...	We don't care if we please you.
We cannot understand your...	You're not thinking clearly.
We differ from you...	So you must be wrong.
We question your...	Are you lying?
We repeated to you...	We told you this before!
When you question our decision...	We're right.
You apparently overlooked...	Careless!
You are wrong...	As usual.
You did not include...	Careless again.
You do not understand...	Dumbbell!
You failed to...	Can't you do it right?
You forgot to...	Ignoramus!
Your complaint...	Crybaby!
Your demand...	Don't be so bossy.
Your disregard...	Pay attention.
Your dissatisfaction...	Whine! Whine!
Your failure to...	You bombed again!

Humor in Negatives

Acceptable Humor

At a time when smoking was permitted on airplanes, a flight attendant's voice was heard on the intercom of a plane in flight: "Smoking in smoking sections only. No smoking at any time in lavatories. Violators of these regulations will be asked to step outside."

Caution should be used in employing **humor in negative situations.** Very often, the matter under discussion is too serious for the receiver to want to hear jokes about it. But under certain circumstances, humor can be used extremely effectively. This is usually more acceptable when the message is well meant and when it is certain that the message will be received in the manner in which it is intended. Also, it helps if the writer and receiver are acquainted.

Members of the career education department of one college were continually plagued by having other staff members block their driveway. Routine memos had produced fair results, but there were still trespassers, particularly the driver of a certain red Porsche. One morning, a member of the staff used a felt tip pen (with water-soluble ink) to draw a wide dotted line across the hood of the part of the car that protruded into the driveway and attached the following note under the windshield wiper:

> Attention Mr. Mike Davis
> Plant Maintenance
> Rio Hondo College
>
>   Please issue a work order for the necessary cutting of that portion of automobile projecting across the access road to Room T-106. See line of cut across hood of 1970 Porsche, red color.
> From: Larry Fickle
> Welding–Tech Dept.

The next day Mr. Fickle found the following note in his mailbox:

>   Imagine my surprise when I went out to the parking lot and found my car so neatly trimmed off. Fortunately, the motor is in the back and I was able to make it home. But imagine the sight it must have been to the other drivers to see a little gray-haired lady in half a car tooling down the freeway doing wheelies!
> But I do know where to park what's left of my car from now on.
> My best,

An effective whimsical approach was the request an oceanfront hotel posted to put across a negative message to guests:

> NO-NO'S: Barbecues, sleeping bags, surfboards in rooms (we have storage facilities).

Unacceptable Humor

Usually it does not take much talent to show humor at the expense of other people. Rather, it takes more talent plus good sense to restrain yourself from ridiculing another person just for a cheap laugh. The nineteenth-century American educator Horace Mann, who is considered the father of American public education, said: "Avoid witticisms at the expense of others." Among other matters we should avoid, we should not resort to humor that focuses attention on a person's race, sex, handicap, sexual preference or religion because it usually offends.

Candor

When things go wrong, there can be a tendency to "beat around the bush" or "pass the buck." However, when a person is ethical and therefore honest about a situation, even if it is not favorable, that person is respected for being candid. Openly and honestly admitting to a less-than-desirable fact can give people trust and confidence in you.

We should maintain our dignity, avoiding alibis and sour grapes. Others will recognize our honesty in a painful situation.

Hiding Behind Company Policy

In a cartoon, the character Bullwinkle was asked, "What's the reason?" "There's no reason," Bullwinkle replied, "it's just policy."

Unfortunately, this is what a person usually thinks when **company policy** is given as the only reason for the refusal of a request or for any other negative communication. The automatic impression is apt to be, "That's a poor policy, and it ought to be changed."

Therefore, rather than hide behind the excuse of company policy, the negative reply should explain reasons for the answer in terms the reader can understand and accept.

Computer Form Letters

The public is learning to accept form letters because people recognize that these letters save money for a business. However, the old aversion to such letters still exists to some extent—welcome the **computer form letter.**

As stated earlier, a computer makes it possible to prepare form letters that are individualized so that letters do not have the fill-in-the-blanks appearance. Two negative computer form letters with specific information for one reader have been set out later in this chapter.

Forestalling Complaint Letters

In the natural course of business, things occasionally go wrong. Delays in shipments to and from your business, production delays or foul-ups, even acts of God—fire, flood, earthquake, and so forth—can be hazards. The aircraft industry coined a word for an error that seems attributable to no identifiable cause: a *glitch*. To promote good will and prevent people from becoming annoyed or angered, try to **forestall complaint letters** before they take pen, typewriter, keyboard, or telephone in hand.

Anticipate Developments

To forestall complaints, we should **anticipate developments** as much as we can.

The number of service calls dropped dramatically when one major manufacturer began to include the following form with the delivery of any appliance. When necessary, additional information for a specific appliance is added.

Before You Call For Service:

As many as 25% of service calls are not due to improper appliance performance. Before you call for service, check the following:

Is unit unplugged?

Has fuse blown or is circuit breaker tripped? (Check outlet with another appliance or lamp.)

Check controls of unit.

To give subscribers beforehand knowledge of the predicament in which a book club found itself, the following form was sent to all club members:

SPECIAL NOTICE

Dear Member:

The recent floods caused by Hurricane Hugo devastated widespread areas of the eastern section of the country.

Our warehouse and shipping facilities and the serving post office are located in areas that were directly in the path of the storm, and unfortunately, they suffered considerable damage. We are making every effort to restore our facilities, but if you should notice a delay in our service, we hope you'll be patient and will understand that we are doing our best to resume normal operations.

Thank you for your patience and cooperation.

Membership Secretary

The following note was attached to pieces of wicker furniture being shipped to customers. The negative message is so well disguised that readers would probably accept it totally. Also notice the uplift ending looking toward the future:

> Congratulations!
>
> Congratulations on your purchase! With proper care, you will probably enjoy your wicker furniture for many years. Please realize that no piece of wicker, no matter how carefully woven, will be like any other, and each will have its imperfections which are part of its charm. In no way was any part machine made, and its beauty lies in its handwoven artistry, using a natural fiber to create the piece you now own.
>
> You will find that wicker is extremely durable, and with proper care will not break or wear out.

Write in "Plain Talk"

Business must learn that an amazing number of complaint letters are written because previous communications have not been written clearly, causing serious **brain drain.** To forestall complaints, we must be sure letters and memorandums from our offices are written in **"plain talk."** Great care must be taken not only in preparing individual letters, but especially in preparing forms and form letters, because of their repeated usage. Be sure that all terms are easily understandable by laymen, avoiding unnecessary technical terms and gobbledygook.

Firms are learning to follow the lead of insurance companies that are changing their policies to remove legalese and are rewording them in language the lay person can understand.

Caveat Emptor vs. Caveat Venditor

The old business concept of **caveat emptor,** "let the buyer beware," is generally outmoded today because of the highly competitive nature of business and industry and because of increasing consumer protection activities. Business people learn that following ethical practices retains customers.

In order to maintain the good will of customers, most businesses, including major retail chains, operate on the basis that "the customer is always right," or *caveat venditor,* "let the *seller* beware." The theory followed here is that when a customer makes a complaint, in that customer's mind the complaint is justified. Therefore, all but the most flagrantly false claims are satisfied.

In responding to customer requests, claims, or complaints, these businesses find it an economic necessity to draw the line somewhere, so they try to make adjustment decisions that are fair to both the customers and the firm. This makes it necessary to write adjustment letters to customers.

Makeup of "No" Letters

A "no" letter or negative message can be made up from these guidelines that were mentioned earlier:

- **The buffer:** Should begin with a neutral statement with which both reader and writer can agree, and should continue with statements "buffering" the coming refusal—that is, setting the stage. The buffer usually includes some or all of the reasons for the refusals.

- **Negative message:** "No" should be brief and clear, but in no way offensive. Then quickly move on to closing.

- **Pleasant closing:** Give any additional explanation that might be needed, then close. As this is the last part the receiver will read, closing should be pleasant, leaving a good final impression as far as possible. *Do not repeat the negative.*

Examples of "No" Letters

Probably the best way to learn how to write good negative messages is to study some specific types. Common "no" replies are refusals of requests, claims, or complaints; adjustments partially complying with requests; nonroutine order acknowledgments; and answering the "crackpot." Another type of "no" letter is the complaint letter you write yourself.

Refusals of Requests, Claims, or Complaints

Some business people dislike refusals so much that they try to avoid writing them altogether. However, writing them sometimes becomes necessary. A **refusal** that retains a customer's good will, and therefore the customer, can be prepared only when the writer has the correct mental attitude. Although the writer may feel that the situation justifies frankness, or even rudeness, the hope of preserving a good business image should prevent such an approach. True, some requests are ridiculous. But a humorous, cutting, or pointed comment would probably lose that customer as well as the customer's friends or relatives.

A refusal of a request, claim or complaint can follow the pattern of the "no" letter, with buffer, brief negative message, and pleasant closing. The closing can do any of the following:

- Suggest an alternative.
- Send an acceptable substitute for what was requested.
- Resell, suggesting future business under other circumstances.
- Wish them well in their plan without repeating your inability to assist.
- Discuss something off the subject, but acceptable.

Following are three refusals with the buffer, negative message and closing labeled.

Letter 1

Buffer (reader can agree) ⟶ Yes, Mr. Nichols, we at American Home Service surely wish to retain our reputation as being the best friends of the do-it-yourself homeowner. One of the greatest services to the public, we believe, is maintaining low prices throughout our store.

Negative message (brief) ⟶ Therefore, we cannot make a refund to you on the partial panels of plywood. We do not have storage facilities for all sizes of paneling and, as a matter of fact, are often unable to sell off the scraps we have left from our regular store merchandise.

Polite closing ⟶ May we suggest, Mr. Nichols, that you try to find a place to store this paneling for your own possible use in the future. We have had many customers return after a period of time seeking to match some previously purchased woods. Because available supplies differ over the years, this is not always easy to do.

Letter 2

Buffer (reader should agree) ⟶ Your survey of business reports should be of great interest to all businesses in our area.

Negative message (brief) ⟶ However, because Axelradd Furniture Company is a wholly family-owned business enterprise, we do not publish reports for distribution to the public.

Polite closing ⟶ May we wish you luck in completing your study. And we surely hope you have success in completing your work toward your college degree.

Letter 3

Buffer (reader ⟶   I agree with you, Ms. Bronson, that we should all do our best to support a cause
would agree)   that is worthy of our time and money. Certainly, I feel that your project of supporting
underveloped nations is worthwhile.

Negative ⟶   When our firm was founded, all joint partners agreed that, rather than spread our
message   support thinly among many good causes, we would give what we could to two community projects: the annual Community Fund drive and the Backman Geriatrics Ward at
the local county hospital. Our support of these two worthwhile causes takes all the
time, money, and effort our small organization can afford.

Polite closing ⟶   I must say that I have noted with interest some of the successes already obtained
by the efforts of your organization, and I do wish you well in your fund drive.

Partial Adjustment Replies to Requests, Claims, or Complaints

Frequently, in reply to a request, claim or complaint, you may avoid an outright refusal by offering to comply with part of what was requested. This is called a **partial adjustment.** (Regular adjustment letters are covered in Chapter 6.)

In writing the partial adjustment, emphasize what can be done and deemphasize what
cannot be done. A full explanation of the reason for the partial refusal should be given
without offending the reader. It is very important that this letter lets the receiver know
that your company looks forward to continuing to do business in the future.

Nonroutine Order Acknowledgments

Quite often it is necessary to make a **nonroutine order acknowledgment** when there
must be a long delay in shipment or when it is impossible to make shipment at all. These
letters are written because the order received was incomplete, the merchandise ordered is
temporarily out of stock, or the order must be delayed or refused for some other specific
reason. These nonroutine acknowledgments are most effective when handled as negative
communications, following the pattern: buffer, negative message, cordial closing.

Acknowledging Incomplete Orders

Too often, a customer sends an **incomplete order** that does not contain all the information necessary for shipping the merchandise desired, and it is necessary to telephone or
write a letter requesting the missing details. Only a poorly run business will return the
order—it may never come back! A picture of the order might be returned, or a form letter
can be sent simply asking details that were not included in the original order.

Be careful with the tone of this letter, because the potential customer has, in fact,
made a mistake in failing to supply all necessary information. Regardless of the temptation, avoid an accusing tone, and try to avoid direct criticism. Write this letter with the
"you attitude" toward the customer. That is, it is to the customer's advantage that additional information is furnished: "So that you may receive the merchandise promptly, could
you please send this information." No matter how tempted you are, avoid a "between the
lines" tone that suggests, "Hey, you dumbbell, you forgot to tell us everything we need to
know!"

Here is one place where the passive form instead of the active form may be preferred
in sentence structure:

Not this   You did not specify color when you ordered the argyle sweater,
catalogue #3215, size 12. Would you please send us this information.

Improved	Could you please tell us the color desired for the argyle sweater, catalogue #3215, size 12.
Not this	You forgot to tell us how payment for this merchandise is to be made.
Improved	Will payment be made by personal check, bank draft, credit card, or by some other means?

Back Ordering Merchandise

When an article is temporarily out of stock and cannot be shipped within a time that is reasonable for that particular type of merchandise, **back ordering** is a good procedure to follow. To back order means to inform the customer of the situation, saying that you will be able to supply the merchandise by a certain date. You should also say that it will be shipped at that time unless the customer sends notification to the contrary. Or you may ask permission to back order the merchandise.

In a letter telling of delayed shipment, it is wise to use resale material promoting merchandise such as that on the order and other items you have available. In this manner you reinforce the ideas that caused the customer to do business with you in the first place.

Because back order situations are common in business, resale information is often written in a form letter. Figure 7.3 is a back order letter prepared on a **computer mail merge system.** With a computer properly programmed, the specific information in a *list document* can be merged with general information of a *main document,* making the resulting letter an attractive personalized letter rather than a common form letter with specific information typed separately or handwritten in blanks.

Following is another back order letter that could be typed individually. Or a form letter could be printed or typed with spaces left blank so that the specific information can be typed or written in the blanks (italicized areas).

Thank you for your order for *twelve two-pound Arizona Best date-nut loaves.*

Because of the overwhelming demand for this popular item, our supply is depleted, but we are filling orders in turn and we will be able to ship yours on or before *December 10.* Unless you notify us otherwise, we will make shipment at that time.

We do appreciate receiving another *holiday* order from you.

Substitutions for Orders

For any of a number of reasons, it may be impossible to ship the specific item requested, and the seller may be able to offer a suitable substitute. In this situation, the acknowledgment letter should tell the reason for the substitution. It should also fully explain similarities and differences between the product suggested and the one ordered. The closing section of this letter should ask for an immediate reply and suggest an order. Following is an acknowledgment letter suggesting a substitution:

Thank you for your order for 5,000 number 5001 Leviton electrical switches for use in your Littleton School construction.

The Leviton merchandise is of excellent quality, but we cannot obtain it because of the trucking strike. There is no way we can predict when Leviton products will be available.

From the experience of other customers, we have found that Ideal switches can be substituted without loss of quality, and at the same price.

May we ship you 5,000 number 5-Ivory Ideal switches by the first available delivery?

List Document

1
March 2, 19XX

2
Ms. Haber Dasher
12345 Going Way
Norcross, Georgia 30093

3
Ms. Dasher

4
mug and plate sets

5
39412

6
March 25, 19XX

7
Ms. Dasher

Buffer   ———→
(Pleasant)

Negative   ———→
(Brief)

Pleasant closing looking
looking to future   ———→
Plus resale

Enclosure

Main Document

1

2
Dear   3

Thank you for your order for   4   , our catalogue
    5   .
Unfortunately, we are temporarily out of this item.
Additional supplies have been ordered, and we expect to
ship your merchandise on or before   6   .

If you cannot wait until our expected shipping date,
please mail the enclosed stamped card asking for a refund.
We will return a check promptly. If we do not hear from
you, we will assume you are willing to wait.

Again,   7   , thank you for your order. We
hope you enjoy reviewing our new spring catalogue which
will be mailed by April 1, 19XX.

Cordially,

J. P. Morgan
Manager, Order Department

Enc.

FIGURE 7.3
Example of a back order letter prepared by
mail merge showing how a list document with
personalized information for one receiver can
be merged into a main document (form letter).

Sometimes a substitution can be sent automatically when it is known that the customer will accept it without question. However, the substitution should be explained fully:

Today we are shipping your order #3908.

We have taken the liberty of substituting stock item #180329 bond paper for your requested #18328, as the stock number we are sending has replaced the former item. The new paper has proven superior to the former.

We do appreciate your order and look forward to continued business with the office staff of Bellows Chevrolet.

Combination of Routine Orders, Incomplete Orders, Back Orders, and Substitutions for Parts of Orders

Although most orders are shipped out automatically, the order acknowledgment letter must sometimes be a combination of two or more types of acknowledgments if all the merchandise is not being shipped immediately. When this happens the most effective letter will, in separate paragraphs, list and itemize each article, making all information pertaining to each article completely clear. The reader should have no question concerning any part of this order.

Refusing Orders

There are times in almost any business when an order must be refused. Some reasons are these:

1. You cannot approve customer's credit. (Writing letters declining credit is covered in Chapter 9.)
2. You do not carry the merchandise desired and do not have a suitable substitute.
3. You do not sell direct; customer must order through the proper distributor or retailer.
4. Sale would be illegal.

This negative letter should end with a positive tone, such as wishing the receiver luck in purchasing under other conditions or locating merchandise elsewhere, or giving specific information about where and how to make the purchase with another firm. This latter information must definitely be given if you are a manufacturer or wholesaler and are recommending a distributor or retailer who sells your own merchandise.

Following is a letter **declining an order,** which follows the negative communication pattern:

Upbeat opening ⟶	We appreciate your interest in purchasing a Cherry Hill bookcase, Model 117C.
Negative brief and clear ⟶	However, as manufacturers, we do not trade directly with retail customers. You will be able to get this bookcase in one of the retail stores that carry Cherry Hill furniture. We are enclosing a brochure that lists the names and locations of such dealers in your area.
Upbeat closing— looking to future ⟶	If any store is out of stock, we have ample supplies in our warehouse. You could have the store order the bookcase and it could be in your home in four to six weeks. Sincerely,

Enc.

Your Own Complaint Letter

As a business person, you will occasionally find yourself on the "opposite end of the stick," having to write a letter of complaint. Always be aware that if you write at the height of displeasure or anger, your letter might be put in someone else's "crackpot" file, and there may be that negative picture circulating—no one knows how far. You may experience great joy and relief in blowing off, but there can be repercussions. The complaint letter can be handled most effectively if you write when your thoughts are collected and your temper is cool.

Complain—to Whom?

Should you complain to a high official, or should you go through regular channels? John A. Goodman, whose occupation is specializing in complaints, suggests you first contact the head of the customer service department. This department has an established network for handling complaints. Mr. Goodman, president of TARP, a company that does consumer behavior studies, says you should go to the top only when dissatisfied with service from the regular complaint people. Going to the top first might only delay matters, he says.[1]

Then, if regular channels fail, take time to find the name of the top official of the organization, such as the president of the company or the chairman of the board. Do not write to an office, like "Dear President," or "Dear Chairman of the Board," but write directly to that person by name.

Writing Your Own Complaint Letter

Start your letter with a neutral statement with which your reader can agree, such as, "In the rush of business, we all know things can sometimes get out of hand," or, "I am sure that you want to maintain the good reputation that your company has always enjoyed with its customers." You might say, "I certainly hope to continue our business association in the future as we have in the past." Then state your case, giving all the facts necessary to make your point, and say clearly what action you would like taken. If you remain cool and logical, your letter should not stir up heightened emotions in your reader and should create a better chance to get the complaint settled in a satisfactory manner.

This letter can be closed with an optimistic attitude toward the future. "We believe that in fairness we can expect...," or, "If you continue to give us the same type of reliable service that we have learned to expect from your firm, we believe you will agree to do this." Ask, don't command, and use positive terms such as "please," "we will appreciate," "we would like," and so forth.

The Chinese have a proverb: "In the midst of great joy, do not promise to give a man anything; in the midst of great anger, do not answer a man's letter."

Sample Complaint Letter for Personal Use

Figure 7.4 is a sample complaint letter that can be used as a form letter for your personal or career business correspondence throughout the years ahead. This letter can be copied verbatim (with your own fill-ins) because it is from a United States Government publication.[2]

[1]"The Months Ahead," *Changing Times,* July 1983, p. 9.
[2]Office of the Special Adviser to the President for Consumer Affairs, *Consumer's Resource Handbook,* (The White House, Washington, D.C., 1987), p. 3.

(Your Address)
(Your City, State, ZIP Code)
(Date)

(Name of Contact Person)
(Title)
(Company Name)
(Street Address)
(City, State, ZIP Code)

Dear (Contact Person):

- **describe your purchase**

- **name of product, serial numbers**

- **include date and location of purchase**

Last week I purchased (or had repaired) a (name of the product with serial or model number or service performed). I made this purchase at (location, date, and other important details of the transaction).

Unfortunately, your product (or service) has not performed satisfactorily (or the service was inadequate) because (state the problem).

- **state the problem**

- **give the history**

- **ask for specific action**

- **enclose copies of documents**

Therefore, to solve the problem, I would appreciate your (state the specific action you want). Enclosed are copies (copies—NOT originals) of my records (receipts, guarantees, warranties, cancelled checks, contracts, model and serial numbers, and any other documents).

I am looking forward to your reply and resolution of my problem, and will wait (set time limit) before seeking third-party assistance. Contact me at the above address or by phone at (home and office numbers—with area codes).

- **allow time for action or response**

- **include how you can be reached**

Sincerely,

(Your name)
(Your account number,
   if appropriate)

Keep copies of your letter and all related documents and information

FIGURE 7.4
United States government prepared form letter
that can be used for making complaints.

Be certain you supply all the information suggested within the parentheses such as your complete address (people forget to do this), a complete description of service or product including serial or model number; describe problem clearly; name specific action you want taken; include *copies* of all pertinent records. Do not send *original* records.

For a listing of companies and their officers, check the reference section of your college or public library for these sources: *Standard & Poor's Register of Corporations, Directors and Executives; Standard Directory of Advertisers; Thomas Register of American*

Manufacturers; Trade Names Directory. A telephone call to the reference desk of your library will usually get you this information.

The Message with the "Bee Sting"

Never, repeat, **never** post a notice, write a memo, write a letter, make a report, or give any other message that sends that tempting unwritten or unspoken snide remark or negative jab.

Figure 7.5 is an example of a message like this, which could be described as having a **"bee sting."** Such messages are borne of frustration that things or people are not working out the way they should. As mentioned in Chapter 3, be careful not to send unwritten negative messages "between the lines." People do have some self-respect, and rather than complying, they may respond with some spiteful reaction.

Answering—or not Answering—the "Crackpot"

Almost every office—business, industry, government, profession—has what is sometimes called the "zero file," the file of letters from **"crackpots,"** who usually can be easily identified. These are the unreasonable letters from unreasoning or angry people whose

FIGURE 7.5
A message with a "bee sting."

PLEASE NO LOOSE TRASH!

WHAT DOES IT TAKE TO GET YOUR ATTENTION TO COMPLY???

communications are hardly worthy of response. Some businesses do not even file these letters but discard them as soon as they are received. Other businesses or government offices, however, have a policy of answering all communications and, for this type of letter, will send off a very perfunctory reply, discouraging continued correspondence, such as:

> Thank you for your letter.
> We are taking the matter under advisement.

If this sounds routine, it is meant to be. Time is too valuable to be spent on unnecessary letter writing. A letter similar to this one would be appropriate in any instance in which your company simply desires to acknowledge receipt of a letter and end correspondence on the matter.

If a letter expresses contempt or attacks you or your company's reputation, never reply with a similar letter. Otherwise, you might leave yourself open to discipline on the job, or you might even be subject to court action for libel.

Some time ago during a Panama Canal controversy, an aide to a United States senator did reply in an uncomplimentary manner to five or six letters that he felt were unnecessarily critical on the matter. For instance, to one resident of an Eastern state, he wrote that her state was a "melting pot for neurotics, cranks, and other individuals with subnormal mentalities." Although mailed as personal letters at his own expense, these letters caused the aide to be suspended without pay for 60 days. His freedom of the mails cost him $6,000.

The Negative Negative Letter

Perhaps there is no need to give instructions on how to write the **negative negative letter.** You may never be justified in writing such a letter. But at times, almost anyone might feel fully justified in "letting it all hang out," and write a letter in which the good will tone is totally ignored. Such a letter should be written only if the following two provisions hold:

1. Something *constructive* may come from it.
2. No illegal threats are made.

Chapter 3, on good will tone in letters, cautions against writing letters in the heat of anger, pointing out that your anger might cool. Also, you might be embarrassed later because people know you at your worst. Remember there is an old saying, "It is better to have the good will of a cur dog than its ill will." And again, you must think of the possibility that legal action will be taken against you if you say anything that might be interpreted as an illegal threat or defamation of character.

Such a negative letter should be considered—we say *considered*—only when all other communication has failed. Then:

1. Cool off. Perhaps put it off until tomorrow, or the next day, or next month.
2. If you must write, make the message clear and brief.
3. Explain steps you have taken that have been ignored.
4. Make the strongest *legal* threat that you can make to get compliance.
5. If you do not get satisfaction, follow through on number 4. Or else FORGET IT!

The Bachelors and the Buffer

Two bachelors lived with their mother. One of the brothers had to leave town and gave the responsibility of caring for his cat to the other, Sam. A few nights later, the absent brother phoned and during the call asked how his cat was. "He died," said Sam.

"Wow!" was the response. "When you have news like that, Sam, you should lead into it gently."

"What do you mean?" his brother asked.

"Well, you might have said something like, 'Last night your cat was up on the roof...' and then gone on to tell the news as less of a shock."

A couple of nights later, the traveling brother called home again. Upon hearing his voice, Sam said, "Well, last night Mother was up on the roof...."

Checkpoints for "No" Letters

1. Identify reader(s) and write at that level.
2. Is the appearance satisfactory?
3. Does the message carry good will for you and/or your firm?
4. Is the message clear and complete? Check your outline.
5. Is there a buffer before the negative information?
6. Is the negative statement brief and clear?
7. Is the closing pleasant, possibly looking toward the future?
8. Eliminate unnecessary words, phrases, clauses.
9. Could any statement be interpreted as discourteous?
10. Check to see that you have few, if any, passive sentences.
11. For variety in sentence form, see that some sentences start with descriptive words, phrases, or clauses.
12. Where possible, change negative words or statements to positive.
13. Recheck for correct grammar and spelling.

Writing Assignments

1. You were chairman of the program for the Illinois City Managers' Association, which had its last meeting on March 13 and 14, 19XX, in the Krayton Hotel, 2108 Washington Boulevard, Detroit, Michigan 48231. Write to the manager of the hotel, Mr. Robert Hinshaw, telling him that you were dissatisfied with the meeting room accommodations because the public address system did not work satisfactorily and the room temperature could not be adjusted to the comfort of those in the meetings. You would like to know what assurance you can have that these matters will not recur at other meetings you would like to hold at the Krayton. Start with something pleasant.

2. A recent fire has damaged your warehouse in Buena Park, California. Temporarily, shipments to the West Coast will have to be sent from the Phoenix, Arizona, warehouse. Compose a letter that can be sent to regular customers telling them why shipments might be delayed. Make up the name and address of an imaginary client and prepare a copy to him or her.

3. John Palladine, the president of the El Camino College Business Club at El Camino College, 16007 South Crenshaw Boulevard, Los Angeles, California 90506, has asked you to speak to the next meeting of the business club at the college at noon, October 30, 19XX. Write a letter *refusing this request.* Remember that you are interested in the group because you were president of the club when you were on campus.

4. A mail order customer has returned a pair of shoes and asked for a refund, saying that the shoes are the wrong size. The shoes show evidence of use, as the heels are worn and one toe is scuffed. *Refuse this request* and return the shoes, but try to retain the customer's good will.

5. It is the policy of your business to answer all letters, regardless of their tone and content. You have received a complaint from some possibly irrational person whose letter started, "What's wrong with you people, anyway?" and proceeded in a similar manner. The letter claims that an order of a dozen "supposedly *fresh* roses" remained fresh only two days, and the customer asks to have his $29.95 for the purchase returned. Write a letter of refusal.

6. An irate customer has returned some carved mahogany bookends for refund, claiming that they were damaged when she received them. There is a deep scratch on the surface of one of the bookends. Since your store deals only in items of high value, you personally check every item carefully before having it wrapped for mailing. Write a letter stating that you cannot accept the returned merchandise and suggesting that the customer have the bookend refinished professionally.

7. As supervisor of the mail order department, you have received another incomplete order from O. D. Schwartz, purchasing agent of J. C. Nichols Company. This time, he did not indicate the make of computer printer being ordered. Further, he did not indicate with which computer the printer should be compatible. Write a letter asking for the make and complete specifications of the printer, along with your catalogue number. Ask for an immediate reply so that you can make delivery as soon as possible.

8. As manager of Panorama Towers, it is your duty to remind tenants that each must use only the parking space assigned to him or her, and that the front area lot is for 20-minute convenience parking only. Write this form letter, which will be sent to all tenants. Thank the tenants for their cooperation while the parking lot was being constructed, and close with some pleasant comment about future operations or tenancy in the condominiums.

Chapter 7 *Writing Improvement Exercise*

Negative → Positive

Negative	Why not visit our store?
Positive	Come in and visit our store.
Negative	You won't regret buying this Skill Saw.
Positive	You'll be glad you bought this Skill Saw.
Negative	We are sorry you are dissatisfied.
Positive	We appreciate your frank comments.

In all business writing, an effort should be made to assume PMA, positive mental attitude, even when dealing with negative situations. There is the story that a pessimist says, "The glass is half empty," while the optimist says, "The glass is half full." Or, you might say, an optimist sees the roses; a pessimist feels the thorns.

It is this optimistic attitude that should be conveyed in our business messages, whether they are interoffice memorandums or letters and reports to outsiders. Before a communication is sent out, it should be checked for negative-sounding statements, and negatives should be dropped or rephrased positively, if possible.

Sometimes it is a challenge to try to make a potentially negative situation sound better. A young girl applying for her first position did this successfully when, instead of referring to her lack of experience, she wrote on her application, "I have no bad habits to unlearn." And an older woman, concerned about competing with younger job applicants, improved a potentially negative situation by stating, "My children are grown and I am free to re-enter the career world." Another woman, resuming her career after 25 years as a housewife, was asked, "What have you to offer us?" Her convincing reply: "Maturity."

Actually changing a few negative statements to positive ones should help make this feature of writing become almost automatic. Here are examples of how the exercises in this section might be completed. Of course, there are other acceptable changes than those given.

1. Change a negative statement to a positive statement.
    a. You will not be sorry if you purchase our Speedelectric Typewriter. → You may be the proud owner of a new Speedelectric Typewriter.
    b. Won't you please let us know? → Please let us know.
    c. Why not mail in a check? → Please mail in a check.
    d. The Senate failed to confirm three of the President's thirteen nominees. → The Senate confirmed ten of the President's thirteen nominees.

2. To make a statement sound better, avoid saying what cannot be done and try to say what can be done. Emphasize the positive; deemphasize the negative.
    a. We cannot give the discount rate on orders under $50. → We can give the discount rate on orders over $50.
    b. We cannot ship the order before the end of the month. → We can ship the order by the first of next month.
    c. Employee coffee breaks should not be longer than 15 minutes. → Each employee may take a 15-minute coffee break twice a day.

3. Don't suggest a negative.
    a. Do you mind if I use your phone? → May I please use your phone?
    b. I hope you are not too busy at this time to see me concerning a position with your firm. → I will be available for an interview at your convenience.

Chapter 7 *Writing Improvement Worksheet*

Negative → Positive

Change the following sentences to more positive statements. Acceptable revisions may vary.

Change a negative statement to a positive one.

1. You did not specify whether you want 16- or 20-pound bond paper for your letterhead stationery. → _____

_____

2. I can type only 40 words per minute. → _____

_____

3. You will not regret buying our Office Hot Soup and Beverage Server. → _____

_____

4. Half the people present voted against your proposal. → _____

_____

_____

5. We have a large backlog of orders and will fill yours as soon as your number comes up on our list. → _____

_____

Avoid saying what can't be done and emphasize what can be done.

6. You will not qualify for our discount rate until your orders exceed $200 a month. →

_____

_____

_____

7. I cannot complete this work while this meeting is in session. → _____

_____

_____

8. We cannot set the report in type until all the revisions are received. → _____

_____

_____

Chapter 7   Writing Improvement Worksheet (*Continued*)

9. Why don't you bank trainees set up a workable break schedule?→

_____

_____

10. Our warranty on computer parts covers only 90 days.→_____

_____

11. At our monthly Board meetings, we will not cover new topics that were not submitted in time to be included on the agenda.→_____

_____

_____

12. If you had read the memo, you would have seen that the last sentence mentions our meeting date had been changed to June 3.→_____

_____

_____

13. You should be more careful and include more men on the executive committee.→

_____

_____

14. If you had returned the merchandise within two weeks, we could give you a full refund instead of an exchange.→_____

_____

15. Why don't you pay attention when your supervisor is making work assignments?→

_____

_____

Don't suggest a negative. Improve these sentences.

16. I hope you won't think this is rude, but can you tell me how many people attended your meeting?→_____

_____

17. You may not like it, but your order will be a week late.→_____

_____

18. Will it bother you if I work at your desk?→_____

_____

19. Would you mind getting this out before you leave tonight?→_____

_____

_____

20. There is a 50% chance of rain tomorrow.→_____

_____

REVIEW AND DISCUSSION

Chapter 7 *The Negative Communication: The "No" Letter*

Make answers to these exercises as brief as possible.

1. Why should we try to write negative letters with a positive attitude? _____

2. Make an outline for a negative letter or make a drawing of a "praise sandwich," identifying what should be in the opening, middle, and closing.

3. How is the first part of the negative message, the buffer, used? _____

4. How should the negative letter close? _____

5. "Ordinarily a negative business message should be filled with negative words and phrases." Why or why not? _____

6. What does *connotation* of a word mean? _____

7. Give three words or phrases not listed in the book that have negative connotations to you. _____

8. Can humor be used effectively in negative communications? _____

9. What is *candor* and what is the advantage of using it in your own negative situations? _____

Chapter 7   The Negative Communication: The "No" Letter (*Continued*)

10. Why is "company policy" a poor explanation of the reason behind a "no" message?
    _____
    _____

11. Can computers set up letters to look individualized rather than looking like standard form letters? _____

12. What is "plain talk"? _____
    _____

13. Under what circumstances should letters be written to forestall complaint letters?
    _____
    _____

14. Some firms that seek good will of their customers handle necessary legal terminology by _____
    _____

15. Define *caveat venditor*. _____

16. Explain how a computer letter is prepared by a "mail merge" system. _____
    _____
    _____

17. Give three circumstances under which a company might refuse an order. _____
    _____
    _____
    _____

18. For your own complaint letter, authorities suggest you first (try regular complaint channels; contact a top official).

19. Complaint letters are most effective when you write (to an official by name; to an official title or position).

20. From page 144 showing a "message with a bee sting," write here a brief courteous statement to replace the "bee sting." _____
    _____

CHAPTER 8
Sales Letters and Persuasive Requests

> *Some see private enterprise as a predatory target to be shot, others as a cow to be milked, but few are those who see it as a sturdy horse pulling the wagon.*
>
> Winston Churchill

Writing sales letters is a talent that can be used in many ways. The "C" letter, or sales letter, is widely used for selling goods and services. Also, this letter pattern can be followed in many other situations, such as in making persuasive claims and requests. This means that the sales letter formula can be used to persuade others to grant a claim you have made that was disputed.

Another type of "selling" message is a persuasive request for agreement on any type of business or personal question that the reader or listener cannot be expected to go along with unless you make a strong presentation. Your success on the job could often depend upon your being able to "sell" an idea.

Further, the employment application letter is a special type of sales letter wherein the product you are selling is yourself. These letters are covered in Chapter 13 on employment communications.

Writing sales letters is called **direct mail advertising.** Direct mail is inexpensive compared to costs of other types of advertising, such as television, radio, newspaper, outdoor (billboards), and so forth. Through sales letters, a firm, large or small, can reach select audiences chosen for best expected return for the advertising dollar.

Being able to write effective sales letters can help in different types of careers. Direct mail advertising is usually the first kind of advertising done by any small business. Then later, perhaps when the firm is operating on a much larger financial scale, it will continue to use some forms of direct mail advertising. Because of this, there is a great need for people who are able to write sales letters for their own firms, for another small or larger company, or for themselves.

Another way in which proficiency in writing sales letters might benefit a person is in a personally owned **mail order business.** Of course, considerable study must be made before launching such a career. Information concerning opportunities for employment in direct mail advertising, as well as information concerning the starting of one's own mail order business, can be obtained through writing the Direct Mail Advertising Association at 230 Park Avenue, New York, N.Y. 10017.

Because of their inherent advantages, properly planned sales letters can bring a large return for the investment. A mailing is selective; that is, it can be prepared for one person or for a special segment of the market. Therefore, it can be very specific in its message.

Sales letters have three general functions:

1. **Getting sales leads:** following up requests for more information, such as brochures or samples, or asking for a call by a sales representative

2. **Bringing people into your place of business:** introducing a new product or service; inviting people to special demonstrations, exhibits, or even parties

3. **Selling by mail** (mail order selling): actually completing the entire process of advertising, selling, and ordering through the mail

> *The codfish lays ten thousand eggs,*
> *The homely hen lays one.*
> *The codfish never cackles*
> *To tell you what she's done.*
> *And so we scorn the codfish*
> *While the humble hen we prize.*
> *Which only goes to show you*
> *That it pays to advertise.*
>
> *Old rhyme*

Selling in Today's Market

The business scene is in a constant state of change. In today's market, there are new and changing products. Currently, a major trend is the sale of new and expanded services, along with continued sale of the products.

Advertising is essential to the free enterprise system, helping keep businesses competitive. As the worldwide market grows and changes, advertising helps raise the standard of living, making people aware of newly available products and services. They are also informed of improvements in older products and the obsolescence of others.

For instance, just think of the improvements made in a very short time in such common items as hand-held calculators and desktop computers. Without advertising to inform people of the improved miniaturization, increased types of functions, and decrease in cost of these items, most people would not be aware of these features. When Maytag and others began advertising their wonderful electric wringer washing machines, our grandmothers and great-grandmothers threw away their washboards.

The market will always have a place for people who are sales professionals. But well written sales letters, widely used and effective, become increasingly important.

Successful Sales Letter: Product, Prospect, Price

Success of a sales letter, as with any other method of advertising, comes from identifying a **product** or **service** that appeals to a particular number of sales **prospects** at a suitable **price.** When the correct marketing mix of product (or service), prospect, and price exists, the expense of preparing and distributing sales letters is justified.

Successful Sales Letters: The Product or Service

The first step in planning a sales letter is to study the product or service to be marketed. In order to do this, the person planning the letter should try as much as possible to become personally familiar with the item under consideration. If you are selling books, you should read them; food, you should eat it; wearing apparel, wear it; laundry service, use it. If it is a product that you cannot test yourself, such as children's shoes or dog food, test it as much as possible on other suitable subjects.

When you live with the item you are trying to sell, you may discover facets for promotion that even the manufacturer does not know. Further, you should discover that certain elements can be emphasized and others deemphasized. The more thorough your knowledge of a product or service, the better equipped you are to write about it. Another important matter to consider is timing. For example, normally you would not try to sell snow tires in summer.

The chief question to answer is, "Will the people buy it?" People will buy it if they are satisfied they will benefit from its use and if the price is right.

Successful Sales Letters: The Sales Prospects

Once it has been determined that a product or service is worthy of promotion, you should identify the prospects to whom the sales letter should be sent. Although the general public may believe that sales letter prospect lists are taken at random from the telephone book, in most instances this would be too expensive. Mailings of sales letters, particularly as postage rates increase, are generally sent to a special segment of the market. To minimize costs in large mailings, it is helpful to identify the expected "heavy users"—that is, the segment of the market that would be the main purchasers—and mail letters only to them.

Test mailings of letters have proved that there is a considerably higher rate of return on letters addressed to individuals by name. Therefore, it is advisable to consider obtaining a mailing prospect list so that specific names and addresses can be used.

When specific names and addresses are not used, and sales letters are sent "blind"— that is, to "Occupant" or "Resident"—an effort can be made to individualize the letter so that it appears it is addressed to a specific person. One device that is used to give a letter the appearance of being individually addressed is the simulated inside address. This impression is created by writing some introductory words or phrases in the position of the inside address of the letter and following it with an appropriate salutation. An example of this device is:

> To you
> If you are owned
> By a cat
>
> Dear Cat Lover:

Sales Mailing Lists

The best **mailing list** of prospects is often the easiest to obtain. It is the list of the firm's current and past customers. However, you may get other good lists of prospects chosen for occupation, area of residence, income, family size and age of family members, hobby and recreation interests, or other characteristics. Some of these lists are free, and others, such as lists of book club members or magazine subscribers, must be purchased. Following are some sources:

Telephone company	Many local telephone companies provide frequently revised telephone directories with phone customers arranged by street and district. Such a directory can usually be rented for a small cost.
Membership lists	Officers of churches, service clubs, or social, professional, or business organizations will often supply you with current lists of members.
Credit rating books	Standard & Poor's, Dun & Bradstreet, and other widely used reference sources are of value in building a worthwhile list of names by income.
Directories	The city directory is useful in selecting prospects by occupation, home-ownership, and size of family. Trade and professional directories provide worthwhile prospects, including top executives of local companies.
Public records	Generally, public records may be examined without cost, and they are extremely accurate sources for names. They include tax lists, license and permit records, property valuations, and street lists, when available.
Local newspapers	These contain news of births, promotions, transfers, business and other activities that could add potential customers to your mailing list.
List brokers	If you want to get started right away on some special promotional activity, you can get lists from a broker—who is a specialist in compiling mailing lists of general and specific markets.[1]

A study should be made to determine the **target market** for a mailing list for any specific product or service. The following factors should determine the mailings for your sales promotion:

1. Where do potential buyers live?
2. What is their buying power?
3. Under what conditions can they use your product or service?
4. Do general conditions in the target area favor your promotion? For example, economic conditions; climate, season, or region for types of clothing, sports equipment; and acceptance of this type of product from other producers.

Computerized Sales Mailing Lists

Most of the preceding mailing lists are available on computer disks. These disks give you the opportunity to send out large numbers of sales letters addressed to specific individuals.

For example, suppose you were selling a new training program in the Atlanta area and you wanted to send personalized sales letters to local training directors. To find your target market you might start by contacting a local professional association for trainers (such as the American Society for Training and Development) or a magazine that reaches training directors, such as *Training* magazine. Such organizations and publications will rent you their mailing lists or the parts of it that are in the ZIP codes of the Atlanta area.

Use of selective **computerized lists** of names and addresses puts your mail directly in the hands of **heavy users,** people who most likely have an interest in your project. It also

---

[1]"How to use the Mails Profitably" (Stamford, Conn.: Pitney-Bowes, Inc., n. d.), p. 6.

gets your mail out of the possible **junk** category of "Occupant" or "Resident" mailings, which often aren't even opened.

Test Mailings of Sales Letters

Various formats of essentially the same sales letter are used for **test mailings** to learn which format brings in the best reader response. Detailed records are kept of the comparative responses to each format. This information is obtained by changing the return coupon or order form in some detail, such as having it addressed to a different department number or a different box number. Sometimes an identifying number or symbol is printed in small type in a corner of the mailing piece that is returned by the reader.

When it is determined which format brought the best reader response, then mailings, sometimes nationwide, are made of this best-selling letter. If other formats receive an acceptable return from the sample of readers, they are often filed for future use in another mailing to a large customer list.

Usually, the parts of the letter that are tested most are the attention-getters—the envelope, possible enclosures, and the first part of the letter itself. The success of the entire letter depends upon getting the receiver to read it and not cast it aside.

It is advisable to pretest results of different formats for even a small mailing.

Successful Sales Letters: The Price

Once a product or service has been identified and a prospect list for sending out a sales letter has been selected, the mailing should be prepared only after a **price** for the commodity is set within which the operation can expect to show a satisfactory margin of profit. The cost of the mailing itself is determined by simple mail order arithmetic. If a mailing costs $1,000 and it results in 200 orders, the cost per order is $5. This figure is justified only when the total profit per sale is a sufficient margin over the $5 cost per order.

Frequently, a firm makes a test mailing, or several test mailings, before committing itself to an expensive mailing campaign. "Expensive," of course, is a relative term. For a person beginning a small business, $300 for the preparation and mailing of a first sales letter may be a considerable expense. For a larger business, the term is equated with much higher figures.

The Purpose of the Sales Letter

Sales letters must be written with the knowledge that they are in stiff competition with the wastebasket. This type of mail is sometimes identified by the unflattering term *junk mail*—although once you have successfully done business by direct mail, you will hesitate to think of it as junk.

An independent research firm recently conducted a survey that revealed the following:

3 out of 4 people open and read thoroughly, or at least glance at, advertising and sales letters.

3 out of 4 open and read thoroughly, or glance at, catalogues.

3 out of 4 people use samples received.

1 out of 2 people usually use coupons.

The Advertising Style Spiral

Figure 8.1 is the author's graph of an advertising style spiral. The *new style* in advertising at first is an **innovation;** if effective, it invites **imitation;** if very effective, it can become a standard style of advertising and moves into the area of **competition,** where most advertising styles remain the longest. Then, if overused, the once innovative style enters a stage of **saturation,** where it tends to repel the buying public. At this point, the market is ready for a different innovation, and the advertising style spiral starts again. It can be readily observed that different styles proceed around the advertising spiral at differing rates of speed.

The spiral of sales letter styles, or any advertising style, can be unending, or it can stop at any stage of the spiral. The Southern California politician who sent voters in his district a letter with his advertising on an enclosed kitchen potholder used an advertising style that was an innovation in area politics. When his opponent copied this selling letter idea, the ad went into the imitation stage. However, partly because of the cost of large mailings, this style did not proceed into common usage, or the competition area of the cycle, and of course went no further.

At one time, the style of placing special designs and printing on the evelopes of sales letters was an innovation. This style has progressed from innovation through imitation, and into competition. Perhaps it is entering a stage of saturation, because it is becoming

FIGURE 8.1
The advertising style spiral, showing a new
style going through the stages of innovation,
imitation, competition, and saturation, with
another new style continuing around the spiral
as a different innovation.

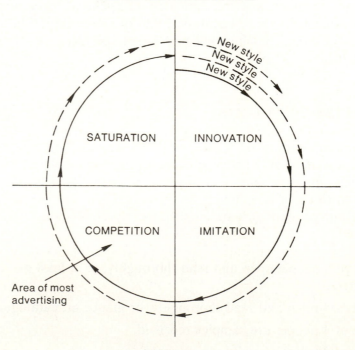

THE ADVERTISING SPIRAL

so common. However, as long as it is believed that the design attracts even a small percentage of readers to study the message inside, designs will undoubtedly be used on sales letter envelopes.

In writing sales letters, we should seek effective innovative sales letter styles, avoiding, if possible, styles that have been used a great deal, particularly those that might be considered to be in the saturation stage of the advertising spiral.

The Sales Letter Pattern

From a thorough study of the item that you are trying to sell, you must come up with one or more ideas that can be used as **attention-getters.** Also, you must have ideas that can be used to build up both the reader's **interest** in the product and his or her **desire** to own or use it. For a persuasive request, you must present ideas that will build up the reader's interest in your proposal and also build up a desire to do what **action** is being asked.

Figure 8.2 is a good **pattern for a "C" letter,** the selling letter, which follows this plan: (1) attention-getter, (2) interest and desire buildup, and (3) action hook.

This letter pattern is sometimes referred to as the AIDA plan, for its elements. The star is for getting *Attention;* the circles are for the buildup of *Interest* and *Desire;* the hook indicates the reader is to be "grabbed" and moved to *Action.*

The entire letter should be written in the "you attitude," emphasizing interests and benefits to the reader. The position of the information in a selling letter determines whether that information is being used to attract *attention,* create *interest* and *desire,* or move the reader to *action.*

The first part of the letter must get the reader's attention, or the rest of the letter will probably not be read. As noted, attention-getters frequently begin even on the envelope. The middle part is long or short, depending upon what is being sold, how it is being pro-

FIGURE 8.2
*Diagram of a selling letter, sometimes called
the AIDA selling letter plan.*

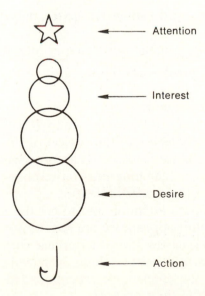

Sales Letter Pattern

Attention

Interest

Desire

Action

moted, and to whom it is being sold. The last part of the letter is what the reader will probably remember best. This section should, in as few words as possible, move the reader to specific action, giving all details necessary for that action.

Addressing the Letter

"Occupant" or "Resident"—No!

It seems that the world probably could not revolve without a certain percentage of "Occupant" or "Resident" mailings. However, these numbers are being reduced because memory typewriters, word processors and computers simplify the process of inserting individual names and addresses economically. Using one of these systems helps personalize the mail and can help stop the reader from giving your letter a quick brushoff.

By all means, individually prepared letters should use the name of the receiver both in the address lines and in the salutation.

Mistakes in multiple mailings.

Check carefully for spelling and number errors when using the merge letter format for filling in different names and addresses on copies of the same letter in **multiple mailings** (as shown in Chapter 6). Otherwise, your efforts to please your readers by personalizing the mail can go awry and offend. This text author, named Hemphill, has received mail addressed: "Hempstead," "Hemple," "Henfil," "Hempfield," "Henpel," "Hempill" and so on. Don McCormick, while a graduate student in Organizational Behavior, received a letter addressed to "Professor Cevmuick, Dept. of Original Behavior." Also, on merge letters, check that the computer is programmed to read lines and commas correctly. An editor with Prentice Hall named "Rymer" often gets letters addressed "Rhymes." (Pretty appropriate!) A city manager named Tom Orr received a letter properly addressed to him, but the letter started: "Dear Mr. City."

While such mistakes may get a few laughs around the office, they probably won't generate a desire for the receiver to accommodate the lazy, careless or cheap sender.

The First Section: The Attention-Getter

The first element, the **attention-getter,** must perform both the following functions:

- It must tie into the product or service or idea that the letter is promoting.
- It must bring the reader into the picture.

Usually, the big questions in the mind of the person reading the sales letter are, "What is the purpose of this message—and WHAT'S IN IT FOR ME???" If the attention-getters do not directly lead into the subject of the letter, the reader's attitude is apt to be "So what!" And the letter is tossed. If an otherwise good attention-getter is used, such as a funny story or an eyecatching illustration, but it has no relation to the selling matter, you've probably lost the reader's attention.

To get the reader's attention and to get the reader involved, some of the traditional rules of business letter appearance are sometimes badly bent or even broken. A firm that employs a conservative, traditional letterhead for standard mailings might use a variety of striking designs, such as bright colors, oversized print, or vivid illustrations. Results are far different from the appearance recommended for standard business correspondence, but they usually serve their purpose.

Attention-Getters on Envelopes

It has become a common practice to have attention-getters on the outside of the selling letter envelope in the form of printing, illustration, or splashes of color. This attack is most successful when it follows the precepts of tying into the matter being promoted and involving the reader. Listed here are some attention-getters used on envelopes as slogans, questions, or leading statements:

$100,000 CASH OR ONE OF 8,835 PRIZES!

PRIVILEGED INFORMATION!

Test ride this motorbike today!

This may be your last chance!

Join your neighbors in an evening of fun and education.

Latest reports on next year's cars.

Enclosed: Flight Ticket, Round Trip. Two Persons.

Please RSVP. Pencil enclosed.

Figure 8.3 shows other examples of attention-getters on envelopes.

Attention-Getters in Letters

Because the first paragraph will usually determine whether or not the rest of the letter will be read, this is the most important part of the letter. Here you must hold the reader's attention.

There are many emotional or rational appeals that can be used to gain attention. (See the section of this chapter, on page 163, "Identifying appeals that attract prospects.") However, care should be taken to avoid gimmicks that have been used so much that they are in the saturation stage of the advertising spiral. Here are some good examples of attention-getters:

Offer of a gift:

The card in the window of this letter will bring the the Handy Tool Set illustrated above. Please accept this with our compliments.

Sex:

[A picture of an attractive young woman (Suzanne Sommers) as part of a hardware display.]

Flattery:

If the list upon which I found your name is any indication, this is not the first—nor will it be the last—subscription letter you receive. Quite frankly, your education and income set you apart from the general population and make you a highly rated prospect for everything from magazines to mutual funds.

Pride:

For only the price of a Skylark, you can own a Buick!

This is not a
Free sample, but...

money-saving
holiday gift rate

SI is up for renewal—
a pencil is enclosed for your instructions

Your
key
to
success
is inside...

PRICE BREAKTHROUGH!
a TRUE QUAD Music System
at a regular stereo price!

New boom and inflation ahead . . .
and what you can do about it.

(see details inside)

Give a Gift
of Wildlife

You've got money coming...

FIGURE 8.3
Examples of attention-getters on envelopes.

His or her better self:

As you know, the asthmatic children of Sahuaro School are boys and girls of every race, color, and religion, who came to the school because they couldn't gasp enough air into their frightened lungs to say even the first syllable of the most important word they know, "Mother."

Bargain:

Give me your permission . . . and I will send you a His 'N' Her Car Coat ensemble in the popular NEW "crushed Buckskin" leather-look for the unbelievable price of only $69.95!

Special interests:

Do you love fishing, boating, water skiing, swimming?...and have you found your favorite public beaches and waterways getting impossibly crowded and more hectic each year?

Another method of getting the reader's attention early in the letter, as mentioned previously, is to avoid "Occupant" or "Resident" in the address and use the reader's name not only in the inside address but also early in the body of the letter. The reader's name can be dropped in at appropriate points in the letter. It is said that to the average person, the sweetest sound in the world is the sound of his or her own name.

Frequently, **enclosures** are also used to gain attention. Or, because they often give information about the product or are actual examples of the product, such as a swatch of fabric or paint, enclosures might be considered part of the buildup of *interest* and *desire,* which is continued in the middle section of the letter.

The Middle Section: Interest and Desire Buildup

The buildup of both the reader's **interest** in a product or service and the **desire** to own or use it follows the introductory section. This is also the section of a persuasive request where you try to build up the reader's interest by presenting appeals to convince the reader to agree to your request. You should include all the details you decide should be used, and follow a good plan. Superfluous details must be omitted, but all necessary information should be included.

There are many ways in which to appeal to the reader's interest, one of which may have been used in the attention-getter.

Identifying Appeals that Attract Prospects

In general, people respond to two basic types of **appeals**: emotional and rational. For your letter to be successful, study the positive emotional and rational appeals that you can tie in with your product or service.

Emotional appeals involve our basic senses of feeling, seeing, tasting, smelling, and hearing. Some strong emotional drives appeal to our feelings of love and friendship, pride, fear, pleasure, safety, and appearance.

Rational appeals include such matters as making money, saving money, getting more for the dollar spent, maintaining a respectable position among family and friends, doing a good job, saving time and energy, protecting the environment, and getting greater use out of a product.

There are many other emotional and rational appeals to people. Study your product or service, or the project or favor you are requesting, and determine the best appeals for specific prospects.

1. Promise money, a bonus, a gift, or a prize.

2. Promise personal safety or property safety.

3. Promise economy—a bargain.

4. Flatter the reader—appeal to pride.

5. Promise their children a better world.

6. Appeal to a special interest: occupation, community service, hobbies, home improvement, etc.

7. Appeal to a person's better self—charities, community service, civic responsibility.

8. Appeal to the sense of humor—use an appropriate story or cartoon.

Different Appeals for Different People

We must recognize that all people do not view the same object in the same way. See the line drawings here that show the possible differing attitudes toward the family car. Whether selling cars or other merchandise, we must try an appropriate appeal for specific prospective buyers.

Some believe that all selling letters should be short, since readers will not spend a great deal of time reading them. But a study of sales letters will show that long letters, as much as three or four pages, are frequently sent to get new subscribers to some of our major magazines. We must acknowledge that a great deal of research is done before preparing and sending these letters.

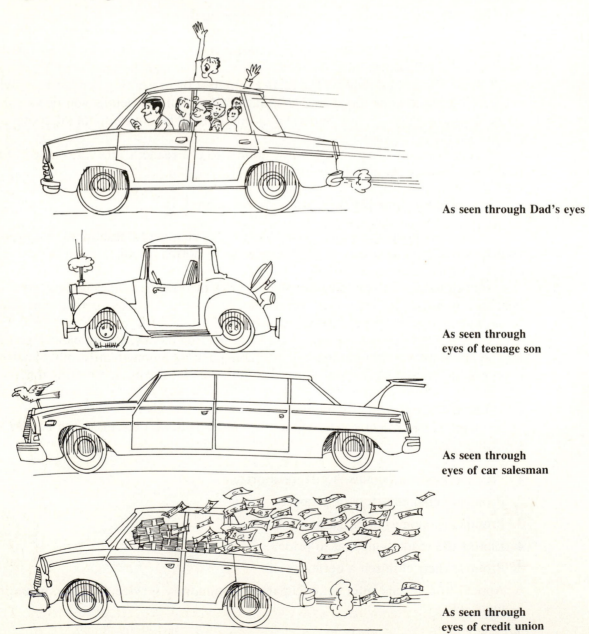

As seen through Dad's eyes

As seen through
eyes of teenage son

As seen through
eyes of car salesman

As seen through
eyes of credit union

Long letters might also be sent to potential subscribers to book clubs, and to possible purchasers of items like technical and professional materials. It might be expected that these prospects will be willing to read more to learn a wealth of detail. Other types of sales letters may also require lengthy presentations.

But if the material can be explained briefly, a short letter is preferred by almost all readers, and it is recommended that most selling letters should be short—no longer than one page.

Following is the middle section of a letter offering a complimentary tool set as an attention-getter with the hope of building interest and desire in purchasing insurance:

> With this practical gift you will also receive details about another fine tool—one that will help you *measure* and *build* your entire family's security. The John Bancock Family Plan makes it simple and sure with a plan tailor-made to fit *your* family's needs.
>
> The plan includes Father, Mother, and *all* children under age 18. You'll see how its flexibility adapts to any expansion in your immediate family circle, at *no* extra cost.
>
> Future children will be included when 15 days old—fully protected until the 25th birthday.
>
> This worthwhile protection *really* grows with your family, *every step of the way* . . . provides guaranteed security for your loved ones—and builds for your own future at the same time!

Here are the selling parts of a letter planned to build interest in and desire for enrollment in a data-processing course:

> In 10 workshop days you'll learn how to plan a logical systems study . . . how to review a system . . . how to conduct a survey and make recommendations to management . . . you'll gain an understanding of what management wants out of systems. You'll leave the workshop ready to perform with minimum help as a systems analyst.
>
> Fast Start shaves months of trial and error into 10 intense days! It has won national acclaim as the fastest way to get a person productive in systems work.

After the introductory paragraph, a letter promoting resort property reads:

> Can you remember the way it was 14,000,000 people ago? And do you know when that was?
>
> Can you remember Lido Isle when the only building you could see from the sand dunes was the Lido Isle Recreation Building?
>
> Consider today's waterfront lot prices: out of this world in many areas—but not at Canyon Lake.
>
> What we have to offer now is the opening of the very best section of WATERFRONT lots at Canyon Lake—only about 150 in all. Excellent long-term financing available.
>
> How would you like owning a choice waterfront lot here for summer swimming, fishing, boating, water skiing—maybe building later for retirement?

The Closing Section: The Action "Hook"

The closing section of the sales letter, the **action hook** shown in Figure 8.2, is diagrammed as a hook to indicate that it must "grab" and move the reader to action.

The hook should be specific as illustrated by this story:

Once a business man paid a writing consultant to edit a letter he had written to his senator asking for help with a problem that he obviously considered important. The final paragraph of the letter read, "Could you please do something about this?"

The consultant left the bulk of the letter almost as it had been prepared, but said to the man, "You realize, of course, that the senator has many different matters on his mind, and it will take time for him or his aide to study your letter—if they are able to give it much time at all. Why not say specifically what you would like the senator to do?" After a short discussion, a clear closing paragraph was composed, explaining the action the writer wished to have taken. Within a short time the senator replied to the letter, saying he had contacted a certain government agency, which sent very helpful assistance to the businessman.

The price of the item being promoted is often mentioned in the last paragraph of the letter. Except for certain prestige items, it is generally wise to make the price sound reasonable. One device is to bring the dollar amount down in a manner similar to this: Instead of saying "six dollars a month," say, "only twenty cents a day."

As far as possible, the closing hook of the letter should do five things. It should:

1. Tell the reader specifically what to do.
2. Tell how to do it.
3. Make it easy, or make it sound easy—the word *just* is often used effectively.
4. Make the price sound right—perhaps use the word *only*.
5. Urge the reader to do it soon (before it is forgotten); sometimes a deadline is given.

This section is the final part of the letter except for possible postscripts. The closing should be brief, preferably one sentence or a short paragraph that fulfills all five specifications.

To make ordering easy, coupons or prepaid postal cards or envelopes are often included as part of the letter. Above all, as in the letter to the senator, the specific action desired should be made clear.

Following are some letter endings that can serve as good examples of the sales hook. To show how frequently and effectively they are used, the words *you* and *your* have been printed here in italics.

To be sure of receiving *your* Permanent Press Flannel Slacks while the supply lasts, just mail *your* free trial order form TODAY.

We'll be looking for *your* card in the mail. Please mail it today. Postage has already been paid. Thank *you*.

An order form is enclosed, along with a postage-paid return envelope. Do initial and return the order form today. We'll be looking for *you* to enjoy refreshments and pick up *your* free gift.

But PLEASE be sure to bring this letter. Present it to the guard at our entry gate. It will identify *you*. Note directions and map on back of enclosure. We're looking forward to seeing *you!*

To order, simply remove the Half-Price Savings Certificate near the back of this book and drop it in the mail. *Your* name and address are already on it, postage is paid, and *you* needn't send any money now—we'll bill *you* after *you've* received *your* first issue of *Apartment Ideas.*

Figure 8.4 is a good example of a short letter that would be considered very satisfactory for the product being sold, a gas climate control system. This letter could be sent to all gas customers of the firm. Note the perforations that permit a tear-off return card at the end of the letter, making replying easy.

```
Dear Customer:

YEAR ROUND CLIMATE CONTROL is now available for your home.

Fresh, circulating air keeps your whole house warm in the winter
and cool in the summer. (We know we don't have to tell you
the advantages of being cool when it's hot. Remember last summer?)

Your CLIMATE CONTROL package will also include special low
gas rates during the summer months for gas used for air conditioning.
And as you know, gas air conditioning is more dependable and
lasts longer because it has fewer moving parts.

Right now, and during the next few months, installers are not as busy
and can provide you with fast, dependable service. So think ahead and
let us help you begin planning your own YEAR ROUND CLIMATE
CONTROL now. You'll be glad you planned for summer this winter.

For complete information, return the tear-off portion below with
your gas bill.

- - - - - - - - - - - - - - - - - - - - - - - - - - - - - - - - - -

Please tell me more about CLIMATE CONTROL for my home.
I understand this does not obligate me in any way.

Name_____

Address_____

City_____ Zip Code_____
                                                          A.M.
Telephone_____ Best time to call_____ P.M.
```

FIGURE 8.4
**Selling letter with perforated reply card
attached.**

Forms of the Sales Letter

There is a wide choice of letter forms that can be used for the sales letter, from a postal card to a multipage production. Figure 8.5 shows the most common forms of mailings: (A) single mailing card; (B) one-fold mailer; (C) two-fold (3-section) mailing card or letter; (D) two-fold (4-section); (E) French fold; (F) four-page letter; (G) broadside.

Persuasive Claims

Sometimes you may realize that the receiver of a claim you make may be reluctant to grant it automatically. These situations would call for a **persuasive claim** letter. You know that you must make a strong case to get what you want. Therefore, you should try a C–type selling letter, to persuade the other person. (Routine or direct claims that are usually granted promptly are covered in Chapter 6.)

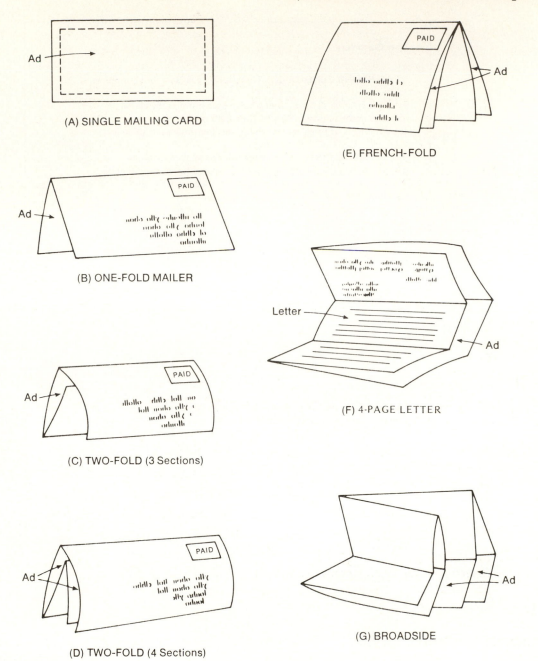

(A) SINGLE MAILING CARD

(B) ONE-FOLD MAILER

(C) TWO-FOLD (3 Sections)

(D) TWO-FOLD (4 Sections)

(E) FRENCH-FOLD

(F) 4-PAGE LETTER

(G) BROADSIDE

FIGURE 8.5
Card and letter forms that can be used for
sales letters [Courtesy: **Direct Mail Advertising**
Association, Inc.].

The first section of the letter should start with some statement you feel the reader will agree with. You might make reference to previous business transacted between the two of you that has been completely satisfactory. Or you might say something like, "I know that you want your customers to be satisfied with the performance of your . . ." This sentence introduces the topic in a positive manner.

The second section of this letter should state clearly, briefly and *calmly* all the facts that are pertinent to your claim. This section should also be as brief as possible. Yet it may take several paragraphs all leading to the responsibility of the reader to grant the claim. Enclose *copies* of any papers that support your claim. Do *not* send original papers.

The closing section should tie the first two sections together, saying specifically what you want done. Do not say something like "I think you should do something about this." Rather, as stated, by having made a logical explanation leading to the other person's responsibility, say exactly what you want done.

Following is a persuasive claim written after a routine claim for an insurance refund was ignored.

Date: December 1, 19XX
Re: POLICY #678910 Mr. Joseph Jacobsen

My father, Joseph Jacobsen has had a life insurance policy #23456 with Blank Insurance Company since 19XX and we have had a good business relationship with you.   ←**Pleasant opening**

However, on September 3, 19XX we applied for a Skilled Nursing Care Facility policy for him and gave your agent, Jeremia Jack, a personal check for $860 for this coverage for one year. At the time Mr. Jack advised us that because of my father's health history, he might not qualify for this particular policy and we were prepared for this refusal.   ←**Complete details (brief)**

However, we received our cancelled check in late September but have received no policy. Mr. Jack has not answered my letter nor our phone messages left on his answering machine.

We are enclosing a copy of the front and back of our cancelled $860 check made out to your company and also a copy of the form signed when we applied with Mr. Jack for your policy.   ←**Copies of proof**

We feel that blank Insurance Company must send us the approved Nursing Care insurance policy or refund our $860 immediately.   ←**Action**

Very truly yours,

Enc. 2

Persuasive Requests

In any career you may have occasion to make a special request to get someone to do you a favor or perform some act, and it would take special motivation to get that person's agreement. A **persuasive request** that follows the form of a selling letter would usually be a good pattern to follow to get desired results.

For example, many companies have social organizations, and special urging is frequently needed to prod people to attend. Following is a most persuasive request.

Dear Leila,

It's been such a long time since we have seen you. We are approaching Delta Pi's 35th anniversary, and your presence would help make it a complete success. ←**Attention getter**

Time after time at each meeting, your friends and colleagues have inquired about your whereabouts and asked that a special invitation be sent to you for this 35th anniversary. ←**Buildup of interest and desire**

The formal announcement with details is enclosed, ready to be returned in the mail.

Would you please mark your calendar to be sure you do not miss this event and the chance to renew friendships with your fellow members. ←**Action hook**

I am sure that everyone will be delighted to see you and that you will have an enjoyable time. ←**Pleasant closing looking to future**

Sincerely[2]

Here is another persuasive request.

Dear Dr. Baird

As a member of the Professional Business Association, I was present at the annual Michigan conference held last spring in Detroit. I was personally delighted to see you receive the Outstanding Professional Woman of the Year award for our State. ←**Should get attention**

Our local members would be honored if you would be the main speaker at our Rapid Brooks Professional Business Association meeting on October 3, 19XX. This is our annual organizational meeting and an important event on our calendar. If you can come, perhaps you would like to speak about your hobby, graphology. You made this intriguing statement: "Graphology is as exact—or inexact—as any other science." Or you may prefer to choose another topic from your business and travel experiences. ←**Building up interest and desire**

We will gladly furnish travel expenses, meals and a waterfront room at Edgewater Tilton Hotel where our meeting will be held. We are able to offer you a $300 honorarium for your presentation. ←**More buildup**

Dr. Baird, we would be honored and grateful to hear from you soon telling us that we can go ahead and announce your participation in our program. ←**Action hook**

Respectfully,

---

[2]Courtesy Janet Matsuyama, Fullerton College

Your Own Look at Mail Order Buying

We can all expect to receive many sales letters in our lifetimes. While we are studying how to prepare such letters, it might be worthwhile to study them for a moment from a consumer's standpoint for our own **mail order buying**.

Most sales offers made by mail are legitimate. However, we should remember the following:

1. Everybody would like to get something for nothing; actually, you are not going to get a vacation or anything else free.

2. Land frauds continue to snag the gullible. Federal and state laws have been passed to protect the public, but all offers should be investigated thoroughly *on the site*. If you are seriously interested, consult a properly qualified lawyer plus city and/or county legal records.

3. If the quality of an article you see advertised seems miraculous, you needn't necessarily believe in miracles.

4. In trying to make a killing, you might lose your shirt.

5. Even questionable deals can sound good on paper—especially if you have the attitude, "My mind's made up; don't confuse me with the facts."

Don't be victimized. Movie star Clint Eastwood is quoted as saying, "You can fool some of the people some of the time, and usually that's enough to make a pretty good buck."

Checkpoints for Sales Letters and Persuasive Requests

1. Identify reader(s) and write at that level.

2. Is the appearance satisfactory?

3. Does the letter carry a good will tone for you and/or your firm?

4. Is the message clear and complete? Check your outline or notes.

5. Does the letter follow the AIDA (Attention, Interest, Desire, Action) plan?

6. Have you used a fresh, effective selling or persuasive approach?

7. Eliminate unnecessary words.

8. Recheck for any statement that might be interpreted as discourteous.

9. If the passive sentence form is overused, change some sentences to active.

10. For variety in sentence form, some sentences should start with descriptive words, phrases, or clauses.

11. Restate negatives in positive terms.

12. Check for a "you attitude." Are statements made in the reader's interest instead of the writer's interest?

13. Recheck for grammar and spelling.

Writing Assignments

1. After working part-time for a neighborhood florist, you have been able to purchase the business from the elderly couple who owned it. In your plan for expansion, you want to promote "flowers of the month" to try to sell to residents of the area. From the telephone company, you have obtained names and addresses of nearby residents, predominantly apartment dwellers. You plan to feature such bouquets or plants as azaleas in January, violets in February, roses in June, chrysanthemums in September, and poinsettias in December.

   a. Write a letter introducing and promoting the general plan of your "flowers of the month" campaign.

   b. Write a letter promoting a particular flower for a specific month.

2. You have a list of all the freshmen at your local community college. Write a letter promoting this year's model of the Speedelectric portable typewriter. Make up special selling features that you feel will help sell the machine to this age group.

3. Write a sales letter for Neutrogenus soap. This is a rich, transparent, amber-colored bar soap that cleans thoroughly without being drying or irritating. It is a chemically balanced soap, beneficial to all complexions, and contains glycerine, an ingredient found in many hand and body lotions. Users write in that it is excellent for clearing teen-age complexion problems, and it also keeps the skin of older people smooth and nice. There is no better soap for babies, and men find it refreshing to use as a shaving lather. The soap sells for $1 a bar. You have a list of people living in the upper-middle-class and upper-class areas of Dallas, Texas. Prepare a letter to send to these people, using individual names and addresses.

4. You are one of the three students at Cruz college who are preparing the college's first poetry magazine, which will sell for $2. The poetry is the original, previously unpublished work of Cruz students. If successful, the publication of the magazine will become an annual event. Your promotion funds are limited, so you have decided to prepare a sales letter on the magazine to be distributed to mailboxes of all students on campus. You will also be able to place copies of the letter at strategic places around the campus. Write this letter.

5. Choose a product or service, real or imaginary, that would be of interest to college students, and write a letter selling it to these students.

6. You own and operate a pet store in the New Rockwood Shopping Center, and from the licensing bureau you have obtained the names and addresses of pet owners in the ZIP codes in your area. Write a letter that can be sent to all names on this list to advise them of your newly opened store and the pets and pet products you carry. Also tell them of any special services you offer.

7. You have recently been hired by the May Company Department Store as college shop coordinator. Write a letter that will be sent to all homes in the community. Announce the opening of the new college shop with wearing apparel for college women. Mention the hours that the store is open and that ample parking is available.

8. You are secretary to the community relations director of your college and have been asked to compose a letter inviting members of the community to an arts and crafts show and sale of students' work. The show will be October 30 and 31 from 10 a.m. to 10 p.m. Light refreshments may be purchased. The show is under the direction of Miss Nancy Redburn, Community Relations Director. Decide what type of arts and crafts will be shown for selling, and make up the letter.

9. Write a form letter that will be sent to all customers of the AyZee Plumbing Company, along with a copy of the new 19XX catalogue. Use resale information in the letter.

Chapter 8 *Writing Improvement Exercise*

"We Attitude" → "You Attitude"

The story is told of a highly successful sales consultant who moves around the country on assignment. Whenever he arrives in a new territory, he places a certain cartoon on his bulletin board. The cartoon shows a tough-looking buyer demanding across his desk, "What's in it for me???"

When you begin to write a business letter, you might benefit from remembering this picture of the "tough-looking buyer." A letter satisfactorily answers his question, "What's in it for me?" when it has the "**you attitude**." This attitude reflects the interests of the reader and is far more appealing than the letter with the "we attitude," which reflects the interests of the writer. The "you attitude" generally satisfies the tough customer as well as the not-so-tough customer or reader, who is also primarily interested in potential benefits to himself or herself.

Although anyone who is doing business with you knows that you are in business to make a profit for yourself, your company, and your employees, correspondence need not call attention to this fact. Rather, you should simply try to phrase your letters in terms of the reader's interests.

In business writing, of course, it is permissible to use the first-person forms—*I, we, my, our,* and so forth. But the purpose of this exercise is to emphasize the potential advantage of phrasing letters, particularly letters of a selling or persuasive nature, in terms of *you* and *yours.*

Following are examples of changing "we" sentences to "you" sentences:

We believe our Baccutron is the best battery-operated watch on the market. → You may enjoy the luxury and accuracy of your own Baccutron watch.

We have been in the dry-cleaning business here for 25 years. → You can rely on a dry-cleaning firm that has been in business in your town for the past 25 years.

We believe you will like our newest model Speedelectric typewriter, which has a blank key that can be equipped with a special letter or symbol. → For your own personal use, the Speedelectric typewriter has a blank key that can be equipped with a special symbol of your choice.

Our store is overstocked with portable color TVs, and we must try to make room for other merchandise. → You may save money by getting a new color portable TV during our stock reduction sale.

Chapter 8 *Writing Improvement Worksheet*

"We Attitude" → "You Attitude"

Rewrite the following sentences from the "we attitude" to the "you attitude." Suggestion: Try to think of an advantage to the reader, and use that idea. You will be writing "mini-commercials."

1. We have put all our floor models on sale to make room in our showrooms for our new spring consoles. → _____
   _____
   _____

2. Our laboratory has worked three years to develop our newest Vitamin-Pack, which we feel will give people the pick-up they need. → _____
   _____
   _____

3. We believe we have the best color TV on the market. → _____
   _____
   _____

4. We also sell an edger that can be attached to any lawnmower. → _____
   _____
   _____

5. We are anxious to have you try our new Doggie Bisquit that we have just added to our line. → _____
   _____
   _____

6. We have been selling real estate in this area for 20 years. → _____
   _____
   _____

7. I have had three years' experience as a program analyst. → _____
   _____
   _____

8. We have a seven-piece cutlery set that comes with a free knife sharpener. → _____
_____
_____

9. Our policy is for the customer to sign the sales slip to make sure the purchase is recorded on the correct account. → _____
_____
_____

10. Our company has flexible scheduling of hours, so that we offer employees different shifts of their choice. → _____
_____
_____

11. After their initial probationary period, we try to give a new bank employees an assignment in a branch bank of their choice. → _____
_____
_____

12. We would like to put your name on our list to get advance notice of our sales. →
_____
_____
_____

13. We offer the Comfort-Aire ladies' pump in five colors. → _____
_____

14. Our yummy Yule-log chocolate cake has vanilla cream filling and snow-white frosting. → _____
_____

15. I believe my skill as a computer analyst will help me advance to a higher position. →
_____
_____

REVIEW AND DISCUSSION

Chapter 8 *Sales Letters and Persuasive Requests*

1. The book names two types of careers that require ability in writing selling letters. What are they? _____

_____

2. Name three functions of sales letters. _____

_____

3. Success of a sales letter depends on identifying *product, prospects,* and _____

_____

4. How should you familiarize yourself with the product or service you are trying to sell?

_____

_____

5. Name five sources of names and addresses for use in mailing sales letters.

_____

_____

_____

6. What are the advantages of using computerized sales mailing lists?

_____

_____

7. Name, in order, the four stages of the advertising style spiral. _____

_____

8. Bring to class an ad from a printed source, and identify its stage of the advertising style spiral.

9. What is the purpose of test mailings of sales letters? _____

_____

Chapter 8   Sales Letters and Persuasive Requests (*Continued*)

10. Diagram the sales letter pattern and identify each of the main elements.

11. Name the two functions of the sales letter attention-getters. _____

_____

12. Bring to class one letter with an outstanding attention-getter on the envelope, as an enclosure, or in the first paragraph of the letter.

13. Name five appeals to the reader that are recommended as being effective in sales let-ters. Be brief. _____

_____

_____

14. Is the use of "Resident" or "Occupant" in the address of sales letters preferred to the use of a person's name? Explain. _____

_____

15. Name the five things the action element of the sales letter should do. _____

_____

_____

16. What devices are sometimes used in sales letters to make ordering sound easy?

_____

_____

17. You need not be suspicious that people may try to use the mails to defraud you. True or False?

18, 19, 20. Change these statements to "You attitude."

18. Our price for bulk orders of one-pound Choco-lat bars is $4.50, and they can retail for $8.95. → _____

_____

19. My interest in mechanical operations has always made it easy for me to learn how new machines work. → _____

_____

20. Our banks will now be open ten more hours each week. → _____

_____

CHAPTER 9
Credit Letters and Collection Letters

> *The two most beautiful words in the English language are: "Check enclosed."*
> Dorothy Parker, 1893–1967, American poet and short story writer

Successful operation of a business depends largely upon the harmonious interaction of three departments of that business: sales, credit, and collection.

Many problems of the credit and collection departments would not occur if sales forces were not too aggressive. Similarly, the work of the collection department would be simplified if the credit department were extremely cautious in granting credit. But actually, most businesses would suffer, perhaps to extinction, if salespeople were not properly forceful. Further, a great percentage of total business would be lost if credit were not granted to certain marginal credit risks. Although credit privileges must be granted with care, figures show that the total credit losses for any given year amount to less than 0.5 percent of sales.

Is it necessary to use credit in business?

As a matter of fact, more than 85 percent of business operates on a credit basis, from the small individual shop owner to the large corporation. Credit is a way of life.

CREDIT LETTERS

The Four Cs of Credit

Most studies state that credit should be granted by evaluating the applicant under the four Cs of credit: character, capital, capacity, and conditions.

1. **Character:** the person's basic ethics, such as honesty, dependability, and sense of moral values, as indicated by a past credit record.

2. **Capital:** the money behind the debtor. This may be cash, securities, real estate holdings, copyrights, etc. In case of necessity, these could be turned into cash. When a per-

son is being judged for credit potential, capital holdings should be rated for liquidity—that is, the ease with which they can be converted to cash.

3. **Capacity:** current or anticipated earnings as wages, salary, royalties, or cash returns on investment.

4. **Conditions:** any conditions that are not directly related to the credit applicant but could affect the applicant's credit picture, such as general economic conditions, regional economic conditons, or the employment situation in a given industry.

Legal Aspects of Credit Letters

Your **credit letters** that ask for or supply information on the credit record or credit potential of an applicant must fit into the legal category of a **privileged communication.** A privileged communication should be furnished only to *somebody who has an interest to protect.* This information cannot be given for a random inquiry made out of curiosity or malice.

In making your report, check records to see that your information conforms with facts. In legal terminology, you should report what a *prudent* person would report. You can give personal evaluations and opinions to authorized inquiries, as long as they are given in good faith, without malice. You should protect the interests of both the applicant and the person making the inquiry.

Anyone handling credit applications or credit reports must be familiar with the provisions of the **Consumer Credit Protection Act** of 1969 and its amendments. A copy of this act can be obtained free by writing the Board of Governors, Federal Reserve System, Washington, D.C. 20551.

Following are some major provisions of this legislation:

1. The credit applicant must be informed that a check is being made of his or her credit.

2. The person or agency making the report must be reasonably sure that information furnished will be used only for the stated reason for which it was requested.

3. Consumers may at any time or for any reason examine their credit records of debt as recorded by any credit reporting agency. If a recent negative report has been made on the applicant, this examination may be made free of charge. Otherwise, the reporting agency may charge a reasonable fee. The applicant has the right to have inaccurate or incomplete information reinvestigated. If information is inaccurate or cannot be verified, it must be removed from the file. If there is a dispute about the information, the applicant may have his or her own version added to the file, and this information must be included in subsequent reports on that person. Consumers can get the names of all who have received copies of reports.

4. Credit reporting agencies must not report adverse information that is more than seven years old, except for bankruptcies, which may be reported for fourteen years.

Recent amendments to the Consumer Credit Protection Act provide that:

A retailer must resolve a customer's credit inquiry within 90 days after the inquiry is made.

A retailer may not refuse credit on the basis of sex or marital status.

A creditor must supply a written statement of reasons for denying or terminating credit if a rejected applicant requests such explanation.

Granting Retail Credit

Different methods are used in getting credit information for retail customers and for trade or mercantile accounts.

Information for Granting Retail Credit

The chief sources of information concerning the retail credit applicant's ability to pay are the following:

The customer, the best source for information on the applicant: The credit applicant can furnish details about employment, residence, financial responsibilities, indebtedness, and so forth.

her firms with which the applicant has done or is doing business, and/or credit card information.

Employer, for verification of employment and earnings.

Local retail credit association.

Associated Credit Bureaus, Inc.

To remove some of the mystery surrounding the operation of **credit bureaus,** the Associated Credit Bureaus, Inc., has published a brochure, available to the public, which identifies the information compiled by a credit bureau: proper identification of the customer, including full name, address, and spouse's name; present employment information; personal history, including the customer's former address, former employer, spouse's employer, number of dependents, and so on; credit history, indicating in what manner the customer has paid bills in the past; and public record information covering lawsuits, judgments, and other litigation that may have some bearing on the person's ability to pay bills.

The information of the credit bureau is available only to those business firms that prove to the bureau that they have some legitimate business need for the information.

Trade Credit Information

Getting **trade credit** information about another business firm usually involves a more detailed study, using many sources.

The credit manager of a large Eastern firm says that financial conditions of businesses change rapidly and trade credit statements, "like eggs, age fast." Every effort must be made to keep information current.

Sales representatives of your own firm can be your best sources of up-to-date information. They can report on such matters as condition of the premises, changes in product or service lines, and changes in personnel, ownership, or management.

Valuable sources of information on the trade account also include those furnished by the account itself, such as references, financial data, and suppliers. National trade reporting services like Dun & Bradstreet, Moody's Investors Service, Inc., and Standard and Poor's Corporation can furnish reports. Further, information obtained from private or mutual trade agencies for a particular industry can be helpful.

Applying for Credit

Today, most credit applications are made by filling in a form furnished by the business. Occasionally, it is necessary to write a letter applying for credit.

The **credit application letter** would be a simple "A" type letter: State clearly in the first sentence that it is a letter applying for credit; give full name, address, telephone number, place of employment, and previous and/or current credit account references. Any other information that might be helpful should be supplied. If you are new in the area, give all pertinent information relative to your prior place of residence.

The Letter Granting Credit

Although the **letter granting credit** is routine, it should certainly express a tone of welcome to the new credit customer. It will also undoubtedly carry with it a spirit of good will if it can be personalized as much as possible, such as having an original signature or using the customer's name in the text. It should go without saying that new cutomers are important to a business, and new customers like to know they are important to you.

Letters granting credit are good news and should be "A" letters, stating immediately that credit has been granted, giving details of credit terms, and closing with a lift that looks toward a pleasant business relationship. Promotional resale materials might be included.

A good example of a letter granting credit to a retail customer follows:

> Robertson's welcomes you as a new credit card customer Mrs. Rogers, and we hope you will use your credit privileges freely.
>
> As a credit customer you will regularly receive announcements of private sales that are held for two days before sales events are announced to the public through newspaper ads. You will also receive special announcements of other credit customer benefits, such as fashion showing and Silver Club specials.
>
> With this letter is an announcement of the Private Back-to-School Sale on August 15 and 16. We hope you enjoy having first selection of this merchandise.

Terms of Credit

Details of **credit terms** must be furnished on the credit application, in the letter granting credit, or in some other communication. Letters from wholesalers to dealers should indicate clearly the date from which the credit discount will be figured: delivery date, invoice date, shipping date, receiving date, or e.o.m. (end of month). Also, you should state clearly when the net amount is due if a credit discount is not claimed.

Not this   Our credit terms are the standard 2/10, net 30.

This   Our credit terms are the standard 2/10, net 30, or 2 percent off if paid within ten days of invoice date; net amount due in 30 days of invoice date if cash discount is not claimed.

Interest charges may be given according to the monthly rate, but current law requires that the true *annual* interest rate also be stated clearly.

The Letter Refusing Credit

The letter **refusing credit** is, of course, more difficult to write than the letter granting credit. The refusal letter is a "B" type that must carry the "no" and still try to retain the good will of the credit applicant.

Credit officers should know the philosophy, "Success is not permanent. The same is also true of failure." However, do not make the opening buffer so pleasant that you give the reader a first impression that credit is being granted. Then, the refusal would be more difficult to take. Following is a letter that is probably too cheerful in handling a credit refusal:

> Congratulations! Getting your college degree is a great accomplishment. This degree should enable you to get a good job.
>
> When you get the job, we will be happy to reconsider your application for credit.

Credit refusals should be courteous, written with the knowledge that a poor credit risk today may be a good credit risk tomorrow, next month, or next year. Basically, the intent of this letter should be to try to get the business on a cash basis. A retail customer might be willing to put merchandise on layaway.

Here is a better credit refusal:

Buffer ⟶	Thank you for the order for your company name-imprinted stationery.
	As yours is a new business, we can locate no information upon which to make a credit approval.
Details (Includes resale) ⟶	From our own experience, we know that new businesses generally find it necessary to watch even small expenditures. Could we have permission to send this order C.O.D., as we are sure that ours are the best prices on the market for first-quality stationery. Morton's stationery will give your business associations a good first impression.
Closing— looking to future	We wish you success in your new enterprise, and would like to look forward to a long and pleasant business association.
	May we send the order on cash or C.O.D. terms?

Exchanging Credit Information

Although most **exchange of credit information** is done through credit rating bureaus or rating services, occasionally it is necessary to write letters asking or giving details of an individual's or firm's credit status. These privileged communications must not contain libelous statements. Postcards cannot be used because credit information, although routine, is confidential.

Information in these letters should relate to the following:

1. How long has the applicant had an account with you?
2. What is the usual size of the account?
3. What is the current status of the account?
4. Do you have any special comments about the applicant?

Because letters requesting credit information are usually quite routine, many businesses use a form letter for these inquiries. A typical letter of this nature is shown in Figure 9.1.

APPLICANT: _____

    Applicant wishes to establish a line of credit with us and has given your name as a reference.

    Would you please give us the confidential information requested in the form at the bottom of this page and return this letter in the enclosed business reply envelope.

    We would appreciate your help and would be glad to furnish similar service to you at any time.

Very truly yours,

. . . .

Period of time sold on credit _____ to _____

Credit limit, if any _____

Current amount due _____ Past due _____

               (Discount)

Paying habits (Prompt)

               (Slow)

Comments _____

FIGURE 9.1
A sample request for credit information.

With a letter like that, the original letter (with desired information filled in) may be returned to the sender, saving much of the time of preparing the reply. It also should eliminate the need for the person furnishing information to file the letter. If desired, you can print your own copy of both letters.

COLLECTION LETTERS

Background for Making Collections

If orders are the heart of a business operation, then collections are surely its life-blood. The importance of the duties and responsibilities of collection personnel cannot be overestimated.

We must write collection letters and they must be effective for these reasons:

1. We want the money that is rightfully ours to use for our own purposes.

2. We want to save the expense of further collection letters or collection procedures.

3. We want to regain the business of a customer who is probably doing business elsewhere because of money owed to us.

As a result of the detail work involved, those processing accounts sometimes "can't see the forest for the trees." Occasionally they should mentally step back to observe the collection process objectively. Such periodic review may be far more fruitful than continually making out the same type of collections on the same schedule as has always been done. Well-run organizations regularly check various collection approaches and various types of communications to determine whether or not they are bringing satisfactory results.

Personal contacts by telephone can be more productive than words on a written page, and in-person contacts can be most productive of all. At one time, telegrams were considered valuable and economical aids at the right stage of collecting, but today's telephoned or mailed telegram does not seem to have the effect of the specially delivered message. The personal telephone call can be used effectively at almost any stage of collection. Telephoning has the advantage of getting an immediate response. Of course, long-distance calls can be justified for any but small amounts. With competition among carriers today, you might get reasonable reduced rates for frequent use of long-distance lines.

The person with an innovative plan for collections will be ahead of competitors for the slow-paying account and may be first in line of those debtors who are playing games in paying bills, settling a few at a time.

Classify Your Accounts

Overdue accounts should be classified by type. Late payment from financially well-rated businesses, government agencies, or municipalities can be simply a matter of paperwork and not a lack of funds. A good collection department officer can organize a personal campaign to devise means of making these accounts pay on time.

To help reduce the need for collection notices, a brightly colored sticker telling of the rewards of cash discounts and on-time payments might be gummed or stapled to the statement.

With large organizations that have a consistent record of losing a cash discount because of late but sure payment, a letter might be written to a person in authority suggesting hand-carrying of large account statements to get cash discount benefits. If no improvement results, at least an effort was made.

Consider Making Collections in Person or by Telephone

In business, most collections are made by letter. Even with rising letter-writing costs, this procedure seems to be most economical and usually as effective as necessary. Competitive rates for heavy usage of long distance lines are usually available. However, earlier sections of this text have related that contacting people in person or by telephone might be more effective than writing letters. Evidently people can more easily ignore a letter than they can ignore a live human being in person or over the telephone.

Certainly, a person in charge of collections should periodically try different collection procedures.

After sending one or two notices of overdue payments, you may find that telephoning or even calling in person is often well worth the time and effort. But it is necessary to do some homework before you make any kind of personal call:

1. *Check to see that your information is correct.* Was the material delivered? Checking all numbers, see that billing was correct. Were all payments noted?

2. Check to see if amount due justifies planned collection procedure.

3. Decide who is the right person to contact.

4. Check the past payment record.

5. Figure out a possible different payment plan.

6. Plan your opening statement:
   a. Introduce yourself and identify your firm.
   b. Give the reason for your call.
   c. Wait a moment. Many calls are successfully completed during this pause.

The Federal Communications Commission in Washington, D.C., has issued Public Notice 70–609 telling specifically what types of practices are prohibited when making collections over the telephone. Anyone making such calls should get a copy of this bulletin.

Contact High Officials

The collection call or letter should be to the owner or manager of a small organization. In a larger organization, it should be to a person of high authority, such as comptroller or supervisor of accounts.

Follow Guidelines in Writing Collection Letters

The plan behind writing collection letters is to collect the money and retain the good will of customers.

Important guidelines for writing good collection letters are:

1. Understand that the customer knows he (she) owes and expects to hear from you.

2. Understand also that very few people are dishonest; most pay their bills. There are often good reasons why some people don't pay: carelessness, temporary financial difficulties, temporary personal problems, dissatisfaction with goods or services.

3. Be specific. Do not refer to the "balance," but give the exact amount due. With a large organization, always refer to the customer's purchase order number. Good idea: Send a copy of the order, so all information is at hand.

4. Check that you have billed and shipped according to directions on the purchase order. This is a good plan for all orders. Major accounts operate under strictly defined procedures, and everything must match before an order can be processed for payment.

Using the Collection Letter Series

Collection letters should be written promptly, regularly, and with increasing forcefulness. Records prove that the older an account gets, the less chance there is of collecting it. United States Department of Commerce figures show that for the probability of collecting on it, $1 due becomes worth these amounts:

90¢ after two months

67¢ after six months

45¢ after a year

23¢ after two years

15¢ after three years

1/2¢ after five years

At early stages of collection, letters should be simple reminders. As the unpaid account becomes older, the later-stage letters should be firmer messages of serious steps that may be taken. Collection letters can be set up in a series, according to the tone or level of the communication.

The four stages of the collection letter series are (1) **reminder,** (2) **inquiry and appeal,** (3) **pressure,** and (4) **ultimatum.** If your first-stage reminder letters are ignored, you should proceed through these four stages of the series until a response is received.

More than one letter can be sent in each stage. However, a reasonable time should be allowed between letters, giving the customer a chance to pay. A follow-up letter every five days or so can be frustrating to both sides. Yet, waiting too long may result in the customer's paying another creditor who is more persistent.

Be sure to acknowledge that payment and your letter may have crossed in the mails. Debtors like to know that the people to whom they owe money are aware that this occurrence is common. Figure 9.2 is a copy of a form regularly sent out by one firm for this purpose. Incidentally, one self-designated authority states that the world's biggest lie is "Payment is in the mail." Your letter could move the debtor to make the statement true.

All collection letters can end with a statement like this: "If this notice and your payment have crossed in the mail, please ignore this letter."

Stage 1: Reminder

As soon as an account becomes delinquent, a notification or **reminder** letter should be sent. It is very important that this first collection letter appear routine, so that it will not offend the good customer who has merely overlooked payment or who has had a personal emergency. Although payment should have been made by the due date, you might lose the continued business of a faithful customer if you send what might be considered a premature dunning notice.

Often, this notification simply takes the form of a second copy of the original statement with a stamped notation or a gummed label attached, saying something like, "Second Notice," "Have you overlooked?" or "Please." Figure 9.3 shows a collection of inexpensive gummed labels that can be used effectively in this manner. These labels can be purchased in most stationery or office supply stores.

FIGURE 9.2
Form that is included in collection letters to indicate that
payment and collection letter may have crossed in the mails.

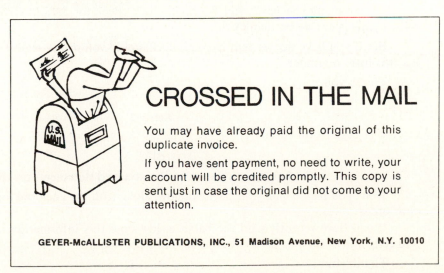

CROSSED IN THE MAIL

You may have already paid the original of this duplicate invoice.

If you have sent payment, no need to write, your account will be credited promptly. This copy is sent just in case the original did not come to your attention.

GEYER-McALLISTER PUBLICATIONS, INC., 51 Madison Avenue, New York, N.Y. 10010

FIGURE 9.3
Gummed labels that can be attached to second copy of customer statement at "reminder" stage of collection.

In other instances, a printed form enclosed in an envelope with a reminding message is often sent:

Most likely the following charges have been overlooked:

| May 15 | $200.00 |
| May 23 | $301.75 |

Here are other examples of collection reminder letters. Italicized information can be personalized for that specific account.

Letter 1

HAVE YOU FORGOTTEN US?

We don't want to take it personally, because we do appreciate the business you have given us. Probably you have already sent us your check for *$148.12* for the past two months' bills. If this is so, we do thank you.

But if you have not yet sent in your check, could you please mail it at once and then forget this little reminder.

Thank you.

Letter 2

We'd like to fill you order...

BUT

...your account balance, as shown on the attached statement, prevents us from doing so.

Won't you please mail your payment now, along with the enclosed form, so we can release your order.

If you have recently paid the balance, just note this information on the enclosed form and return it in the postpaid envelope we have provided.

Thank you!

Letter 3

Apparently through an oversight you have neglected to send us payment for the outstanding balance on your account. The amount, according to our records, is shown on the accompanying statement.

Won't you take care of this now, while the matter has your attention. Just return the enclosed statement with your check or money order, using the envelope provided.

Humor may be effective in early stages of collection procedures, but use it cautiously, because most people do not feel that being reminded of overdue accounts is a humorous matter. Sometimes among members of fraternal organizations or other membership groups, mild humor might be effective. Or some appropriate humorous touches might be used in other cases. Here are two oldies that could be used, together with two more modern messages.

How do you do?
Some pay when due.
Some pay when overdue.
Some never do.
How do you do?
Balance $ _____.

Man is dust.
Dust settles.
Be a man.
Amount due: $ _____.

Hi.
This is your friendly computer. Your loan is past due. If payment is not made, I will have to refer this to a human. Please include the late charge shown below with your payment.

HELLO! I AM THE COMPUTER. As yet, no one but me knows that you have not been making regular payments on this bill. However, if I have not processed a payment from you in 10 days, I will tell a Human who will resort to other means for collection.

Stage 2: Inquiry and Appeal

In this, the second stage of the collection letter series, the **inquiry** and/or **appeal** stage, inquiries or appeals are made to try to draw out a response from the customer who has remained silent. This letter asks for the customer's side of the story before matters get out of hand. Here, you are trying to touch some human chord that will bring action from a customer who has so far ignored you—and possibly other creditors. These letters may take the form of inquiry about the reasons for nonpayment, appeals for response or payment, or a combination of both. Resale material can be used here, confirming the advantages of keeping accounts current so the customer may continue to do business with you.

More than one reminder might be sent. But it is recommended that only one or at the most two letters of inquiry or appeal be sent. This will make it possible to get on into stronger messages of the pressure and ultimatum stages if the customer fails to respond. After all, the original statement has been sent, as well as one or more reminders. At this stage, however, it is a good idea to suggest an excuse for slow payment to help the customer save face. You could still be saving the business of a potentially good account.

Inquiry

For customers with running accounts, at the **inquiry** stage you should send a print-out of recent purchases and payments. They may have a valid question about the activity on the account, and you are trying to get part or all of the money due or get some response that explains the reason for nonpayment.

Or, the customer may in fact be dissatisfied with goods or services received and may be reluctant or too busy to communicate this information. Unusual circumstances may make prompt payment impossible. You are asking for an explanation. The following would serve as good letters of inquiry.

Letter 1

Inquiry ⟶ This is the third time we have reminded you of your overdue account of $200. Surely there must be a logical reason for your not answering our letters.

In view of your past good record with us, we would like to offer to rewrite your credit agreement, perhaps allowing you to make smaller payments over a longer period of time at the same interest rate.

Please come in and make both of us feel better by arranging to settle this account.

Letter 2

We have mailed two monthly statements, and we have also written you on June 30 that your account was overdue. So far, we have received no response.

Inquiry ⟶ We like to assist our customers whenever possible, if we know what the problem is. To do so, we must have partial payment of the account or an explanation for the delay in payment. Meantime, you are missing some really good buys in our Annual
Resale ⟶ Fall Clearance Sale.

Your prompt reply as to the cause for withholding payment is expected.

Appeal.

There are many suggestions that can be used at the **appeal** stage of letter collection. Frequently, inquiries and appeals are combined. Here are some of the most common appeals:

Pride: Self-respect
Economic self-interest: Good credit rating, advantages of continuing to do business with you
Sympathy: "We both have our bills to pay..."
Courtesy: "Do as you would have others do."
Fair play: "We have helped you; now you can help us."

Any one of these appeals could be phrased in many different manners.
The following letter is an inquiry combined with a self-interest appeal:

Buffer ⟶ A few years ago we suffered through our city's first electrical brownout. Today we are "in the dark" again, but in a different manner.

Economic ⟶
self-interest ⟶ Surely, it is in your best interests to maintain the good credit standing you have enjoyed with us and pay this bill today—$301.75—which is now almost two months past due.

Inquiry ⟶ If there is some reason why you haven't paid this bill, let us know what it is and perhaps we can help.

Goodwill ⟶ We have always valued your business and we believe it is in the best interests of
Looking to ⟶ both of us if we continue to do so.
future

Here are two letters that use different appeals in their attempts to get some response:

Letter 1

Sympathy ⟶ Mr. Bucher, you have your bills to pay and we most certainly have ours.

Can't you help both of us by mailing a check for $280, the amount that has been due to us since March 31?

Letter 2

I'd like to take care of the problem you seem to be having with your past due homeowner's payment.

Inquiry ⟶ Let's look at some of the choices you have. If extra cash will help, I'll do my best to arrange it. If your budget isn't working, I'll help you develop a new one. If you're faced with a financial difficulty that extra cash won't solve, I'll try to suggest some practical solutions.

Sympathy ⟶ Over the years we have learned to sympathize with those who have temporary troubles meeting their expenses. I can't help unless I know what your problem is.

Please call or come in today so we can talk things over.

Sincerely,

P.S. Perhaps you don't feel a need to contact me. If so, I'll look for your payment of $_____ no later than January 26, 19XX.

Stage 3: Pressure

If you have heard nothing as a result of your earlier communications, you are dealing with a person with poor paying patterns. Your plan at this stage of the collection procedure is to try to break the ice with some form of **pressure** to try to get a response from the account. In the normal course of business, you would probably telephone the customer or make a call in person. Or you might have another representative of the firm call.

To force action, letters with a stronger tone are sometimes sent. If contact has been made by telephone or in person and no response has resulted, a letter should follow.

The tone of the pressure letter is firmer than that of earlier communications, with a clear understanding that the customer is in the wrong by not having paid the amount due and by not even responding to your many communications.

At this stage, certified letters with a return receipt requested can be effective. You then know that the customer or someone authorized to act in that person's behalf has received your letter. The customer knows it and knows you know it. Although the expenditure for certified letters is minimal, it would not, of course, be recommended for attempting to collect two or three dollars. But for most accounts, it is well justified.

The pressure letter shows little friendly attitude but should in no way offend the customer. This may still eventually be a good customer again if you are patient through some difficulty. But the seriousness of the situation must be made clear. The tone of the following letter is firm, with reference to unspecified action, obviously serious, that might be taken:

The matter of your long overdue balance of $300 has become critical.

We have received no response to several letters we have written, although we have given you every opportunity to let us help you with your financial difficulties.

Frankly, you leave us no alternative but to inform you that unless we hear from you by April 30, we will have to consider other action.

Won't you give this matter urgent attention?

Another letter of the pressure stage of collections follows:

> It has been brought to my attention that your current account is six months overdue. Previous efforts to contact you have gone unanswered. Your account shows a balance of $147.67 on one portable electric typewriter.
>
> I will expect to hear from you by April 24, 19XX, or we will consider more drastic action.

The threat of impairing an individual's or a business's credit record is quite powerful. Most people want to maintain a good credit record to their own advantage, and most businesses cannot remain in operation without one. Therefore, the threat to report an account unfavorably frequently brings the desired results. The following letter has been effective:

> As a businessman, you know the value of a good credit rating. As a matter of fact, today it is all but impossible for a business to operate without the advantages of being able to purchase on credit.
>
> Yet it seems that it will be our unpleasant duty to report your nonpayment of your account of $402.25, due since November 1.
>
> Could we just have partial payment of this amount and a suggestion for scheduling payments that you will be able to meet?

Of course, form letters are used at any stage of the collection letter process. Here is a form letter for the pressure stage, as late stage letters are more difficult to write.

> We are worried because our efforts to reach you concerning the past due condition of your account have not resulted in the balance being reduced to a current condition.

Previous balance	Purchases and Penalties	Credits	Payments	New balance	Amount due
134.44	1.50	.00	.00	135.94	135.94

> Your account has reached the point where we would ordinarily refer it to our Collection Department. However, we at Buffums value your patronage highly, and it is our desire to aid you in maintaining a prompt payment record.
>
> Please contact me so that we can work out some arrangement which will be mutually satisfactory.

Stage 4: Ultimatum

After you have sent one or two gentle reminders, a letter of inquiry and/or appeal, and one or more messages showing firmer pressure, if there is no response, the messages take on a different tone. Letters of **ultimatum** are written at the final stage of the collection letter series.

In preparing these letters, it is helpful to try to get a mental picture of the person to whom you are writing: the poor credit risk. This person is accustomed to getting reminders and has a rather hard shell against most reasoning or appeals. If there is one appeal that is effective, it is **fear**—fear of something that the person does not wish to happen.

The letters written at this stage are among the few kinds that violate the rule of promoting good will. Your competitors are welcome to such customers. They are poor at paying obligations and are too much trouble to the collection department. Further, negatives are more effective here than positives—these cutomers have brushed off your more positive "nice guy" approaches.

The letter of ultimatum can take several forms. It can threaten to turn the account over to collection agencies, or to attorneys for legal action. If legal action is to be taken, the debtor can be reminded that court costs of both the debtor and the creditor will be charged to the debtor. Some merchandise can be repossessed for money due, and in some states, wages can be garnisheed. Since none of these avenues appeal to either the sender or the receiver of the letter of ultimatum, it is imperative that the message be as strong as legally possible to try to effect payment.

Legality is the key. The threat can be only for action that is within the limits of the law, such as a suit to collect a debt on a contract, or other actions as just set out. Libel laws prohibit name calling or threats of damaging a person's reputation. Other laws prohibit threats of violence.

Recent Federal law sets out specific things you cannot do in debt collection:

You may not communicate by postcard (outsiders could read it).

You may not threaten violence.

You may not call repeatedly with intent to annoy.

You may not use obscene language to abuse.

You may not falsely say you are a lawyer.

You may not misrepresent the legal status of a debt.

You may not falsely suggest that the debtor has committed a crime.[1]

Guidelines for writing the letter of ultimatum in collection processes are shown here:

1. Give specific details of the debt: amount due, how long overdue, late payment charges, and interest charges.

2. State clearly that previous notices have been ignored or refused.

3. State clearly what action is desired.

4. State clearly what action you will take if no response is received.

5. Give a specific deadline, such as, "If we have not heard by _____ . . . ." Give the person ample, but not too much, time—about a week or ten days.

Figure 9.4 is an example of an effective letter of ultimatum.
Examples of some effective letters of ultimatum in the collection process follow.

Letter 1

As you have failed to answer our earlier requests for payment of $300.17 now six months overdue, we will be forced to put this matter in the hands of a collection agency.

If by January 31 we do not have in our hands the money due us, you can expect to be contacted by members of Brownson Collectors Group.

Letter 2

You are undoubtedly aware that federal law provides that anyone using the mails to defraud may be fined or imprisoned or both.

We do not like to report a customer to postal authorities, but we feel we have the right to collect what is legally due us. As you have ignored our many letters, we have no alternative, because your merchandise was ordered through the United States mails.

If we have not heard from you by August 23, you will be reported.

[1] Iris I. Varner and Carson H. Varner, "Legal Issues in Business Communications," *The American Business Communication Association Bulletin,* September 1983, p. 14.

"Here's your hat; what's your hurry!"

The Marina
601 Ocean Park Place
Long Beach, California 00800

AUGUST 16, 19XX

Edward Jaxson
Unit #1060

Dear Edward

I received your response explaining your refusal to pay the $5.75 increase in cable TV costs.

This is a problem that is encountered all the time by people living in condos. It is the need to conform and go along with the majority of owners that drives a lot of people away from condo living. I don't use the pool and sauna, but I still must help pay for their upkeep.

Thru July of 19XX the breakdown of your maintenance fee was a follows:

Unit	Parking Space	Cable TV	Basic Maintenance Fee	Total Maintenance Fee
1060	4.33	6.80	75.37	86.50

Starting August 1 your maintenance fee is as follows:

Unit	Parking Space	Cable TV	Basic Maintenance Fee	Total Maintenance Fee
1060	4.33	12.55	75.37	92.25

Let me know how you intend to proceed in this matter. I hope you will not force us to use legal action.

For the Board of Governors

A. D. Dunkin
Treasurer

c   Alfred Hunter—as you suggested
     Law Offices
     141 Beach Boulevard
     Westminister, Calif. 92683

FIGURE 9.4
Ultimatum letter for collection of condo fees.

Letter 3

Because you have failed to pay the premium when due, your policy #121467892 is being canceled today, in line with our formal announcement mailed to you April 30, effective May 20.

Please return our policy immediately in the enclosed envelope so that we may complete cancellation. Please remember that we wanted to keep you as a client—you are the one who is responsible for the cancellation.

Upon receipt of a check for the $97.20 due, we will suggest reinstatement of your policy to the underwriting department.

It might be risky to use humor at this stage. Dartnell Corporation gives us this story:

A few years ago, a furniture company attempted to collect some overdue bills with this threatening letter:

Dear Sir:

What would your friends and neighbors think if our truck pulled into your driveway some afternoon, and our men came into your house to pick up the items of furniture for which you have not paid us?

Shelby Furniture Company

Back came this prompt reply from a customer:

Gentlemen:

I have talked this over with my friends and neighbors and they all agree it would be a pretty lousy trick.

Henry Jones

Checkpoints for Credit Letters

1. Is the appearance satisfactory?

2. Is the message courteous?

3. Is it clear and complete?

4. *Making credit inquiries and granting credit:* Does the first paragraph contain the main message?

5. *Refusing credit:* Is there a buffer beginning and a pleasant closing? Is the refusal stated reasonably and briefly?

6. Eliminate unnecessary words.

7. Recheck for any statement that might be a violation of libel laws.

8. If the passive sentence form is overused, change some sentences to active.

9. For variety in sentence form, some sentences should start with descriptive words, phrases, or clauses.

10. Where possible, change negative statements to positive statements.

11. Check for "you attitude." Are statements made in the reader's interest rather than in the writer's interest?

12. *Repetition:* Remove any word that unnecessarily repeats the sound of another word.

13. Recheck for correct grammar and spelling.

Checkpoints for Collection Letters

1. Identify reader(s) and write at that level.

2. Is the appearance satisfactory?

3. Is the message clear and complete?

4. Does the message carry good will for you and/or your firm? *Exception:* In the late stages of the collection letter series, retaining good will is not a major concern. However, do not make libelous statements or threats of violence.

5. Eliminate unnecesary words.

6. Recheck for any statement that might be interpreted as discourteous.

7. If the passive sentence form is oversused, change some sentences to active.

8. Check for variety in sentence form: some sentences should start with descriptive words, phrases, or clauses.

9. Where possible, change negative words to positive. *Exception:* late stages of collection letter series.

10. Check for a "you attitude." Are statements made in the reader's interest, rather than in the writer's interest?

11. *Repetition:* Remove any needless repetitions of the same or similar words.

12. Recheck grammar and spelling.

Writing Assignments

1. You are employed as general office assistant for C. E. Lukes, D.D.S. Dr. Lukes has suggested that you try to collect his overdue accounts for an agreed percentage of the amount you can collect. The accounts you have range from 30 days to nine months past due. (You are to make up fictitious names and addresses.)

   a. Write a letter to a client whose account is 30 days past due. The amount due is $39.
   b. Write a letter to a client whose account is 60 days past due, amount $172.
   c. Write a letter to another client whose account is 60 days past due, amount $126.
   d. Write a letter to a client whose account is five months past due, amount $126.
   e. Write a letter to a client whose account is nine months past due, amount $163.

2. As vehicle loan officer of First City Bank, you are in charge of collecting loan payments on all motor vehicles. Write a collection letter for each of the following overdue accounts. Make up individual names and addresses:

   a. A 19XX VW with a $123 balance one month past due.
   b. A 19XX Oldsmobile Cutlass with $1330.78 balance. Payment has not been made for three months.
   c. A 19XX Wagoneer Motor Home with a balance of $4,272 on which payments have not been made for six months.

3. You are new to town and want to apply for credit at a local department store. Write to the store of your choice with a request to open an account. Give them information of accounts you have had previously in Tucson, Arizona, at Goldwater's, Rosenzweig's, and Jacome's. Also mention that you have a current Texaco card under your name, account #75 141 3562.

4. Write a letter from the store in the preceding assignment, welcoming the credit applicant as a new customer and enclosing two credit cards. Ask the receiver to have the cards signed immediately by the persons who will be using them.

5. Write a letter from the store in assignment 3, refusing credit to the applicant. The credit information you have received indicates that this person would not be a good credit risk. Be tactful. Suggest business on other terms.

6. You are manager of a department store in a town where there is no retail credit bureau established. Write a letter to Mrs. Mun Tam asking for credit information on a person relatively new to town who has given Mrs. Tam's business, a dress shop, as a credit reference. Tell what information you would like to have.

7. As Mrs. Mun Tam, reply to the letter in number 6, making up your own response.

8. A member of your credit union has ignored the first two payments on a $3,500 loan. You feel she is a good credit risk. Write a letter inquiring about the reason for nonpayment.

9. One of your good old customers has failed to make the past two monthly payments on his Ice-Maker refrigerator, which he purchased eight months ago. Write him a collection letter.

10. You have sent several collection letters to another customer who purchased an Ice-Maker refrigerator and have tried to reach her by telephone, but you have been unsuccessful in getting any response. Write a letter that will be the final communication before the account is turned over to a local repossession agency.

Chapter 9   *Writing Improvement Exercise*

Avoiding Redundancies: Needless Repetition of the Same or Similar Words

Original	The difference in results occurred because the new owners followed different routines.
Improved	The change occurred because the new owners followed different routines.
Original	This term would not be proper terminology.
Improved	This would not be proper terminology.
Original	They are located in convenient locations around the area.
Improved	They are located in convenient places around the area.

Each of the examples above in its original form contains a needless repetition of the same or similar words. One evidence of poor communication style in writing or speaking is such repetition, which is monotonous to the reader or listener. A way to catch this type of usage in written material is to read it aloud, since repetitions are more readily picked up by hearing them.

Some of these sentences can be improved by simply rephrasing them and omitting one of the repetitious words. In other instances, it is necessary to use another word of similar meaning. To find such synonyms and to improve your vocabulary, refer to a dictionary or a thesaurus or both.

Not all word duplications can be considered improper. When properly used intentionally for emphasis, repetition of the same or a similar word can be effective. For example: "Your report is *excellent*, really an *excellent* piece of work." Or, "The critic claimed that new movies are either neurotic, erotic, or tommy-rotic."

Name _____

Date _____ Class Section _____

Chapter 9 *Writing Improvement Worksheet*

Avoiding Redundancies: Needless Repetition of the Same or Similar Words

In the following sentences, underline the words that are the same or similar, then rewrite the sentence in an improved form in the space provided. If the repetition is not apparent, read the sentence aloud. (Not all improvements for a given sentence will be alike.)

1. Gregory initiated the initial action. → _____

_____

2. One important thing she learned was that getting along with people was as important as ability to do the work. → _____

_____

3. Management should set up a program whereby written instructions are set up for each machine operation. → _____

_____

4. Andrew David's stuff is working out working arrangements. → _____

_____

5. Rising costs are mostly due to our own doing. → _____

_____

6. What is the use of studying word usage? → _____

_____

7. He repeats this repetition frequently. → _____

_____

8. The advertising department has laid out the layout for next month's magazine ads. → _____

_____

9. After all the information was obtained, the contract was contracted by the survey team. → _____

_____

10. This provision provides insurance coverage for all dependents. → _____

_____

Chapter 9   Writing Improvement Worksheet (*Continued*)

11. The sectional weather roundup will not be available this morning owing to un-availability. → _____

                                           _____

12. He said that he feels that this is a good solution. → _____

                                           _____

13. Ask them to make a record of each recording sold between 6 and 9 p.m. → _____

                                           _____

14. They want us to send two copies to them too. → _____

                                           _____

15. Reporters reported detailed activities of each candidate. → _____

                                           _____

REVIEW AND DISCUSSION

Chapter 9 *Credit Letters and Collection Letters*

Give concise responses to the following:

1. For successful operation of a business, three departments must work closely together. What are they? _____

2. What percentage of accounts are usually uncollectable? _____

3. _____ percent of business operates on credit.

4. Name the "four Cs of credit," and define each. _____
   _____
   _____
   _____
   _____

5. Name four sources of retail credit information. _____
   _____
   _____

6. Name three sources of trade credit information. _____
   _____

7. Letters granting credit are ("A," routine, good news; "B," negative; "C," selling) messages. _____

8. Is it acceptable to explain credit terms simply as "1/10, net 60"? Why, or why not?
   _____

9. Letters refusing credit are (A; B; C) messages. _____

10. Name the four topics that should be covered in exchanging credit information.
    _____
    _____
    _____
    _____

Chapter 9   Credit Letters and Collection Letters (*Continued*)

11. Give three reasons why collection letters must be written and must be effective.

    _____

    _____

    _____

12. What do well-run organizations do to see that collection letters are continuing to be
    effective? _____

    _____

13. What type of telephone service is usually available for heavy usage of long-distance
    telephone lines? _____

14. In collections, personal oral contacts are usually (more; less) effective than written
    contacts. _____

15. Sometimes late payments from well-rated businesses or government agencies are not
    due to lack of money but are due to _____

    _____

16. Collection letters should be written to (high officials; people in lower levels of respon-
    sibility). _____

17. Give four guidelines for writing good collection letters. Be brief. _____

    _____

    _____

    _____

18. The text says: "Collection letters should be written promptly, regularly, and with

    _____ "

19. The older an account gets, the (more; less) chance there is of collecting on it.

    _____

20. Name the four stages of the collection letter series. _____

    _____

21. Why should the first collection letter appear routine? _____

    _____

22. How do most people feel about using humor in collection letters? _____

    _____

23. Name three types of inquiries or appeals that can be used in the "inquiry and appeal"
    stage of collections. _____

    _____

    _____

Chapter 9   Credit Letters and Collection Letters (*Continued*)

24. Name three types of ultimatums that can be used in the last stage of the collection letter series. _____

_____

25. List five guidelines for writing a good ultimatum collection letter. Be brief.

_____

_____

_____

_____

_____

26, 27, 28, 29, 30. Make each of the following sentences shorter and clearer by drawing a line through any unnecessary redundancy or by rewriting the entire sentence.

26. We will be happy and delighted to attend your fund raising event. → _____

_____

27. Let us know if his talk is stimulating and thought-provoking. → _____

_____

28. Getting approval for writing the report was both difficult and rugged. → _____

_____

29. My cousins and the children of all my aunts and uncles attended the services. →

_____

30. I can assure you that you will receive the shipment immediately without any further delay. → _____

CHAPTER 10
Memorandums

> "The horror of that moment," the King
> went on, "I shall never, never forget!"
> "You will, though," the Queen said, "if you
> don't make a memorandum of it."
>
> *Through the Looking Glass [1872]*
> *Lewis Carroll [Charles Lutwidge Dodgson]*

Memorandums can be forceful communications within any organization. The following story is one example.

For a time during World War II, the Federal Bureau of Investigation was heavily involved in international espionage. Selected largely for their competence in foreign languages, special agents were quickly given training in foreign espionage. Stripped of all identification with the FBI and assigned logical "covers," they were dispatched on far-flung missions.

Officials at headquarters in Washington, D.C., were gratified at the work that was being accomplished. But after a time, they decided that they must follow the domestic plan of sending inspectors unannounced to check on these foreign agents where they were assigned.

One such inspector arrived in Buenos Aires, Argentina, contacted an undercover agent and began routine inspection procedures. But the agent, well trained, refused to admit any past or present connection with the FBI. He stood his ground, knowing that Germany had well-trained undercover agents in South America—he had tailed some of them. The inspector, meanwhile, showed all types of identification, told public and private details of the Bureau's operation, named locations of its offices, recited long lists of Bureau employees, and so on and on.

But the espionage agent held firm. Hours of frustration passed. Finally, the inspector picked up his briefcase in disgust, and said, "Well, there's nothing I can do. I'll just have to write a memo."

"Come back! Come back!" cried the agent. "When you say that, *now* I know you are with the Bureau!"

Few memos have such dramatic impact. Most are about routine matters and therefore can be read and destroyed immediately. However, memos help keep an office operation running smoothly. Some memorandums should be filed for future reference, and a few are of critical importance.

Importance of Memorandums

Only recently has it been realized that business communications classes should devote more time and attention to the preparation of memorandums.

Surveys in various businesses and other organizations have shown that in many offices, far more memorandums than letters are written. One survey showed that of 20 forms of written communications, top personnel ranked memos first as the most frequently written.

For communicating within an organization, memorandums and printed forms are the chief types of written communications between individuals and also between offices.

Your Memorandums = Your Reputation

The memorandums you write can have a great effect upon your general reputation. Upper management and administrators often have very little concrete information upon which to judge the job performance of people working for them. There is a saying in business, "By their memorandums shall ye know them."

To some extent, your fellow workers may also get to know you by your memos. And eventually, as you progress toward supervisory and management positions yourself, your memorandums will often determine your effectiveness with subordinates.

Studies relating to content of effective letters also apply to content of memorandums. Certainly we should create and maintain good will within an organization by employing a good will tone in interoffice writing. Also, sucessful operation of business demands that the message of any memorandum be clear and complete.

Advantages of the Memorandum Form

The chief advantages of the memorandum form are as follows:

1. *The memorandum invites brevity*. It is the no-frills communication that almost invariably includes the necessary information and nothing more.

2. *The memorandum is convenient.* The chief notations at the top of the memo give ready reference to its subject matter, and the major area is left free for the message. Although usually typed, these messages can be written in pen or pencil.

3. *The memorandum is inexpensive.* Because the memorandum is generally circulated within an organization, computer memos on a screen or printed memos can be trashed immediately.

4. *The memorandum can be used as a record of information to be filed for future reference.* As noted, most memos can be destroyed immediately. At times, however, memo records of day to day transactions in person or by telephone can be very helpful. Unnecessary memos stored on computer disks or paper can consume valuable storage space.

Appearance of Memorandums

Typical Memorandum Format

Following is a typical heading for a memorandum with or without file number. The balance of the sheet would be left blank. Any office can use full sheets or half sheets with a heading similar to this. For the unusually long memorandum of more than one page, blank sheets with or without a one line heading can be used for attached pages.

INTEROFFICE MEMORANDUM

To: _____   File #_____

From: _____   Date: _____

                                   Subject: _____

Routine Message Memorandum Forms

Routine message memorandum forms prepared for a specific office are sometimes used. Such forms can be made out according to messages that are commonly transmitted in that office. However, among businesses, most routine messages are quite similar. Figure 10.1 is typical of preplanned message forms. You can see that most messages could be composed quickly by simply checking the appropriate box or boxes. The bottom half-sheet is left blank for supporting details, if there are any.

Intra-Office Routing Slips

Intra-office **routing slips** are used for sending information and/or materials around to several individuals within a given office. Figure 10.2 is an example of a typical intra-office routing slip. These memorandum forms can be composed for the needs of any office. However, it can be helpful to see other such slips for ideas on what to include.

Simple messages can be written on routing slips or the slips can be attached to material that is to be seen or read by many people on the staff. A line can be drawn through the name of any person or persons who are not to receive this particular message.

Routing slips can be changed and updated for new office situations, especially for changes in personnel. Therefore, they should be printed in limited numbers.

Good Will Tone for In-Company Communications

The "Good Old Days"

Looking at the memorandum in Figure 10.3, written in 1870, we can recognize that the tone of employee communications of today is or should be different from the tone of such an old memorandum.

Memos at All Levels

Memorandums are written to people at all levels. As stated earlier, you—and your job performance—will frequently be judged by the memos you write.

RIO HONDO COLLEGE
BUSINESS DEPARTMENT

TO: _____   DATE: _____

FROM: _____

FOR YOUR

( ) APPROVAL
( ) FILES
( ) INFORMATION
( ) REPLY - SIGNATURE
( ) SUGGESTIONS
( ) RECOMMENDATIONS
( )

PLEASE

( ) PHONE ME REGARDING THIS
( ) SEE ME REGARDING THIS
( ) CIRCULATE
( ) TAKE NECESSARY ACTION
( ) RETURN
( ) FILE OR DESTROY
( )

FIGURE 10.1
Memorandum form with routine messages preprinted.
Notice space left for any needed additional message.

Treating others with respect and courtesy is the key to success in getting along with people on or off the job. On the job, whether dealing with your superiors, with your peers, or with those who work for you, writing with a good will tone showing respect will usually reward you with better understanding and cooperation. Also, you should always show that you are following ethical practices.

To get cooperation or agreement from others, also use an uplifting, positive tone. This plan, too, applies in preparing communications that go up the ladder, down the ladder or straight across the board to fellow employees.

Check your message carefully to remove any planned or unplanned negative overtones. Remember, a sarcastic tone will sound out loud and clear, sometimes obscuring the rest of the message. Such negative between the lines messages can boomerang and hurt you. Also, you should always show that you are following ethical practices.

Humor used appropriately is especially recommended and appreciated in internal communications at any level. You can give the reader or readers a brief lift from reading the bulk of other memos that can be so deadly dull. Your humor can also help make your own day.

PHYLLIS PEARCE
DEPARTMENT CHAIRPERSON

Date _____

	To	Initials	Date
_____	Becker	_____	_____
_____	Bristol	_____	_____
_____	Fraser	_____	_____
_____	Hempstead	_____	_____
_____	Hunter, E.	_____	_____
_____	Hunter, G.	_____	_____
_____	Kreitz	_____	_____
_____	Long	_____	_____
_____	Myers	_____	_____
_____	Podewitz	_____	_____
_____	Rhoads	_____	_____
_____	Sakata	_____	_____
_____	Wejmar	_____	_____
_____	Williams	_____	_____

_____ Please see me.   _____   Read, initial, and
                                                 pass to next person.
_____ For your files.

_____ For your signature.

_____ For your information.

_____ For your suggestions.

_____ Please handle.

Comments:

FIGURE 10.2
An example of an office routing slip.

Memos to Your Superiors

Naturally, you should show respect toward people who must judge you and your work. A special memo here can often end with "Respectfully" or "Respectfully submitted."

Memos to Co-Workers

We should also be respectful of our fellow workers as well as those working for us. Others at your own level might hurt you if in writing or speaking you do not treat them

---

OUR CODE

INSTRUCTIONS TO EMPLOYEES

(Issued in 1870 by P. W. Madsen of the Madsen Furniture Company, Salt Lake City, Utah.)

Our Business Code:

Store open at 7:00 a.m. and close at 8:00 p.m. except on Saturday, then store open at 7:00 a.m. and close at 9:00 p.m. This is in effect the year round. This store will remain closed each sabbath.

Duties of Employees

Sweep floors, dust furniture, office shelves and show cases. Remember, "Cleanliness is next to Godliness." Trim wicks, clean chimneys and fill lamps. Make your pens carefully (but you may whittle the quills to suit your individual taste). Open the windows for fresh air. Each clerk should bring in one bucket of water and one scuttle of coal. These things are necessary to prepare us for the day's business. Any employee who smokes Spanish cigars, uses liquor in any form, gets shaved at the barber shop, or frequents pool halls or public dance halls will give his employer every reason to suspicion his integrity, worthy intentions and his all around honesty.

Each employee is expected to pay his tithing, that is 10% of his annual income to the Church. No matter what one's income might be, you should not contribute less than $25 per year to the Church. Each employee will attend Sacrament meeting and adequate time will be given to each employee to attend Fast Meeting. Also you are expected to attend your Sunday School. Men employees will be given one evening off each week for courting purposes. Two evenings each week if they go regularly to Church duties. After any employee has spent his 13 hours of labor in the store, he should then spend his leisure time in the reading of good books, and the contemplating of the Glories and building up of the Kingdom of God.

(Signed) P. W. Madsen

FIGURE 10.3
Communication to employees, dated 1870.

with respect. In considering people for advancement, the opinions of fellow workers is usually considered.

Memos to Those Working for You

Hiring, replacing and training employees is a major expense of any organization. Therefore, supervisors and managers must be concerned that communications to employees, even negative communications, are written in a courteous tone.

A positive, respectful memorandum, telephone call, bulletin, letter or other communication should stand a good chance of persuading others that you are considerate, and this tone should help get the work done satisfactorily.

Then look at it selfishly: Opinions of those under your supervision will often be sought when officials are looking for someone to advance to higher positions. Getting along with people is a prerequisite for most promotions.

Today's Communications from Management

In contrast to the "good old days" memo shown earlier, today's memos have a different style.

Pointing out that *managing* does not mean *ordering,* the following six guidelines for communications to employees are condensed from an article in an *American Business Communication Association Bulletin:*

1. **Provide adequate information.** Do not assume that an employee only needs to know how—and does not need to know why.

2. **Be truthful.** A manager needs to retain the confidence of subordinates.

3. **Be clear.** Eliminate gobbledygook or ambiguous language. Otherwise, employees may begin to ignore the manager's messages, and management–subordinate communication breaks down.

4. **Maintain employee understanding of company goals.** Show employees the relationship between their individual tasks and the goals of the company. Focus on the connection between individual roles and corporate planning.

5. **Motivate rather than order.** Effective motivation shows employees not only how the action fits the company goals, but how the action will benefit them; effective employee motivation is based on logical explanation supported by facts.

6. **Provide opportunity for feedback.** Employees should know there is a path for upward communication and that management wants to hear from them.[1]

"The Ultimate Memo"[2]

With the flexibility of computers and word processors, strikingly new and different memos are being prepared. Jim Bartimo, contributing editor of *Personal Computer* magazine, tells how to make up what he calls "**The Ultimate Memo.**" Bartimo points out that different typefaces and sizes with added white space can make a memo stand out.

He emphasizes the value of leaving **white space,** saying that "too much gray is boring." Further, he suggests that besides using different typefaces, we can center headings, possibly setting them in bold face. Also, on many machines, important items can be set in reverse type which has white lettering in a band of black. With some machines, graphics can be added within the text, quickly calling attention to their content.

"Keep paragraphs short, since paragraph breaks provide needed white space," Bartimo cautions. Also, he says that we should make sure all margins are at least one inch wide. Standard headers and footers (upper and lower margins) can be set so all pages look alike.

On the word processor or computer we can make a special file called "Letter," "Format," or "Design" to store any page makeup we especially like and may want to use again. The message of the original memo can be temporarily erased while its format is being saved to the special file.

"The end result of putting your software and printer through hoops is the kind of documents people like to read. This can be critical to the success of a project...." says Bartimo.

---

[1]Diana C. Reep, "The Manager's Message—Teaching the Internal Memo," *The American Business Communication Association Bulletin,* March 1984, pp. 11–13.

[2]Jim Bartimo, "The Ultimate Memo," *Personal Computing,* September 1986, pp. 100–111.

Clear and Complete Messages in Memorandums

Most memorandums carry "A" messages, **routine information,** but sometimes they can carry less routine information, such as negative messages or messages of persuasion. Almost any memorandum could follow the appropriate plan of a routine message, a negative message, or a selling letter.

"A" Messages: Routine Information, "Yes" or Good News Memorandums

Most memorandums fit into this category. Employees are, or should be, busy. Therefore the message should be direct and clear.

Figure 10.4 is an example of an "A" message, a good news message. Figure 10.5 is a routine information memorandum with a place for a return message. Notice that in both memos, the main message comes early, so people need not wade through extraneous matter.

"B" Messages: Negative Memorandums

For **negative** messages to others in your organization, try to use a touch of humor, if possible. This can give a lift to the reader and writer, and can also help develop a positive attitude toward you personally. Figure 10.6 is an example of such a negative message.

Figure 10.7 is another example of a negative message under different circumstances. In cases of really bad news, as this one probably is, it is inadvisable to use humor. The closing of a business and the possible loss of jobs are typical matters that don't invite humor.

Notice that Figures 10.6 and 10.7 each has a buffer that leads somewhat softly into the negatives, giving the bad news briefly and clearly without dragging in too many details. Then they close with a message that is suitably upbeat.

MEMORANDUM

To: All Employees   Date: August 15, 19XX
From: Marilyn Spooner   Subject: New Parking Spaces

Good news!

Our addition to the employee parking lot will be finished by September 1, 19XX. No more walking through mud and guck this winter if you had to park in the old parking area.

We trust you understand that additional parking facilities were needed because of the successful sales of our line of Cord-Wear and the additional staff needed in all departments.

September is nearly here. Just cross your fingers that we don't get a heavy storm meantime! Bear with us just a few more days.

FIGURE 10.4
Routine information memorandum , an "A" memorandum.

```
                LEMON GROVE COMMUNITY COLLEGE DISTRICT
                      Office of Personnel Services


     To:      All Faculty
     From:    Brian Waver
     Date:    September 10, 19XX
     Subject: Release of Information


     Article 16 of our current contract between Lemon Grove College District and
     Lemon Grove College Faculty Association requires that the District provide the
     Association with a list of the names and job titles of all unit members. It
     further requires the District to provide the Association with home addresses
     and home telephone numbers of unit members who authorize the release of
     such information.

     If you wish us to provide the association with your address and telephone
     number, please complete the following form and return it to the Personnel
     Office by Friday, September 28, 19XX.


     kg


     _____
     _____


     I authorize Lemon Grove Community College District to release my address and
     telephone number to the Lemon Grove College Faculty Association as follows:

     Name: _____
            (Please print)

     Address: _____

              _____

     Telephone: _____

                                   _____
                                   Signature
```

FIGURE 10.5
*Routine information memorandum—"A" message with room
for return message.*

"C" Messages: Persuasive Request Memorandums

Sometimes it is helpful or even necessary to send memorandums that attempt to sell others on a certain plan or idea. These memorandums, of course, could be classified as **persuasive requests** and could be written on the same "C" letter plan as other sales letters.

This type of message can usually be most effective following this pattern, highlighting the advantages to the firm and/or individual for whom it is written (the "you attitude"). This would be the first part, the "attention-getter." Following would be the interest–desire buildup, explaining specifically the advantages of the plan. Also, it should state as briefly as possible how the plan could be implemented.

TO: Summer Business Faculty

FROM: Phyllis Pearce, Dept. Chair

DATE: June 22, 19XX

SUBJECT: Eating and drinking in classrooms

Students are leaving coffee cups, empty cola containers, and trash in the classrooms. If you allow eating and drinking in the classroom, please use good judgment and make students clean up after themselves. It may interest you to know that cola spilled on the floor eats off the finish; coffee does not.

I would prefer that you not allow students to drink cola in the classrooms. The empty containers draw ants, and we have enough problems without attracting little critters who are not interested in an education.

Not an order

Closing humor

PMP:ct

FIGURE 10.6
Negative memorandum that closes with a humorous touch.

KARL'S VINE STREET BOOKSTORE
INTEROFFICE MEMORANDUM

TO: All employees   DATE: June 1, 19XX

FROM: Harold F. Karl   SUBJECT: Store closing
       Owner-Manager

As our long-time employees know, it has always been our policy to inform employees of important developments as soon as possible. We try to notify you officially before news gets on the grapevine, but do not always meet with success.

We are all aware of the general reduction in sales since the discount bookstore down the street (I won't name it) first opened its doors. Because you have all helped us develop a large clientele over the years, we have known many prosperous seasons. As you may have already predicted, we now find it necessary to close our doors at our beloved Vine Street location.

This decision to close is welcome news to none of us, but we can find no alternative.

Meantime, those of you with longest seniority will be offered positions in other Karl's branch stores. For the rest, we will give all the aid possible to assist you in finding a new position elsewhere. I will be talking personally with each one. Our best wishes go with you.

Cordially,

Buffer

Negative-brief and clear

As upbeat as possible

FIGURE 10.7
Negative memorandum that contains really bad news.

The last section of this memorandum–request should state clearly what action should be taken. Also, it is usually appropriate to explain costs and/or savings. If applicable, give a deadline.

Such an important communication might be prepared hurriedly. But it should never be submitted in final draft to others until you have studied it thoroughly for clear content, good will tone, and grammar. Then prepare a revised copy. Success of your project could depend upon the wording of this memo.

Figures 10.8, 10.9 and 10.10 are examples of "C" memorandums—persuasive requests.

Checkpoints for Memorandums

1. Identify reader(s) and write at that level.

2. Appearance: Less expensive stationery and less expensive means of reproducing can generally be used for memos.

3. Good will tone: It is especially important to check for satisfactory tone in communications to people with whom we work.

4. Message: Make it *clear, complete,* and especially *concise.*

TO: All Employees
FROM: I.M. Earnest, President
DATE: June, 19XX

We all recognize that each person has different tastes in many matters. Of course, one way in which we show our individuality is in our manner of dress.

   Now, summer is upon us, and a craving to get out of the cocoons of winter is universal. While lighter dresses and suits are certainly necessary and acceptable, could we just be a little more cautious in some choices: no strapless tops—in fact, shoulder lines should be more than a strap. Also, please, no deep cle_____, I mean, no deep necklines. We feel people should watch their necklines so that others won't.

   And a few of you venturesome males have been adorning the torso with shirts more appropriate to the sands of Hawaii. Maybe our opposition is partly envy. In all, could we leave casual dress for casual places.

   We all realize that our firm is expected to present a certain businesslike image to our customers and the public, and we will appreciate your cooperation.

PS   Of course, it is come-as-you-like at the company-sponsored picnic next month.

Annotations (right margin):
- Attention-getter
- (Hoping to build up)
- Interest
- &
- Desire (to conform)
- Action

FIGURE 10.8
"C" memorandum, a persuasive request to get employees to conform to a dress code.

TO: All Employees   DATE: June, 19XX
FROM: CFH   SUBJECT: Overload on copying machines

If we want to have monies to spend in areas we feel are most important, we are all finding we must cut some corners.

Attention-getter

Since the recent cutback in overseas orders, it is necessary to watch costs carefully. Duplicating material on our department copying machines costs .00 per page; however, our duplicating department reproduces materials at only .00 per page.

Interest

We know the difference in these two amounts seems minimal. But with our heavy production, that difference really adds up.

and

Could you cooperate with us and try to have most of your copying done by Mrs. Stauffer and her fine duplicating department staff. They need only a 24-hour turnaround time.

Desire

We will appreciate your continued help in one more small—but getting bigger—method of watching costs.

Action

FIGURE 10.9
Persuasive request concerning an office expense.

DATE   October 30, 19XX
TO   Josephine Broderick, Vice President
                Advertising Department
FROM   Matthew Blanchford
                Account Executive
SUBJECT New Advertising Campaign

Following our discussion at the Coral Gables meeting, where new ideas were invited, I am respectfully setting out a suggestion for a new ad campaign.

Attention

Could we consider publicizing the customer courtesy being taught our employees in special classes on this aspect of their work. I believe the public would be favorably impressed.

Interest and Desire Buildup

We are all aware of the superior training our employees receive, and I believe the public should be made aware of it. Your department could choose lively scenes and dialogue for ads demonstrating our employee courtesy.

Action

I would be happy to discuss this idea further with you.

Action

FIGURE 10.10
Persuasive request "selling" idea of a new advertising campaign.

5. For an "A," "B", or "C" message, follow the checkpoints for writing that type of message.

6. Check for grammar and spelling (your memorandums = your reputation).

Writing Assignments

1. You are the personnel director of a Denver bank and have been asked to select a secretary for a special one-month assignment to San Francisco. The person will receive air fare and per diem living expenses. There could be competition for this assignment. Write a memo to John Mohr, Officer in Charge, naming the person you select and telling why you chose this person.

2. As company social director, write a memo to all employees announcing the annual fall potluck picnic, to be held Saturday, September 17, in a nearby park (name the park). The company will furnish hamburgers, buns, soft drinks, watermelons, and prizes for games.

3. You are assistant manager of a branch bank. From your office at the back of the bank, you are able to see most teller stations. You have observed that Marie V., a new employee, takes breaks of 25 to 30 minutes instead of the allowed 15 minutes. Also, she does not greet customers in a friendly manner, despite her recent training. When you mentioned these matters to the bank manager, she asked you to write a memo to make a record of this information. Prepare that memo.

4. You have observed that some members of the word processing department are overstaying their one-hour lunch period. Also, if you are not on the floor, a few have begun to bring back a beverage to drink at their work stations, a complete violation of rules. Warning people has not corrected these practices. Write a memo to urge employees to comply with company rules regarding these two matters.

5. Your supervisor has assigned you the duty of writing office memorandums. Your first assignment is requesting employees to follow fire-prevention procedures more carefully. Recently, in violation of fire codes, several doors to stairways have been propped open, which would allow a potential fire to spread quickly to several floors. Also, at different places around the plant, boxes of merchandise and supplies have been clogging aisles that should be left open for quick exit in case of fire. Write the memorandum.

6. As chair of the Employees' Association of your firm, write a memorandum to try to persuade employees to sign up for a four-day, 40-hour workweek. Think of possible advantages of such a plan, and try to sell the employees on the idea.

7. You are head of the loan department of your credit union. The credit union manager is planning to expand use of microcomputers in your department. Write a formal memorandum to members of your department explaining the plan and setting forth its advantages. Also explain that employees using new equipment will receive training on company time. Remove the fears that any jobs will be lost as a result of installing the new equipment.

8. The manager of your section was unable to attend the last general meeting of company managers and had asked you to attend in her place. Write a memorandum reporting major matters covered at the meeting. Use your imagination.

Chapter 10 *Writing Improvement Exercise*

Avoiding Redundancies:
Needless Repetition of Words or Ideas with Similar Meanings

"The weather is damp and wet."

"I am tired and exhausted."

Each of the sentences above contains a repetition or a redundancy. In other words, each sentence needlessly contains a word that has essentially the same meaning as another word that has just been used. These sentences would be better if stated:

"The weather is damp" *or* "The weather is wet."

"I am tired" *or* "I am exhausted."

A professional writer or speaker avoids the use of redundancies, but owing to various pressures, speakers and writers occasionally make these grammatical lapses. Redundancies are also sometimes used as "filler" words, so that a person who has little to say can appear to be saying more.

Good business writing seeks just the opposite. Here, words should be used economically—two words should not be used where one will do. Following are some examples of redundancies, all of which were taken from current writing and speaking:

1. But all these recommendations, however, will be put into effect. (*but* or *however*)

2. Basically, there are two fundamental reasons for following their progress. (*basics* are *fundamentals*.)

3. It was claimed that women charged with the exact same crime as men received longer sentences. (*exact* or *same*)

4. This matter is being used as a political football for various different reasons. (*various* or *different*)

5. They are laboring under a false deception. (What is a true deception?)

6. The senator has a new and innovative approach to the problem. (Something *new* is *innovative*.)

7. Everything is agreeable and satisfactory. (*agreeable* or *satisfactory*)

8. Today's game will be broadcast at 3 p.m. this afternoon. (*p.m.* or *afternoon*)

9. I got a rebate back on my federal income tax. (*rebate* or *money back*)

10. We'll also broadcast from the locker room of the losing team, too. (*also* or *too*)

11. The alleged rumor is that the boss is dating his secretary. (*It is alleged* or *The rumor is*)

12. James reported the chance of a possible strike threat. (*the chance of* or a *possible*)

Chapter 10 *Writing Improvement Worksheet*

**Avoiding Redundancies: Needless Repetition
of Words or Ideas with Similar Meanings**

Make the following sentences shorter and clearer by drawing a line through any needless repetition.

1. I can take the bus and get to a variety of different places.

2. The company is still flourishing today.

3. We found this ancient old office memorandum.

4. This is the same identical piece of information that you got.

5. Frequently, profit anticipations of a business often do not materialize.

6. Friendly Inn policies are formulated by the governors and directors at an annual meeting held each year.

7. Don't be an impediment or hindrance to the campaign.

8. A full and complete report will be presented at that time.

9. Possibly they will perhaps be able to set the March meeting.

10. I believe these experiences have prepared and qualified me for a position as assistant manager.

11. I am appreciative and grateful that you attended our recent conference last week. It was obvious and easy to see that the session you led was very successful, as well as being well received.

12. You have said too much—it was more than was needed.

13. Our hero did not expect that his best friend would perform a dishonest act of betrayal.

14. Scott openly and freely discussed his pending legal action.

15. An unknown stranger contributed $50 to Edgerton's campaign fund.

16. We are sure that without a doubt we can remedy this situation.

17. They seem to be sorry and concerned about the results.

18. Each and every bit of evidence was presented.

19. Your firm and ours can cooperate together and agree.

20. We were pleased and happy to hear from you.

Review and Discussion

Chapter 10 *Memorandums*

Give very concise answers to the following.

1. Should memorandums be filed? Explain. _____
_____
_____

2. For communicating within an organization, what two types of written messages are
the most common? _____
_____

3. *Because memorandums are generally used only within an organization, it is not necessary
to be concerned about their tone.* Explain why this statement is or is not true. _____
_____
_____

4. Name four advantages of using the memorandum form.
_____
_____

5. How are intra-office routing slips used? _____
_____

6. In the 1870 Memorandum to employees, what would you find most objectionable?
_____

7. Speaking of writing memorandums to people at all levels, the text says "Treating others with _____" usually produces desired results.

8. Other than their salaries and fringe benefits, in what three ways are employees a major
expense to an organization? _____
_____

Chapter 10   Memorandums (*Continued*)

9. Of the six points suggested for today's communications from management, which point do you believe is violated most frequently? Give an example. _____

   _____

   _____

   _____

10. Speaking of "The Ultimate Memo," an editor emphasizes the value of white space. What is his reason? _____

    _____

11. Most memorandums fit the ("A" routine information), ("B" negative), ("C" selling) message plan.

12. For a persuasive request memo, the text suggests you follow the ("A" "B" "C") letter plan.

13. The first part of a persuasive request is usually an effective attention-getter if it highlights what? _____

    _____

14. What can be included in the middle section of this memo?

    _____

    _____

15. Give three or four points that could be covered in the last section.

    _____

    _____

    _____

16. A redundancy is (unnecessary repetition of a word or idea) (careless writing or speaking) (repeating yourself) (all of these).

17. Yogi Berra once said, "Here we go again—*déjá vu.*" For better grammar, Yogi might have said, "_____."

18, 19, 20. Eliminate the redundancies in these sentences:

18. Each and every criticism struck at the real problem.

19. Management sadly regrets that work hours must be extended.

20. We are sure without a doubt that regular hours will be resumed next month.

CHAPTER 11
Oral Communications

The ability to communicate orally is helpful in many careers, particularly careers in business. Business students are urged to take college courses that include training in various types of speaking, such as classes in speech, salesmanship, and business behavior. Summary discussions of major types of oral communications important in the business scene will be presented here: telephoning, dictating, leading and participating in meetings and conferences, feeding the grapevine, winning the confrontation, making speeches, and listening.

Telephoning

Telephone techniques are extremely important in any business. A telephone call is frequently the first contact a customer has with a firm, and poor telephone manners—even by the switchboard operator—can obviously lose the caller's good will and change a

customer's mind about dealing with that firm. Each person along the line of the call must recognize that the company is being judged by its employees' telephone manners.

In a booklet entitled, "Every Time You Talk on the Telephone, You Really Are the Company," the General Telephone Company gives the following excellent advice:

Greet the caller pleasantly. Be enthusiastic and yet sincere. Such treatment makes customers like you and more apt to call again.

Use the caller's name. There's no sweeter music to a person than the sound of his or her own name. And speak to the person at the other end of the line, not to the telephone.

Treat every call as an important call—because it is important to the person calling you. When the customer feels that you are giving **individual** rather than **routine** consideration, you'll create more confidence in you and your company.

Be tactful. When it's necessary to refuse a request because of company policy, give a full and sympathetic explanation. Avoid expressions such as "you have to" or "you must." A reply such as, "If you'll come in Monday we'll be happy to check that for you," is better than, "You'll have to come in Monday if you want that checked."

Apologize for errors or delays. Maybe things won't always go right, but you can always be courteous. And if you're really sincere and natural, you won't sound artificially sorry.

Keep your promises. If you make any promises to call back with more information, do everything you can to follow through. A broken promise may mean a lost customer.

Suggest an appropriate time for callback. When you leave a message for someone to return a call and you expect to be out of your office for a while, it is courteous to suggest a time for calling back; for example, say, "Please tell him I'll be in after lunch."

Treat your co-workers like customers. Handle inside calls with as much care as calls from the outside. Remember, you're building your personal telephone reputation too.

Take time to be helpful. Brighten up your day by pleasant telephone contacts. It really doesn't take much more time to be helpful. It's better to spend minutes to keep a customer happy than months to regain good will.

Use basic phrases of courtesy. Say, "Please," "Thank you," and "You're welcome." The use of such phrases is one way to put a smile in your voice. **THERE'S ALWAYS TIME FOR COURTESY....**

As pointed out in Chapter 1 on the theory of communications, face to face dialogue is in many ways more effective than other means of communicating. The other person is there—you can observe reactions, and there is immediate feedback from both sides. In the normal course of events, you will discontinue the conversation by mutual agreement. In telephoning, we must try to overcome some of the handicaps of not seeing each other in person.

The Name of the Game is Names

Most telephone calls, of course, are made between people who know each other's identity. But too often, telephone calls giving or asking information are made without identifying the caller or the person answering the call. Business telephone calls, whether they are for personal business or otherwise, are most effective when both speakers know the **name** of the party on the other end of the line. Get the name of the other person even though you may only be seeking or giving routine information and it doesn't seem necessary to identify yourself or the person at the other end of the line. After all, a telephone call can become disconnected. Or you may need to get additional information later. It can be next to impossible to get reconnected with the right person in any way but by having the correct name. Also, calls can be transferred to many different departments, sometimes incorrectly. Having the name of the person to whom you were speaking makes reconnection easy.

Memorandum Forms for Telephone Calls

All offices should have **telephone call memorandum forms** similar to that in Figure 11.1, which contains blanks for typical information that should be written down for missed telephone calls: name of person calling firm, name of person called, date of call, time of call, and message. Obviously, all the information is important, even the notation concerning the time of the message. The two parties involved may have contacted each other in person, and it might be important for the one getting the message to know if the call came in before or after the other contact. Telephone memorandum forms can be purchased in bulk from a stationer or office supplies dealer, or they can be run off on the office copying equipment.

FIGURE 11.1
Example of telephone memorandum form.

To _____

Date _____ Time _____

WHILE YOU WERE OUT

M _____

of _____

Phone _____

TELEPHONED	PLEASE CALL
CALLED TO SEE YOU	WILL CALL AGAIN
WANTS TO SEE YOU	RETURNED YOUR CALL

Message _____

_____

_____

_____

_____
Operator

Telephone Logs

Different offices maintain different types of telephone call records. Most keep date and time information on long distance and toll calls so that a central office can check the accuracy of telephone charges being made to the company. Many firms and individuals keep **telephone logs** of all calls made and received, information that can be helpful in future plans and in correspondence. Logs also corroborate other records of telephone charges and can be of legal assistance in checking telephone company charges.

Dictation

Thanks to the efficiency of electronic typing equipment, many supervisors, managers, or other executives today can compose much of their own work rapidly and efficiently. However, for those who compose slowly at a typewriter or word processor, if possible, **dictation** should be done into a tape recorder or dictation machine, with transcription being done on a word processor or a computer.

If you are new at dictation, you will probably not have perfect results at first—no one expects it of you. Practice—even dry run practice—helps. It is amazing how dictation improves with such practice. You will dictate well if you follow these guidelines.

Before Dictation

1. Choose a quiet place for dictation, free from distraction.

2. Prepare for dictation by having necessary materials and enclosures at hand.

3. Have a list of points to be covered; these may be notations on letters that you are answering.

4. Develop rapport with your secretary and/or efficiency in the use of dictation equipment. A good secretary should be treasured and treated with respect. In return, your secretary will respect you and will be one of your greatest assets on the job. In dictating to a machine, get adequate instructions and take the small amount of time needed to make yourself a pro in handling this equipment.

During Dictation

1. Keep background noise down.

2. Dictate at a moderate speed; it is better to be slow, clear, and sure than to be too speedy.

3. Take care not to clip your voice when using the on/off switch.

4. Begin each tape by saying what type of document you are about to dictate. This helps a word processing secretary select the right disk for the machine.

5. Explain any special paper or format needed.

6. If you make a mistake, erase it and record over it. Don't tell the transcriber to "change that to . . . ."

7. Do not speed up when reading printed matter, If possible, furnish copy of printed matter to transcriber and save dictation time.

8. Turn unit off when you pause for a long time.

9. At end of document, say, "End of memo" or something similar.

10. Unless you want dictation stored in the machine memory, have secretary erase after use, or someone else could retranscribe your old information.

Even the best secretary appreciates having you spell out not only names and addresses but also any other terms or words that might be misunderstood. Use the phonetic alphabet of telephone operators, shown in Figure 11.2, for letters that may be misunderstood. If there is a question in your mind about anything you have said, do not hesitate to ask the secretary to read it back. Or learn the simple machine operation procedures that enable you to go back and listen to your dictation, erasing and redictating to make any desired improvements.

After Dictation

Read before you sign. Nobody is perfect—not you, your secretary, nor a typist. Proofread everything you have dictated before you sign it. You and your firm are legally responsible for anything you sign. If there are any necessary corrections that cannot be made neatly, a fresh copy should be made.

Participation in Meetings and Conferences

Our discussion of participation in meetings and conferences can be set up under two headings: suggestions for the conference leader, and suggestions for other conference members.

The Conference Leader

To accomplish the purposes of the meeting and to hold the respect of members attending, the leader has several responsibilities in carrying out plans of the meeting. Some duties may be delegated, but they are ultimately the responsibility of the leader.

- The conference leader should set the time and place of the meeting and supply these details to those who are to attend in sufficient time for them to make plans to be there.
- The leader should prepare a meeting agenda—that is, a list of matters to be discussed and work to be done at the meeting. Copies of the agenda should be distributed to potential conference members either prior to the meeting or when they arrive, according

FIGURE 11.2
Phonetic alphabet used by telephone operators.

A	Alice	J	James	S	Samuel
B	Bertha	K	Kate	T	Thomas
C	Charles	L	Lewis	U	Utah
D	David	M	Mary	V	Victor
E	Edward	N	Nellie	W	William
F	Frank	O	Oliver	X	X-ray
G	George	P	Peter	Y	Young
H	Henry	Q	Quaker	Z	Zebra
I	Ida	R	Robert		

to the topics being covered. This gives members time to study it enough to plan their own participation. It is very effective to give members a tentative agenda in advance, asking for suggestions to be included in the final copy that will be used as a blueprint for the meeting.

• A conference should be called for a specific purpose or specific purposes, not because "it's about time we got together." If there is no purpose for calling a regularly scheduled conference, it should be canceled.

Maintaining Order

Maintaining order at the meeting is the responsibility of the leader. Parliamentary procedures are recommended for most meetings, since they not only give fair rulings on procedure but tend to smooth out disagreements among members.

In a small meeting, the leader is usually in charge of procedure. If unsure in this regard, the leader should assign this task in advance to another member who will study parliamentary procedure so that rulings can be respected and followed. In larger conferences, it is helpful to have a regular parliamentarian appointed who is (or will become) well grounded in procedural format. However, at all times the leader is in charge of the meeting and uses the parliamentarian only for reference.

Marguerite Grumme, parliamentarian, states:

The four basic principles of parliamentary law:

1. Courtesy and justice to all.
2. Consider one thing at a time.
3. The minority must be heard.
4. The majority must prevail.

Note: Parliamentary law is common sense used in a gracious manner.[1]

If parliamentary procedure is not followed strictly, the preceding four principles can serve as an excellent framework for group discussions and decisions. If parliamentary procedure is followed, it should be for the entire meeting and not merely at the whim of the conference leader.

Conducting the Meeting

As leader, you will gain confidence if you follow these guidelines:

• You are in charge of the discussion at all times, but you must show concern for others in attendance. Relinquish the floor properly to others. Avoid letting a few individuals monopolize discussions, and try to draw out comments from the more retiring persons.

• If you do not wish to take notes or minutes yourself, assign this duty to a responsible person. Notes should be taken; memory should not be trusted for details.

• Watch the time lapse, keeping your eye on the agenda.

• If a follow-up meeting is to be held with the same group, set an approximate or specific time and place for it after consulting with members present.

[1]Marguerite Grumme, *Basic Principles of Parliamentary Law and Protocol,* 3rd ed. (published privately at St. Louis, Missouri), p. 3.

- When matters have been taken care of, conclude the meeting. Ample time should be scheduled for all meetings, but avoid the hazards of Parkinson's Law. This law states, "Work expands so as to fill the time available for its completion." If the full time set aside has not expired when business of the meeting is completed, conclude the conference, giving members welcome free time.

Handling Guest Speakers

Guest speakers usually do not appreciate sitting through proceedings in which they are not directly involved. Try to plan the agenda to avoid having these guests listen to the long (usually boring) reading of minutes, treasurer's report, business matters, and so forth. Such planning might help give the speaker a better attitude about addressing your group. Further, word gets around the speakers' circuit, and you may find it possible to attract speakers who would otherwise not be interested.

The Conference Members

Conference members are responsible for bringing to the meeting any information in their possession that will aid the purposes for which the meeting is called. Each is also responsible for listening to others and for asking pertinent questions at the proper time.

All conference members owe respect to others in attendance, even though they may not agree with what another is saying. Improper conduct at meetings or conferences reflects negatively on job performance and may even hurt possibilities for promotion.

The Office Grapevine

Grapevines exist wherever people gather, and one of the ripest seems to be the **office grapevine,** office gossip. The term "grapevine" originated during the American Civil War and at first meant a false report circulated as a hoax. It was then called the "grape-vine telegraph." Today on the job management accepts its existence. Sometimes the most judicious supervisors and managers learn to use the grapevine to their own advantage by circulating rumors, trying to test how workers would react if rumor became fact.

However, 75 percent of the stories circulated on the grapevine are accurate, according to a study performed over several years. It concluded that wise managers learn to cultivate the office and factory grapevine, using it to their advantage because they cannot abolish it. The study states that the grapevine is as hard to kill as the mythical glass snake which, when struck, broke into a thousand pieces and grew a new snake from each piece.

Over the years, many officials have learned that the best antidote for negative effects of false rumors is to keep people informed. Having workers feel they are part of the organization helps them get more out of their work. In this way they feel respected, do a better job and are more productive.

Winning the Confrontation

In business and personal lives, **confrontations** can occur. Patience and preparation can help you win. Avoid arguments, but if you find yourself suddenly in a confrontation, follow these steps:

1. When a confrontation starts, take a deep breath. This will help you relax and gather your thoughts.

2. Identify what you want to accomplish and concentrate on that objective.

3. Speak clearly, concisely, using easily understood terms.

4. Maintain eye contact, showing you honestly believe in what you are saying and cannot be intimidated.

5. Hold your temper—don't snap or yell at the other person.

6. If the opponent's position is weak, ask him/her to repeat that position. This might show how weak that position is, and you are gaining time to plan your strategy.

7. Pause. You can think of positive comments and counter the negatives.

8. Continue to concentrate on your objective.

Keep in mind that your performance will probably be described to others and remembered. Senator Barry Goldwater once said, "The important thing is to learn, become more gracious, and die as a gentleman."

Talks and Speeches

Speaking before a group, like many other communication processes, can best be improved with practice. As already mentioned, business students are encouraged to take courses in speech. It is also helpful to study **speeches** by others, noting their favorable and unfavorable aspects.

Planning the Speech

Having something worthwhile to say is the best possible asset for any public speaker.

Like a good letter or report, a good speech takes planning. Actually, a speech might be considered the oral presentation of a written report; it can certainly be prepared largely in the same manner. First, make a good outline. Set up a central idea and then give introduction, details, and summary in an organized manner. (The topic of preparing reports is covered in Chapters 15 and 16.)

Notes can be helpful if you do not keep your eyes glued to them. Any notes or cards should be moved noiselessly and unobtrusively. Otherwise, listeners may feel the notes are more important than the audience or your message. Some speakers use a special large type for their notes.

Putting your notes on 3 by 5 or 4 by 6 cards that have been arranged in numerical order is a good system. By jotting down just one phrase on a card, you will not glance at your notes and be confused as to which phrases you have already covered. Whether you use note cards or sheets of paper, you should never read your presentation word for word. Reading can bore your audience and make your presentation difficult to follow. Using brief note cards as reminders allows you to speak naturally and focus more of your attention on the audience.

Using a Microphone

If you are using a microphone, be sure that it is operating properly so that the entire audience is able to hear. It is always perfectly correct—actually, imperative if there is a doubt—to ask if everyone can hear you. If the answer is negative, show respect for the comfort and concern of your audience and get all the help you can in trying to rectify the problem.

A well known man had traveled from Washington, D.C., to a Rocky Mountain state solely for the purpose of making an outdoor speech. But he was forced to cut his speech short when high winds made it impossible for the large audience to hear him, even with the public address system. People in the back had begun to talk, disturbing others. Later he said, "I didn't blame them."

You can build self-confidence before speaking over a microphone if you arrange a practice. Even a few short minutes can be very helpful while you learn to adjust the microphone to your height and to determine the proper distance, usually a handspan, between your mouth and the microphone.

Some large auditoriums are equipped with electronic sound systems with microphones that can be attached to a lapel, collar or neckline of the speaker's apparel. Women should plan to wear an outfit with a small pocket convenient for holding the power pack that activates the mike. This is generally not a problem for men.

Bringing Life to a Speech

You can usually **bring life to a speech** by telling a story, joke or by giving an appropriate quotation. Also, almost any speaker will help the audience remember what is said by using visual aids. Listeners can follow your speech more easily if you give them an outline. Further, slides, films, video tapes, flip charts, transparencies, or a blackboard are essential to some presentations and are helpful to most others. Improvements are constantly being made in visual aids. Each season much equipment becomes simpler to operate, as well as more compact and lighter to carry.

Handouts are usually welcomed by audiences, whether they are summaries of the talk, information on the background of the speaker, additional sources of information on the topic, or appropriate gadgets.

Stand Up! Speak Up! Shut Up!

Stand Up!

As speaker, you should stand up comfortably, firm on your feet, showing confidence in your appearance. Of course, you should be dressed appropriately for the occasion. When in doubt about proper dress, inquire for suggestions from the program chairman or some other person in authority. In various organizations, at various times of day or night, and in various parts of a town, a country, or the world, different dress might be recommended for what essentially seems to be the same type of occasion.

Speak Up!

Speak up so that people can hear you and get your message. This is done through many conscious efforts, such as speaking clearly, speaking loudly enough for those assembled to hear, maintaining eye contact with your audience, and avoiding a monotone and any annoying mannerisms.

Speak clearly. To get your message across and to be courteous to your audience, you should speak clearly by enunciating carefully and speaking slowly enough to be understood. If you mumble or mutter, or if you talk too fast, you may lose the attention of the audience.

Speak loud enough so that everyone present can hear you. It is usually possible to train yourself to project your voice so that even a relatively large audience can hear and understand you, with or without the use of amplifiers.

Speak directly to the audience by maintaining eye contact. Let your eyes wander around the group, stopping momentarily on different individuals, bringing people into the picture and giving them a feeling of audience participation.

Do not speak in a monotone. A change in the pitch of your voice will prevent your putting the audience to sleep by an incessant drone or singsong, and it will also relax you and your vocal cords.

Avoid annoying mannerisms of action or speech. Listeners may find themselves watching or listening for action or speech mannerisms that are unusual. Avoid these.
William J. McCullough, a recognized authority on public speaking, gives these points:

Avoid mispronunciations or glaring errors in grammar.

Avoid profane or vulgar expressions; the laugh isn't worth it.

Avoid holding the lectern or desk for long periods of time.

Avoid playing with things.

Avoid pacing back and forth.

Avoid memorizing a speech....The bulk of your speech should be extemporaneous.

Avoid reading your speech.

Avoid alcohol. "If you drink, don't attempt to make a speech...."[2]

Give your audience a chance for input. If the situation permits, give your audience a chance for input. People are there because of a special interest or involvement in your speech topic. Their questions and comments may improve your presentation. Do not let this practice get out of hand, however. Keeping to time restrictions is your responsibility.

---

[2]William J. McCullough, *Hold Your Audience* (Englewood Cliffs, N.J.: Prentice-Hall, 1978), pp. 167ff.

Shut Up!

The effectiveness of a message can be lost and public relations damaged when a speaker drags on, reducing the audience to fidgeting boredom. One of the most helpful suggestions for making a good speech that will be well received is this: Say what you have to say and SHUT UP!

President Franklin D. Roosevelt said it this way, "Be sincere; be brief; be seated."

Listening

It takes two to speak the truth—one to speak and another to listen.

Henry David Thoreau

Common sense tells us that on most jobs a high percentage of time is spent **listening**. Surveys show that most of those at executive levels spend at least one-fourth of their time listening.

Business communication classes traditionally concentrate on writing, because of the acknowledged need for improved writing. However, much communication in business is spoken, as we all recognize. As oral communication is studied thoroughly, it becomes apparent that poor listening is a major culprit in the lack of understanding between speaker and audience—sender and receiver—whether the audience be one or many.

TV Interviewing as a Model for Listening

We may gain some insight into how to improve our listening skills if we take a look at one of our more or less refined forms of listening, the **television interview.**

Bill Moyers, respected for his effectiveness as an interviewer on national TV, recently said that two things make you a good interviewer—in other words, a good listener:

1. Pay attention.
2. Anticipate.

Moyers says he interviews according to a plan expressed by champion hockey player, Wayne Gretzky, who said, "I skate to where the puck is going to be, not to where it's been."

Just so in listening on the job: Anticipating does force us to pay attention, and we can try to see if the speaker says what we expect or want to hear. If we have anticipated correctly, we are gratified. If we do not hear what we expected, we have to be alert to hear other ideas, possibly leading to a good question-and-answer session.

Listening for Major Points

A main reason for poor listening is failure to identify major points. (This is why giving audience members an outline or list of major topics helps hold an audience and helps them remember.) Listening for major points helps you identify facts that support a point. Our minds can move much faster than anyone can speak, and your mind can wander far away from what you are hearing. Concentrating on major points pulls your mind back to what is being said.

As you listen for major points, you can begin to identify the major plan. When listening to a speech, you usually hear the speaker first make an introduction to what will be presented, then give the body of the presentation, then fill it out with a summary. Anticipating the progress of even a long presentation can help you tune in on what is coming.

Taking Notes

Should you take notes? In one-to-one interviews or in small or large conferences, diligent note-takers can lose the train of thought of a speaker. Good notes are taken when you listen a lot and write little. Then, the sooner you review your notes in private, the easier it is for you to fill in useful information.

"Hearing" Between-the-Lines Messages

In his writing and speaking, Norman B. Sigband of the University of Southern California emphasizes the advantages if you "listen to what you can't hear." His expression means watching for body language, listening for voice intonations, and so forth, to get those between-the-lines messages that can be extremely meaningful.

Asking Questions

Don't be afraid to ask questions. In a two-person interview or explanation, or in a large conference, if you feel the need for clarification and have the opportunity, ask questions. Good listeners ask good questions, and any speaker will be glad to clarify points. Even in a large group, you might say something like, "Could I get something cleared up? I lost the train of thought when you got into . . ." You will usually hear a muffled wave of agreement from others in the audience who similarly got lost.

As people realize that everything spoken is not immediately understood, we will probably have more open discussions with people asking to have points clarified. This will lead to better understanding by everyone.

Getting around Barriers to Good Listening

Recognize that there are many possible **barriers to good listening**. For example, your attention span suffers if you let personal prejudices against a speaker stop you from concentrating on what is being said. Also, good mental discipline forces you to concentrate on your work when you have personal or job problems. When listening, try to ignore personal problems and prejudices, other conversations, airplanes overhead, slamming doors, and so forth. Are you, the listener-receiver, getting the message of the speaker-sender?

Interrupting

The claim is made that we listen at only a 50 percent efficiency rate. Another chief block to understanding is **interrupting**. Some people are more guilty than others of interrupting—a rude habit. If you are a guilty one, do everything in your power *not* to interrupt, no matter what.

Often we don't understand because we bring up another topic right in the middle of what someone else is saying. Or we have the audacity to complete a statement that another person is making, giving the impression that we think we can say it better than the speaker. People who are bothered by constant interruptions often fail to get their messages across, to the detriment of both speaker and potential listener.

Summarizing

As previously suggested, concentrate on what you are hearing by trying to anticipate what is going to be said. Listen for major points and between-the-line messages. Take brief notes if they will be helpful. Ask questions. Consciously block out anything that interferes with your understanding of what is being said. This happens too often: "I know that you heard what I said, but I don't believe you understand what I meant."

Oral Communication Assignments

1. Outline information to be included in a form letter of your own making, and dictate the letter onto a machine.

2. Select a topic from those suggested for reports at the end of Chapter 16 and prepare a short speech to be presented to the class.

3. You are chairman of the next meeting of the class. Prepare an agenda of matters you would like covered in the class.

4. From the local telephone company, get any printed material it has for public distribution that will be helpful in learning to conduct telephone calls properly.

5. Take notes of one class meeting, either in business communications or in another class. Outline the notes as minutes of the class meeting.

6. Watch a news commentator on television for at least a 30-minute program, and give an oral report to the class about his or her most effective and least effective speaking mannerisms.

7. Prepare an agenda for the next meeting of any organization to which you belong.

8. If you are preparing a written report for this or any other class, make an oral report to this class summarizing that report.

9. If you are to make an oral presentation on the job, practice by first giving it to the class, getting suggestions for improvements. (Of course, information cannot be confidential.)

10. Get a copy of a public corporation's annual report. (Most libraries will have some of these reports.) Give a five-minute speech on the activities of the firm, possibly emphasizing its products and financial standing. Use at least one visual aid for your presentation.

Chapter 11 *Writing Improvement Exercise*

Agreement of Pronoun with the Word It Stands for; Sexism in Pronoun Usage

Each leader will be responsible for the people in (*her*, their) section.

The invoice, together with the copies, should be returned to (*its*, their) sender.

Each employee selected (his, her, their, *a*) preferred vacation.

Businesspeople find that a common error in grammar is incorrect use of singular or plural pronouns. Also, an objection has recently developed to the use of a masculine pronoun (he | him | his) when the person the pronoun stands for could be either male or female.

A pronoun should agree in number with the word it stands for—its antecedent. If the antecedent is singular, the pronoun should be singular. If the antecedent is plural, the pronoun should be plural. And we should reword our writing so that a masculine pronoun does not stand for both male and female.

1. Pronoun agreement with antecedent: general

   a. Mr. Crawford and Mr. Dowling offered (his, their) assistance in tabulating the votes.

   b. A new workman must do (his, their) best to learn the job quickly.

   c. Neither woman wished to boast about (her, their) individual success.

   d. I thought I lost my office key; (it was, they were) hanging on my desk drawer.

   e. We take pride in (ourselves, ourself).

   f. Each woman set (their, her) own pace in the fashion world.

2. Sexism in pronoun usage. Traditionally, the masculine pronouns *he/him/his/himself* have been used as both masculine and feminine. However, with the increasing number of women in the workplace, we are requested to avoid such usage because it implies that women are being left out.
   Here are three simple ways that will help avoid sexism in most pronoun usages:
   a. Change the antecedent and singular pronoun *he/him/his/himself* to plural *they/them/ their/theirs/themselves*
   b. Change the wording to avoid using the masculine pronoun.
   c. Change *he/him/his/himself* to *you, one,* or (infrequently because these usages are wordy) *he or she/him or her/ his or her/his or hers/himself or herself.*

   Here are examples of such usages:

   Each student should bring <u>his</u> own blue book. →
   Students should bring <u>their</u> own notebooks. (Singular → plural.)
   Each student should bring <u>a</u> blue book. (Pronoun removed).

   Every supervisor was given <u>his</u> assignments. →
   All supervisors were given <u>their</u> assignments. (Singular → plural.)
   Every supervisor was given an assignment. (Pronoun removed.)

   Each tour member is responsible for <u>himself</u>. →
   All tour members are responsible for <u>themselves</u>. (Singular → plural.)
   Everyone is responsible for <u>himself or herself</u>. (Reworded).

   The chief engineer must initiate a new project <u>himself</u>. →
   Chief engineers must initiate new projects <u>themselves</u>. (Singular → plural).
   Only the chief engineer may initiate <u>a</u> new project. (Prnoun removed).

Each manager will report progress of <u>his</u> current projects. →

Managers will report progress of <u>their</u> current projects. (Singular → plural).

Managers will report progress of current projects (Pronoun removed.)

If a student wants an appointment, <u>he</u> may see me after class. →

If you want an appointment, see me after class. (Reworded.)

Anyone who wants an appointment may see me after class. (Reworded.)

Chapter 11 *Writing Improvement Worksheet*

Agreement of Pronoun with the Word It Stands for; Sexism in Pronoun Usage

1. Draw a line through the incorrect terms. You might draw an arrow from the antecedent to the pronoun.
   a. Everybody on the team earned (their, his) medal.
   b. Someone should give (his, their, her, a) seat to the elderly gentleman.
   c. Several wanted (his, her, his or her, their) instructions in writing.
   d. We promised (ourself, ourselves) that we would do superior work.
   e. All of you on this crew can be proud of (yourself, yourselfs, yourselves).
   f. Each student has turned in (her, his, the) assignment.
   g. Many players made (their selections, a selection, his or her selection) from the equipment on stage.
   h. Everyone on the staff should indicate (their, his, her, his or her) preferred vacation dates.
   i. Which designer selected this material as (her, their) preference?
   j. Terry and Koji cannot find (their driver's license, her driver's license, their driver's licenses).

2. Rewrite each of the following sentences and change the italicized pronoun by one of the following methods:
   a. Change the antecedent and the italicized pronoun to plural.
   b. Change the wording so that the pronoun may be omitted.
   c. Change the italicized pronoun to *you, one,* or *her or she, him or her.*
      (1) Each photographer received *his* assignment.

      _____

      (2) Any tour leader can collect tickets from the people in *her* group.

      _____

      (3) Every member of the conservation corps was rewarded for *his* efforts.

      _____

      (4) Each of you can place *his* own book back on the shelf.

      _____

      (5) Any official can call a special meeting *himself.*

      _____

Name _____

Date _____ Class Section _____

REVIEW AND DISCUSSION

Chapter 11 *Oral Communication*

1. Why are business students urged to take courses in various types of speaking?

   _____

   _____

2. Name five types of oral communication that are important to the business person.

   _____

   _____

3. The General Telephone Company gives the reason for learning to handle telephone calls in business correctly in the title of its booklet, "Every Time You Talk on the Telephone, You _____."

4. The text suggests that on business telephone calls, you should usually try to get the name of the person to whom you are talking. Why?

   _____

   _____

   _____

5. Give five specific items of information that should be included on any telephone memorandum form.

   _____

   _____

   _____

6. How can a person learn to improve business dictation?

   _____

7. What are the five steps that the text gives for good dictation?

   _____

   _____

   _____

   _____

Chapter 11   Oral Communication (*Continued*)

8. Why is the conference leader responsible for carrying out the plans of the meeting?

   _____

   _____

9. How is a meeting agenda used?

   _____

   _____

10. If there is no specific purpose for a conference, should it be held?

    _____

11. Who has responsibility for maintaining order at a meeting?

    _____

12. Marguerite Grumme, parliamentarian, gives four basic principles of parliametary law. What are they? _____

    _____

    _____

    _____

13. Who has responsibility for seeing that notes of a meeting are taken?

    _____

14. What are the two major responsibilities of conference members?

    _____

    _____

    _____

15. Is it possible to kill the office grapevine? _____

16. What is a good antidote to the negative effect of office rumors?

    _____

17. What should you concentrate on in any confrontation? _____

    _____

18. How can you learn to improve your manner of speaking before a group?

    _____

19. Planning a good speech is like planning a good _____.

20. Is it permissible to use notes when making speeches? _____

21. List four ways of enlivening a speech.

    _____

    _____

    _____

    _____

22. The text furnishes three basics of giving a good speech. What are they?

_____

_____

_____

23. What does "eye contact" mean? _____

_____

24. Why should you avoid annoying mannerisms in your speaking?

_____

25. Name at least six steps the book gives to help you listen effectively.

_____

_____

26. If the antecedent of a pronoun is singular, the pronouns should be _____ .

27, 28, 29, 30. Reword these sentences to eliminate sexism.

27. Here is help if a person is learning English as (his, her, a, their) second language.

28. The supervisor must approve the work schedule himself.

29. If anyone wants to volunteer for this hazardous assignment, he can talk to me himself.

30. If a student wants to discuss their grade, he can see me after class.

CHAPTER 12
Employment Guides:
Finding a Job; Holding a Job; Earning a Promotion; Changing Jobs

---

Work spares us from three great evils: boredom, vice, and need.

Voltaire,
eighteenth-century French writer and philosopher

If we study the nonworking minority of people, we learn that they usually lead lives of emptiness and frustration. There are many nonworkers at both ends of the economic scale—those of the unemployed poor "gray ghetto," and those of the unemployed wealthy "golden ghetto." Such people often lead lives that few can envy. Psychiatrists classify both groups as being emotional zombies, uninterested in work, self-centered, often depressed, bored, shallow, and short on ideals, values, or goals.

Most of us see our college education as eventually leading to employment. To help you take your place among the working majority, this chapter discusses how to apply for a job, how to be a satisfactory employee, and how to earn promotion. Also, we will discuss when and how to change jobs. These steps involve all types of communication principles—visual, oral, and written.

Finding Yourself

The decision of what career to follow should be each person's own choice. However, this decision should not be made arbitrarily, without considering important influencing factors. You should judge your own desires, capabilities, and limitations. Then, to avoid lifelong frustration, you should try to fit your own background and desires into the current employment scene.

Plato, the ancient Greek philosopher, said, "No two persons are born exactly alike, but each differs from each in natural endowments, one being suited for one occupation and another for another." Following a lifetime career that is personally unrewarding can lead to unhappiness and disappointment. You should try to identify your own preferences in such general matters as the following:

Working conditions. Do you like working with other people? Do you like meeting the public? Do you prefer working alone?

Work location. Do you want the advantages and disadvantages of working in or near a large metropolitan area? Do you prefer the advantages and disadvantages of working in a small town or rural area?

Work hours. Will you accept long hours that might result from being promoted to additional responsibilities? Or would you prefer more free time that might come from refusal to accept promotion? Can you accept the discipline of working hours prescribed by others, as most work demands? Or do you insist on setting your own schedule?

When you evaluate these general questions relating to working conditions and personal preferences, you are better able to judge yourself and your own qualifications for a particular type of work.

Education and Training

We are all aware that certain occupations require particular backgrounds of education or training. Such fields as the professions—engineering, law, medicine, education—demand specific college degrees. If any of these is your choice, your plans are under way to fulfilling your goal. Few shortcuts can be taken.

Many business, industrial, and technical positions also require specific education or training—accounting, data processing, medical technology, secretarial, and real estate, to name a few. Statistics still show that, on the average, the college-trained person will earn two or three times as much money in a lifetime as the non-college-trained. Many of today's larger firms conduct their own formalized management training programs, preferring to hire people with a college background whom they can train in the specifics of the particular company.

Experience

If you hope to get good full-time employment at the completion of your education, seek some part-time employment in the interim, even if you have no financial need. Although the employment may not be related to the hoped-for career, a good recommendation from any former employer is worth having, because it shows your ability in a working situation.

A person looking for work may be confronted with the problem of being unable to list any work experience on a job application form. Applicants often ask, "How can I get experience without experience?" It really is possible to get a job without having worked previously. Even if you have not yet worked for pay, it is valuable to be able to show a potential employer some past record of working successfully with others. If the job market is tight, consider volunteer work, because it, too, can result in favorable employment references. And successful involvement in worthwhile community or campus activities will give the future employer a positive picture of you as an individual. (The Writing Improvement Exercise at the end of Chapter 7 gives the successful experiences of three people, both young and older, who initially believed they had limited backgrounds for applying for work. They successfully turned their negatives into positives.)

Personality

Personality is a major factor influencing success in any employment. Therefore, before you seek employment, study yourself to see if you are the type of person an employer would want to hire. Look for such personal traits as these:

Being neat, clean, well-groomed, dependable, punctual, and resourceful

Having confidence, drive, a positive attitude, an even disposition, good command of the English language, and ability to work under pressure

Some personality traits are more important in certain job situations than in others. But on any job where you come in contact with people, your personality strongly influences your success regardless of how well you perform your work. You must look at yourself as having both positive and negative character traits. You must realize that the greater the positive nature of your personality, the greater the possibility of your being hired for a position, being retained in it, and being promoted to a better position. You may see yourself as lacking personality traits that should help make you a satisfactory employee in the career you would like to follow. If this is the case, you would undoubtedly benefit from determined efforts at self-improvement.

Opinions of Others

In studying yourself and your career plans, you should seek the opinions of others, such as employment counselors, teachers, religious leaders, community members, and interested friends and relatives. These people may or may not have as much education as you do; they may or may not have the intelligence you do; but they will have the wisdom of years of experience, both in their own lives and in observing the lives of others.

Finding a Career

There is some advantage in choosing to follow the **"family business,"** or any other type of career with which you have had first-hand contact. Over a period of time you may have picked up knowledge and skills that give you some proficiency not possessed by those who have not lived in or around that particular atmosphere. You may have what amounts to an internship or apprenticeship in a profession, business, or trade that would make it easy for you to gain true competence in that field.

Ultimately, however, weighing all factors objectively, you should choose the type of work that will be satisfying to you. It may not be the same work as that of your father or mother, your favorite aunt or uncle, or anyone else with whom you are acquainted. Spending years at an occupation that conflicts with your true interests or abilities can bring about a physical, mental, or emotional breakdown in your later life. It is hazardous to be locked into work that is too challenging. But it may be even more hazardous to try to spend your life in a career that is neither sufficiently challenging nor rewarding for you.

Employment Counseling

Some people can make these career judgments completely on their own. But many benefit from employment counseling experts. You can contact any college nearby (you often need not be a student or former student). Someone there can counsel you or refer you to a job counselor. Also, in some locations, state job services give free aptitude tests. Aptitude tests might reveal you have a good potential for a field you have never considered. Or the tests and counseling might lead you to stay in the field where you have been.

Counseling services have information on employment possibilities in given fields and also in given geographical areas. Federal government studies are available. The most thorough of these is the U.S. Department of Labor's *Occupational Outlook Handbook,* available in the reference section of your library. This handbook gives up-to-date descriptions of hundreds of occupations, with details of type of work performed, training and education needed, salary to be expected, and employment outlook (*excellent, good, may have to hunt some,* or *poor*).

Some college and private employment advising services now have this type of information available on computers to make specific information readily available to you in a printout.

Personal Recruitment

Some firms specialize in finding employees for other companies, and the people who do the actual looking for employees are called **"headhunters."** Companies that do head-hunting by computer are becoming common. With this system, a computer matchmaker firm sends out client companies' job openings to college and private job placement centers, where the matches are made. Results are praised for speed and efficiency by both the companies and career counselors. Announcements are posted on bulletin boards and in binders that you can study for job openings.

A major New York life insurance firm recently reported they got their top new agent—rookie of the year—through such a computer service. Also, a "nanny" institute in Beverly Hills where they train nannies for child care, reported excellent results, especially in finding office and clerical help.

A Movie Star's Career Choice

Jack Lemmon, the movie star, tells a story of how his father helped him get started in acting. At an early point in his career, Lemmon asked his father for a $300 loan. His father was vice-president of a large company that made doughnut machines and all sorts of baked goods; he had started at the bottom and worked up.

Lemmon's father said, "OK, you don't want to start in my business. You want to act."

"I said, 'Yes.'

"'Do you need to do that?'

"I answered, 'Yes, I really need to find out if I can get anywhere in acting.'

"'You love it?'

"I said, 'Yes, I love it.' I had already done summer stock and some other stuff.

"He handed me the $300 and said, 'The day I don't find romance in a loaf of bread, I'm going to quit.'

"It was a marvelous, marvelous line. What he was saying was that whatever the _____ you do is not as important as loving it."

Selecting a career is a matter of checks and balances, of weighing one factor against another. You yourself must live with the eventual decision. This decision not only guides you toward open fields of interest; it also tends to determine your lifetime income and often your position in your community.

Equip yourself for the type of career that is right for you. Then, following that career should lead to a life of fulfilling satisfaction that is worth years of study in school and postponement of other aims.

The Job Market

Unless you are a person of unlimited wealth—and can be sure you will stay that way—you will be wise to study the job market before making a career decision. Being honest, we know that some fields today are overcrowded; others are undersupplied. If you ignore the information you get and still stay in an employment field that has stiff competition for the few job openings there are, don't cry. You must have known what you were getting into.

Job prospects for the 90s are good for accountants, engineers, nurses, communications and computer people, scientists, mathematicians, teachers, paralegals. Also, specific industries that have good prospects are recycling and waste disposal firms, financial services, long-term care for elderly, high tech machinery, health care, child care, prepared meals, cleaning services. (People are becoming more willing and able to pay for services.)

Study the demand in a particular field and the potential supply of applicants, study yourself, and make a choice. Career counseling services and the *Occupational Outlook Handbook* mentioned earlier can help you.

Importance of Money

Selecting a career can involve many choices regarding both the field and one's own particular role or roles in that field. Although it must be acknowledged that money buys the necessities and luxuries of life, the amount of **money** you will be able to make over your lifetime in each possible line of employment should not be the overriding reason for making a choice. Much more is at stake here than the money you will earn; for instance, the manner in which you will use your talents, the way you will spend many waking hours, and even many of your dreams at night.

Neither should entry level income be the deciding factor of job choice. Some firms may offer higher-than-average entry level income with scarce opportunity for advancement beyond the entry position. On the other hand, one national electrical supply firm insists that all new employees start in warehouse positions at low pay, to learn the business "from the ground up." Some employees stay at this level only a few weeks or months before progressing into other positions in the firm, in such fields as accounting, data processing, selling, public relations, and administration. Eventually, many reach high-level executive positions.

Finding a Job

Surveys of job seekers and job finders show that the more serious study a person puts into the important task of finding a job, the more satisfying is the result. Spend plenty of time in preparation. Study yourself, the type of work you want, and why you want it. Basically, understand that you must try to present yourself more favorably than your competition.

Keep Your Eyes Open

Self Analysis

First of all, take time to write down carefully a personal inventory of your own pluses and minuses. Here are 12 points to cover:

1. Long- and short-range goals—responsibilities, money, security, fame.
2. Strengths: What have you enjoyed doing in the past?
3. Weaknesses: What have you *not* enjoyed doing in the past?
4. Finances—needs and desires.
5. Interests.
6. Appearance: Can you improve it for acceptance on the job market?
7. Health: Do you need to improve it?
8. Education and training: List academic and vocational courses that you have particularly enjoyed and in which you have done particularly well. List academic and vocational courses in which you did poorly.
9. Experience: List each job experience and skill you have used, assessing each favorably or unfavorably according to your personal tastes.
10. Hobby interests: Some could eventually be of help on a job.
11. Type of company: small, large, medium-sized? Perhaps you would prefer going into business for yourself.
12. Family situation affecting the employment picture.

By studying your answers to these 12 points, you should get a good picture of the type of work that fits you best and therefore should be the work at which you would best succeed.

Job Sources

Few people realize how many job sources there are. The following list contains several suggestions for you to explore and by becoming familiar with a field, you may even add others on your own.

1. **Friends, relatives, neighbors, business contacts of your own.**—Such people often know of job opportunities.
2. **College placement bureau.**—Numerous employers contact these agencies looking for students with various types of backgrounds.
3. **Public library.**—Talk to a librarian about your project. You may be surprised at the wealth of information in your library that relates to possible employers. (See *Moody's Industrials, Standard & Poor's, Dunn & Bradstreet,* and others.)
4. **Business periodicals.**—Libraries will contain copies of *The Wall Street Journal, National Business Employment Weekly* (published by *The Wall Street Journal*), *Business Week, Nation's Business* and more.
5. **Newspaper ads.**
6. **News items.**—Current news developments can sometimes lead to jobs, such as new business and government job developments.
7. **Public employment agencies.**

8. **Private employment agencies.**—Many firms do not like to spend their own time in employee searches; therefore, you may find excellent positions offered through such agencies. Some require a fee; some do not. *Do not pay a high fee or sign a contract to pay a high fee unless it is guaranteed in writing that you will be offered a job of your choice.*

9. **Drop-ins on prospective employers.**—Appearing in person can be more favorable than telephone or letter contacts.

10. **Telephone inquiries.**—If a position in a distant place especially interests you, you might consider stretching the truth and say something like: "I expect to be in your area next week and would appreciate it if I could talk with you about . . . ."

11. **Trade and industrial organizations such as retail trade marts, insurance organizations and computer science associations.**—Retail and insurance employers and many others regularly hire large numbers of employees in a wide range of work assignments.

12. **Civil service—municipal, state, county, and federal.**—A large percentage of college graduates and others are hired each year by government agencies. Job notices may be found in an agency's headquarters, in job information centers or in post offices. Also, public libraries contain job descriptions, salary ranges and sample examinations. All state and national government agencies are required by law to list their available jobs with state unemployment offices.

13. **Organizations.**—Church, YMCA, YWCA, professional associations and career planning centers especially set up for women, and for men and women over 40.

14. **Direct mail.**—Applying for a job by mail often puts you in competition with large numbers of people. Therefore, your application must be particularly expressive and impressive. For details, see the material in Chapter 13 about writing employment application resumés and letters.

15. **Yellow pages of telephone books.**

16. **U.S. Census Bureau.**

The Job Hunt

Sometimes it is an employees' job market—jobs are relatively easy to find. At other times, finding the right job can be a difficult battle. But in good times and bad, education, experience, and personality are put to the test, and the person with the best background will be given first chance at available positions. Even in the worst of times, there are some jobs available.

The **job hunt** can be wearisome, and a person can be conditioned physically and psychologically to only a limited number of turndowns in a given period. But the person who perseveres lands the job—sometimes a better position than the one originally sought.

The job hunt can be one of life's toughest battles, and in this battle being persistent— fighting for a job—can get you the job you want.

James J. ("Gentleman Jim") Corbett, world heavyweight boxing champion at the turn of the century, said:

> Fight one more round. When your feet are so tired that you have to shuffle back to the center of the ring, fight one more round. When your arms are so tired that you can hardly lift your hands to come on guard, fight one more round. When your nose is bleeding and your eyes are black and you are so tired that you wish your opponent would crack you one on the jaw and put you to sleep, fight one more round—remembering that the man who fights one more round is never whipped.

On Being Persistent

Robert O. Snelling, head of a private employment service company with 500 offices across the country, was asked, "What are the mistakes young people most frequently make when they apply for jobs?" He gave this classic advice:

> One common mistake is not being insistent enough—not fighting for an available job. I see this all the time among the sons and daughters of friends and neighbors. The youngsters apply for a job, and I ask them what happened. Often the reply is "Well, they said they'll call me if they want me." When I ask what they're going to do next, they say, "I'll wait to hear about this first opening, but meanwhile I'll apply to other companies."
>
> I tell these youngsters they're taking the wrong tack. They should go back to the first place and tell the employer, "I really want that job." Then they should follow up with a phone call and then with a letter saying, "I want that job. Here's why I'm qualified."
>
> It's amazing to me that young folks won't fight to get a job they really want.[1]

Employers want evidence that a person really wants a specific job.

One young woman who planned a career in journalism learned that the university campus correspondent for a daily newspaper was a graduating senior. Figuring that there should be an opening for this position, she mustered her courage, walked into the newspaper office, and approached the news editor. After listening to her, he pulled his glasses down over his nose, stared her straight in the eye, and said, "You know, of course, that all the other high school journalism seniors in the state are probably applying for that job!"

Returning the stare, she said, "I believe I could do the job as well as any of them." Before she left, she received permission to check in to see if the position had been filled.

And check she did. Every few weeks she dropped in, until the editor would say, "Oh—you again!"

But she got the job.

Frequently, at the completion of education and training, people find it impossible to get employment that they feel adequately suits their background. If this occurs, you should not be too discouraged. One young man, a particularly creative type with a major in theatre arts and a minor in advertising, sought unsuccessfully for the kind of position he wanted. Eventually, in desperation, he accepted a position as meter reader for a power company. After a period of wearing out shoe leather and enduring innumerable assaults from neighborhood dogs, he was advanced to an office position doing routine accounting work. There, through a company bulletin, he learned of an opening in the marketing department—the type of position for which he felt particularly well qualified. Since the firm practiced in-house promotion, he was interviewed for the position, and within 2 1/2 years after his initial employment, he began a new career as an assistant account executive in advertising.

In another instance, a woman whose children were grown became tired of volunteer work and sought employment for pay. She had an interest in writing but had found little opportunity to develop it. The best position offered her was as typist and file clerk in the Utah state fish and game department. Gradually she progressed from one position to another, taking some night courses at a nearby university. After a few years, she became editor of the state's fish and game magazine, a popular publication with worldwide circulation. Today she is a published poet, children's nature story writer, and author of three books published by a major New York publisher.

---

[1]"Are There Jobs Enough for All?" copyrighted interview in *U.S. News & World Report,* October 30, 1972, p. 72.

The Over-the-Hill Job Hunters

While God and nature give to the young the plentiful advantages of youth, many employers point out reasons for their preference in hiring the **over-the-hill employee.**

These more mature job seekers are recognized as expecting the *work* that goes with the job. They usually are more appreciative of being hired, and therefore are more loyal to those who hire them. Thus, they are less likely to job hop. They probably will not miss work to care for small children. Further, tests have shown that people in their 50s learn at the same rate as 16-year-olds.

Older workers seeking employment should follow these suggestions.

DON'T emphasize your age or possible disabilities.

DON'T lecture the interviewer about new laws that favor the hiring of older people.

DO study this Chapter and Chapter 13 for guides in your job search.

DO consider volunteer work. Work experience and contacts you make can lead to paid employment.

In all, most employers recognize the advantages of hiring older applicants.

Holding a Job

So now you have your first job and you think that's that. You will soon discover that holding a job takes as much effort as finding one. You must make a continuing effort to perform your duties responsibly. Your success or failure depends upon you. As with most other things, what you get out of a job depends upon what you put into it. You can tell whether or not you can hold your job by asking yourself these questions:

Do I have the qualifications to hold this job?

Do I want to hold this job?

Can I get along with my boss and my fellow employees?

If the answers to all the preceding questions are yes, you will probably hold this job successfully. If the answer to the first question is no and you want the job, you must get additional training or education. If the answer to either of the other questions is no, you should look into yourself for a change in attitude or a change in jobs. Employers have seen too many people who want the *job* but don't want the *work.*

Appearance is also important. A person may not be expected to spend an excessive amount of money for clothes, but a certain standard should be maintained. For both men and women, appearance on the job can be critical. Good introductions to the subject of proper business clothing are the two popular books by John Malloy: *Dress for Success* (for men's wear) and *Dress for Success for Women.*

However do not overdress on the job. People who overspend on clothing set themselves apart from their fellow employees, which can be difficult for relationships among personnel and even with superiors.

No matter what type of work you do, your success will depend largely upon getting along with people—your boss, your fellow employees, and those who work for you. Actually, in casual conversations and otherwise, people who work for you can be making comments to your superiors about you and your job performance. If you work with a pleasant, positive, courteous attitude, feeling sure that you *can* succeed, you *will* succeed.

Earning a Promotion

If you are successful on the job, the next question concerns whether or not you will be considered for promotion. Promotions usually go to the employees who show the following attributes.

Productivity

Productivity is the bottom line for judging most employees—how much work does that person do? Mistakes cost money, and a seemingly productive worker who makes more than a tolerable number of errors cannot expect to be kept on the job, much less promoted.

Motivation

Motivation—or drive—comes from a person's attitude toward the job itself. Motivation is a sincere desire to succeed. The salesperson who sells the most, whether the oldest or youngest on the staff, will be a person who is highly motivated.

Initiative

Initiative means doing things without being told—taking the extra step. Initiative also means observing what is going on around you and being interested in the best companywide performance. It means helping another worker under pressure without being told, if your work load will permit it. It means asking questions and being willing to make decisions when needed. Some people are good at analyzing problems but have no idea how to correct them. Such people are usually kept in the back room, and decision makers use their ideas in instituting changes.

People with initiative often seem to accomplish the impossible when plans seem to have bogged down completely.

Reliability

Time is money, and people who are late often waste not only their own time but also the time of others. A record of tardiness and too many absences has stopped the advancement of many employees.

Reliability also involves promptness with your work. When a job you have been given must be completed by a certain time or a certain day, be sure you have it done by then. This may require pacing yourself carefully and perhaps putting off other work that does not have such a deadline.

All in all, reliability is one of the most valuable human characteristics, in or out of business. If you can be counted upon, if you are dependable in any normal situation, this quality can outweigh many other minor ones.

Industriousness

Industriousness is the willingness to become totally involved in your work—the willingness to work long, hard hours. Refusal to work overtime shows a lack of interest in the progress of the firm. J. C. Penney once said, "I would like to warn any embryonic executives right now that unless they are willing to drench themselves in their work beyond the capacity of the average man, they are just not cut out for positions at the top."

Use of Good English

As noted earlier in Chapter 4, to thrive in the American career world, a person, native-born American or foreigner, must have good command of the English language.

Work Ethic

In his *Autobiography* (1731–1759) Benjamin Franklin said:

> When men are employed, they are best contented; for on the days they worked they were good-natured and cheerful, and, with the consciousness of having done a good day's work, they spent the evening jollily; but on our idle days they were mutinous and quarrelsome.

Changing Jobs

The Backward Step

Sometimes it is necessary to take a **backward step** when job demands force a person to leave and accept a different type of employment with a lower salary. Often this step can be an anticipated development for which long-range plans can be made. Or sometimes, the backward step is temporary, and the person is able to get into a new field and gradually build up to or beyond previous earnings and position.

Many people, old or young, may at some time have to accept job setbacks because of diminishing physical capacities, business or corporate problems or mergers, technological or other changes. But it is the person with intelligence, courage and determination who stands the best chance to recover and achieve new heights of success. In the uncommon person, adversity is said to be a source of strength.

Recovering from Losing a Job

If it's you who has just lost a job, it may right now seem impossible to believe that it may have been a "blessing in disguise." But this is frequently the case, and sometimes even in the middle of this dismal picture, there is a sense of relief in not being tied into work you did not like. It may take time to realize that **loss of a job** often occurs because a person really did not want to stay on that job, for whatever reason.

At such a time, take stock of yourself, and *write down* answers to these questions:

What are my career options?

What type of work would I enjoy doing?

What type of work would I *not* enjoy doing?

Am I trained for my choice of work? (This could lead to a hunt for interim employment during retraining.)

What type of opportunities should I seek?

What type of opportunities should I stay away from?

Making the Change

Changing jobs is an act that should never be approached lightly or considered haphazardly. However, circumstances sometimes force a person to seek new employment. At other times, a person may feel that a voluntary change should be made.

Before you make a move to change your type or place of employment, you should make a serious study of your current employment and your reasons for wanting to leave. If, after such study, you are convinced you should work elsewhere, you should have your new position firmly lined up before quitting your old job. It is always easier to get a job when you are already employed. If you are still on the job, it is evidence of satisfactory performance.

Sometimes you may cross off a certain type of work because you tried the right job at the wrong time or place. Working at it part time or full time while in school, possibly compounded by family responsibilities, might for a time dim the appeal of the most attractive career. After trying other lines of employment, you may find yourself best suited to your original school-time work, after all. Or perhaps success seemed too easy in some type of employment. Maybe you should try it again, for you could be headed toward higher goals than you originally anticipated.

There can be many reasons for changing jobs. Usually it is done because of a change in personal objectives and goals, sociological changes, or technological advancements. With continuing developments in computer science, nuclear power, laser technology and superconductivity, people should look ahead to foresee how these changes can affect the job picture.

Take this Test before Changing Jobs

An article in Kiplinger's *Changing Times,* "Are You and Your Job Cut Out for Each Other?" covers the topic of changing employment by presenting a self-check test for evaluating yourself and your job. This article points out that the choice of a career means "logging 90,000 hours, possibly more, at work. While we do it for money, we also work to fill deepseated needs for recognition, advancement, learning, and social relationships."

Although this article was written some time ago, its value is timeless, and it can serve you and others now and for the rest of your lives.

If you are employed and are wondering if you should look for another job, try taking the following test, which, with permission of the publisher, has been slightly abridged from the test in that article.

The Job Itself

1. *Overall, do you find your work at least moderately satisfying?* (Yes _____ No _____)

2. *Are you confident that the skills you've acquired will keep you employable even in bad times?* (Yes _____ No _____)

3. *Are at least some aspects of your work different from what you were doing five years ago?* (Yes _____ No _____)

4. *Are you earning as much as co-workers who have equal training and experience?* (Yes _____ No _____)

5. *Assuming you're interested in a promotion, is the way clear for one?* (Yes _____ No _____)

The Company You Work For

6. *Is your company well established, successful, and in a strong competitive position?* (Yes _____ No _____) There are advantages and disadvantages to working for a small firm new to its field. If it succeeds, you could rise fast. But many small businesses fail or are swallowed up by larger firms. The outlook is generally best in established companies that keep up to date.

7. *Are pay increases and fringe benefits as good as or better than average?* (Yes _____ No _____)

8. *Is the firm's general practice to promote from within on the basis of merit?* (Yes _____ No _____) Seniority should carry you part of the way, but ideally, ability is the clincher in determining who is chosen.

9. *Is your employer respected by you, the community, and other firms in the industry?* (Yes _____ No _____) It's natural to want to be proud of what you do and your employer's products or services. If the product is shoddy, you may mumble when people ask where you work. You'll be happier if you can find an employer whose goals and ideals—possibly even political and social outlook—coincide with your own.

10. *Is the division you're in an essential company operation?* (Yes _____ No _____) When a firm must retrench in bad times, unnecessary functions are the first to get the ax.

The Industry You Work In

11. *Does your industry's chief product or service meet an enduring need?* (Yes _____ No _____) There's money in fads, but not over the long haul. Best job protection is offered by producers of standard items.

12. *Is your industry or occupational group expected to expand in size in the years just ahead?* (Yes _____ No _____)

13. *Has your industry already adjusted to technological change so that few additional job shifts are likely to be caused by it?* (Yes _____ No _____) Hundreds of clerks have been replaced by electronic computing machines and other devices. It is difficult to foretell which jobs technology will create or destroy. Be on the lookout for signs of change.

14. *Is your industry large enough to absorb you elsewhere in the event your company fails or you get the itch to switch?* (Yes _____ No _____)

15. *Are there related industries that could also use your services with little or no retraining?* (Yes _____ No _____)

Scoring. Count three points for each "no" answer in the "your job" section, two points for each "no" in the "your company" section, and one for each "no" in the "your industry" section. Add the total.

A total score of around ten points indicates that you should be on the lookout for a more suitable position, most likely outside your present company.

Fifteen or more points means that you should be on the pavement actively searching. With so many things going against you, another job at the same pay is likely to be better than the one you have. But don't quit until you have a solid offer and until you've subjected the new job to the same kind of scrutiny.

If your score is under ten, congratulations. No job is perfect, of course. If you're relatively happy most of the time where you are, stay put. If not, happy hunting.[2]

Watch Yourself When (If) You Leave

Unfortunately, sometimes a primary reason for wanting to leave a position is the desire to tell off someone in authority about all the negative aspects of the position, the firm, and the people working there. But in the long run, this can only hurt you, since at

---

[2]"Are You and Your Job Cut Out for Each Other?" *Changing Times*, August 1972, p. 41ff

some time in the future, you will need references attesting to your performance on the job and your ability to get along with people. If inability to get along with people is a major reason for leaving a position ("It was *only* a matter of personality conflict"), be careful. The next employment interviewer may seriously question your claim that the responsibility rested entirely with others—even if it did. People shy away from hiring someone who might bring such potential personality problems.

The wise employee who decides for any reason to seek employment elsewhere controls personal feelings, calmly assesses the situation, finds other employment (listing the current employer as a reference), turns in a pleasant resignation, and is off to a new assignment.

Welcoming the New Employee

Do you remember your first day on a new job? Or perhaps you have not yet had this experience. Everything is strange. Not just your job, but the building you work in, the area where you work, and the people around you. Obviously, any friendly gesture is welcome.

One phase of employee communication that should be practiced by all is that of **welcoming the new employee.** The success of newcomers will help your company and, in the long run, should help you.

Let's say that you are now an established employee. A new woman is starting her first day of work at a desk in the same office as yours. There are many ways in which you can give that new employee the boost that may assist her in becoming an effective working member of the team.

"Hello"

Greet the newcomer and introduce yourself, or repeat your name if you met previously. Welcome her aboard, and get her acquainted with a few people who work nearby. Repeat the newcomer's name to them and identify them in some manner, such as saying what type of work they do or making some pleasant personal comment that will help individualize them. This will prevent the new employee from feeling engulfed in a sea of strangers.

The Grand Tour

Don't just explain where things are, but take time to point out to the newcomer the location of such things as the cafeteria, the stockroom, the restroom area, and the employee parking lot. Show her the location of manuals or other instructions that will aid in her daily work.

Lunch Hour, Coffee Break

During her first days on the job, frequently invite the new employee to join you and your friends at lunch or for other break periods. Then draw her into the conversation occasionally, so that she does not feel like an outsider. Don't worry that you will always have to include her with your group whether you want to or not. As she gradually moves among other people, she will find a group of her own.

Friendly Help

For the first few days on a job, an employee is hesitant to ask help of anyone, especially of an immediate superior. Without intruding, try to offer any suggestions that you believe will be of assistance. Also, encourage the new employee to refer to higher officials at the proper time. At the end of the day, take time to seek her out for a friendly "good night."

Loneliness is said to be the world's most prevalent disease. The new employee needs your help, patience, and friendship.

Writing assignments for chapters 12 and 13 are at the end of chapter 13.

Chapter 12 *Writing Improvement Exercise*

Pronouns in Subject and Object Form

Usually, the acceptable use of pronouns is not a problem. However, there are two chief places where pronouns might raise a question. The first and most common is when a pronoun is joined to another noun or pronoun (**compounds**).

Pronouns in Compound Usage

Compounds are formed by joining parts of a sentence with the words like *and, or, nor*. Here are examples of compounds:

John *and* I   John *and* me

she *or* you   her *or* you

they *or* he   them *or* him

When a pronoun is joined to noun or another pronoun, it is usually very easy to select the preferred pronoun by mentally leaving out the other word or words of the compound momentarily and selecting the preferred form of the pronoun.

The two chief pronoun forms that might give trouble are subject and object:

Subject	*Object*
I	me
we	us
you	you
he	him
she	her
it	it
they	them

1. *Pronoun as compound direct object. (Direct object receives action.)*
The coach sent Lou and (he, him) to the showers.
The coach sent . . . him to the showers.
The coach sent Lou and him to the showers.

We appointed (she, her) and her assistant.
We appointed her....
We appointed her and her assistant.

2. *Compound object of a preposition.*
   They assigned the work to Dean and (she, her).
   They assigned the work to ... her.
   They assigned the work to Dean and her.

   For (we, us) and our crew, it was a piece of cake.
   For us ..., it was a piece of cake.
   For us and our crew, it was a piece of cake.

3. *Pronoun as compound subject (more than one subject).*
   (Her, She) and Curt read his poetry.
   She ... read his poetry.
   She and Curt read his poetry.

   (He, Him) and (I, me) can complete the project.
   He ... can complete the project.
   ... I can complete the project.
   He and I can complete the project.

   With choosing the pronoun when it is part of a compound subject, a question can arise. When part of the compound is dropped, the subject can momentarily change from plural to singular. Then, you must mentally change the *verb* to the singular form to select the preferred pronoun. *(Selecting the correct pronoun really can become an easy habit).*

   Karen and (I, me) *are* taking the lead.
   ... I *am* taking the lead.
   Karen and I *are* taking the lead.

   Jeff and (he, him) *work* the late shift.
   ... he *works* the late shift.
   Jeff and he *work* the late shift.

Pronouns are Appositives

   Pronouns are sometimes followed by appositives. That is, they are sometimes followed by a noun that gives additional meaning to the pronoun. Here too, there can be a question about choosing the better form. A simple solution is to temporarily drop the noun appositive, letting your "ear" select the preferred form.

   (We, Us) workers at Hemp Company make the finest West Texas rope.
   We ... make the finest West Texas rope.
   We *workers* at Hemp Company make the finest West Texas rope.

   Please send fax copies to (us, we) *arthitects.*
   Please send fax copies to us....
   Please send fax copies to us *architects.*

Chapter 12 *Writing Improvement Worksheet*

Pronouns in Subject and Object Form

Select the correct form of the pronoun by crossing out the incorrect form.

Compound Subject

1. (He, Him) and (she, her) will attend the concert together.
2. Mr. Prince and (I, me) have worked together for some time.
3. Miss Marvin and (they, them) will start their own agency.
4. Did you and (he, him) write your own speeches?
5. Chris and (me, I) are preparing a new agenda.

Compound Direct Object

6. The president sent Hoskins and (I, me) to the meeting.
7. Yesterday the supervisor selected Ruben and (he, him) as shop foremen.
8. They introduced Jean and (she, her) during coffee break.
9. Janice invited (him, he) and (me, I) to the ceremony.
10. We met (he, him) and Matthew at the entry door.
11. We want (she, her) and Andrew for the opening ceremonies.

Compound Object of Preposition

12. Between you and (I, me), I am in favor of Mr. Charles.
13. Give this bouquet to (she, her) and Doris.
14. Let's hope the matter is settled in favor of (they, them) and their staff.
15. These designs were especially prepared for Ari and (she, her).
16. Between Don and (I, me), there is no sharp difference.

Pronouns with Appositives

17. (We, Us) secretaries are prepared to assist them.
18. The work should be assigned to (us, we), the ones who are responsible.
19. Please help (we, us) employees in our negotiations.
20. (She, Her), the person in charge, is expected to be on time.

REVIEW AND DISCUSSION

Chapter 12 *Employment Guides*

1. The French philosopher Voltaire said that "work spares us from three great evils." What are they?

   _____

2. Name someone in public or private life who seems to suffer one or more of these evils.

   _____

3. What four matters should a person study when choosing a career?

   _____

   _____

   _____

4. On the average, the college-trained person still earns _____ times as much as the non-college-trained.

5. Name two advantages of part-time work.

   _____

   _____

6. How can a record of volunteer work aid a person seeking employment?

   _____

   _____

7. What course should you follow if you feel you are not the type of person that someone would employ?

   _____

   _____

8. What are the advantages of following the "family business" or any other business with which you have a long-time familiarity?

   _____

   _____

9. Why is it important that you try to follow a career that is right for you?

   _____

   _____

Chapter 12   Employment Guides (*Continued*)

10. Name at least five fields that should have good job opportunities in the 90s.

_____

_____

11. Should salary be the only consideration when selecting a career? Why/Why not?

_____

12. Should entry-level income be the major consideration in selecting a position? Explain.

_____

_____

13. Name ten sources of job information.

_____

_____

_____

14. Is it ever advisable to use the influence of friends or relatives, if available, in seeking employment?

_____

15. Robert O. Snelling, employment counselor, says young people make a common mistake in applying for jobs. What is that mistake?

_____

16. The text says that most employers are learning that discrimination against older applicants is _____.

17. What three questions can you ask to determine your capability for holding a job?

_____

_____

_____

18. Why is a person's appearance on the job important?

_____

_____

19. Is it possible for a job to have some undesirable features and still rate as being satisfactory employment? _____

20. Why should you "Watch yourself when you leave"?

_____

_____

21. Why is a record of "personality conflict" a difficult trait to be reported on an employment record?

_____

_____

Chapter 12   Employment Guides (*Continued*)

22. Why should you try to make a new employee feel welcome?

_____

_____

Choose the preferred pronoun by drawing a line through the other form:

23. Between George and (I, me), we know we can meet the deadline.
24. George and (I, me) received the best assignments.
25. Please give this assignment to (we, us) word processors.
26. We left (she, her) and her sister at the station.
27. Divide the assignments between (he, him) and Jarvis.
28. Sometimes they asked Hilda and (I, me) to sing, poor things.
29. Did you and (him, he) get your assignments?
30. Among (we, us) homeowners, we must watch taxes.

CHAPTER 13
Employment Resumés and Application Letters:
Miscellaneous Employment Communications

> *The harder you work, the luckier you get.*
> Gary Player, *professional golfer*

The Employment Resumé

Almost everyone who works for someone else will at some time have to prepare an employment **resumé** (REZ-oom-ay). You may be asked to furnish one at the time of an employment interview. Or, if you are applying for a position by mail, you may follow the standard procedure of enclosing a resumé with your letter of application. A resumé is sometimes called by another name, such as *data sheet, vita, or bio* (biography).

This form is a summary presentation of your background and employment qualifications. It should be prepared before the letter of application is written. Properly prepared, it sets out in a logical, organized manner major facts concerning an applicant that should be of interest to a potential employer. Therefore, it furnishes a good outline for choosing the parts of this information that should be highlighted by being included in the letter of application.

Because your employment resumé can determine whether or not you will get a job, a professional writing consultant might charge you a high fee for preparing one. However, studying a few examples and seeing how they are written should make you able to write a professional resumé for yourself.

Any communication so important in applying for a job should not be written hurriedly. Take care to compose one or more rough drafts of each section, and select the best of each for inclusion in the final draft.

As you study how to make up a resumé, look at the examples shown in Figures 13.1 and 13.2.

Problem Areas in Resumés

In a survey of the 500 largest corporations in the United States as listed in the Fortune directory, chief personnel officers of those corporations listed these problem areas as showing too often in resumés:

MARIA HELEN GOMEZ

POSITION SOUGHT: SECRETARY AT ACME FOODS

45 Olympia Avenue
West Grove, Penn. 19390
(215) 555-1239

<u>Education</u>	19XX–19XX: Cerritos College, Norwalk, California. AA degree; Administrative Secretary major.

Courses taken that would be useful in secretarial work:

Advanced Shorthand	Administrative Secretary
Advanced Word Processing	Machine Calculation
Business English (grammar)	Office Services
Business Communications (writing)	Basic Accounting
Machine Transcription	Human Relations in Business

19XX–19XX: Downey High School, Downey, California. Graduated; pre-college major.

<u>Experience</u>	19XX–present: Student assistant in office of Business Division, Cerritos College. General office duties: take shorthand; answer telephone; act as receptionist; file.

19XX–19XX: Volunteer worker in office of Principal, Warren High School, Downey, California.

<u>Special Qualifications</u>	Bilingual: Competency in writing and speaking both English and Spanish.

<u>Personal</u>	Health excellent Age 20 Height 5′ 7″ Single	Hobbies: Tennis; styling own clothes. Memberships: Alpha Gamma Sigma college honor society; Phi Beta Lambda, college business fraternity. FBLA, high school business club.

<u>References</u>	Mrs. Margaret W. Baird, secretarial instructor, Business Division, Carritos College, 11110 East Alondra Blvd., Norwalk, California 90650. Telephone: (213) 860-2451

Mrs. Merle Davidson, Office Manager, Warren High School, 8131 East DePalma Street, Downey, California 90241. Telephone: (213) 923-6711.

FIGURE 13.1
Employment application resumé or data sheet.

RESUME: ROBERT D. ARMSTEAD

1522 South Jellison Avenue
Rowland Heights, California 91748
(213) 964-0000

CAREER ACCOMPLISHMENTS

In each of my three years as department manager of J.C. Penney, Culver City, California, my departments had significant sales gains while total store showed losses. Prior to my arrival my department had also shown losses.

EDUCATION

9/XX–present   CALIFORNIA STATE POLYTECHNIC UNIVERSITY, POMONA, Pomona, California. Will receive B.S. degree in Business Administration in June 19XX. Current grade point average 3.9 on 4-point scale.

2/XX–6/XX   RIO HONDO COLLEGE, Whittier, California. GPA 3.9. Completed lower division requirements.

EXPERIENCE: J.C. PENNEY COMPANY

Left retail management position in January 19XX, to complete my B.S. degree.

2/XX–present   Selling Specialist, Sporting Goods Department, Puenta Hills Mall, City of Industry, California.

6/XX–2/XX   Management Trainee: Earned early promotion to Department Manager, Stonewood Shopping Center, Downey, California. Duties: Responsible for purchasing, merchandise assortment planning, hiring, training, and managing up to 25 employees.

HONORS AND ACTIVITIES

Dean's Honor List since beginning Cal Poly. Member of Data Processing Management Association, university data processing club.

Enjoy family activities, snow skiing, singing and playing a folk guitar. Won two prizes for original oil paintings. Elected president of Key Club, high school honor club.

PERSONAL

Health: excellent   Hobbies: Jogging; spectator sports;
Age 28   photography.
Height 6′   Job preference: Like it here; willing
Weight 180   to relocate

REFERENCES

References will be forwarded on request.

FIGURE 13.2
Employment application resumé or data sheet.

- Applicants fail to list career objectives and specific job objectives.
- They have no knowledge of the company to which they are applying.
- They oversell themselves and are vague instead of specific about how their qualifications fit job requirements.
- Their spelling, grammar, and writing ability are poor.[1]

Appearance

The **appearance** of your resumé may be crucial. It is foolish to make up one that is less than perfect looking. You should be aware that an employer may be so deluged with resumés that any excuse, reasonable or unreasonable, may narrow the number of prospective job candidates. A resumé that is too long, is on cheap paper, or is typed with dirty keys or even a single typo will often be rejected without being read. Right or wrong, employers look at your resumé to judge how you present yourself. Too often, they are harsher here than they are in person.

Be brief. One personnel interviewer says, "We get hundreds of job applications from college students. If the resumé is longer than one page, I don't take time to read it." The vice president of another company says, "If a resumé is too long, I probably wont't read it. Even the best job applicant can get the message across in two pages."

Later, after years of experience, you should certainly make your resumé longer than one page if you have significant details to present. Try to picture what competing applicants are listing and show your possible superiority. Be honest but don't be modest. Tell of career accomplishments, evidence of leadership, how many subordinates you had, and contributions you made to company success. If something is worth saying, say it. Don't make the potential interviewer try to read any additional information into it. Other applications may be clearer and more specific.

In any resumé eliminate minor details and mention only matters that will be of help in getting a position. *Make good use of* "**white space**"; that is, leave top, bottom, and side margins of at least 1 1/4 inches. Also, leave blank lines between sections. This white space shows off individual parts, making the paper easier to read and more inviting. The person reading the resumé knows you are available for an interview if more information is wanted.

Nevertheless, in being brief, do not list a person's last name without giving the first name or initials. Also, do not use confusing abbreviations or titles for business, campus, or other organizations.

Not This	*This*
Dr. Reeves, veterinarian	Dr. D. J. Reeves, veterinarian
Ms. Frances	Ms. Holly Frances
B of A	Bank of America
Alpha Gamma Sigma	Alpha Gamma Sigma, community college honor society
VA	Veterans Administration
GPA	grade point average

---

[1]Nelda Spinks and Barron Wells, "Letters of Application and Resumés: A Comparison of Corporate Views," *The Bulletin of the Association for Business Communication,* September 1987, page 15.

Paper and Printing

For attractive appearance, use a word processor with a letter-quality printer or a good typewriter. (If you do not have access to one of these, you will find it worthwhile to pay the small charge of a secretarial service for making a final draft.) Be sure the printing element of the machine is clean for sharp, clear print. Shadows or dark spaces in the enclosed parts of such letters as *a, o, e, d,* and *b* give an unprofessional appearance to any material.

Be sure that you use first quality paper, preferably rag content bond, for your resumé. Do not use duplicator or mimeograph-quality paper, even if it is of a special color of your choice. Use white paper. Or, to make your application stand out from others, you might select first-quality paper of a soft shade of gray, tan, or blue. Sharp, deeper colors might turn the reader off, unless you are applying for a creative position such as in advertising.

If you have several copies of your resumé printed, be sure that copies are similarly on letter-quality bond paper. Good copies can be made for a minimal cost. Purchase extra paper and matching envelopes for cover application letter and mailing.

Good Will Tone

Make the resumé or data sheet "you-oriented." That is, set material out according to the reader's interests—what will help make someone hire you because you fit that person's needs.

Don't be modest. You are selling yourself. State your case clearly and forcefully. On the other hand, don't brag. One person in charge of company personnel said, "Don't make it sound as if you can jump over mountains or, if you can't jump over them, you can move them."

Format

There is no single good format for setting up your resumé. You might center your headings or place them at the margin. Material might be set out in sentence format or in columns. Look at business communications book illustrations, or make up a distinctive, attractive plan of your own. Remember to leave a lot of white space in margins and between paragraphs, making the resumé appealing and easy to read.

Again: *Be brief.* Unnecessary details that cloud the forcefulness of necessary information weaken the entire communication.

The message or content of the resumé can be set up in sections: *heading, special qualifications* (if any), *education, experience, career accomplishments* (if any), *personal details,* and *references.*

To make up your resumé, refer to information in your employment profile as set out for the first section of Chapter 12, "Employment Guides."

Heading

For the heading, set out your name, address, and telephone number clearly at the top so it identifies you and shows you are available for contact.

Authorities disagree about the advantages of setting out your employment objective. Most say it is advantageous because it shows you have a goal. Others say that in early employment stating a specific objective may exclude you from other fields that may lead to a better future. If you have a specific position in mind, include an employment objective.

One applicant who was successful in obtaining a highly contested position in city management did not list an employment objective on his resumé. When asked this question in the interview, he replied, "Well, if you and I are happy with my work here, I may stay until I am an old man. Then again, I may eventually leave for a position in another field. Or, I may just use this position as a stepping stone to another position in city management."

He was later told that only a few applicants were called in for a second interview. A member of the interviewing committee said one reason he got the job was that the committee felt he was the only one of the group who gave an honest answer to this question.

After the heading, the sections under *special qualifications* or *career accomplishments, education,* and *experience,* should be set up in order of their importance, with details of the section that will best impress a potential employer being listed first.

Special Qualifications or Career Accomplishments

One of these two headings should be set out next, if you have background material that suits such a classification. Figure 13.2 shows the section *Career Accomplishments* first, because it was judged worthy of this emphasis.

Following are examples of qualifications that can be considered of high value on the employment market and could be listed under one of the headings above:

- Outstanding employment in a specific field
- Competent bilingual or multilingual ability
- Writing ability and experience (with examples)
- Artistic ability (with portfolio)
- Research in a specific field
- Work with someone outstanding in a field

Competence in a foreign language could be a valuable special qualification. The job markets of today and the future show a need for people with foreign language skills. With recent waves of immigration from Asia, Latin America and Eastern Europe, business persons increasingly find themselves in a "global village," managing El Salvadoran employees working for a Vietnamese boss or working side by side with Russian co-workers.

One expert on international travel emphasizes that the tourist industry is thriving, with great promise for new employees in the future. But few Americans bother to learn foreign languages, making great employment opportunities for people who speak English and another language or other languages.

U.S. businesses and industries continue to expand into many foreign markets, and the number of foreign-owned companies is growing in the United States. As we have been showing, we are experiencing a constantly growing need for people with bilingual or multilingual ability. Learning a foreign language or polishing up on one could be extremely worthwhile.

Education

For most college students with no special qualifications, or applicable work experience, education would be listed first.

Set out information concerning your education in reverse chronological order, with your current or most recent education first. This is of most interest to an employer. If some time has elapsed since high school and there is a record of college work, leave out high school information. Identify fully any degree you have received and the town and state of educational institutions you attended.

Listing Courses

List specific courses you have completed that would directly help in performing duties of the position you are seeking. Completion of courses in business writing, public speaking, and data processing should be listed. Today, aptitude in these subjects is helpful in a high percentage of business positions.

Do not list courses by number, such as "Marketing 101." Instead, list each course by its full title, such as "Survey of Marketing," because course numbers probably mean nothing to others. If you have attained a certain level of competency in office skills or in operating data processing equipment or office machines, list your ability according to tests you have passed or certificates you have received. If you wish to state your grade point average, identify it as "grade point average" and not as "GPA."

No diplomas or degrees? List special courses you may have taken. Completion of any training shows perseverance. List special talents you have shown such as selling the most tickets to a fund raiser, assembling or repairing a motorcycle or other complicated machinery.

Experience

Work experience. Work experience is invaluable in employment applications. As with data referring to education, list the most recent or current employment first, then go in reverse chronological order, ending with the earliest. If part-time work is not related to the position sought, do not list it if there is a sufficient record of full-time work. All full-time employment should be reported, as well as terms of military service, because long gaps in a record may arouse questions. This is also the place to report volunteer work if paid work experience is nonexistent or limited. Include the following with each employment position, giving information briefly and eliminating unnecessary details:

- Job title
- Date of employment
- Firm name (no abbreviations) with city or town
- Duties performed

Be consistent in sentence or phrase format in all sections of the resumé. In explanation of duties performed, the following lists of verbs might be handy. Use them as verbal phrases, avoiding the overuse of "I" with complete sentences: "*Compiled information for department report. Planned daily work routine for five employees. Maintained....*"

The following verbs describe skills that are transferable from one job or career field to another. Use them in your resumé to describe your experience.[2]

achieved	designed	interviewed	provided
adapted	determined	invented	purchased
administered	developed	investigated	recommended
advised	directed	led	recorded
analyzed	distributed	maintained	reported

[2]Courtesy Career Center, Rio Hondo College.

assembled	documented	managed	researched
assorted	edited	monitored	reviewed
classified	established	motivated	revised
communicated	estimated	negotiated	scheduled
compared	examined	obtained	selected
compiled	gathered	operated	served
conducted	guided	ordered	sorted
constructed	handled	organized	stocked
consulted	hired	performed	supervised
contracted	implemented	planned	trained
coordinated	improved	prepared	translated
counseled	increased	produced	utilized
created	inspected	programmed	wrote
delegated	installed	promoted	

Military Service. Military experience could lead off your resumé if your work experience is limited. Emphasize courses completed, skills learned, promotions earned and leadership shown.

Volunteer Work. Make your volunteer work work for you. Besides the self-satisfaction you received in performing volunteer work, listing this activity can be of value to you if your work experience is limited or nonexistent. Name the organization for which you work, your position, your duties, and any commendation you may have received. Satisfactory performance of volunteer work shows that you were a responsible, willing worker who therefore should be able to perform on the job. It also is a favorable statement about you and your personality.

Personal Details

Basically, unless there is a bona fide need for a given position, employment interviewers are forbidden by law to ask for the following personal information before, during, or after employment: height, weight, race, creed, color, national origin, sex, marital status, children and who takes care of them, or handicap.

On the other hand, employers like to see you as a whole person. Thinking of your future success on the job, potential employers are interested in answers to many of the preceding questions, even if they cannot ask for them.

Therefore, in the "Personal" section, it is legal for you to voluntarily furnish standard information plus answers to any of the preceding questions or other questions that you believe might be helpful in getting you the job or, at least, will not be harmful.

A given organization may have need for a person with diverse talents, so consider listing hobbies and other pastime interests. Include such items as artistic capabilities, campus or community organizations in which you are or have been active and the type of work done, publications worked on and type of work you did (writing, editing, selling ads) etc. Some of your best assets could be revealed here.

One young woman, recently graduated with a degree in health science, wanted to work in pharmaceutical sales. For lack of experience, she was quickly turned down by two companies. At the third interview she emphasized her extracurricular activities and was chosen from 600 applicants because she was so active on campus.

To repeat: Employers want to know the whole person. Listing extracurricular activities could reward you with a job.

When given, personal details should be listed briefly and modestly. (None of the "People tell me I am good looking" sort of thing on a business application.) You might give hobbies, sports, and organizations in which you are active. Such information should be clear, and sports should be listed as *active* or *spectator* if both types are shown. This would preclude the puzzling notation made by one college freshman: "Favorite sports: tennis, baseball, bullfighting."

When listing organizations to which you belong, identify clearly the name and type of each organization. Not everyone who reads the resume will be able to determine what an organization is if it is identified only be name, initials, or Greek letters. A teacher new to California was mystified by students' listing participation on a "CIF" team or "CIF" pep squad. Questioning revealed that these initials refer to the highly competitive state-wide sports championship playoffs, but most students did not know that CIF stands for California Interscholastic Federation. The teacher concluded that "'CIF' is like heaven—nobody knows what it is, but everyone wants to go there!"

References

Many employment resumés do not give names of references. Instead, a statement like this is made: "References will be furnished if requested."

If you do give references, try to give three and list them last. There they serve as natural lead-ins for the employer to telephone or write the people listed.

Give the name of a supervisor or administrator who can vouch for your job proficiency in preference to the name of a fellow worker or a higher official who might not remember you personally. If you have no previous employment or other suggested references, you might list names of instructors, religious leaders, youth activities leaders, business people with whom you or your family have traded, friends, or neighbors. Do not give names of relatives as references.

If you do not want your current employer advised that you are seeking employment elsewhere, make a statement like, "Please do not contact my present employer," and be ready to explain your request to an interviewer.

For each reference, give the appropriate title, such as Dr., Mr., Ms., Miss, or Mrs., together with the first name or initials; address complete with ZIP Code; telephone number, including area code; and your association with that person. Omission of any of the details of a reference might make the person reading it feel that is would be easier to inquire about another potential hiree.

You should request a person's permission before using his or her name as a reference. Most people will willingly do you this favor. An example of a request for letter of reference is given later in this chapter. Also shown is the type of information you might ask to have included in such a letter.

Editing the Resumé and Application Letter

It is an excellent idea to make a neat rough draft of your planned resumé and application letter. For editing show them to a teacher, counselor, business person (perhaps one of your references) or another whose opinions you value. An experienced person can often help you avoid mistakes by seeing them from another point of view. After they are thoroughly studied by yourself and others, you are ready to make the final copies.

The Employment Application Letter

Address your letter of employment application to a person by name. Several personnel officials who were asked about this matter agreed that a letter that is not addressed to the specific official by name is often disregarded. One officer said, "If you really want a job, take the time to look up the name of the proper official who would receive the letter." This information can be obtained from the company by telephone or letter. For a large organization, you will find personnel officers listed in business directories in the library.

After setting out the information for a good employment resumé or data sheet, you have the information before you for writing a good letter of employment application. This letter is truly a "C" letter, a selling letter. As stated before, the product you are selling is yourself.

All the basic qualities of a good letter apply here. Appearance is important, because from this letter a judgment will be made of you personally. The clear and complete message that must be given is that you are applying for a position for which you feel qualified, and you would like to be granted an interview to discuss this matter. As part of the message, you should present an abbreviated version of some major points in your resumé that would aid you in getting the job. Naturally, the letter must be written in a good will tone. You should show an interest in the firm and have some knowledge about it. In addition, you might show a special interest in the type of position you are seeking.

The tone of the letter should be as natural as possible, as if you were talking directly to the person who is to read it. However, avoid being too casual or informal. Avoid using contractions.

The employment application letter that encloses a resumé should be short, almost always just one page. Fuller details are set out in the enclosure, and you should always mention the enclosure. As much as possible, this letter should have the *you attitude* instead of the *me attitude*. This way, you *stress how your qualifications can benefit the employer instead of how you would expect to benefit from the employment.*

This letter is about you, and use of the words *I, me, my,* and *mine* is necessary. However, avoid overusing these words, and in particular limit the number of sentences that begin with *I.*

Figures 13.3 and 13.4 are examples of good employment application letters.

The standard formula for writing a selling letter can be followed: attention-getter, buildup of interest and desire, and action closing.

Attention-Getter

State clearly that you are applying for a position. If possible, name some factor that especially qualifies you for the position or that makes you want to work for the firm to which you are applying. Show some specific interest in or knowledge of the firm.

Interest and Desire Buildup

To build up in the reader an interest in you and a desire to employ you, choose from your resumé the most pertinent facts that qualify you to hold the position sought. Make your request plain, and make it with the "you attitude," as already noted. That is, make it from the viewpoint of the potential advantages to the firm, not to you. If you refer to yourself, be sure not to brag. For example, instead of saying, "I believe I have a pleasant personality," say something like, "I enjoy working with people and feel that I get along well with others."

1314 Gladys Avenue
Long Beach, California 90803
May 15, 19XX

Dr. Armand C. Teague
Professor of Marketing
California State University
   at Long Beach
6101 East Seventh Street
Long Beach, California 90801

Dear Dr. Teague:

   Through your bulletin posted at the CSULB placement bureau I learned that you are looking for a student to work part time as an assistant in charge of marketing research. I believe that my educational background and my experience working with people could be put to good advantage for you in your research work.

   On June 15 I expect to receive an AA degree with a marketing specialty from Rio Hondo College, Whittier. As my resumé shows, I have been holding two part-time jobs: one as assistant to a professor of marketing at Rio Hondo College, one as night supervisor at a local pet clinic. My work at the clinic is mostly summers and holidays. I would prefer to do more work in the marketing field.

   I feel that I work well with people, and in my position at the college supervise the work of a crew of three students.

   The resumé you requested is enclosed. You may reach me or leave a message at my home telephone: (213) 555-4567. May I see you soon?

                                        Sincerely,

Enc.

FIGURE 13.3
An example of an employment application letter.

Action Closing

   The purpose of the combination letter of application and job resumé is to get an appointment for an employment interview. The closing section of the letter should make this request clear. Also, give information that makes it easy for the potential employer to contact you, either by giving your telephone number and address here or by mentioning that this information is on your enclosed resumé. If the times that you can be reached at the telephone number are limited, give this information clearly.

Roger E. Morrison
3103 Lexington Avenue
Baltimore, Maryland 87577

Mr. James T. Jones
Professional Recruitment Counselor
Jones Manufacturing Company
200 North Park Avenue
Baltimore, Maryland 87577

Dear Mr. Jones:

Your advertisement for a Payroll Manager in the *Baltimore Sun* on Sunday, January 25, 19XX interests me considerably. I feel my background is well suited to the position you describe.

My experience has been very diversified in the following areas:

Office and computer terminal equipment
Payroll systems and payroll taxation
Accounting and taxation problem solving
Supervision of 10 staff people

I have a Bachelor of Science degree in Business Administration with heavy accent on financial courses. My experience has been in payroll for more than five years with two years of this time being spent with computerized systems. I would be happy to negotiate salary with you.

A resumé is enclosed which summarizes my background and experience. May I have the opportunity to further discuss my qualifications in a personal interview?

Sincerely,

Roger E. Morrison

Enclosure

FIGURE 13.4
Employment application letter.

Signature

The letter must be signed in either blue or black ink. If a woman wishes, she can type a title (Ms., Miss, Mrs.,) before her name, below her signature. A man would not have a title typed before his name unless he has a first name that might be used for a man or woman, such as *Leslie, Terry, Lynn, Pat,* or *Lee.*

A person with a professional degree could give this information by having his or her name typed below the signature space with the standard abbreviation for the degree shown (Ph.D., M.D., CPA, J.D., etc.). Here is an example:

Christopher T. Rynerson

Christopher T. Rynerson, J.D.

The Employment Interview

At a recent advisory committee meeting of business executives and college business division faculty members, the business people were asked, "How can we help our graduates compete on the job market?" Replying for the group, one man advised:

Teach them how to present themselves properly at a **job interview**.

So much has to be decided in the brief time of employment interviews that it may not seem fair. But the individual's appearance and also that person's ability to participate in an interview both at the time of employment and later during personnel progress reports on the job can be more important than educational background. We will hire a two-year college graduate in preference to the four-year individual if the two-year person has a good appearance, speaks up and looks you in the eye, and in general makes a positive impression. The person who dresses carelessly, mumbles answers, slouches in a chair, and evades looking you in the eye will be passed by regardless of otherwise good qualifications.

In regard to people being interviewed for a job, a national survey of employment interviewers listed the following qualities in order of their relative importance: (1) appearance, (2) manner of dress, (3) personality, (4) speech and voice, (5) manners, and (6) skills.

How NOT to get the job.

Planning Ahead

Before the interview, you can take steps to aid you in presenting yourself favorably and give you self-confidence during the interview.

Study the Company

A man who had been interviewing UCLA students for a major national corporation said that if any applicant had shown some knowledge of his firm, he would have hired that person on the spot. He objected to the fact that everyone interviewed seemed interested only in personal job goals and was not applying because of any interest in the organization.

Your college placement bureau will have information on companies interviewing students. Libraries carry books and periodicals with information about specific companies. Again, ask your librarian. The company itself may, on request, furnish employment brochures and annual reports that are very informative.

Prepare Yourself

It would seem unnecessary to mention the importance of a person's appearance at a job interview. But another personnel officer who interviews graduating applicants said, "You wouldn't believe the appearance of some of our job applicants—even graduates of universities and junior colleges."

You should dress for the job you want, not for the job you have. A day or two in advance, check to see that your clothes are clean and neatly pressed, and that your shoes are shined and new looking. If necessary, it may be advisable to go into debt to get one suitable outfit for making that good first impression. The choice of clothing for this purpose should be conservative. A suit for men is not always necessary; attractive go-togethers of jacket, slacks, shirt, and tie will usually do nicely. The style and cut of hair for both men and women should also be conservative. If a man does not choose to be clean shaven, his beard and/or mustache should be neat and trimmed. Women should consider a little shaping of their hair, and should use only a minimum of makeup.

If possible, bring a portfolio of your work and any written job references you may have. Also, you might bring a copy of a resumé in case it is requested, or other xerographed materials you may wish to leave with the interviewer. On a card or a small piece of paper you might bring a short list of questions you may wish to ask, or you should have in mind some appropriate questions. You will be given an opportunity to ask them. Do have a pen or a pencil with you, as you may be asked to fill out an application blank or an interview form. Asking to borrow this equipment gives a negative impression.

Timing the Interview

Selecting the day and time of an interview can be important. Also, there are additional matters that should be planned in advance.

Try to Choose Your Day

Because the job interview is important to you, try to make it on a Tuesday, Wednesday, or Thursday. Try to avoid Mondays—we all know about "blue Mondays," when both you and your interviewer might not be at your best. Also try to avoid Fridays, when the interviewer's mind may be full of plans for the weekend, and "If this applicant weren't here today, I could have left already." However, if you must make your appointment on a Monday or Friday, you could be very successful. Much satisfactory business is done on these days.

Be on Time

The interviewer's time is valuable, and in evaluating an applicant, tardiness for an appointment may be overemphasized. Give yourself ample time for the vagaries of traffic and parking. Try to arrive in time to catch your breath, check on your appearance, and relax a few minutes. In the waiting room, there may be reading materials available that can give you current information on the organization that you can discuss with the interviewer. Be sure to phone the day before to confirm your appointment.

Being Interviewed

Let the Interviewer Lead the Interview

Resist the temptation to take over the lead in the interview unless encouraged to do so, and do not ask too many questions relating to job benefits. The interviewer gets an extremely negative picture of an applicant whose questions relate mostly to such matters as vacations, insurance, sick benefits, and stock options. You should show more interest in the company and your possible position in it. Toward the end of the interview, it is usually proper to discuss potential salary, if this matter has not been discussed previously. However, a few extremely conservative companies have a sharply negative attitude toward such a question.

Figure 13.5 is a list of questions frequently asked during employment interviews.

Keep Calm

Some nervousness during an employment interview is expected and accepted. If some embarrassment arises, try to recover gracefully. For example, as one applicant for a position with an airline entered the door of the personnel director, he tripped on a rug and fell flat on the floor. His aplomb at recovering from such an experience probably helped him get the job.

Answering Questions Briefly and Honestly, State Your Case as Clearly as Possible

Answer questions briefly and honestly; do not boast; do not be too humble. Show that you are making a straightforward appeal for the position and that you feel qualified to fill it.

A nationwide authority on hiring practices says that the thing to keep uppermost in mind is that typical employers are looking for reasons to hire you—they may be desperate for good workers, so they are begging you to tell about yourself.

Don't Try for Pity

If you feel that a bid for pity is one of the chief appeals you can make for being hired for a position, don't make it! If the interviewing official represents a large corporation, the firm is probably suffering through enough people problems already, and they certainly

Questions Most Asked During Interviews[3]

1. What are your future vocational plans?

2. In what type of position are you most interested?

3. Why do you think you might like to work for our company?

4. What jobs have you held? How were they obtained? Why did you leave?

5. Why did you choose your particular field of work?

6. What percentage of your college expenses did you earn? How?

7. What do you know about our company?

8. What qualifications do you have that make you feel you will be successful in your field?

9. What salary do you expect?

10. What are your avocations?

11. Do you prefer any specific geographic location? Why?

12. How did you rank in your graduation class in high school? Where did you rank in college?

13. What do you think determines an individual's progress in a good company?

14. What personal characteristics are necessary for success in your chosen field?

15. Why do you think you would like this particular job?

16. Are you looking for a permanent or temporary job?

17. Do you prefer working with others or by yourself?

18. What is the most important aspect of the work you do?

19. Can you take instructions without feeling upset?

20. Did you enjoy your last job? Why?

21. What have you learned from some of the jobs you have held?

22. Can you get recommendations from previous employers?

23. What interests you about our product or service?

24. What do you know about opportunities in the field in which you are trained?

25. Do you like routine work?

26. Do you like regular hours?

27. What is your major weakness?

28. Define cooperation?

29. Do you demand attention?

30. Do you have an analytical mind?

31. Are you eager to please?

32. What do you do to keep in good physical condition?

33. Have you any serious illness or injury?

FIGURE 13.5
**Questions frequently asked during employment
interviews.**

[3]"Questions Most Asked During Interviews," *You and Your First Job,* Personnel and Industrial Relations Association, Inc., Los Angeles, California, undated, page 12.

34. Are you willing to go where the company sends you?

35. Is it an effort for you to be tolerant of persons with a background and interests different from your own?

36. What books have you read recently?

37. What type of people seem to rub you the wrong way?

38. Do you enjoy sports as a participant? As an observer?

39. What jobs have you enjoyed the most? The least? Why?

40. What are your own special abilities?

41. What job in our company do you want to work toward?

42. Would you prefer a large or small company? Why?

43. What is your idea of how industry operates today?

44. Do you like to travel?

45. How about overtime work?

46. What kind of work interests you?

48. Are you interested in research?

49. To what extent do you use liquor?

50. What have you done that shows initiative and willingness to work?

FIGURE 13.5
(Continued)

do not want you to add to them. And if you are applying for a position with a smaller firm where contacts may be closer, the person who will make the hiring decisions is probably even less inclined to want someone who may seriously handicap business operations because of financial or family difficulties.

If You Take a Test...

If you take a **test** during the interviewing process, follow these guidelines:

1. Listen to instructions and read printed instructions thoroughly.

2. Read each question through.

3. Write legibly.

4. Don't dwell too long on one question.

Do Not Overstay Your Alloted Time

Be alert for signals that the interview is near a conclusion, but try not to leave until you are satisfied that you have furnished an effective presentation of all information and material that could help you get the job. Tedious repetitions will do little to assist your cause, unless the interviewer is clearly interested in hearing them.

Reason for Leaving

You need not volunteer a **reason for leaving a previous position.** However, if you are queried on this matter, make your answer as positive as possible and do not "bad mouth" your previous employer. Your interviewer might think that this may be the way you would describe leaving this new position. Remember, many people have been fired a time or two—your listener may have had this very experience. It is known that this can be a lesson well learned.

On Leaving, Sincerely Thank the Interviewer for His or Her Time

Besides sincerely **thanking the interviewer** for his or her time, it is also proper to thank the receptionist who conducted you to the interview, if it is convenient to do so.

Instructions for writing a thank you letter are given later under the "Miscellaneous Employment Communications" section.

Why They Don't Hire

In a study of reasons for *not* hiring applicants, 166 employers were contacted. Figure 13.6 lists negative factors, in order of frequency, mentioned as reasons for not hiring. Notice that negative personality factors and lack of communication skills were the two most common reasons that applicants failed to get the job.

Miscellaneous Employment Communications

Follow-Up Communications

After the job interview, be sure to write a **letter of thanks** to the person who talked to you. This letter should be brief and will serve two purposes: (1) to thank the interviewer, and (2) to remind that person that you still want the job. This letter also helps

FIGURE 13.6
In a survey of 166 employers, these reasons were given for not hiring applicants. Reasons are shown in order of frequency given.

Why They Weren't Hired

Reasons	Frequency of Mention
Negative personality or poor impression: lack of motivation, ambition, maturity, aggressiveness, or enthusiasm	110
Poor communication skills	62
Lack of competence—inadequate preparation	56
Low grades—poor grades in major field	38
Unidentified goals	32
Unrealistic expectations	28
Lack of interest in type of work	25
Unwillingness to travel or to relocate	23
Poor preparation for the interview	14

Source: Frank S. Endicott, *The Endicott Report: Trends in the Employment of College and University Graduates in Business and Industry* (Evanston, Ill.: Northwestern University), p. 8.

keep your file active and shows that you are aggressively interested, something the employer would like to know. Further, even if someone else is hired, your letter helps keep you a step ahead of others if another opening occurs. This letter should have an upbeat, positive tone.

One employment interviewer tells the story of interviewing 15 college students on a Friday morning. When he returned to his office Monday, on his desk were letters from three of these applicants thanking him for the interview. These were the first three applicants he considered. Two were hired for the two positions.

Figures 13.7 and 13.8 are letters that thank the employment interviewer.

There is another type of follow-up employment letter. If you have applied for a position and have not heard that it has been filled, after a short period of time you should telephone to ask if it is still open. If it is, your next step is to try for another interview, expressing your continued interest in the position and your confidence in your ability to fill it. If it is not open, you should ask to be kept in mind if something else in your field opens. Further, you should continue to look for employment with the firm as long as you are interested and you feel there is any possibility of your being hired.

One woman applying for an executive position with Los Angeles County did not fit all the background requirements, yet in many ways she did qualify. Eventually, after more than 18 months of courteous, patient persistence, she was hired for the position. For many

FIGURE 13.7
Employment interview thank you letter.

                                                          Your address with ZIP Code
                                                          Your telephone with area code
                                                          Date

Mr. John E. Onthespot
Kimball Electronics
141 West Eighth Avenue
Oshkosh, Wisconsin

Dear Mr. Onthespot

    I do thank you for taking time today to talk with me about joining the Management Training Program there at Kimball Electronics.

    My experience in electronics combined with my earlier two years in personnel work as shown on my resumé should give me a strong background for this program.

    Mr. Onthespot, I surely hope we will be working together in the future and that I will hear from you soon.

                                        Cordially,

                                        (Signature)

                                        Your name

Your address with ZIP Code
Your telephone with area code
Date

Miss Ann T. Locks
Personnel Director
Acme Electronics
3400 Palo Verde Avenue
Tucson, Arizona 85726

Dear Miss Locks

Thank you so much for our interview today. I enjoyed meeting you and learning more about Acme Electronics.

Now I am even more interested in being part of your sales force. Acme's plan to increase the market area interests me, and the expansion sounds exciting. As I told you, I am single and available for travel.

Again, I do appreciate the opportunity with you. I hope to hear from you soon.

Respectfully,

(Signature)

Your name

FIGURE 13.8
Employment interview thank you letter.

years she served the county in an executive capacity and was the pride of those who had hired her.

Refusal of a Job Offer

Usually, a refusal of a job offer is made orally in person or by telephone. This personal interview should be a natural, open explanation of the reasons for not accepting the position. It is always easier to explain a matter if you are candid about the reasons, whether they involve making a personal change of plans or taking a position that seems better to you.

Sometimes a job refusal brings forth a better offer than the original. Here again, it is risky to try this as a ploy. A better offer may or may not be made, and you will have refused the original offer.

Occasionally it is necessary to write a letter refusing a position that has been offered to you. When writing this letter, keep in mind the possibility that some day in the near or far future, you may have business contacts with the person or firm to whom you are writing. You may even, at some later date, desire to reapply for a position with this same firm. By the good will of a well prepared job refusal, you can try to keep the door open for any future developments.

Following is an example of a job offer refusal:

Dear Mr. Kirby:

Neutral, leading to negative	→	Little did I think when I was talking to you last Wednesday that if you offered me a position with Kirby and Kirby I would even consider not accepting that position.
Explanation of negative	→	However, just this morning I was offered a similar position with a manufacturing firm in Abilene, Texas, my wife's home town. I believe you can understand why I am accepting it.
Negative	→	
Pleasant closing	→	While my wife and I will both be glad to return to our native state, I would otherwise have been very happy to be working with you. I do thank you for your time in considering me for employment with your company.

Very sincerely yours,

Turndown of Job Applicant

The **turndown letter** of a job applicant is a negative message that should be handled most delicately. If at all possible, it should contain a compliment and/or some word of encouragement. Naturally, this is a "bad news" message, but the applicant undoubtedly felt qualified for the position and should get some hope so that the turndown message does not create a deep hole for that person to crawl into. This letter is best when it ends on some kind of alternative suggestion or other uplift.

Examples of employment turndowns are hard to find, but here are some that have been used satisfactorily. Notice that all these messages are short, not dragging out the negative. Some are results of intense work of committees or other groups.

Letter 1

Thank you for taking the time to send your resumé for our consideration. However, at this particular time, ther are no openings for your area of expertise. [This last could be more specific.]

We will keep your information on file, and should there be any positions available that would be suitable, we will contact you.

Again, thank you for your interest in our company.

Letter 2

We appreciate your taking time to apply for the position of Knowledge Engineering Consultant.

We received many highly qualified applications such as yours. However, your background does not fit our rather specific requirements.

May we otherwise wish you success in your career.

Letter 3

We received your resumé and wish to thank you for expression of interest in our firm.

Your experience and background are quite impressive. However, there does not appear to be a match between your skills and our present needs.

Should our needs change so that we could take advantage of your qualifications, we will contact you.

Again, thank you for your interest in ZOO, Inc. We wish you success in finding a new and challenging position.

Letter 4

Thank you for applying for a position in _____. We were very pleased to receive many high quality applications for our department position.

Our MHR members reviewed the applications and we are inviting several candidates for interviews. Your application was not among those chosen at this stage.

We appreciate your interest in our firm and wish you much success in your career.

The last of these letters is an obvious "kiss off," but it would be perfectly proper to follow up by telephone or letter any of the other replies until you are satisfied that the position for which you applied is filled and that there are no other positions for which you qualify.

Many people eventually get the job after an initial turndown. Robert O. Snelling, the nationally known job counselor, said one common mistake job applicants make "is not being insistent enough—not fighting for an available job." (See page 284.)

Asking for a Raise

Many people—especially women—do not know how to bargain for a raise.

But there can come a time when you feel undervalued on the job. First, you should do some homework. Get good information about what people in comparable jobs are making in your company and at other companies. Such information is hard to get, and you may have to resort to social occasions when conversations are more relaxed.

Then, approach your boss and ask if the firm is satisfied with your work and if you have a future there. If the answer is yes, simply say, "I am underpaid. What can we do about it?"

You may get a satisfactory answer, or you may get a promise for a raise in the future. If the latter, you can probably have some patience, but maybe you should be looking elsewhere.

Don't whine. Don't plead the high cost of living—this doesn't influence facts about your value to the organization. Don't plead the high amount of your indebtedness—this could lead you right out the door.

Do have a specific amount of raise that you believe would be fair, and be ready to negotiate.

Requests for Employment Reference

Sometimes it is necessary to write letters **requesting employment references.** At times, you will be requesting that the letter of reference be written to a particular potential employer. At other times, you may ask for a letter addressed to you or "to whom it may concern." You can carry these letters as part of your portfolio, or you can forward copies to interested persons. If the letter is not addressed to a specific individual or firm, you may leave copies with interviewers.

Your request for a reference letter should be brief, polite, and direct. It is an "A" letter, in which you immediately state the purpose of the letter, closing on a friendly tone of gratitude. It should follow these guidelines:

State that you would like a letter of reference and give the particular reason for your request.

Explain how you want the letter addressed. If you want it sent to a particular person, give that person's first name or initials so that a letter can be addressed to him or her properly. Be sure to give the complete address, including city, state, and ZIP Code, even if it is to be addressed to the city in which you are living.

List specifically the type of information you would like included in your letter, such as the dates of employment and the nature of your duties. To facilitate checking the records, furnish approximate dates of employment. It is also helpful if you mention specific responsibilities you had that you wish mentioned in the letter, to jog the memory of the person answering.

Include any appropriate personal comments to help close the letter on an "up" note.

In some manner, close with an expression of appreciation for this favor.

A letter requesting a reference might read:

Dear Mr. Cooper:

    I would appreciate it very much if you could write a letter of reference to help me obtain a position with Hostetter Manufacturing Company.

    The position I am seeking with Hostetter is in the accounting department, and I would be handling all accounts receivable. The letter should be addressed

Mr. T. Hee, Personnel Manager
Hostetter Manufacturing Company
Suite 1301, Majors Towers
Philadelphia, Pennsylvania 00000

My employment with you, as you may recall, was during the summers of 19XX and 19XX. During this time I posted all accounts receivable and accounts payable and also performed general filing and typing duties.

    I enjoyed working for you, Mr. Cooper, and this is part of the reason I am seeking full-time work in an accounting position. Also, the money surely helped me in completing my education.

    If you would write a letter verifying my employment with you, I would be very grateful.

                                Sincerely,

Letters of Reference

Standard Information

Letters of reference need planning so that they will be brief, honest, specific, and sincere. It is rarely necessary to write a negative letter in this situation. A person will usually not list you as a reference unless you can be expected to give a good recommendation. Today especially, people must be acutely aware of the possibility of legal action that might be taken to elicit proof of any negative statements that are made.

This letter should cover the points requested by the job applicant, and should also include other comments you would like to make. The major consideration in preparing this letter is that it should sound sincere.

This information is usually desired in an employment reference letter: dates of employment, nature of duties, manner in which the employee performed the work, special abilities of the employee that would be of interest to an employer, and personality traits of a positive nature, such as neatness, drive, imagination, punctuality, resourcefulness, and dependability.

The following letters are examples of favorable employment references. Any such letters can be fleshed out to include more favorable comments.

To Whom It May Concern

I gladly recommend _____ as a potential employee.

_____ has been in my classes for two semesters and has proven himself to be a dependable, hard-working student. He is in the upper quarter of the class. Also, he is pleasant to know and would be an agreeable person to have as an employee.

Sincerely,

Dear Ms. Sussman:

I am writing to recommend that you favorably consider Debbie Jacobsen for employment in your firm. She has been a completely satisfactory part-time employee here at Ross hardware for nearly two years.

Debbie is an efficient, competent worker who gets along well with fellow employees and customers. Her reliability and punctuality are excellent, and we can count on having her here to get our work completed on time.

Her duties here consist of greeting customers in person and on the telephone, typing, and other secretarial activities. Debbie willingly accepts assignments under time pressure and produces excellent work on time. We will certainly miss her fine work and also her pleasant personality.

Cordially,

Sometimes it is necessary to dismiss an employee for reasons not related to the employee or the job performance, such as when there is a cutback in work. At such times, it can be helpful to furnish any affected employee with a letter of reference explaining the reason for the termination. Such a letter might read as follows:

To Whom It May Concern:

Recently, due to a major cutback in government spending in our region, many people have moved out and we have been forced to reduce our sales staff.

One of the people affected was Mr. Eric G. Cain, who was one of our newest employees. During his year in our employment, Mr. Cain was a very effective salesman who not only handled old accounts well but succeeded in bringing in more than his share of new customers.

Mr. Cain is an honest, reliable employee who gained the respect and friendship of all those who worked with him. We are sorry that we are unable to retain him. We would be happy to recommend him for another position.

We will be glad to furnish additional recommendations for him by telephone or letter.

Sincerely,

Legal Guidelines in Letters of Reference

If you do have reservations about making a full recommendation, you might consider that everyone deserves another chance and that anyone can improve. Emphasize positive attributes.

However, when asked to recommend a truly poor worker, you should be selective and not write a letter for that person. In this way you prevent such workers from being able to jump from job to job.

In writing potentially negative letters of reference, be sure to follow these legal guidelines.

1. Direct any communication only to a person who has specific need for it.

2. Do not volunteer any information. Answer only the questions asked.

3. Provide only reference data that relates to the job and job performance.

4. Document any potentially negative information. "Three workers asked not to be placed on shift with Ms. _____." "Mr. _____ did not attend required re-training courses."

5. To avoid legal entanglements if your opinion is asked, instead of making a negative comment you might "damn with faint praise."

6. "Would you rehire this person?" is a trap question. Don't fall in the trap. Watch any negative.

7. Do not answer any "off the record" questions.

8. State that the information you are providing is confidential and should be treated as such. To avoid the appearance that you are providing information voluntarily, explain that the letter is "in answer to your request and is to be used for professional purposes only."

Letter Requesting Permission to Use Name as Reference

A letter requesting to use a person's name as a reference should be short, with as little or as much detail as is needed. Following is a letter sent to a former instructor:

Dear Mrs. Hunter:

I am applying for a word processing position that is now open at Myers Corporation.

Since I was a student in your word processing program in 19XX and received excellent practical instruction on the operation of many different machines, I would like to use your name as a reference.

I have enclosed a self-addressed envelope for your reply.

Cordially,

Resignations

A heavy record of frequent job-hopping does not look good to a potential employer. Yet occasionally you may find it necessary or desirable to make a change in employment. If you can make your **resignation** in person, this method is preferred, with the natural discussion and feedback that are possible. For your own good, you should approach this important interview with an extremely positive mental attitude. Do not give vent to any grievances you have unless you feel that they can be interpreted as constructive criticism. When the employer is later contacted for a job reference for you, that person's most vivid recollection may relate to this resignation interview.

An employment resignation may bring forth a counterproposal so attractive that you may decide to remain in your current employment. Do not let this be the primary reason for submitting your resignation, however, because your plan might backfire and you might find yourself out on the street sooner than expected.

Sometimes it is necessary to resign by letter. This communication should be patterned as a "B" letter, a negative message. You can assume that it will be necessary to replace you and that your employer will regret losing you and the training you have received in the organization. The "B" letter of resignation should have three parts:

Opening: neutral, pleasant statement probably relating to experience with the firm.

Middle: clear statement or resignation, with reasons given in positive terms.

Closing: "up" tone, making positive statements about work, firm, and employees. Offer to train replacement; if it is not presumptuous, suggest a replacement; express appreciation for employment with firm.

Two letters of resignation follow:

Dear Mr. Brando:

Neutral, pleasant →	For the past four years I have enjoyed my work with Brando Brothers and have also enjoyed the association with the many fine employees here.
Lead into negative →	Recently, however, I was offered the position of Junior Management Consultant with Farrell-Lynch, Inc., and I feel that this larger firm can offer me considerable chance for advancement.
Negative (resignation) →	I would like to resign the end of this month. I believe that this will give you time to find my replacement.
Pleasant closing →	I do thank you personally, Mr. Brando, for a pleasant association with your firm.

Sincerely,

Dear Mr. Plunkett:

Neutral, pleasant →	When we came to Burlington on a skiing vacation, we did not expect that we would try to make it our permanent home. However, we like Burlington so
Lead into negative →	well that my husband interviewed for a position. As a result, he will be a reporter and assistant editor on the local newspaper staff, and I will be a part-
Negative (resignation) →	time legal secretary while I learn the work of a woman who will retire in a few months.
	As this letter should reach you two weeks before the end of my vacation, I hope that this will give you time to find my replacement.
	I am truly sorry to leave the employ of Fargo Wells, because I have enjoyed my work there and certainly like all the people with whom I worked. Please give my best wishes to the other members of the firm, and also to Mrs. Plunkett.
Pleasant looking to future →	I surely appreciate the training I received in the Legal Department, Mr. Plunkett, and I wish you continued success with Fargo Wells.

Cordially,

Employment Resume Checkpoints

1. Identify your reader(s) and write at that level.

2. Appearance:
   a. Is it short?
   b. Is it neat, clean, and attractive?

    c. Is it uncrowded, with margins of at least 1 1/4 inches?

    d. Is there at least one blank line between sections?

3. Good will tone:

    a. Is material set out courteously according to interests of employer?

    b. Minimize use of *I, me, my,* and *mine.*

4. Clear and complete message:

    a. Have you set out information concisely under appropriate headings?

    b. Are education and employment listed with most recent or current experience first?

    c. If resume is overlong, reread it to eliminate information least helpful in securing the position.

5. Writing improvement points: Recheck for all writing improvement points, especially correct grammar and spelling.

Employment Application Letter Checkpoints

1. Identify your reader(s) and write at that level.

2. Appearance?

3. Good will:

    a. Have you shown interest in and/or knowledge of the firm?

    b. Have you tried to point your background toward needs of the potential employer?

    c. Minimize use of *I, me, my,* and *mine.*

4. Clear and complete message: Follow the AIDA plan.

    a. Attention: Focus on the firm or your special background.

    b. Interest and desire buildup: What especially qualifies you for the position that will make them *interested* in you and should make them *desire* to hire you?

    c. Action: Is the closing designed to move the reader to action?

5. Writing improvement points: Check for all writing improvement points, especially grammar and spelling.

Writing Assignments

1. Make up an employment resumé and application letter that you might use either (a) at the completion of your college work this year, or (b) at the completion of your college work some time in the future. If you wish, you may use your imagination for details. Try to make the assignment something that will eventually be useful for you.

2. Write a letter requesting an employment reference for the job for which you are applying in assignment 1. If you are currently employed, write a letter that you might actually use. If you are not employed, use an imaginary situation.

3. Write a letter supposedly to an instructor, asking to use his or her name as a reference on an employment application.

4. You have a small accounting firm and have employed a student part time as receptionist and typist. She has also done some basic bookkeeping for you. Since she worked for you, she has received a B.S. degree in accounting and has applied for full-time work as a junior accountant. Write her a letter of reference for this position.

5. It is early Friday evening. This morning you were interviewed for a position with Rockefeller Corporation, 1111 Vine Street, Your Town, Your State (with ZIP code). Your interviewer was John Jacob Astor, Director of Personnel. You want to have a let-

ter on his desk Monday morning. Write Mr. Astor thanking him for the interview. Make up an explanation about why you are now more than ever interested in becoming a member of the staff of Rockefeller.

6. A week ago you applied for a position that you would really like to obtain, and you have had no response. Write a follow-up letter to the person who interviewed you and thank her for her time in granting you the interview. Also inform her of your desire to obtain the position, and ask if you could come in again to discuss the possibility of getting the job.

7. Write a letter of reference for yourself that you would like to have prepared for you some time in the future when you have completed the education and training for the position you eventually wish to hold. (Believe it or not, this situation frequently happens when an employee is doing completely satisfactory work but is seeking a higher position.) Of course for this assignment, you will have to fictionalize some details of matters that in your background have not yet been completed.

Chapter 13   *Writing Improvement Exercise*

Using a Thesaurus to Improve Your Vocabulary

Winston Churchill, a master in the use of the English language, said, "Short words are best, and the old words when short are best of all." Our study of the Fog Index in Chapter 16 supports this idea by encouraging the use of a long word only when a short word will not do.

At the same time, our study here on how to use a thesaurus will demonstrate three distinct advantages of finding and using longer words when they are needed. First, synonyms from a thesaurus will improve your vocabulary by showing a choice of words of specific meaning to help make your speaking and writing clear and precise. As you will see from the following examples and from your own homework for this exercise, so-called synonyms do not have exactly the same specific meaning. It is up to you to choose the best word for your own purpose, referring to a dictionary if necessary. If English is your second language, you must be especially sure that any synonym you choose is correct for the meaning you want.

Second, learning to find and use synonyms from a thesaurus or dictionary will help you avoid overuse of the same common words or terms. Third and last, enlarging your vocabulary with a command of specific words when needed improves your speaking and writing, marking you as a better-educated person.

A thesaurus also contains a limited number of antonyms for most words. This information, of course, can be helpful at times.

There are a few different thesauruses (or thesauri) on the market today. The old standby—*Roget's International Thesaurus,* published by Thomas Y. Crowell Company—is widely used and respected. Although not providing as many choices as the larger hardcover books, pocket-size paperback editions provide a good help.

Following are selections from Charlton Laird's reference book, *Webster's New World Thesaurus* (New York: Simon and Schuster, 1971):

believe, *v.* 1. [To accept as true]—*Syn.* accept, hold, think, conclude, have faith, be convinced, be certain of, deem, understand, regard, take at one's word, consider, affirm, be of the opinion, postulate, opine, conceive, give credence to, have no doubt, rest assured, swear by, take one's word for, cherish a belief, keep the faith, be credulous, entertain *or* nurture a belief.[4]— *Ant.* doubt, deny, suspect.

2. [To assume]—*Syn. suppose, guess, gather; see* **assume** 1.

sweet, *modifier.* 1. [Sweet in taste]—*Syn.* toothsome, sugary, luscious, candied, sweet as honey, sweet as sugar, like honey, like sugar, honeyed, saccharine, cloying, like nectar, delicious; see also **rich** 4.—*Ant.* sour, bitter, sharp.

2. [Sweet in disposition]—*Syn.* agreeable, pleasing, engaging, winning, delightful, patient, reasonable, gentle, kind, generous, unselfish, sweet-tempered, even-tempered, good-humored, considerate, thoughtful, companionable; see also **friendly** 1.—*Ant.* selfish, repulsive, inconsiderate.

3. [Not salt]—*Syn.* fresh, unsalted, uncured, unseasoned, freshened.—*Ant.* salty, pickled, briny.

4. [Dear]—*Syn.* sympathetic, loving, winsome; see **beloved**.

hungry, *modifier.*—*Syn.* starved, famished, craving, ravenous, desirous, hankering, unsatisfied, unfilled, starving, edacious, insatiate, voracious, of keen appetite, famishing, half-starved, hungered, ravening, omnivorous, carnivorous, supperless, greedy as a hog, dinnerless, piggish, hoggish, peckish, half-famished; on an empty stomach; hungry as a wolf, empty; see also **greedy** 2.—*Ant.* satisfied, full fed.

---

[4]See dictionary for usage.

Chapter 13 *Writing Improvement Worksheet*

Using a Thesaurus to Improve Your Vocabulary

Using a thesaurus for reference, find at least ten synonyms for each of the following words:

1. awful _____

_____

_____

2. friend _____

_____

_____

3. happy _____

_____

_____

4. like (verb) _____

_____

_____

5. long (modifier) _____

_____

_____

6. stupid _____

_____

_____

7. thing _____

_____

_____

8. neat _____

_____

_____

Chapter 13   Writing Improvement Worksheet (*Continued*)

9. weird _____

   _____

   _____

10. wonderful _____

    _____

    _____

REVIEW AND DISCUSSION

Chapter 13 *Employment Resumés and Application Letters*

Give brief answers.

1. Today's typical employment application letter consists of two parts. What are they?

_____

_____

2. What does "white space" mean in relation to written or printed communications?

_____

3. What are the main sections of an employment resumé or data sheet?

_____

_____

4. What should be included in the heading of the resumé?

_____

_____

5. If you took a course titled, "Speech 118: Public Address," how would you list it on a resumé?

_____

6. In what order should educational and employment background be presented on a resumé?

_____

7. Name three specific types of information you should list about any employment.

_____

_____

_____

8. Name five qualities that could be considered for inclusion under "Special Qualifications."

_____

_____

_____

Chapter 13   Employment Resumés and Application Letters (*Continued*)

9. Why might it be to your advantage to give some details under a "Personal" heading?

   _____

   _____

10. On a resumé it is (not acceptable, acceptable, acceptable and often recommended) that you give information that by law cannot be asked by a potential employer. Under-line the best answer.

11. Why are references usually listed last? _____

    _____

12. Whose names can you list as references if you have had no previous employment?

    _____

    _____

13. What pattern should the application letter follow?

    _____

14. What can be the source of information for your letter of application?

    _____

15. What is the best tone for a letter of application? (Formal; natural; casual)

16. How should a letter of application be signed?

    _____

17. In planning ahead for a job interview, there are two areas in which you should pre-pare. Name them.

    _____

18. The text lists eight steps to help carry you well into and through your interview. List them.

    _____

    _____

    _____

    _____

19. Is a record of frequent job-hopping usually in your favor in seeking employment? Why, or why not?

    _____

    _____

20. Why is it advisable to follow up an employment application when you have had no response?

    _____

    _____

21, 22, 23, 24, 25. Check a thesaurus and list at least five synonyms for each of these words:

21. appreciate _____

_____

22. lazy _____

_____

23. fantastic _____

_____

24. good (modifier) _____

_____

25. funny _____

_____

CHAPTER 14
Letters You Don't Have to Write, But Should

> *I will pay more for the ability to deal with people than any other ability in the world.*
> John D. Rockefeller, U.S. industrialist and philanthropist, 1839–1937

It is difficult to set a dollar value on that intangible asset of a business, **good will.** But when a business is sold, the new owners will pay money for the privilege of operating the business under the old name if that name has a favorable reputation. At such a time, an estimate of a reasonable value is placed on this asset, and the value of good will is included in the selling price as part of the cost of taking over the business. The new owners can then use the name to their own advantage.

In the crush of making money, business people should not concentrate so much on other important aspects of business that they overlook the value of creating and maintaining good will among present, past, and potential customers and among employees. Although this text cautions against writing unnecessary letters, there are times when a personal message, although not really necessary, would be welcomed and should be written. Customers usually receive only two types of communications from a business: either those trying to sell goods and services or those trying to collect money. Other types of communications are rare and are therefore appreciated.

Much of business has become so large and impersonal that sometimes we do not show the thoughtful personal consideration of people that we should. One top executive of a large corporation says he spends a high percentage of his time writing "letters you don't have to write, but *should.*"

Personal Communications within an Organization

Besides pleasing employees, which is exceedingly important, showing good will to them helps a business prosper because employees, of course, have much to do with the successful operation of any business. Lines of communication can be kept open between employer and employee by the judicious writing of personal letters or notes that show an interest in the other's well-being. An occasional **letter from an employer to an employee** noting a special event would undoubtedly be well received.

An occasional letter from an **employee to an employer** may also indeed be welcome. Even in a large business this act gives a favorable impression to an employer who is aware that it is impossible to become well acquainted with all employees. A letter might be written to compliment an employer on such an occasion as an honor received, a promotion, a speech, or some other notable personal event in his or her life or in the life of a member of the family. After all, the boss, too, is a human being! This letter should not be too effusive—just short and clear.

Types of Special Good Will Letters

Remember—customers are your most priceless possession. Next best are the customers who bought from you in the past but have stopped.

Be aware that **special good will letters—courtesy letters**—are appropriate not only for many business situations but also for professional and personal contacts. These are letters you don't have to write, but should.

Thank You Letters and Other Letters of Appreciation

Thank you letters and other **letters of appreciation** are probably the most common type of special good will letters written in business. These letters can be sent to show appreciation for such things as doing business with the firm, completing payments on an installment account, paying open accounts on time, performing work beyond regular duties, doing favors, or doing anything else that is especially appreciated.

Here are some typical letters in this category:

Letter 1

On behalf of the management and the entire staff of the Queen Mary Restaurants, we would like to thank you for affording us the pleasure of hosting your recent dinner.

It was a pleasure working with you, and whenever we can be of further assistance to you in any way, do not hesitate to contact us.

Thank you again, and we shall look forward to serving you again in the near future.

Letter 2

Dear Friend and Good Customer:

There's no use taking a whole page to tell you what I want to say, so I'll just skip down to here and say it.

Your account is really appreciated. Anytime I can be of assistance to you, please let me know.

Letter 3

Thank you for opening a new account with Bank of South America. It is a pleasure to serve you, and we look forward to a long and cordial relationship.

If at any time we can assist you in any of your other banking needs, please do not hesitate to call upon me.

Letter 4

Dear Friends:

Today I am back at work feeling better than ever, and I can tell you it's a good feeling. Health is a big blessing. No one knows more than I how fortunate I am.

Having friends is another big blessing, and I want each of you to know how grateful I am for your prayers and good wishes. I received so many cards and get-well messages it would be impossible to acknowledge them all, so I am taking this means to thank you and tell you how much I appreciate your thinking of me.

There has never been any doubt in my mind that _____ is the greatest family in the world—always concerned and caring for its own. We have excellent benefits, but you have shown me that our concern for one another is the greatest benefit of all—and that's a benefit that money can't buy. I am truly grateful.

It's good to be back!

Sincerely,

[Personal note to individual recipient.]
P.S. Thanks for your nice letter. I appreciated hearing from you.

Letter 5

Dear Mr. and Mrs. Hansen:

This is just a short note to let you know I very much appreciate the concern you expressed to me in Mrs. Hansen's letter of July 12. This has been a tragedy for the family, and we sincerely appreciate all the support we have received from family and friends.

Thank you for your thoughts.

Sincerely,

Letters of Congratulations

Letters of **congratulations** are some of the more common good will messages. They are sent for reasons like promotion, anniversary (personal or business), birthday, wedding, length of service, civic honor, published writing, research, or an exceptionally fine piece of work.

Here are typical congratulation letters:

Letter 1

Congratulations on moving into the new headquarters of your bank. The building is very attractive, and it should be a pleasure to do business with you there. It is really a fine addition to our community.

I will expect to call on you one of the first days the building is open for business.

Letter 2

Dear John,

Well, it really doesn't seem as if it was fifteen years ago that I interviewed you for your first position with Bankers Trust and Company. But it surely was, and I have enjoyed watching you grow with the organization, assuming different new duties and performing them well.

It will be my pleasure to be among those honoring you at the annual employee awards dinner-dance.

I just wanted to send you a note of congratulations and say how much I personally appreciate your work with us.

Letter 3

It has just been brought to my attention that last Friday evening you received the Silver Beaver Award in honor of your active participation as a leader in the Boy Scouts of America for the past fifteen years.

I am sure your work with the Scouts has not only been of much value to the boys, but also been gratifying to you. I am also gratified to have such a person as a member of our staff.

I certainly congratulate you on receiving this distinction, and wish you continued success and enjoyment in your work in our community.

Letter 4

Congratulations on your daughter's graduation. You must be very proud of her. Congratulations to her—and also to her parents!

Letters of Welcome

People always like to know that they are **welcome** as customers, as members of a group, as members of a community, or as new employees.

Here are some example letters of welcome:

Letter 1

Mr. Tom Padia, the president of our local bank, just informed me that you have recently moved into our community. I wish to welcome you here. Big Springs has much to offer its residents, and the friendliness of our people is just one of its attributes.

I hope you enjoy living among us, and if I may be of service to you in establishing your business, please let me know.

Letter 2

We are pleased to welcome you as a member of the Brandywine Museum of Art and to send you your official membership card.

Over the coming year, through the monthly calendar, you will be kept informed of special exhibitions and other events of particular interest to members.

On behalf of the Trustees, the staff, and the more than 2,000 members of the Museum, I extend warm thanks for your support and a firm hope that you will find your personal association with the Museum an enriching and stimulating one.

Letters of Concern

Letters of **personal concern** might be appropriately written on many different types of occasions, such as illness or injury, closing of a business, inactivity of an account, or damage of goods. The tone of this letter varies with the occasion and the relationship between the individuals involved. Five such letters are given here:

Letter 1

I just became aware of your recent operation through a communication from Ms. Angelo.

My initial thought was to contact your wife to inquire of your condition, but I realized such a contact from a person she hardly knows would scarcely be appreciated. I did call your secretary and was advised that your condition is improving splendidly and that you will probably be able to return to the office within the next two or three weeks. Needless to say, this assurance caused me much relief.

While I realize the unlikely need, if there is any way I may be of service to you personally, I would consider it an honor to accept.

It is my sincere hope that when you receive this letter you are feeling your old self again.

Letter 2

Well Lou!

We all knew you wanted to watch the World Series this week, but breaking your leg so you could do it was a bit much!

Seriously, I am sorry that you had an accident, and it certainly can't be fun. But we are pleased to hear that you are well on the mend.

We all miss you around here, and hope to see you back soon.

Best wishes,

Letter 3

WE'VE MISSED YOU—

When we closed our books today, we found that your account has not been used for some time. Naturally, we are greatly concerned, because we value each of our patrons and miss them when they fail to visit us regularly.

Right now we are showing so many lovely new fashions at affordable prices that we are sure you will agree it's a good time for you to use your account again.

We trust that you will find it convenient to call on us soon. Just use your charge card. Your account is ready and waiting.

Letter 4

Dear Dr. Albanese:

Tom and I are very grateful that Bob and Julie Ede recently referred you to us as our dentist. We surely appreciate the professional help you and your staff are giving to both of us.

Yesterday Julie told me that the young Albanese woman who recently was the innocent victim of that shooting is your cousin.

Tom and I both express our regret that the incident occurred, and we want you to know of our concern for you and all your family.

Best personal wishes,

Letter 5

We were very sorry to learn of the flood that did so much damage to your warehouse. We hope that our man there, Martin Francis, arrived in time to be of some help to you.

Do be assured that any offer of assistance he makes to you is authorized by our entire organization.

We'll be happy to see you continue your operations as soon as possible.

Letter 6

The good will of old friends is of great value to us. And when we do not hear from our friends for a long time, it causes us concern. Because your last order was in July 19XX, we can't help wondering if our services to you may have faltered in some way unknown to us.

If it is simply that you haven't had the need of our services lately, you will be glad to know, I'm sure, that we have recently increased our capacity with additional equipment, incorporated a number of new features, and streamlined systems in our plant, which other customers are already finding most profitable.

Your good will and friendship are worth much to us, and we want to serve you well. May we look forward to the pleasure of hearing from you again soon?

Sincerely,

Letters of Condolence

At a time of bereavement, a person appreciates getting a card, but a personal letter of **condolence** from a friend or a business associate is appreciated even more. Because these letters are somewhat difficult to write, and also because they come at a time of deep emotional disturbance, they are probably more welcome than others.

There are certain guidelines that will help you compose such a letter. First, avoid long recitations of details that could sadden the reader. Avoid reference to anguish, loss, or suffering, and perhaps try to promote the thought that a person's good influence continues in the hearts and minds of those who knew him or her. You should not write of people's religious beliefs unless you are very close and fully understand their feelings. This is not the time to try to promote your own religious values.

A short message is very acceptable. The most important thing is that you took the time and effort to send the letter. Here are letters you might follow as examples:

Letter 1

I was deeply saddened by the sudden loss of my good friend, Eugene.

He was a strong and effective leader who had accomplished much, both in his business and community life. We will all certainly miss him.

I send my personal concern to you, Beth, and to your children.

Letter 2

I just learned that you lost your mother last week and want to add my personal concern to those from your many other friends.

We all remember your mother as a friend of everyone—she left a good influence on those who knew her.

I will be sure to call on you the next time I am in town.

Seasonal Greetings

Many businesses send holiday cards and letters, mostly end-of-the-year or New Year greetings. Businesses should avoid religious references, concentrating instead on such phrases as "Season's Greetings," and "Happy Holidays." These can take any form, from a printed card to a personally written letter. This message should avoid maudlin sentimentality but should sound sincere.

Longhand Correspondence

There is still a place in business for **longhand correspondence**, although this form should rarely be used. But when someone does you a particular favor or supports a cause in which you have a personal interest, you might send off a brief longhand note. The fact that you took the extra time and attention to prepare this communication will not go unnoticed.

> Dear Ms. Long:
>
> Thank you very much for your letter of March 19 and the thoughts expressed therein.
>
> It is always a pleasure to have interested students visit my courtroom, especially when their instructor has prepared the class well, as you obviously had. I was happy to have had a little time to visit with them between cases. This luxury is not always available.
>
> Again, my deepest appreciation for your kind remarks. Come again!
>
> Most sincerely,

FIGURE 14.1
Longhand letter from a Superior Court judge.

Figure 14.1 is a copy of a longhand letter written by a Superior Court judge to a college instructor who had taken her class to visit his courtroom. Writing the letter took some of his valued time, but it does make a good impression.

Communicating with Public Officials[1]

We can make this truly a government "of the people, by the people, and for the people" by communicating frequently with our elected officials. How? By letter, telegram, phone, and personal visit.

Letters

Letters are probably the most effective means in most cases. A congressman recently stated that "letters are one of the best gauges of public opinion on issues that a busy

[1]Courtesy of Lois M. Plowman, Professor of Business Communications, Cerritos College.

member can have during a decision making period. While this is time-consuming to the citizen, it is valuable to the representative—and therefore, I encourage letters and welcome them."

A senator said, "...citizens concerned about specific legislation should make their views known before the legislation is acted upon in Congress." This is important at *any* level of government.

Here are some guidelines for writing letters to our elected officials:

1. *Identify yourself.* State not only your name and address, but also which of your life roles you are representing. For example, you are requesting action as a businessman (give kind), parent, teacher, student, doctor, lawyer, officer of some organization, etc.

2. *Specify your concern.* If it is in regard to a bill, state the number and author if possible.

3. *Write briefly.* It is preferred that you limit your letter to one page. Give reasons for your position.

4. *Give facts.* Back your reasons for your position with facts, if you have them.

5. *Be courteous.* Show appreciation for the public servant's efforts. In no way be threatening.

6. *Cover one issue in one letter.* If you have concerns about unrelated items, write a separate letter for each issue. In other words, if you are writing a letter about legislation regarding oil rights, this same letter should not include your concern about sending troops to Angola. Instead, write two letters.

7. *The letter should be original with you.* There is strong aversion to form letters. One congressman has said that more attention is given to a handwritten letter than to other kinds of letters. Congressmen know that it is fairly easy to get people to sign a form letter that they may not really understand or that may not truly reflect their views.

8. *There should be only one signature to a letter.*

9. *Use the correct name and spelling of the official being addressed.* You can get help on this from the following sources:
   a. Your local library (college or city). Ask the librarian over the telephone or visit the library.
   b. The local office of the official involved. Look in the telephone directory under the unit of government involved. For example, if you live in Jefferson County and it is a county matter, look under "Jefferson"; look under "United States" for a federal office; under the state's name for a state office.
   c. The city clerk in your city hall.
   d. The registrar of voters in your county or city.
   e. The League of Women Voters.

10. *Where to write:*
   a. *National affairs:*
      The President of the United States: The President, The White House, Washington, D.C. 20500. Or The Honorable _____, President of the United States, The White House, Washington, D.C. 20500.
      U.S. Senators: United States Senate, Washington, D.C. 20510
      U.S. Representatives: United States House of Representatives, Washington, D.C. 20515.
   b. *State affairs:* State Capitol Building, name of your capital, state, ZIP code.
   c. *Local affairs:* Mayor _____ or Councilman or Councilwoman _____ c/o City Hall, name of your city, state, ZIP code.

Here is an example of a letter one might send to a member of the House of Representatives:

The Honorable Congressman _____
House of Representatives
Washington, D.C. 20515

My dear Sir:

I ask that you oppose HR 2556, sponsored by Mr. Charles Wilson. This bill would close census records, which are now open, after they are 75 years old or older. This bill would not only keep them closed to the public but would also close them even to genealogists and historians.

I believe that the history of our country should be preserved so we can study events of the past to learn from them, thus avoiding mistakes of other times in the present and also benefitting from the solutions of problems of other times. This is the way we make progress.

It is important that every source of information be available so that a true picture of events can be made. How else can history be of value? Let us not close any sources! "And ye shall know the truth, and the truth shall make you free."

Yours respectfully, [Other appropriate closings are, "Sincerely yours," "Very truly yours," etc.]
Mrs. Lois M. Plowman

The federal government does want the average citizen to keep in touch, so much so that it has made available a free pamphlet, which comes out monthly, titled, "How to Keep in Touch with the U.S. Government." You can get on the mailing list by writing to:

Superintendent of Documents
Government Printing Office
Washington, D.C. 20402

Telegrams

Western Union will send a Public Opinion Message to any elected state or Federal official for a reasonable reduced rate. This message can be telephoned in and you will be billed on your phone bill.

Mailgrams

Also at a reasonable rate, Western Union will send a Mailgram electronically to a post office near any addressee. Printed on the distinctive blue and white Mailgram letterhead with envelope, the message will be delivered in the next regular mail, usually the next day, or sometimes the day it is sent.

Writing Assignments

1. You own a printshop. Write a letter of concern to clients who have not done business with you in the past year. Let them know of the improvements in your shop, and tell them that you would like to do more work for them.

2. Mark Janowicz has just completed payments on his 19XX Volkswagen sedan, financed by your agency. Write Mr. Janowicz a brief letter complimenting him on the completion of his contract and the regular manner in which he made his payments.

3. The daughter of one of your employees, Mrs. Bonnie E. Brown, has just been chosen as commencement speaker at the Spring 19XX graduation exercises at the local college. Write a note of congratulations to Mrs. Brown.

4. Write a letter to Tom Padia for him and other members of the accounting division baseball team, which, although not placing as champions, fielded a team once a week for the entire summer season.

5. Write a letter thanking the members of the department where you work for the wedding gift they combined funds to purchase for you and your new bride or groom. Tell them to what use the gift is being put.

6. Prepare a letter to be sent to all employees thanking them for the extra effort they expended during a recent changeover to a central dictation system and for their patience in learning how to work with the new equipment. Mention benefits to them that should result from this changeover.

7. Write a letter that might go to a fellow employee who is in the hospital recovering from surgery.

8. John James, supervisor of your department, has recently lost his mother. Mr. James is out of the state attending services for his mother and taking care of her legal and business matters. Write him a brief letter of condolence.

9. You are manager of the local Volvo agency and have decided to have a special letter printed to send to all recent customers. Make up this letter.

10. As a member of the Lakeside Junior Chamber of Commerce, write a letter of thanks to Ted Snyder, Director of Community Relations, for being the main speaker at the recent meeting of the group, held at the Lakeside Country Club.

11. Write a letter to a public official expressing your concern about a matter in which that person might have some influence. If you actually plan to send the letter, make a note of this information and attach it to your letter so that the instructor will not place grading information on it. You should follow the pattern for a routine information letter, a negative letter, or a selling letter, according to your message. Your letter will be graded according to how well it follows the information contained earlier in this exercise.

12. Write a letter to a public official expressing your appreciation for some action taken by that official.

Chapter 14 *Writing Improvement Exercise*

Misplaced Modifiers

All the sentences in this exercise were actually found in previously printed material.

A modifier should be placed to show clearly what it describes or modifies. If there is confusion about what is being modified, the meaning is usually made clearer by moving the modifier closer to the word being described. Or for clarity, it may be necessary to rephrase the entire sentence.

A modifier may be a word, a phrase, or a clause. Here are examples of unclear modifying with revisions for clearer meaning:

> Original   The cowboy roped the calf *on the palomino pony.*
>
> Improved   The cowboy *on the palomino pony* roped the calf.

Original   A university student was convicted of grand theft *just 24 hours after his trial went to the jury.*

Improved   *Just 24 hours after his trial went to the jury,* a university student was convicted of grant theft.

Original   One acre overlooking a waterfall for an unusual buyer, *shaped triangular.*

Improved   For an unusual buyer: *One triangular-shaped* acre overlooking a waterfall.

Original   That is the toughest decision *almost* that we have made.

Improved   That is *almost* the toughest decision that we have made.

Original   He *only* sang for his family.

Improved   He sang *only* for his family.

Original   After hanging on the bulletin board for two weeks, the mail clerk removed the announcement.

Improved   After the announcement had hung on the bulletin board for two weeks, the mail clerk removed it.

Chapter 14 *Writing Improvement Worksheet*

Misplaced Modifiers

Rewrite these sentences to show clearly what is being modified by the italicized modifiers.

1. During the campaign I *nearly* called a thousand people. _____
_____

2. She has *only* memorized the first scene. _____
_____

3. The crash victims needed medics to take care of them *badly*. _____
_____
_____

4. I finished early because the foreman *only* told me to clean this room. _____
_____
_____

5. He told me what to do *with a smile*. _____
_____

6. His book came out after retirement *in a new edition*. _____
_____
_____

7. They announced that they planned to enlarge the warehouse *at the board meeting*.
_____
_____

8. She lifted a photograph *from a grimy shelf that also held engine parts* and brushed off the dust. _____
_____

9. The trainer led the lion *cracking a whip*. _____
_____

10. I *scarcely* know a dozen members of the group. _____
_____

11. We have published a booklet about our stocks and bonds, *which we will send upon request.* _____

_____

_____

12. What is the company policy on correcting shipping errors *that they want us to follow?*

_____

_____

_____

13. The supervisor checked the week's work order and overtime schedule *with a frown.*

_____

_____

14. I *only* asked for one copy. _____

15. The young lady will lead the elephant *dressed in a sequined bikini.* _____

_____

_____

16. *Lying underneath the couch,* Julie found the letter. _____

_____

_____

17. *Running down a winding path,* the haunted house was discovered by Benji. _____

_____

18. This is the domestic crisis center for battered wives *that we helped get started last year.*

_____

_____

19. The teacher said that a colleague of hers was hospitalized *at school* for emergency surgery. _____

_____

_____

20. Mr. Bampkins said he has discussed filling the drainage ditch *with his partners.*

_____

_____

REVIEW AND DISCUSSION

Chapter 14 *Letters You Don't Have to Write, but Should*

1. What is "good will" in business?

   _____

   _____

2. Is a dollar amount ever placed on the value of business good will? Explain.

   _____

   _____

3. What are the two types of communications that customers usually receive from a business?

   _____

4. Although mails and desks are frequently overcrowded with communications, why should we occasionally take time to write the "letters you don't have to write, but *should*"?

   _____

   _____

5. Name some occasions that might prompt an employer to write a special good will letter to an employee.

   _____

   _____

6. Is it ever proper for an employee to write a good will letter to his employer? Explain.

   _____

   _____

   _____

7. Name five occasions for which a thank you letter might be written.

   _____

   _____

   _____

Chapter 14 Letters You Don't Have to Write, but Should (*Continued*)

8. Name five occasions for which a letter of congratulations might be written.

_____

_____

_____

9. Give guidelines to help someone write a letter of condolence.

_____

_____

_____

10. Is longhand correspondence ever acceptable in today's business? Explain.

_____

_____

11. Do you believe public officials pay attention to messages they receive from their constituents? _____

12. If you want to write to the same official about two different matters, how many letters should you write? _____

13, 14, 15. Rewrite these sentences to show the actual meaning more clearly.

13. They supposedly supplied Hughes, who died while enroute to Houston from Acapulco, with codein. _____

_____

14. Mr. Simpkins has a wife and three children, all under four.

_____

_____

15. Did the man have a mustache that got out of the car? _____

_____

CHAPTER 15
Planning the Business Report or the Term Paper

> *Once begun, half done.*
> *Old proverb*

Advantages to the Student, Job Applicant, and Employee

The advantages to the student in learning how to write effective reports or term papers are in three chief areas: (1) as a student, (2) as a job applicant, and (3) as an employee.

For the Student

Colleges are placing more emphasis on writing courses because employers emphasize business's need for writers and because people in technical, scientific, and professional fields recognize the same need. Students who learn to organize and write good, clear reports can noticeably raise their grades in classes that require any kind of writing, particularly the writing of reports.

For the Job Applicant

With many firms conducting their own courses in language skills, such as English grammar and writing, the job applicant who already has an ability to organize information and write good reports will frequently be hired and/or promoted ahead of those who cannot. Although writing ability is helpful in preparing daily business correspondence, there is also a great demand for the person who can prepare longer letters, sometimes called report-letters, and the essential reports of business and industry.

For the Employee

Business reports must be written for three reasons:

- For management to know what is taking place, for its own efficient operation and for meeting competition
- For legal obligations to investors, government, customers, employees, and suppliers
- For customer relations and various public information uses

On the job, employees must frequently turn in many different types of reports. Upper management studies these reports not only for the information contained in them but also for leads in locating people who can write clearly and concisely. The employee may feel that routine reports are filed away where no one sees them. But to high-level officials, these reports are often their only concrete evidence of a person's progress on the job. The person who carefully prepares routine reports will be singled out for consideration when promotions arise.

Unnecessary Reports

Business leaders caution that today, too many reports are being produced and circulated. Too many reports are being furnished to people who don't need them and won't read them. The result is that essential reading is sometimes overlooked in the morass of reports. This comes from two causes: (1) Unnecessary, overlapping, irrelevant reports are being prepared; and (2) copies of necessary reports are being circulated not only to those who have need for them, but also to those who neither need nor want them.

One airline recently reduced its report budget by 43 percent when it inaugurated a system of monitoring distribution of reports according to circulation and use. Through its findings, the company eliminated the preparation of some reports and curtailed distribution of many copies of others. Figure 15.1 is a copy of an "Evaluation of Report" form that can be attached to a report to determine if each person who receives it needs or uses it.

Also, we must be cautious of being wooed too often by the siren call of electronic data processing. EDP enables us to record and classify data much more quickly and efficiently than was possible earlier. But a result has been that, by pushing a few buttons, voluminous reports are frequently prepared and distributed when they are in no way helpful to the business enterprise.

Research

In general, two types of research are conducted, primary and secondary. Primary research—obtaining original data—is done from observational studies, in-plant surveys, opinion polls, and experimental research with actual testing of solutions. Secondary research—written from studies made and reported by others—is usually done from public and private library sources.

Chapter 15 and 16 of this text will deal chiefly with the second method, library research, with references to gathering data by the other methods. In reporting much primary research, many procedures here can be followed. Primary or original research often also includes some secondary research, reference to other printed materials.

```
┌─────────────────────────────────────────────────────────────────────────────┐
│                          EVALUATION OF REPORT                                 │
│  Ref. SPLIT 1-02-011                                                          │
│  ┌──────────────────────────────────────┬─────────────────────────────────┐  │
│  │ TO:                                   │ FROM:                           │  │
│  │                                       │                                 │  │
│  │                                       │                                 │  │
│  └──────────────────────────────────────┴─────────────────────────────────┘  │
│  TITLE OF REPORT:                                                             │
├───────────────────────────────────────────────────────────────────────────────┤
│  PLEASE ANSWER THE FOLLOWING QUESTIONS AND RETURN THIS FORM TO THE SENDER.     │
│  IF YOUR ANSWER TO THE FIRST QUESTION IS "NO", NO FURTHER ANSWERS ARE REQUIRED.│
└───────────────────────────────────────────────────────────────────────────────┘
```

| DO YOU REQUIRE THIS REPORT? YES ☐ NO ☐ | IF YES, AT WHAT FREQUENCY? WK ☐ MO ☐ YR ☐ OTHER (EXPLAIN) |

IS PRESENT FORMAT ACCEPTABLE?   YES ☐   NO ☐   (IF "NO", SPECIFY CHANGES DESIRED)

ARE OTHER REPORTS, FORMS, ETC. PREPARED FROM THIS REPORT? YES ☐   NO ☐   (IF "YES", ENUMERATE)

IF YOU KNOW OF ANY OTHER REPORT THAT DUPLICATES INFORMATION IN THIS ONE, INDICATE.
TITLE:

PREPARED BY:

BRIEFLY JUSTIFY YOUR REQUIREMENT FOR THIS REPORT

FIGURE 15.1
A report evaluation form that can be attached to a
report to determine the need for it.

Steps in Seeking Solutions to Problems or Completing Other Research

To solve your problem or complete your research for your report topic, take the following steps:

Identify the problem or the research topic.

Identify the people who will read and use the report.

Identify the parts of the problem.

Ask questions about each part.

Write down what you know—and what you must find out.

Allow for limitations on time, money, and availablity of data.

Get authorization to prepare the report.

Identify the Problem or the Research Topic

The most helpful step in writing any report is to clearly identify the problem or the research topic. Everything in the report must hinge upon this central idea. Making a brief statement of this problem or research subject is very helpful. It becomes the central idea of the report and, even though this statement may never be used in the actual report, it will give you a framework into which all the research and writing must fit. It should be kept uppermost in the mind of anyone working on the report. In this manner you are able to zero in on wanted material and eliminate extraneous information.

A common error in students' choices for term papers or graduate dissertations is that the selection of topics is too broad for the planned presentation. Undergraduate students often try to choose a term paper project that would be more suitable for a graduate dissertation—or more. For example, one college sophomore wrote on his 3 by 5 term paper proposal card, "Data Processing"; another wrote "Explorations in Outer Space."

To help choose a topic you can cover properly, write down the name of the field of study you want to research, such as "Data Processing." Then list subtopics under your chosen title that would interest you for doing research. On broad topics, you and your instructor might agree on a sub-subtopic for your paper.

Identify Those Who Will Read and Use the Report

Identification of the people who will read and use the report will affect the information to be included and will help determine the detail into which the report must go. Further, it will affect the physical aspects of the report, such as method of printing, types of illustrations, quality of paper, types of covers, and tone of writing. An in-house report might economize on printing, illustrations, paper, and cover, and it might have a relaxed, informal tone. Reports for clients, customers, board of directors, and government agencies would probably receive more formal treatment in these areas.

Identify Parts of the Problem

Any problem or research topic can be studied and reported more easily when it is broken down into small segments, making it easier to find solutions. This is particularly true when the large unanswered problem seems almost beyond comprehension. Step-by-step solution of these parts can be combined into the solution of the whole.

Ask Questions about Each Part

As each part is identified, list questions that can be helpful in finding the solution. Questioning may eliminate some parts and add others not previously listed.

Write Down What You Know and What You Must Find Out

Make notes on what you know and what you need to find out about each part of the problem or topic. At this stage, business often uses the advantages of brainstorming or "think tanks"—freewheeling, open-end group discussions with few limits on ideas and suggestions. Brainstorming usually helps clear the air, resulting in significant help in the search for solutions.

Allow for Limitations on Time, Money, and Availability of Data

Reports must be structured within certain limits of time, money, and availability of data. This applies to all reports, from the college term paper to the annual report of a major corporation.

Businesses must especially recognize limitations of time and money in respect to the value of the research and report writing being done. Any type of report must be of sufficient interest and value to justify the expenditure of time and talent required.

Get Authorization to Prepare the Report

If proper authorization to prepare the report has not been received before this time, specific authority should be obtained before more work is completed. An instructor should agree that the planned topic will be acceptable and of proper length and depth for class requirements. Properly authorized personnel must give approval for a go-ahead on the business report project.

Sources of Information

Now you are ready to begin research for the project.

Business reports must above all else be accurate and up to date. As a rule of thumb, use no reference that is more than five years old unless it is an exceptional case or the data are needed for historical comparison. The business scene changes rapidly, and in some fields of study, information even one year old is outdated. Further, factual information must be documented with reference to its source by the use of footnotes if there can be any question about its accuracy, or if further study of that information might be made by readers.

Reference Librarian

Probably your best help in doing library research is the reference librarian. One librarian says, "If you don't know, ask." Another says, "Don't leave without asking." Reference librarians are trained to help researchers locate information. They will guide you to locating sources you ask for, and probably will guide you to sources you had not considered. As a matter of fact, your first step in doing library research might be to explain your topic to the reference librarian and ask for help. "You'll be glad you did."

Periodicals

All libraries, including public, corporate, and other private libraries, have three basic classifications of materials: periodicals, references, and books in stacks.

For business reports, much information might come from authoritative periodicals— magazines and newspapers—because they are, by their nature, of more recent publication than most other sources.

Periodical indexes. A comparatively new type of periodical index is the *Magazine Index*. Prepared on a computer and updated monthly, this index is viewed on a microfilm screen. You can easily call up five years' indexing of subject matter in magazines, and it is efficiently cross-indexed like other periodical indexes.

Other helpful indexes for researching business or industrial subjects are listed here. Probably the most helpful will be the *Business Periodical Index* and the *Reader's Guide to Periodical Literature*.

Name of Index	*Periodicals Indexed*
Applied Science and Technology Index	Engineering, trade, business
Business Periodicals Index	Business, industrial, trade
Humanities Index	History, economics, international relations, political science
New York Times Index	*New York Times,* including business section of *Times;* oriented to eastern U.S. and international business
Reader's Guide to Periodical Literature	General periodicals on all subject matters; covers major business periodicals

Business periodicals. These are the major authoritative business periodicals:

Business Week	Weekly business news magazine
Changing Times	Kiplinger's monthly business magazine for general readership
Dun's Business Monthly	Periodical for business executives; regional coverage
Forbes	Magazine for business executives published every two weeks
Fortune	Magazine containing articles on business firms and business problems published every two weeks
Harvard Business Review	Magazine on business activities published every two months
Money	Monthly business and investment magazine for general readership
Nation's Business	Published by U.S. Chamber of Commerce; articles on business for general readership
The Wall Street Journal	Daily Monday–Friday business and financial newspaper, which also contains general news; regional issues

Besides these major business periodicals, the library may contain copies of other magazines and journals pertaining to business in general, as well as those devoted solely to a particular field of business. Library indexes should be studied for names of such periodicals. Each library makes its own selection of materials found on its shelves; these decisions are usually made according to demand.

The library can be checked for periodicals in many different categories, such as these:

Accounting	Industry	Office management
Advertising	Insurance	Personnel
Computers	Labor and labor relations	Retailing
Economics	Law	Secretarial science
Finance	Marketing	Transportation
Food	Mines and minerals	Word processing

Reference Materials

Business directories and business encyclopedias can be of great help in writing business reports. The corporation directories are good general references.

Corporation directories list information on specific corporations and businesses by name, as well as listing government units that offer opportunities for investment. These directories will give such information as the address of a business main office and divisions, its current status, its history, types of products or services, and detailed financial statistics. Your reference librarian can help you locate current major corporation directories.

Other corporate directory references can be found in these areas:

Automotive and aviation	Import and export
Chemical and engineering	Metals and machinery
Coal and mining	Mining
Drugs	Petroleum
Electronics and data processing	Textiles and apparel
Food and food processing	

Books in Stacks

Fiction books are shelved alphabetically by author.

Library card catalogues or bound catalogues list each non-fiction book under three different classifications: author, title, and subject.

To aid us in locating them, nonfiction books are placed in library stacks according to subject matter. The two major classification systems used are the Library of Congress and the Dewey Decimal systems.

The Library of Congress system. College, state, and federal libraries are increasingly adopting the Library of Congress system of classification. This system facilitates interlibrary lending opportunities offered by the automated system of the Library of Congress so that through your own library you can borrow books from other libraries. This system uses letters of the alphabet combined with arabic numerals to place materials in specific categories. Following are the Library of Congress classifications.

A	General, Work, Polygraphy
B	Philosophy, Religion
C	History—Auxiliary Sciences
D	Universal and Old World History
E–F	America
G	Geography, Anthropology, Folklore, Customs, Sports and Games
H	Business, Political Science
K	Law
L	Education
M	Music
N	Fine Arts
P	Language and Literature
Q	Science
R	Medicine
S	Agriculture
T	Technology
U	Military Science
V	Naval Science
Z	Bibliography and Library Science

The Dewey Decimal system. The Dewey Decimal system, the most widely used library classification system in the United States, is based on a progressive use of arabic numbers 0 to 9.

Most information of interest to business and industrial research is listed under the classifications "300: The Social Sciences," and "600: Technology (Applied Sciences)." The following list contains the major classifications of the Dewey Decimal system and also includes subheadings of the 300 and 600 classifications:

000	GENERALITIES	
100	PHILOSOPHY AND RELATED DISCIPLINES	
200	RELIGION	
300	THE SOCIAL SCIENCES	
	310	Statistical method and statistics
	320	Political science
	330	Economics

340 Law
350 Public administration
360 Welfare and association
370 Education
380 Commerce
390 Customs and folklore
400 LANGUAGE
500 PURE SCIENCES
600 TECHNOLOGY (APPLIED SCIENCES)
610 Medical sciences
620 Engineering and allied operations
630 Agriculture and agricultural industries
640 Domestic arts and sciences (home economics)
650 Communications, business
660 Chemical technology, etc.
670 Manufactures
680 Mechanical trades
690 Building
700 THE ARTS
800 LITERATURE AND RHETORIC
900 GENERAL GEOGRAPHY AND HISTORY, etc.

Doing Library Research

Research Notes

For a short report. As you look up a source of written information, make out library research notes on cards measuring 3 by 5 or 4 by 6 inches. Or you may prefer to keep notes on note pads or $8\frac{1}{2}$ by 11 inch standard-size paper. However, you will find the cards handy for carrying and for stacking in order of presentation of the material when you are writing the report. Figure 15.2 is an example of a typical library research card.

You will not only use this card as a reference while writing the report; you may also find it useful if you wish further details from this source, or if you need to recheck the information on it with other materials that seem to conflict with it.

The card information can be set out in sections:

At the top of the card in the left corner, list a key word or phrase identifying the part of the report that this card covers. Placing this information here makes it easy for you to stack cards (or pages) in the order in which their information will appear in the report.

In the upper right corner, put the library call number for possible future reference.

From the title page of the book or periodical, copy the full name of the author, full title, name of publisher, place and date of publication, and the page number(s) on which the material appears. This information may be used for reference, footnotes, and/or bibliography. If several cards are made from the same source, abbreviate this information by listing just the name of the author, or key words in the title of the article if the author's name is not given. Always note exact page numbers.

Leaving one blank line below this source identification material, write pertinent research information on the rest of the card and on the back of the card, if necessary. More than one card may be used for lengthy material.

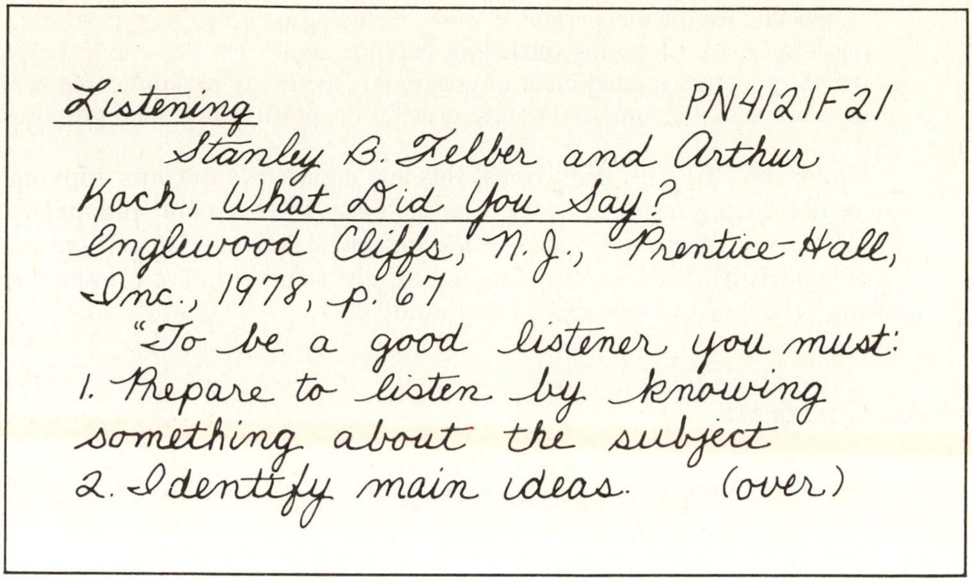
Listening PN4121F21
Stanley B. Felber and Arthur Koch, What Did You Say? Englewood Cliffs, N.J., Prentice-Hall, Inc., 1978, p. 67
"To be a good listener you must:
1. Prepare to listen by knowing something about the subject
2. Identify main ideas. (over)

FIGURE 15.2
Example of library research card for report writing.

For a longer report. For a longer report, it might be more helpful to keep two sets of research cards: One set of 3 by 5 inch bibliography cards would contain full information as shown in Figure 15.2—name of author, full title of source, place of publication, publisher, and date of publication. However, your research notes would not be put on these bibliography cards.

The second set of larger, 4 by 6-inch cards would be used for all research notes. Both front and back of these cards might be used. You could identify the source of this information at the *bottom* of these cards in abbreviated form, such as *Felber and Koch, p. 67.* Each large card should also have at the top the title of the major section of the report to which the card refers.

Organizing Notes

To help make a good plan or outline for the report, these note cards can then be compiled under the major headings. By placing the note cards in a logical order of development of the report, you are organized and ready to write the outline. Subheadings can be made up from the organization under the major headings.

With notes in order and outline written, you are ready to write your report. Chapter 16 contains detailed information about writing a report.

Copyright Laws

Copyright laws are passed to protect writers and other creators from those who would appropriate their work without paying for it. Because technological changes have made copying and sending printed and recorded materials much easier than in times past, newer laws have been passed. Supporting and updating old copyright laws, Section 107 of Public Law 94-553, reads in part:

...the fair use of a copyrighted work, including such use by reproducing copies...for purposes such as...teaching (including multiple copies for classroom use), scholarship, or research, is not an infringement of copyright. [Factors to be considered shall include] whether such use is of a commercial nature or is for nonprofit educational purposes....

Under its "fair use" provisions, this law apparently permits copying of printed materials for use during research, providing such use is noncommercial and *does not deprive the copyright owner from money that would otherwise be derived from the sale of the material.*

"Plagiarism" discussed in Chapter 16, gives further caution and explanation against "quoting other writers without giving credit."

Writing Assignments

Writing assignments for Chapters 15 and 16 are at the end of Chapter 16.

REVIEW AND DISCUSSION

Chapter 15 *Planning the Business Report or the Term Paper*

1. Tell how report writing ability can help you as a student.

   ——————————————————————————————————————

   ——————————————————————————————————————

2. Business people say that ability to write reports is important because reports have to be written for three reasons. What are the reasons?

   ——————————————————————————————————————

   ——————————————————————————————————————

   ——————————————————————————————————————

3. Tell how report writing ability can help you as a job applicant.

   ——————————————————————————————————————

   ——————————————————————————————————————

4. Tell how report writing ability can help you as an employee.

   ——————————————————————————————————————

   ——————————————————————————————————————

5. What do business leaders say are two causes of excessive report writing and report circulation?

   ——————————————————————————————————————

   ——————————————————————————————————————

6. When the airline officials studied the distribution and use of their reports, they reduced their report budget by ——— percent.

7. Name four methods of conducting research for reports.

   ——————————————————————————————————————

   ——————————————————————————————————————

   ——————————————————————————————————————

   ——————————————————————————————————————

8. What is the most helpful step in solving any problem?

_____

_____

_____

9. Give the six steps to follow in seeking solutions to problems.

_____

_____

_____

_____

10. Why should you always identify the people who will use the report?

_____

_____

_____

11. When a problem is so large it seems almost unsolvable, what is a good method to follow for its solution?

_____

_____

12. What is a common error that students make in choosing a topic for reports they are preparing?

_____

13. What are the criteria for determining the amount of time and money that can be spent on preparing a report?

_____

_____

14. As a rule of thumb, references used in writing a business report generally should not be more than ____ years old.

15. Name the three basic classifications of printed library materials.

_____

_____

16. Which of the three preceding classifications is most current?

_____

17. Under what three categories are non-fiction books in the library stacks catalogued?

_____

18. Colleges and government agencies are increasingly beginning to classify materials under the _____ system. Why? _____

_____

_____

Chapter 15   Planning the Business Report or the Term Paper (*Continued*)

19. Identify the information that should be included on a card or other note that will be used as reference in writing a report.

     _____

     _____

     _____

20. Under the *fair use* provisions of current copyright laws, we are permitted to copy printed materials for use during research and for educational purposes, providing this

    use is noncommercial and _____

    _____

    _____

CHAPTER 16
Writing a Business Report or a Term Paper; Writing Proposals

> At a pub in Dublin known as a haunt of the late Irish poet, Brendan Behan, men around the bar were discussing the talent of writing. One "wee lad of 60," Jocko, concluded: "Ah, now. You know it's not the writin' down. It's the assembly."

WRITING A BUSINESS REPORT OR A TERM PAPER

What do you do when all you have is a jumble of ideas, plus a handful of notes that must be enlarged into a complete, understandable report?

When Writing Comes Hard

If you are like most people, writing your first business report or term paper comes hard. Just keep in mind that the purpose of writing the report or paper is to set out ideas clearly so that readers can easily understand what you have written. Also, recognize that good organization simplifies the entire process.

So how do you organize? Following ideas set out in the preceding chapter, take these early steps:

1. Define the problem or make a statement of the purpose of the report.
2. As you do research, keep notes.
3. Make a report outline or make a list of the main headings of your report which may or may not be placed in final order.
4. Identify your reader(s) and write to that audience.
5. As you work, check and change your outline to conform with what you discover.
6. As you work, label your research papers at the top as belonging under one of the main headings of the outline or the list.

First: Define the Problem or Make a Statement of the Purpose

Certainly, the first step in solving any problem is to define the problem. Odd as it may seem, in both our personal lives and in our careers, we waste much time and effort trying to solve a problem when we have not actually faced up to what the problem is. So it bears repeating: The first step in solving any problem is to define the problem.

Many reports are written not to solve a problem, but to set out facts or ideas. If your report is of this nature, *make a statement of the purpose of the report.*

Capsulize that problem or statement in as few words as possible, so that it is clear and you can readily recall it to mind. Everything that appears in the report should be pertinent to this announced problem or purpose. As you do your research, you may constantly need to ask yourself, "Does this relate to my basic problem (purpose)?"

Second: Keep Notes

Make sure you have notes on everything you have learned on the subject. While you were doing your research, these notes should have been put on cards or pieces of paper. Don't worry yet about good grammar, complete sentences, neatness, and so forth. Keep a folder or file box where you can collect all the notes or other relevant material over a period of time.

Third: Make a Report Outline

As the self-proclaimed critic in the story that introduces this chapter said, "... it's not the writin' down. It's the assembly."

Make your first phase report outline from your list of notes. Remember: Your outline is not cast in concrete. As your work continues, you will probably adjust and change it, adding, subtracting, and altering its order. Writing down this first phase report outline with major divisions gives you a skeleton that you can flesh out as you complete your research. Also, your report may change as you get different information on the ideas you first had in mind. These major report outline divisions could eventually be the headings in the table of contents at the beginning of the report to help readers find specific parts.

Order of Presentation

Choose a logical order of presentation of material. Because the purpose of preparing the report is to have material that will be read and understood by other people, one step must lead to the next and then on to the next. Select a method of presentation that will set out your major points and conclusions best, such as one of the following:

The inductive problem solving technique. This method is sometimes called the scientific "parts to whole" method. All positions relating to the problem—pro and con positions or arguments—are clearly identified. Then all these "parts" or positions are evaluated, even those that initially seem least appealing.

At this point of making important decisions, a **free-wheeling unrestrained discussion** by people involved (sometimes called "brainstorming," "bull session," or "toro ballistics") can bring forth the best solution. During these sessions, members are free to toss in any ideas, even seemingly lunatic ones. All options are considered in making a decision about the "whole," the problem.

In using this method, some members may learn that a position they have previously held must be scrapped because evidence proved the earlier position invalid. (Exception: When the dissenter signs everyone's paycheck.)*

The deductive problem solving technique: This technique can be called the "whole to parts" method. An answer (the whole) is agreed upon and then all positions that support that conclusion are considered and stated. Potential arguments against the agreed-upon decision are ignored. This might be called the nonscientific method of decision making. Unfortunately, costly business, industry, government and personal life problems are sometimes "solved" by this deductive problem solving technique.

Cause → effect. Many reports are written in the cause → effect style: As a result of this, this, and this, the following happened (or may happen).

Chronological order. This type of report is easiest to organize but is of course not appropriate to all studies. Matters are related in the order of occurrence.

Geographical order. Geographical order reports state matters by areas or regions, such as showing activities of various branches of a firm. As much as possible, all matters reported from each area should be given in similar order making them easier to find and compare.

Outline Forms

The three most common outline forms for reports are alphanumeric, Roman numeral and decimal.

The Alphanumeric Outline. An easy report outline format to follow employs alphanumeric symbols (combining alphabet and number symbols).

For example, using alphanumerics, an outline of types of business communications might read:

Types of Business Communications

A. Nonverbal communications
   1. Body language
   2. Illustrations
B. Verbal communications
   1. Oral
      a. Telephone calls
      b. Conferences
      c. Dictation
         (1) to a machine
         (2) to a secretary
      d. Speeches
      e. Listening

---

*Before Henry Ford's time all cars were basically custom built. Ford was the first to effectively use the assembly line for manufacturing cars. All Ford cars were similar and sold at a low price, making them available to the average person. After much success, executives asked for a meeting to discuss making cars of different colors to satisfy their customers. Ford's reply, which held because he owned the company: "People can have any color they want, as long as it is black."

     2. Written
       a. Letters
       b. Memorandums
       c. Reports

The Roman Numeral Outline. This same outline might be set up using the Roman numeral outline system:

Types of Business Communications

   I. Nonverbal communications
    A. Body language
    B. Illustrations
  II. Verbal communications
    A. Oral
      1. Telephone calls
      2. Conferences
      3. Dictation
        a. to a machine
        b. to a secretary
      4. Speeches
      5. Listening
    B. Written
      1. Letters
      2. Memorandums
      3. Reports

The Decimal Outline. The decimal system of outlining, seen in scientific and technical papers, and frequently in academic work, is increasing in popularity. It would show the same outline as follows:

Types of Business Communications

  1.0 Nonverbal communications
    1.1 Body language
    1.2 Illustrations
  2.0 Verbal communications
    2.1 Oral
      2.11 Telephone calls
      2.12 Conferences
      2.13 Dictation
        2.13.1 to a machine
        2.13.2 to a secretary
      2.14 Speeches
      2.15 Listening
    2.2 Written
      2.21 Letters
      2.22 Memorandums
      2.23 Reports

Fourth: Identify Your Readers and Write to Their Level

Decide how much detail you must include to serve your readers properly.

Fifth: As You Work, Check and Change Your Outline

Now, take a good look at your outline. Have you kept your reader or readers in mind so that the report will be understood from the viewpoint of your audience? Is it set out in a sensible order that will lead a reader logically from one idea to another throughout the entire report?

Use numbers and/or letters to label parts of the outline. These symbols show the relation of parts of a report to each other and show when you have covered one section or subsection and are going into another.

Preparing a report outline may seem to be a tedious, unnecessary step. However, having an outline to follow simplifies your writing. Just as a builder follows a blueprint, a good writer usually follows an outline.

Sixth: As You Work, Label Your Research Papers

Label your research cards and notes with tag lines that match major headings in your outline. Then stack your cards and notes according to their corresponding position in your outline. At this point you will probably add or delete some headings or subheadings in your outline to follow your research discoveries.

Making a Rough Draft of the Report

Now, referring to your outline and your research papers, start to write your report.

In making your report, never submit the first draft as a final copy. Always prepare a **rough draft** of the entire report. Don't feel that you are exhibiting amateurism because you make a first "practice" copy. Far from it. Harry Shaw is an internationally known editor and author of respected books on writing. He has also taught writing classes at both New York and Columbia universities. Shaw states, "There is no such thing as good writing. There is only good rewriting."

Shaw says further that those who are unwilling to revise and rewrite are skipping a major step in becoming better writers. He recites the experiences of other professional writers:

William Faulkner on his novel, *Sound and Fury:* "I wrote it five times."

Thornton Wilder, dramatist and novelist: "There are passages in every novel whose first writing is the last. But it's the joint and cement between those passages that take a great deal of rewriting."

Frank O'Connor, short story writer, when asked about rewriting, said that he did so "endlessly, endlessly, endlessly."

James Thurber, asked if the act of writing was easy for him: "It's mostly a question of rewriting. It's part of a constant attempt to make the finished version smooth, to make it seem effortless." He told of having rewritten one story 15 times.[1]

Before writing your first draft, however, read through the rest of this section.

[1] Harry Shaw, *20 Steps to Better Writing* (Totowa, N.J.: Littlefield, Adams & Co., 1978), p. 124ff.

Open-Minded Attitude

A responsible researcher has an open-minded attitude, and recognizes that there may be some biases or pet theories relating to certain studies. To conduct valid research, report theories that are supported by facts. If opinions or biases are given, they should be shown as such and should not be given the weight of being factual. Otherwise, an entire study loses credibility—the parts that are valid as well as those that are not. Such research reporting is considered unprofessional and should not be done.

If you hide facts or problems in trying to prove your point, most readers will become suspicious of your one-sidedness. Instead, deal gracefully and intelligently with opposing viewpoints. You will strike your readers as being fair-minded, ethical, and balanced.

Reporting Opinions

Opinions from authoritative sources are valuable in research. As for including your own opinion, anyone seriously interested in writing should study Strunk and White's *The Elements of Style.* In this classic authority, we are told:

> Unless there is good reason for its being there, do not inject [your own] opinion into a piece of writing. We all have opinions about almost everything, and the temptation to toss them in is great. To air one's views gratuitously, however, is to imply that the demand for them is brisk . . .[2]

Relevance vs. Irrelevance

When you make a study for a report, you may find a great deal of material that seems interesting but is not relevant to the study. To determine whether or not this material should be reported, go back to the first part of the outline, the statement of purpose, and decide whether or not this information is relevant to that purpose. Even if the material is extremely interesting, leave it out if it is not pertinent. You might, of course, take notes for use at another time or place. If material is quasi-relevant to the topic at hand and if it warrants such treatment, you might consider making a footnote reference to it on the same page as the material to which it most closely relates.

Plagiarism

In Chapter 15, you were informed that it is legal and ethical for you to copy written material while doing research if you are not copying so much that you are preventing the sale of a copy of the original work. When you report information found in other sources, paraphrase the writing of others—that is, state the information in your own words.

Do not appropriate the writing of another person and try to pass it off as your own. To quote another person word for word without giving credit is to plagiarize. There are laws against plagiarism—that is, quoting other writers without giving credit. For term papers and most business reports, you may quote others without getting their permission, but you should give them credit in some way, either in the context of the report or in a footnote. If material is to be circulated widely, such as in a periodical or book, permission to quote must be sought and granted.

---

[2]William Strunk, Jr., and E. B. White, *The Elements of Style,* 3rd ed. (New York: Macmillan, 1979), p. 80.

Quoting the work of another and pretending it is your own is not only unlawful; it is unethical and damages the reputation of the writer. Further, readers of your material may be quite knowledgeable and may actually recognize the writing as coming from another source. Writing styles do vary. It may be jarring to the reader to go from a student's writing style to the style of a different person—a person who may be a recognized authority in a given field. Your own writing may be quite authoritative, but keep it in your own words.

Tone

Writing Up and Writing Down

Avoid writing up or writing down to your reader. Keeping your audience in mind, make your report understandable and logical. If technical terms must be used, explain them without belittling those who are trying to understand them. How much you must explain is determined by the level of understanding of your readers.

Improve your vocabulary in order to have grasp of the appropriate terms in your field. However, choose a long word only if a short word will not do. After all, the best writing in any field is made up of short, crisp words that are easily understood and well remembered.

Charles T. Brusaw, a recognized authority on business writing, says:

> In business writing, tone can be especially important; just as it can help you gain your reader's sympathy, so it can rub him or her the wrong way. When you write you must always consider your objective; in addition, you must then maintain an appropriate tone....
>
> The tone used in reports should normally be objective and impersonal....The important thing is to make sure that your tone is the one best suited to your objective. To make sure that it is, always keep your reader in mind.[3]

Definitions

Define all terms that may not be understandable to readers of the report. A term should be defined the first time it is used. If you use a number of new terms, you might have an alphabetized glossary at the end of the report where definitions are repeated.

Formal vs. Informal Tone

Business today is often adopting an informal tone in reports by the use of first- and second-person form, saying, "We found that...," or "You will note..." With business's growing interest in better direct communications, you can see why the less formal conversational tone is the trend in business report writing.

However, formal business reports are written in the impersonal, third-person form. In other words, formal reports do not use *I, me, my, we, our, you, your, yours.* Instead of saying, "We found that...," the report would read, "It was found that..." Looking at a few formal business reports will show how effective and easy this writing style is.

The "Breezy" Writing Tone

In business communications, do not use the breezy writing style that you frequently find in bulletins and newsletters distributed among people who are well acquainted. The tone of such writing may be appreciated and accepted within some small groups, but this

[3]Charles T. Brusaw and others, *The Business Writer's Handbook,* 2nd ed. (New York: St. Martin's Press, 1982), pp. 559–60.

style can be deadly in business writing. Walt Whitman has been blamed for this type of writing and for letting loose hordes of stream-of-consciousness "scribblers," because he wrote "spontaneous me."

This is the type of stream-of-consciousness writing that you should avoid altogether in business writing:

> Well, buddies, isn't it about time you heard from your reckless, feckless reporter? That's me—good ol' Dan. And here are some fresh grapes right off the vine (grapevine, get it???).
>
> If you didn't get to our annual Fall roundup, let me tell you, you really missed a bash! 'Frisco never looked better—the Cannery, Pier 39, Golden Gate. To name a few!
>
> Grant M. showed off his latest—car, that is. And Roxie L. kept buttonholing everybody (including yours truly) to give endless details about her latest tour. . . .

Sexism in Writing

Prentice Hall, Inc., gives its authors the following advice on avoiding sexism in writing:

> In your writing, be certain to treat men and women impersonally in regard to occupation, marital status, physical abilities, attitudes, interests, and so on. Depending on the requirements of your subject, avoid attributing particular characteristics to either sex; instead, let your writing convey that one's abilities and achievements are not limited by gender. Your text should support the fact that both sexes play equally important roles in all facets of life and that activities on all levels are open to both women and men alike.

The preceding guidelines could also be followed by writers of business reports and term papers.

Tense

Do not slip from present to past tense in writing the report. Some writers favor using past tense, such as, "This survey *revealed* that . . . " But use of the present tense throughout the report might make the information seem more alive and current: "This study *reveals* that . . . " Whichever form is selected, be consistent. Repeatedly changing from past to present and back to past can be disconcerting to the reader and could detract from the clarity of the report.

Sentence Length

In their manual for training consultants how to write reports clearly, a national business consulting firm strongly recommends short sentences. They suggest that "getting stuck" in the middle of a sentence probably means you have too many ideas in it. The solution: Break it down into two, three, or four sentences; however, don't make the sentences so short that they sound childish or choppy. Their recommended average sentence length: 15 to 20 words.

Readability of Written Material: The Fog Index

Many studies have been made on readability of written material, and there are various yardsticks for judging this quality. One of the most reliable and simplest to use is the Fog Index, originated by Robert Gunning. (*Fog* in this use refers simply to lack of clarity.) Gunning has earned high fees from business and government to rewrite material before publication to make it more readable. Among his clients are *The Wall Street Journal,* General Motors, du Pont, and Standard Oil of New Jersey.

The Fog Index is based on the premise that short words and short sentences result in clear writing. This index number is determined from sentence length and count of long words, and it includes a factor enabling this number to represent the number of years of schooling needed to readily understand the written material. Thus, the higher the Fog Index number, the more difficult the material is to understand.

Many letters and reports sit unread on the desks of business and professional people because the reading index is too high and the material is therefore difficult to understand.

Readability studies show that written material with a Fog Index level above 10 or 11 is difficult to understand and is extremely slow reading even for those with college and advanced degrees. Writing authorities recommend that all writers, including business writers, seek to write at a level no higher than 10.

The Fog Index level of writing is determined by first finding the length of the average sentence in a selected piece of writing and the percentage of difficult words in that segment. From these two figures, the index is determined in this manner:

1. Select a representative sample of the writing. Count 100 words, ending with the sentence that is nearest the 100 count.
   Example: Selected sample contains: 103 words
   Find the average number of words in a sentence by dividing the number of words in the sample by the number of sentences. Count each independent clause as a sentence. *"We came. We saw. We conquered"* would be counted as three sentences whether these clauses were separated by periods, semicolons, or commas.
   Example: There are 5 sentences in the sample:
   $103 \div 5 = $ Average length of sentence   20.6

2. Find the percentage of difficult words in the sample this way: *Of the first 100 words in the sample,* count the words that have three or more syllables. Do not count:
      Capitalized words
      Words that make their third syllable by combining two words, such as
         typewriter or *underlying*
      Verbs that form the third syllable by adding *es* or *ed*
   Example: Number of difficult words: 5

3. Take the figure that represents the average sentence length: 20.6
   Take the figure that represents the percent of difficult words: + 5
   Add these two figures: 25.6

4. Multiply that sum by .4 (In the answer, disregard figures after the decimal).   × .4
                                                        10.24

5. FOG INDEX   10

In order to understand easily the sample of writing studied in this example, the reader would have to have completed at least 10 years of schooling. Reviewing the works of the best writers in the English language will prove that our best writing is around or below the level of ten. Ernest Hemingway said he went to the King James version of the Bible for his instructions in clarity of writing. Here are Fog Index studies from this edition of the Bible, from Hemingway, and from other outstanding writers:

King James Bible	
23rd Psalm	5
Ten Commandments	9
Ernest Hemingway	
Farewell to Arms, first page	10
Old Man and the Sea, selection	3
Lincoln's Gettysburg Address	10
Winston Churchill speeches	
"Blood, sweat, and tears..."	11
"Give us the tools and we will finish the job..."	5
Isaac Asimov	
I, Robot, average of random selections	9
Roger Kahn	
The Boys of Summer, average of random selections	10

Graphics and Visuals

Confucius:

I hear and I forget.
I see and I remember.

On the theory that a picture is worth a thousand words, graphics, or illustrations of every kind, are used in business reports. Although information dealing with figures could be simply set out in paragraph form, for instance, these figures are usually clearer if set out in a table, a chart, or in a bar or line graph. Maps, photographs, and drawings are also used when applicable.

Graphics should not be set out alone in the report. Before each illustration is given, it should be introduced with a summary of its contents. Figure 16.1 is an example of a table set out to make information clear for comparison. Figure 16.2 shows a line graph, a pie chart (generally used for percentage figures), and a bar graph.

FIGURE 16.1
An example of a table showing figures for easy comparison.

KEY INDICATORS FOR MAJOR INDUSTRIAL COUNTRIES

	Real Growth (Percent)			Consumer Prices (Percentage Change)			Current-Account Balance (Billions of U.S. Dollars)		
	1983	1984	1985	1983	1984	1985	1983	1984	1985
United States	3.4	5.8	2.2	3.2	5.0	6.3	−40.8	−79.0	−80.0
Canada	3.0	4.8	3.0	5.8	5.3	6.0	1.3	−1.5	−3.5
France	.7	1.0	2.0	9.3	8.0	7.7	−4.0	−1.0	−3.0
Germany	1.3	3.0	2.5	3.0	2.9	3.1	3.9	4.5	4.0
Italy	−1.2	1.8	2.0	14.7	12.2	11.7	—	−.5	−2.0
Japan	3.0	4.2	3.8	1.5	2.3	2.5	21.0	29.0	25.0
United Kingdom	3.5	3.0	2.2	4.6	5.3	5.6	3.1	2.0	.5
All Countries Above	2.5	4.2	2.5	4.3	5.2	5.9	−15.5	−46.5	−59.0
All Countries Above excluding U.S.	1.9	3.0	2.8	5.4	5.4	5.6	25.3	32.5	21.0
European Countries Above	1.2	2.3	2.2	7.1	6.7	6.7	3.0	5.0	−.5

Sources: Data Resources; International Monetary Fund; SPNB Estimates and Forecasts. Courtesy Economics Department, Security Pacific Bank.

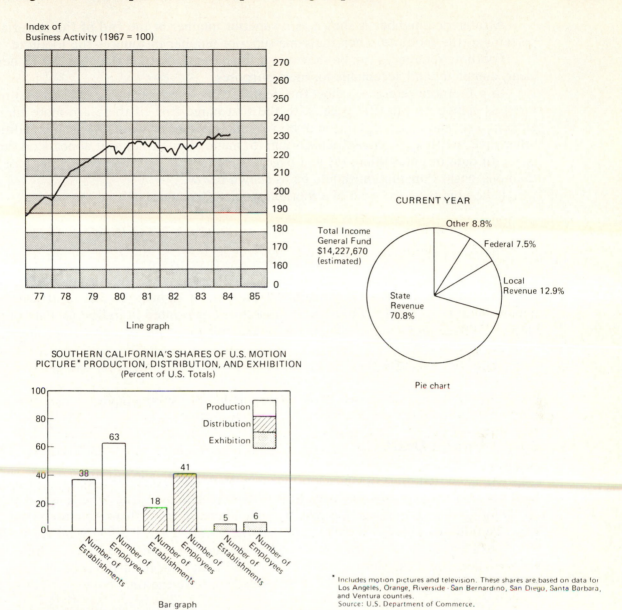

FIGURE 16.2
Examples of line graph, pie chart, and bar graph.

Documentation: Footnotes

To give credit to those whose ideas are being used and to document authority for statements made, footnotes and bibliographies are included as part of a report. Documentation—supplying supporting evidence for what you are saying—is also useful to those who may wish to read further on the subject and would appreciate seeing additional sources.

Footnotes are usually placed within a report; a bibliography is placed at the end of the finished report.

For classroom reports and many business reports, footnotes are usually placed at the bottom of the page on which the reference is made. Technical papers sometimes include footnote documentation within the written material of the report, in brackets at the end of the sentence containing the reference. Longer texts sometimes list all the footnote data in a separate section at the end of the book or report.

A reference number is shown as a superior number at the end of the material that pertains to the footnote. Then the same superior number introduces the footnote.

Footnote references can be shown in different manners, but the ones shown here are clear, complete, and acceptable for most purposes.

In a footnote reference, show the items in this order: (1) name of author(s) or editor(s) as shown on the title page, with the first name first (if there are more than two authors, list "and others"); (2) title of book, underlined or printed in italics; (3) edition, if other than the first; (4) city of publication; (5) name of publisher as it appears on the title page; (6) date of publication; (7) and page number(s)—"p." for one page, "pp." for more than one page. Punctuation should be as shown below.

Following is an example of a footnote copied from page 339.

[3]Charles T. Brusaw and others, *The Business Writer's Handbook,* 2nd ed. (New York: St. Martin's Press, 1982), pp. 559–60.

In a footnote reference to a magazine, newspaper, newsletter, or any other periodical, items can be shown in this manner: (1) author, if shown; (2) title of article, within quotation marks; (3) title of periodical, underlined or printed in italics; (4) date of publication; (5) page number(s). Following is an example of a footnote for a magazine article:

[1]Arthur M. Louis, "The Great Electronic Mail Shootout," *Fortune,* August 20, 1984, pp. 167–68.

Later parts of this chapter show how to make up a bibliography.

Revising Your Rough Draft

After the first draft of your report is completed, set it aside for a while, if possible, to let it cool off so you can come back to it totally fresh. Now is the time to check meticulously for grammar, spelling, and punctuation. Then reread it, checking closely that it follows the outline. This helps make sure that the report tells what you want it to tell and that your ideas proceed logically from one to another. You will also find it helpful at this point to have someone whose opinion you respect read it for form and content. Only after a careful rereading of your own will you be ready to have the final copy typed or printed.

Compiling the Complete Report

After carefully proofreading and correcting the body of your report, you are ready to set up the complete report with title page, table of contents, and so forth.

From the proper authorities, specific instructions can be obtained for setting up the typing, printing, and so forth of a business report. A term paper should be typed double spaced with paragraphs indented. If paragraphs are not indented, there should be a triple space (two blank lines) between paragraphs to make the separations clear.

Major Parts of the Report

The major parts of a business report are the title page, table of contents, introduction and summary, body of the report, bibliography, and report cover. Figure 16.3 is an example of a title page of a report; Figure 16.4 is a sample table of contents; Figure 16.5 is a sample first page. Following are details of the preparation of each part of the report.

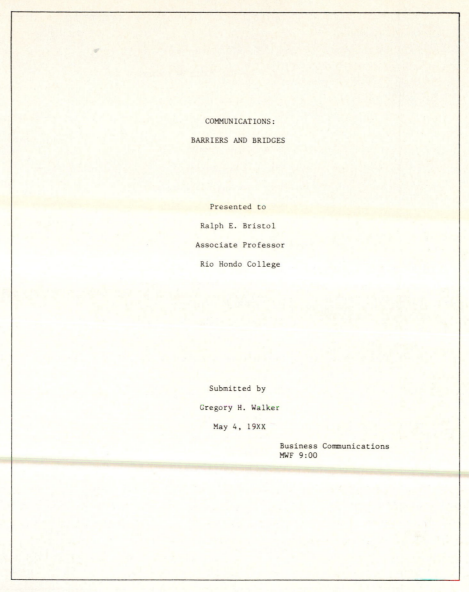

COMMUNICATIONS:

BARRIERS AND BRIDGES

Presented to

Ralph E. Bristol

Associate Professor

Rio Hondo College

Submitted by

Gregory H. Walker

May 4, 19XX

Business Communications
MWF 9:00

FIGURE 16.3
Title page of a report.

Title Page

The title page of the report should be an attractive introduction to the report. Items should be well spaced and well balanced for good visual effect. Information on the title page should include the title of the report, person(s) or firm for whom the report was prepared, name of the person or persons who prepared the report, and date of submission of the report. Other information might be included according to the specific nature of the report. For a classroom assignment, the name of the class for which the report was prepared should be shown.

Table of Contents

As stated previously, the table of contents can be made up from the report outline, but it should be prepared after the entire report has been written, because some adjustments in the outline may have been made as writing progressed. You may add some sec-

TABLE OF CONTENTS

Chapter		Page
I	INTRODUCTION--SUMMARY	1
	What is communication?	1
	How do communications succeed?	2
	How do communications fail?	3
II	COMMUNICATION BRIDGES	4
	The feedback bridge	4
	The bridge of gearing to the receiver	5
	The empathy bridge	6
	The planning bridge	6
III	COMMUNICATION BARRIERS	7
	The listening barrier	7
	Listening capacity	8
	The poor listener	9
	The semantics barrier	10
	The self-interest barrier	11
	The planning barrier	12
IV	CONCLUSION	13
V	BIBLIOGRAPHY	15

FIGURE 16.4
A sample of table of contents page for a report.

tions, combine sections, delete sections, or change their order. But the major purpose of the report must be kept uppermost in mind in making any changes, and only changes that improve the original form should be made.

Introduction and Summary

The person who receives your report wants to know immediately its main message and the specific parts that are of most interest to that person. The introduction-summary, which is the first part of the report, must give this information. It should explain what the report is about and summarize it, giving the purpose and major findings. From this, some readers may see that they need to read the entire report; others may find that they will need to read only specific sections.

```
                         INTRODUCTION


What is communication?

Communication, it has been said, is not a chapter in the book of

management; it is the whole book.  The ability to communicate

effectively is regarded as an essential skill for integrating

the company.


Communication is the transmission and interchange of facts, ideas,

feelings, and courses of action.  Mental or emotional concepts are

conveyed by means of symbols from one person to another, each being

compelled to think in terms of who says what, to whom, how, and with

what effect.  Good communication is the result of clear thinking.


A system of communication developed and maintained in a company

should keep employees informed.  Management can build attitudes,
```

FIGURE 16.5
An example of the first page of a report.

Sometimes, business firms ask for a synopsis of a report, and the introduction-summary can be used as the report synopsis. In other instances, a detailed letter of transmittal may be the first part of the report, and this letter may contain the essentials of the introduction-summary. If a synopsis or a detailed letter of transmittal containing major information introduces the report, it is not necessary to set out this basic information again in summarized form at the beginning of the report. You can then proceed directly to the next major section, the body of the report.

Most business reports are set out as presented in the foregoing paragraphs—that is, with some type of introduction-summary first, followed by details or the body of the report. Two other popular formats are these:

1. Introduction; body of report (details); summary

2. Introduction-summary; series of findings and recommendations

Figure 16.6 is an example of another type of report made by a management consultant. This report shows findings and recommendations.

The Body of the Report

The rough draft of your report, which was covered in an earlier section of this chapter, is, of course, the body of your report. After preparing the front pages of the report, set out this, the main part, always beginning on a new page. Figure 16.5 shows a typical first page for a report. The copy should begin at least two inches from the top of the page; frequently it starts in the middle of the page, as the example shows.

Documentation: Bibliography

The bibliography is a list of all materials used for reference in the report. The bibliography contains essentially the same information for each entry as is contained in the footnote, except that the last name of the author is listed before the first name or initials (for alphabetical listing), and page numbers are not listed. Bibliography entries are listed alphabetically by the name of the author. When there is more than one author for an

FIGURE 16.6
Sample page of findings and recommendations report format.

FINDINGS

It is essential to security of your computer that backup disks be maintained in a separate location. In reviewing your procedures, Mr. Steele reported that backup disks are being stored in the main vault and that backup documentation is also on file. This procedure is to be recommended; however, the surest approach is to allow no one employee access to both off-site and on-site files.

RECOMMENDATIONS

It is recommended that the duplicates being maintained by you be retained in the vault of the State Street Branch, rather than remaining on the premises. This would make certain that a serious catastrophe would not destroy both current copies and backup copies. It would also remove the possibility that one employee could destroy all copies.

FINDINGS

At the present time you have no formal contract arrangement with an outside firm to supply hardware (computer) backup in case of a serious breakdown.

RECOMMENDATIONS

Under the circumstances, it is recommended that the manager of your computer facility continue to make inquiries to insure that backup computer hardware would be available to you in the event of an extended breakdown.

---

entry, the authors after the first one are listed with first name or initials preceding last name. (See the first and fourth entries in the example following.) If no author's name is shown, the entry is listed alphabetically by the title. (See the second entry following.)

For longer bibliographies, entries can be separated under headings like *Books, Periodicals, Government Documents,* and *Unpublished Works.* For a shorter bibliography, all entries can be included in one listing.

Interviews, Print Bibliography. Following is an example of a print bibliography that includes books, periodicals, and a government pamphlet. The hanging-indent paragraph form used here is recommended for bibliographies, because the alphabetical heading can be located most easily.

Barzun, Jacques, and Henry F. Graff. *The Modern Researcher,* 3rd ed. New York: Harcourt Brace Jovanovich, 1977.

"Learning to Live With TV," *Time,* May 28, 1979.

McCullough, William J. *Hold Your Audience: The Way to Success in Public Speaking.* Englewood Cliffs, N.J.: Prentice-Hall, 1978.

Stine, Donna, and Donald Skarzenski. "Priorities for the Business Communication Classroom," *The Journal of Business Communication,* Spring 1979.

U.S. Federal Communications Commission. *Federal Communication Commission Rules and Regulations, Volume IV.* Washington, D.C.: U.S. Government Printing Office, March, 1977.

Zinsser, William. *On Writing Well.* New York: Harper & Row, 1976.

Interview Bibliography. A citation for a personal interview should show the name of the person interviewed, last name first; the type of interview (personal or telephone) and date:

Barrett, John C. Personal interview. August 14, 1990.

Personal interviews can be listed alphabetically with other sources. Or, if there are several interviews, all interviews can be set out together alphabetically under the heading "Interviews."

Report Cover

The cover can be an extremely important part of the report and, for business, should be prepared according to the value of the material inside. For some classroom assignments, no special report cover is required; for others, a special cover is requested. In business, much care and expense are spent in preparation of report covers to identify the report both for future use and for the detailed piece of work that it is. Report covers may be printed and/or embossed, with two- or four-color illustrations. Report covers should be designed to withstand wear.

Minor Parts of the Report

Minor parts not always included in a report are a list of illustrations, a letter of transmittal, miscellaneous items that might be placed in an appendix at the end, a glossary of terms, and an index.

List of Illustrations, Charts, or Graphs

A separate list of illustrations, charts, or graphs is included if several of these items are in the report. This list would immediately follow the table of contents.

Letter of Transmittal

A short letter of transmittal might be part of any report, even one prepared for credit as a classroom assignment, and would usually follow the table of contents or the list of illustrations, if there is one. The message of this letter is basically, "Here is the report I prepared." It might read:

Dear Dr. Albanese:

   Here is the report I prepared as partial fulfillment of requirements for Introduction to Business, Spring 19XX.

   I found the work very interesting, particularly charting the progress of my selected stocks.

Respectfully submitted,

Appendix

Most short reports do not have appendixes, but this section can hold detailed information considered useful but not essential to the basic study of the report. Here you would include a copy of a questionnaire used for a survey, or the full text of some materials that have been only highlighted in the report. In the body of the report, reference must be made to the fact that this information can be found in the appendix.

For example, business communications instructors suggested to me that certain miscellaneous information should be included in a textbook on this subject. It was felt that for study and reference, there should be a list of words commonly misspelled on the business scene with basic spelling rules, and that there should be an abbreviated list of common punctuation rules. These two items were believed to be helpful to the course, although they did not necessarily fit into the format of the text. A vocabulary for desktop publishing was needed for this editor. Therefore, these three items are Appendixes to this book.

Glossary of Terms

The glossary of terms is the last section of a report, with the exception of an index if there is one. If only a few technical terms are used in the report, they can be defined within the text of the report itself or with occasional footnotes. If there is a large number of terms that will not be easily understood by the readers of the report, these terms can all be defined in an alphabetized glossary.

Index

In an extremely long, detailed report, an alphabetical index might be prepared to assist readers in locating specific information. If there is an index, it is at the end of the report.

Order of Major and Minor Report Parts

For a long report, major and minor parts would be included in the following order:

1. Title page
2. Table of contents
3. Table of illustrations, charts, graphs
4. Letter of transmittal

5. Introduction-summary
6. Body of report
7. Bibliography
8. Appendix
9. Glossary of terms
10. Index

Desktop Publishing

A new power tool, desktop publishing, has entered every phase of business communication. This type of publishing is called "desktop" because the materials used can fit on the average desk. Printed material produced will appear the same as if it had been sent out to a print shop.

With the proper combination of software package, microcomputer and laser printer, professional printing can be produced within any office. Besides other work, your microcomputer can produce forms, letterheads, and one-page brochures as well as major reports and proposals. Printing costs are reduced enormously. For example, a report that formerly cost $3000 would cost about $300 produced in-house with desktop equipment.

Also, saving time can be important. A project that might previously have taken two weeks when farmed out to a printer can be completed within three or four days.

With your own desktop publishing you can

- choose varying layouts of pages with columns of different widths.
- combine different sizes and kinds of fonts (type styles) for text, headlines, etc.
- choose even or uneven right margins, or have certain sections even and other sections uneven.
- make layouts for master pages so that an overall style can be set automatically for all pages throughout a publication.
- edit the text during preparation.
- have on one page any combination of text, photos, diagrams or other graphics with explanatory text set in any type style. This information can be placed in any position on or near illustrations.
- use all combinations of the four basic colors (black, red, blue, yellow), to produce any tint for text or illustrations. They can be printed on any type of paper from inexpensive newsprint to more expensive glossy paper like that in many of the better magazines.
- save any page format for future use on other papers.

Competition for the widening desktop publishing market is heavy, and considerable study must be made in your selection of software. Decisions must be made about capabilities, adaptability, cost and ease of mastering software of any new machines purchased.

As in any other field, desktop publishing (DTP) brings us new terms and new usages of old terms. Appendix C provides a DTP vocabulary. Printers have used some of these terms for centuries. So with print shop work coming into offices, office workers will benefit from learning and using the old and the new.

WRITING PROPOSALS

Because of the complexity and high cost of work projects today, detailed written bid proposals are required for selling many products and services. Businesses, industries, government, and individual buyers are demanding that these proposals be written specifically according to their requirements.

There are two types of bid proposals, *unsolicited* and *solicited*.

Unsolicited Proposals

Unsolicited proposals can be handled like *sales letters* (Chapter 8) because you are trying to sell your product or service. According to the nature of what you are proposing, your presentation can be in the form of a detailed letter or a letter with various enclosures that give fuller information.

Enclosures can be photographs, charts, graphs, and so forth. Bold or soft color can be very effective when appropriate. If your proposal involves something that could be helped by including a sample (like selling an artificial grass installation), include the sample. "Hands on" experience can be effective in promoting sales.

The chief aims of your unsolicited proposals are (1) to get their *attention* (2) build up their *interest* in your proposed work and their *desire* to discuss it with you and (3) move them to *action,* that is, to get them to contact you.

If you do not receive a response, phoning or visiting the office could give you an opportunity to discuss the matter personally.

Solicited Proposals

Large organizations (and often smaller ones) will usually initiate **solicited proposals** by issuing a **request for proposal** (RFP). An RFP asks for bids from contractors for each project or each phase of a large project. Commercial, industrial, government and other big customers usually do not do their own research. Instead, they rely on bidders to be knowledgeable about fulfilling their needs for specific types of products and services.

Contracts obtained by successfully responding to such requests for proposals are almost always highly competitive. Therefore, the *proposal you prepare must show how you can satisfy their needs better than any competitor.*

The most important concern in writing a proposal is to follow all guidelines and regulations set out in the (request for proposal) RFP information kit available to bidders. Worthwhile proposals may be turned down if instructions are not followed to the letter.

Format of Proposals

A proposal usually has five parts: heading, introduction, customer's needs, proposed plan, your qualifications. In making your proposal, copy the format of the RFP, using the headings given there, and cover items in that order. Remember, this may be in a different order from a proposal you submitted for similar work for another organization.

Heading

Because an organization might have several requests for proposals circulating, at the top of the first page clearly identify the proposal request you are answering, such as:

A PROPOSAL IN RESPONSE TO RFP #GB-4-1234
TO PLAN AND INSTALL SECURITY PROCEDURES
FOR SKYLINE COMPUTER SYSTEMS

Introduction

While the introduction is the first major part of your proposal, you will probably benefit from writing it after you have completed the other sections. In the introduction you get the customer's attention by promising to satisfy their specified needs; also, you set out additional effective work you can do to benefit them. You should include a summary background of key personnel who will be doing the work. Further, promise that you or your representative will be available for any follow-up work on the project.

Customer's needs

Set out specifically from your own experience and observation what you see as the **customer's needs**, constantly referring to the RFP. Show that you have studied the situation thoroughly and understand how you can solve their problems. Tell of possible future problems related to the matter at hand and how to avoid or correct them. Avoid any discouraging attitude, but approach the work positively, displaying confidence. Showing that you have studied beyond specifications in the proposal will help give the customer the assurance that is wanted. It will also probably put you ahead of some competitors who do not include this factor.

Proposed Plan

The **proposed plan** is the heart of your proposal and this is the place to spend most of your time and talent. In your first drafts, set out the plan that you believe from the beginning to be most logical. Then, set out alternate plans that might be considered by you or your competitors. After studying all possible options, you are ready to choose solutions to make the plan you will offer.

Following the format of the RFP, set out by number exactly how you propose to complete the project. Numbering items helps make discussions with you, your workers and the customers clear.

Set up a reasonable time frame with a schedule for completing each phase of the operation. In stating the time expected for completion of the project, make clear whether it will be calendar days or working days. If your expected time varies from the time projected in the RFP, give clear reasons for the difference. It is best to schedule the number of working days needed for completion of each phase. Uncontrollable factors may cause work interruptions, such as natural disasters that might delay shipments of needed goods or might otherwise delay completion of work. Also, the customer might postpone inspection time, and you will be protected by saying how many working days will be needed for completion of each phase.

Your Qualifications

Here you show **your qualifications** that make your firm a better choice than your competitors.

Describe the type of work your firm performs and your facilities. If you will need to add to your present capacity, tell how it can be done efficiently and effectively. Show that you have thought through all possible developments. Name past and current projects of your firm so the customer can actually check your work, giving names, addresses and phone numbers of references.

Also, it is important that you identify and give background experience of key personnel who will be in charge of the project. Give as much detail as might be helpful. Make this an individual presentation for this customer, not a standard list that can be added to any proposal.

Copies of letters of appreciation from satisfied customers can be strong persuaders.

Summary

Make the entire proposal as attractive as possible. Use the best in-house printing facilities or contract with outside printers to give it a professional appearance. Give special attention to the cover, possibly setting out in vivid color an important diagram or illustration taken from the report. You must catch the attention of the reviewers.

The actual presentation of your proposal should be done in the best possible manner. Hand carry it to the top executive if possible and try to get an interview at that time. If you must mail it, be sure to follow up with a telephone call and see that it has reached the correct destination. Many proposals have been lost because papers were misfiled or delivered to the wrong person.

If you have not received a response within a reasonable time, make one or more follow-up personal or telephone calls. Don't delay these calls too long or a competitor may get ahead of you. As you know, many contracts are group decisions made by people with several different demanding interests. Showing your active interest in getting the contract can jog the memory of a customer. Besides being a reminder that you are ready and eager to do the job, sometimes you are reminding them that a particular job has to be done.

1. Write a library research report of approximately ten pages, completing the following steps:
   a. Select a topic of interest to you.
   b. Get topic approved.
   c. Conduct research in the library and through other reliable printed sources; also, possibly, interviews.
   d. Outline the report to determine order of presentation.
   e. Prepare a rough draft of the report.
   f. Make a final copy of the report.
   The report should contain:
   a. Title page
   b. Table of contents
   c. Report proper
   d. Footnotes—at least three
   e. Graphics (optional)
   f. Bibliography (at least three entries)
   Suggested report topics:
   A study of a career of interest to you.
   A study of an organization for which you might like to work.
   A study of some topic that has come up in class on which you think you would like to read further.
   A study of the life of a successful business leader, or a part of his or her life.

2. Prepare a shortened report format. This report writing assignment will give experience in the mechanical aspects of report preparation with very limited report research and writing. To complete this assignment, select a topic that would be of interest to you if you were writing a report. (For suggestions, see assignment 1.) Then follow these steps:

   a. Prepare a title page of the report.

   b. Prepare a table of contents. This should mainly be fabricated and not necessarily what the table of contents would be if you actually wrote the report. Make it sound logical.

   c. Prepare the first page of the report.

   d. From a magazine, take a xerographic copy of a selection of at least ten lines that might have been part of your report if you had written it in full. Paraphrase this selection—that is, write it in your own words. Turn in both copies as part of your minireport.

   e. Make a footnote reference for this material; also, make a footnote of a book reference and a government source.

   f. Make an alphabetized list of the footnotes in item *e* and prepare a bibliography of them. Use the hanging-indent style.

3. Give a ten minute oral summary of your report.

REVIEW AND DISCUSSION

Chapter 16 *Writing a Business Report or a Term Paper*

1. What is the first step in solving a problem?

_____

2. How can an outline be used in the completed report?

_____

_____

3. Name six different methods of setting out the major points of a report.

_____

_____

_____

_____

4. Which order of presentation is considered scientific reporting?

_____

_____

_____

5. Name the three most common forms of outlining materials. _____

_____

6. Why should you make a rough draft of any report? _____

_____

_____

7. Is it acceptable to give the writer's personal theories and prejudices in a report? Explain.

_____

_____

_____

Chapter 16 Writing a Business Report or a Term Paper (*Continued*)

8. How can you determine whether or not information you discover is relevant to your study and should be reported in it? _____

_____

9. What is plagiarism? _____

_____

10. Business reports today are becoming (more; less) formal.

11. Is it proper to give definitions of terms in a business report? Explain.

_____

_____

12. Why should you be consistent in the use of verb tenses in writing a report?

_____

_____

13. Why are graphics used in reports? _____

_____

14. Name the two types of documentation that are often used in reports.

_____

15. Give three uses for documentation. _____

_____

_____

16. What information is included in a footnote citing a book reference?

_____

_____

17. Name the six major parts of a report. _____

_____

_____

18. What are the advantages of placing a summary at the beginning of a business report?

_____

_____

19. A _____ or a _____ can be used as the introduction-summary.

20. Why is the cover of a report important? _____

_____

21. Name five minor report parts that might be included in any report. _____

_____

_____

Chapter 16   Writing a Business Report or a Term Paper (*Continued*)

22. What type of material might be included in a report appendix? _____
_____

_____

23. What is an RFP and how is it used?
_____

_____

_____

24. When drafting your plan to reply to an RFP, why is it helpful to number the items you propose? _____
_____

25. What two categories of information should be included under "Your Qualifications"?
_____

_____

APPENDIX A
Punctuation

Over a long period of time, the English language has slowly changed. Gradually it has gone from the Old English of the early Anglo-Saxons, through the Middle English of Chaucer during the 1400s, and on through the Early Modern English of Shakespeare's time in the 1600s. Continuing to accept gradual differences slowly over the years, today's Late Modern American English has shifted in many ways from the Early Modern English of Shakespeare's time.

Language authorities say that any grammar form used long enough by enough people eventually becomes standard. That is how changes have taken place over the centuries. You can see such acceptable changes in current respected magazines and newspapers. In our own usage, therefore, we should neither try stubbornly to stay with outdated forms nor lightheartedly adopt all modern innovations.

Today, there is a trend toward omitting some punctuation marks. For instance, leaving out unnecessary commas and hyphens. However, before we decide to follow any new, simplified punctuation style, we must first clearly understand why we use punctuation marks. Early written English did not have punctuation at all as stated in Chapter 4. The *Washington Post Deskbook on Style* says, "The primary purpose of punctuation is to clarify written expression. Tend toward open punctuation (fewer marks) if the meaning is clear."[1]

Use common sense in applying rules of punctuation. Also realize that the simpler usage—less punctuation—is the newer usage. The simpler usage of grammar is almost always preferred over an older style.

Here are a few punctuation rules that will answer many common questions on this subject. For additional information, consult *current* editions of the following: *The Modern Language Style Manual,* a grammar text, or an unabridged or desk-size dictionary that contains punctuation rules.

The Period

1. Use a period at the end of a sentence that is not a question or an exclamation.

2. Use a period after a polite request phrased as a question.

   Would you please send us the complete title of the book you requested.

[1] Robert A. Webb, *The Washington Post Deskbook on Style* (New York: McGraw-Hill, 1978), p. 122.

3. A good current standard-size dictionary will show whether or not you should use periods after abbreviations. If you cannot find an abbreviation listed alphabetically in the main word list, look for it in the special list of abbreviations in the front matter or end matter of the dictionary. Use periods with common abbreviations like these:

a.m.	M.D.
C.O.D.	M.P.
Dr.	Mr.
f.o.b.	Mrs.
ft.	Ms.
gr.	oz.
kilo.	Ph.D.

Commonly used abbreviations for government agencies, military services, and other well-known organizations generally do not have periods. When in doubt, consult a current dictionary for the preferred form.

AFL-CIO	NAACP
CIA	PTA
DAR	USN
FBI	USSR
FHA	VA

4. In a typed manuscript, abbreviations and initials of names do not have space between periods.

U.S.A.
p.m.
A.R. Russon

5. In a typed manuscript, there should be two spaces after a period at the end of a sentence.

The Comma

1. Use a comma before the conjunctions *and, or, nor, but, yet,* and *for* when they join the independent clauses of a compound sentence. Between most short clauses and between many long ones when the meaning is clear, omit the comma.

   We read the report he had made, and everyone approved what he said.
   They were waiting to hear the speech, but we were preparing for the next meeting.
   They arrived and we left immediately.

2. Omit a comma after a short introductory clause or phrase. Use a comma in this position for emphasis, or use a comma here if you would tend to pause at that point in speaking. Also, use the comma if it is needed to make the meaning clear.

   When they arrived we left.
   If you will cooperate with us, we can meet the deadline.
   Last night we received our final instructions.
   Eventually everything worked out all right.

Certainly, our office will cooperate.

As a matter of fact, several notices have been mailed.

If you hit, the umpire will be ready.

3. Use a comma to set off an introductory *yes* or *no*, mild exclamations, and words of direct address. Use a comma after a transitional adverb conjunction such as *however, anyway, nevertheless, therefore, later,* etc., if it is an interrupting element and if in speaking there would normally be a pause at that point.

Yes, they own the laundry.

Oh, I did not know they were in business.

Here, Jerry, is a current list of our customers.

Nevertheless, this is the Internal Revenue Service report.

The judge began to address the jury; therefore the room was quiet.

The attorneys remained calm; actually, they appeared unconcerned.

4. Use a comma to separate parts of dates and addresses.

The first manuscript was mailed on August 10, 1974, from my home.

He lived in a hotel at 19400 Collins Avenue, Miami Beach, Florida for three years.

5. Set off titles and appositives with commas.

I am writing to Dr. Olga Swenson, Dean of Admissions.

This is our chief comptroller, James P. Post.

6. Use a comma to separate words, phrases, and clauses in a series. Do not use a comma before the conjuction at the end of the series unless it is needed for clarity.

We had a choice of hamburgers, hot dogs or pizzas.

The memorandum was carried out this door, down the hall and into the mailroom.

If you outline your letter, draft a copy and then write the final form, you should have a good letter.

Use a comma before conjunctions when needed for clarity: pancakes, waffles, and bacon and eggs.

7. Use a comma to separate coordinate adjectives (adjectives of equal form) modifying the same noun. If you can substitute *and, or* or *nor* for the comma, the adjectives are coordinate.

Her window box holds lush, green, healthy plants.

Margaret has brown, bright, mischievous eyes.

Did you order beige, blue or yellow notepads?

Do not use a comma between noncoordinate adjectives.

Two ancient red clay pots were discovered in the ruins.

We studied the fine old English manuscript.

8. Use a comma or commas to set off nonrestrictive (nonessential) words, phrases or clauses from the rest of the sentence.

The tower, actually, was directly in front of us.

The letter, when it did arrive, was unimportant.

9. Use a comma to set off direct quotations from such expressions as *she said, he replied,* etc.

She said, "We will meet the printing deadline on schedule."

"We will be ready," he answered, "when we receive it."

Do not use a comma to introduce part of a quotation within a sentence.

Churchill is quoted as saying that "old words when short are best of all."

10. In a typed manuscript, a comma is followed by one space.

The Semicolon

1. Use a semicolon between two independent clauses not joined by a coordinating conjunction (*and, or, nor, but, yet,* or *for*).

   Mr. Clark's company is prospering today; he foresaw the current business problems.
   Most managers attended the convention; a few remained at home.

   Note: At the choice of the writer, a period could be used in place of this semicolon, capitalizing the next word for a new sentence. A semicolon is used to show a close relationship between the two thoughts expressed.

2. Use a semicolon to separate independent clauses joined only by conjunctive adverbs (*however, therefore, furthermore, nevertheless, consequently, also, then, moreover,* etc.) In such instances, at the writer's choice, the second clause could be written as a new sentence.

3. Use a semicolon to separate elements of a series when the elements themselves contain one or more commas.

   We went to Englewood Cliffs, New Jersey; Philadelphia, Pennsylvania; Wilmington, Delaware; and Baltimore, Maryland.

4. In a typed manuscript a semicolon is followed by one space.

APPENDIX B
Spelling Rules and Spelling Lists

Learning to Spell

Practice, practice, practice.

This is the best advice to follow if you wish to improve your spelling. As any text on business communication will tell you, in personal and career life you are often judged on how well you can spell. If you are not a good speller, you will certainly benefit from spending the time and effort needed to improve your spelling.

To improve your spelling, say and spell a problem word correctly; write it or type it ten times; look at the correctly spelled word and try to remember how it looks—commit it to visual memory. Above all, keep a dictionary handy for quick reference when you are not sure of the spelling of a word. Good software programs that check spelling are available for computer systems. (One woman executive tells that she is aware of her difficulty with spelling. However, she attributes part of her career success to carrying a small speller's dictionary in her purse or pocket.)

Most improved spelling is achieved by rote, memory—repetition, as just described. However, mastering a few basic spelling rules will help you with a high percentage of questionable spellings.

You may find the rules more helpful if you memorize the pattern of *one word* from each rule. Then apply the principle of spelling that word to the spelling of other words that fit the same rule.

Spelling Rules[1]

Rule 1: Adding a Prefix to a Basic Whole Word

Some long words can be broken into parts, leaving a basic whole word with a prefix. To spell such words correctly, simply add the prefix to the basic word.

book/keeping   mis/understanding
co/axial   re/affirm

[1]From Phyllis Davis Hemphill, *Career English: Skill Development for Better Communication* (Englewood Cliffs, N.J.: Prentice-Hall, Inc., 1980), p. 219ff.

dis/appoint	re/commend
dis/satisfaction	retro/active
extra/ordinary	un/announced
fore/closure	un/known
fore/going	un/necessary
il/legible	un/noticed
inter/state	with/draw
mis/spell	with/held

Rule 2: Words with *ie* or *ei*

I before *e*, except after *c*,
Or when sounded like *a*,
As in neighbor and weigh.

This old rhyme will help you with many words that have the *ie* or *ei* combination. Remember, as the rhyme says, most words with one of these combinations are spelled *ie*, such as these few examples:

achieve	grievance
alien	hosiery
belief	lien
believable	mischief
chief	niece
client	piece
clientele	proprietor
convenience	relief
friend	vacancies

Choose the combination *ei* generally "after *c,* or when sounded like *a*...."

ceiling	beige
conceit	chow mein
conceive	eight
deceit	freight
deceive	neighbor
perceive	sleigh
receipt	vein
receive	weigh
	weight

Exceptions

Memorize these common words that are exceptions to this rule:

either	neither
foreign	seize
height	their
leisure	weird

Some words have the *cie* combination as in *science:*

ancient	efficient
conscience	proficient
conscientious	science
deficient	scientific

Rule 3: Adding Suffix to a Word Ending with *y* Preceded by a Vowel

To add a suffix to a word ending with *y* preceded by a vowel (*a, e, i, o, u*), simply add the suffix to the base word without changing the *y:*

annoy	annoyed, annoying, annoys
attorney	attorneys
convey	conveyed, conveying, conveys
employ	employed, employer, employing, employs
holiday	holidays
journey	journeyed, journeying, journeys
portray	portrayed, portraying, portrays
survey	surveyed, surveying, surveys
valley	valleys

Rule 4: Adding Suffix to a Word Ending with *y* Preceded by a Consonant

To add a suffix to a word ending with *y* preceded by a consonant, generally change the *y* to *i* before adding any suffix except *ing.* The only two common words in the English language with two consecutive *i*'s are *Hawaii* and *skiing.*

accompany	accompanied, accompanies, accompanying
annuity	annuities
apply	applied, applies, application, applying
beneficiary	beneficiaries
busy	busily, business
casualty	casualties
copy	copied, copier, copies, copying
dictionary	dictionaries
discrepancy	discrepancies
necessary	necessarily
opportunity	opportunities
quantity	quantities
satisfy	satisfied, satisfies, satisfying
satisfactory	satisfactorily
vacancy	vacancies

Rule 5: Adding Suffix Beginning with a Vowel (*-ing, -ed, -en, -ance, -ally*)

To add a suffix beginning with a vowel to a word that ends with a single consonant preceded by a single vowel: If the word is of one syllable, double the final consonant.

One Syllable

bag	baggage
drop	dropped
fit	fitted, fitting
get	getting
hop	hopped, hopping
plan	planned, planning
stop	stopped, stopping
wrap	wrapped, wrapping

If the word is of more than one syllable and the accent is on the last syllable follow the same rule by doubling the final consonant.

Multisyllable

admit	ad·mit′tance, ad·mit′ted, ad·mit′ting
allot	al·lot′ted, al·lot′ting
begin	be·gin′ning
confer	con·ferred′, con·fer′ring (con′fer·ence)
control	con·trolled′, con·trol′ling
equip	e·quipped′, e·quip′ping
infer	in·ferred′, in·fer′ring (in′fer·ence)
occur	oc·curred′, oc·cur′rence, oc·cur′ring
omit	o·mit′ted, o·mit′ting
recur	re·curred′, re·cur′rence, re·cur′ring
refer	re·ferred′, re·fer′ring (ref′er·ence)
remit	re·mit′tance, re·mit′ted, re·mit′ting
transfer	trans·ferred′, trans·fer′ring

To add a suffix beginning with a vowel to a word ending with a single consonant preceded by a single vowel, do *not* double the final consonant when the accent is not on the last syllable.

confer	con′fer·ence
exhibit	ex·hib′it·ed, ex·hib′it·ing
infer	in′fer·ence
limit	lim′it·ed, lim′it·ing
profit	prof′it·able, prof′it·ed, prof′it·ing
refer	ref′er·ence

Exceptions

cancel	cancelled or canceled, cancelling or canceling
equal	equalled or equaled, equalling or equaling
travel	travelled or traveled, travelling or traveling

Rule 6: Adding Suffix to a Word That Ends with a Silent *e*

To add a suffix to a word that ends with a silent *e*, keep the *e* if the suffix begins with a consonant.

achieve/ment	hope/ful
approximate/ly	immediate/ly
comparative/ly	love/ly
definite/ly	manage/ment
disburse/ment	nine/teen
ease/ment	nine/ty
encourage/ment	require/ment
endorse/ment	sincere/ly
grate/ful	use/ful

To add a suffix to a word that ends with a silent *e*, drop the *e* if the suffix begins with a vowel.

argue	arguing
arrive	arrival, arriving
believe	believable, believing
collate	collating, collator
come	coming
compare	comparable, comparing
desire	desirable, desiring, desirous
duplicate	duplicating, duplicator
execute	executing, executive, executor
fascinate	fascinating
plane	planing
receive	receiving
write	writing

Exception: If a word ends with *ce* or *ge*, retain the *e* to soften the *c* or *g*.

changeable
chargeable
manageable
noticeable
serviceable

Spelling Lists

The following lists are chiefly compiled from the author's collection of words commonly misspelled on student papers and professional papers submitted for editing. They also come from miscellaneous sources of common spelling errors seen in business and other career writing.

Study 1	*Study 2*	*Study 3*	*Study 4*
1. abandoned	1. accustomed	1. allocate	1. affluent
2. accessible	2. acquaintance	2. allotted	2. agenda
3. accumulate	3. approximately	3. already	3. alien
4. assistance	4. beneficiary	4. apparatus	4. allies
5. beginning	5. calculator	5. beneficial	5. belligerent
6. believes	6. casualty	6. binary	6. committee
7. calendar	7. deficiency	7. concealment	7. congratulate
8. component	8. economical	8. conceive	8. dilapidated
9. concede	9. equitable	9. definitely	9. empathy
10. desirable	10. follow-up	10. effect	10. February
11. enthusiastic	11. grammar	11. excellent	11. flammable
12. envelope	12. inevitable	12. fascinating	12. galaxy
13. environment	13. infinite	13. grievance	13. forcible
14. familiar	14. initial	14. height	14. immediately
15. fiery	15. microcomputer	15. incidentally	15. liberation
16. foreword	16. necessary	16. leisure	16. license
17. handwritten	17. obvious	17. meticulous	17. memorandums
18. imminent	18. privilege	18. millionaire	18. miscellaneous
19. installation	19. requisition	19. nineteenth	19. occasionally
20. interpret	20. restaurant	20. ninety	20. quandary
21. knowledge	21. suitable	21. personnel	21. ramification
22. maintenance	22. trivial	22. pollution	22. satellite
23. personally	23. unforgettable	23. sabotage	23. television
24. ratification	24. whether	24. scarcity	24. undoubtedly
25. vacancies	25. vacuum	25. width	25. willful

Study 5	*Study 6*	*Study 7*	*Study 8*
1. abbreviation	1. accede	1. acceptable	1. accommodation
2. absenteeism	2. accidentally	2. altogether	2. adjustment
3. allowance	3. already	3. ambiguity	3. amateur
4. anonymous	4. aluminum	4. arbitration	4. amendment
5. basically	5. conscientious	5. automation	5. architect
6. census	6. conspicuous	6. believable	6. booster
7. collateral	7. depreciation	7. clientele	7. comparatively
8. disappear	8. embarrass	8. constitution	8. competitive
9. ecology	9. foreign	9. disappointed	9. discrepancy
10. eliminate	10. heretofore	10. executor	10. eminent
11. foreclosure	11. interoffice	11. flexible	11. electronic
12. foregoing	12. intrastate	12. independence	12. formally
13. grateful	13. librarian	13. innovation	13. interdependence
14. helpful	14. manager	14. nonessential	14. journeys
15. illegible	15. omitted	15. parallel	15. manifestation
16. incredible	16. paradoxical	16. precarious	16. morale
17. lien	17. polyester	17. precede	17. opposite
18. manageable	18. reaffirm	18. predominant	18. prerequisite
19. misspell	19. receive	19. recommend	19. proceed
20. occurred	20. seize	20. recommendation	20. rebellious
21. paid	21. seminar	21. separate	21. remunerate
22. pamphlet	22. temperament	22. serviceable	22. requirement
23. reference	23. unique	23. signature	23. similar
24. referred	24. vandalism	24. theory	24. studying
25. satisfactory	25. warranty	25. variable	25. weather

Study 9	Study 10	Study 11	Study 12
1. assembled	1. accompanied	1. appropriate	1. apparel
2. attorneys	2. announcement	2. arguing	2. applicable
3. bookkeeping	3. annuity	3. artificial	3. astronaut
4. conquer	4. antagonistic	4. brochure	4. attached
5. controlling	5. bankruptcy	5. coaxial	5. business
6. convenience	6. chaplain	6. collator	6. contingent
7. crisis	7. chargeable	7. dependent	7. continuous
8. dissatisfaction	8. endorsement	8. dictionary	8. defendant
9. exercise	9. energy	9. easement	9. disbursement
10. extraordinary	10. famous	10. fundamental	10. elementary
11. fuselage	11. hesitant	11. guarantee	11. ethical
12. itinerary	12. litigation	12. interference	12. exaggerate
13. mortgage	13. mathematics	13. invalidate	13. facsimile
14. optimism	14. parentheses	14. loose	14. gratuitous
15. partial	15. phenomenon	15. municipal	15. interrupt
16. prestige	16. processing	16. past due	16. manuscript
17. pursue	17. procrastinate	17. proprietor	17. opportunity
18. recurrence	18. replica	18. psychology	18. participant
19. recycle	19. souvenir	19. questionnaire	19. penalize
20. retroactive	20. statistics	20. reimburse	20. pressurized
21. reveal	21. supersede	21. reimbursement	21. reinforcement
22. succeed	22. surgeon	22. stationery	22. subpoena
23. sympathize	23. unpretentious	23. stewardesses	23. symbolic
24. synonymous	24. vehicle	24. transit	24. symmetrical
25. versus	25. withheld	25. verbatim	25. voluntary

Study 13	Study 14	Study 15
1. auctioneer	1. advice	1. administrative
2. awkward	2. allowed	2. assimilation
3. corporation	3. carefully	3. corroborate
4. existence	4. casualties	4. courageous
5. extemporaneous	5. creditor	5. eligible
6. flourishing	6. dining	6. excusable
7. interstate	7. disastrous	7. extension
8. jeopardize	8. fiscal	8. fortieth
9. lose	9. module	9. guarantee
10. manipulate	10. necessarily	10. itemize
11. mutually	11. official	11. notifying
12. noticeable	12. parliamentarian	12. nuclear
13. overdue	13. peculiar	13. outdated
14. prosecute	14. plaintiff	14. outmoded
15. quantity	15. publicly	15. overpopulation
16. retrieval	16. recent	16. perseverance
17. ridiculous	17. satisfactorily	17. psychological
18. sacrilegious	18. stationary	18. reciprocal
19. synthetic	19. tangible	19. rudiment
20. twentieth	20. thorough	20. voidable
21. utterance	21. underrated	21. Connecticut
22. vicinity	22. unnecessary	22. Hawaii
23. videotape	23. warehouse	23. Massachusetts
24. visible	24. writing	24. Mississippi
25. warrant	25. written	25. Pennsylvania

APPENDIX C
The Vocabulary of DTP

Desktop publishing is replete with jargon. Because it combines computer jargon and publishing jargon, the terminology of desktop publishing can be confusing—especially because those involved in desktop publishing don't always use publishing terms correctly. Vocabulary, however, very often holds the key to achieving the effect because knowing the word may be essential to employing the concept. The following terms are those used most often.[1]

ascender: The part of the character that extends above the x height of the font, as in the lowercase "b."

ASCII: American Standard Code for Information Interchange, the dominant communications protocol for exchanging data between computers. ASCII files usually contain text only without any special formatting.

artwork: Any material, such as drawings, paintings, or photographs, prepared as illustrations for printed matter.

baseline: The imaginary line that the characters rest on in a line of text. The distance from baseline to baseline is *linespacing.* Parts of characters that drop below the baseline are *descenders.*

bit-map: A method of depicting images as a matrix of black dots of the same density—shades of gray are achieved by having fewer dots in a given area.

bleed: The part of illustrations that extend to the edges of the page and are cut off when pages are trimmed for binding.

bold: Type that is heavier and thicker than the rest of the type contained on the page.

buffer: Memory in either a computer or laser printer used to store documents about to be printed.

camera-ready copy: Material in final form, ready to be photographed for offset printing or for duplication by photocopier.

caps and small caps: Two sizes of capital letters made in the same font.

clip art: Art work prepared by professionals ready for use in a variety of documents. Clip art for DTP applications is available as bit-mapped images on computer disk.

coated paper: Any paper with a smooth finish.

condensed: A typeface that is narrower in relation to its height than the standard form of that typeface.

continuous tone: An image containing a range or gradation of tones, such as in a photograph.

contrast: The gradation between shades in halftones.

copyfitting: Determining how much copy will fit in a given space, or adjusting copy through editing or formatting to fit a given space.

[1]This appendix is reprinted with permission from Joel P. Bowman and Debbie A. Renshaw, "Desktop Publishing: Things Gutenberg Never Taught You," *The Journal of Business Communication,* Winter, 1989, pp. 73–77.

crop: Cutting the edges of an illustration to fit a given space.

descender: A part of a character that descends below the baseline, as in the letter "y."

diacritic: Accent marks and other phonetic indicators, more common in European languages than in English.

display face: Any typeface appropriate for headlines. Usually 18 point or larger.

drop-outs: Parts of master copies that do not reproduce (sometimes inserted intentionally).

dummy: A rough layout of a page, document, or publication.

em: A unit of measurement equal to the point size of the current face.

em dash: A dash one em wide—used like a comma or a colon.

en: A unit of measurement equal to half an em.

en dash: Longer than a hyphen, but shorter than an em dash. Used for "through" or "to," as in 9:00–10:00 a.m.

expanded: A typeface that is wider in relation to its height compared with the standard form of that typeface.

flush: Aligned with a margin, without indentation—*flush right* or *flush left*.

folio: The number of each page or a sheet folded twice to make four pages.

font: One size, one style, of one typeface. For example, 10-point Times Roman, and 12-point Times italic are different fonts. Desktop publishing software and literature may use *font* to mean *typeface*.

footline: The bottom line of a page.

hairline: The thinnest rule the equipment being used is able to produce.

galley: Type set in column widths before the columns are made up into pages. Used for proofing and copyfitting.

gutter: The space near the spine (the left side of right pages, the right side of left pages) allowed for binding.

gray scale: A range of gray tones, from white to black.

grid: A design template that divides a page with imaginary horizontal and vertical lines as an aid to aligning type and placing graphic elements.

halftone: A *continuous tone* image composed of very small dots.

imposition: The layout of pages as they will be printed, considering any required folding and cutting.

initial: An opening character of a paragraph or section, often of larger type than that used in the body of the paragraph or section.

italic: A typeface variation in which letters slope forward. True italic typefaces are designed. DTP italic typefaces may be mathematical variations of the standard font of a typeface.

justification: Setting type so that both left and right margins are even.

kern: A part of a letter that extends beyond the body of a type, like the ends of the italic letters, *f* and *j*. The space occupied by such an extension.

kerning: The process of adjusting space between letters.

lasercrud: Poorly designed pages produced by amateurs with laser printers.

leader: A row of dots used to separate items in tables.

leading: Space (traditionally with strips of lead) added between lines of type to adjust linespacing.

linespacing: The distance from the baseline of one line to the baseline of the line below it.

measure: The width of a full line of type on a page.

monofont: A font in which all the characters occupy the same horizontal space regardless of the actual width of the letters. *Courier* is a common monofont.

opacity: A measure of how difficult it is to see through a piece of paper.

optical center: Approximately 1/3 below the top edge of a page.

ornaments: Decoration used in chapter headings.

orphan: A single line of type from the bottom of a paragraph appearing at the top of a column or page.

Page description language (PDL): A generic term used to describe the instructions computers use to communicate with a printer about the appearance of the document on paper.

pagination: Creating pages from text or graphics.

phototypesetter: A device that creates printmasters from camera-ready copy. Phototypesetters usually have print resolution greater than 1,000 dpi.

pica: A unit of measure equal to 1/6th of an inch or 12 points.

point: A unit of measure equal to 1/72nd of an inch.

Postscript: A page description language developed by Adobe Systems—currently the most commonly used PDL for DTP applications.

process colors: Yellow, Magenta, Cyan, and Black—the colors used in four-color separations.

proportional font: Any font in which the characters are not all the same width. Proportional fonts are usually easier to read than monofonts.

ragged: Unaligned type, as in *ragged right, ragged left.*

river: A line or channel of white space in printed matter caused by the spaces between words in several lines.

rule: A line. Can vary in width from *hairline* to a wide, dark bar.

running head: Repeating text at the top of successive pages—often a title or abbreviated title.

scaling: Reducing or enlarging an image or piece of paper.

scanner: A device used to read printed images (including text) and convert them to digital form so that they can be manipulated by computer.

screen: A fine mesh used to create *halftones.*

serifs: Small strokes at the ends of letters in many typefaces.

sexed quotes: Beginning and ending quotation marks that point toward each other instead of being the same—a mark of good DTP practice.

signature: A sheet of paper folded so that, when cut, it will produce a specific number of pages.

small caps: A set of capital letters the size of lowercase letters.

trim size: The final size of an entire page, including all margins, after trimming.

typeface: The general design of a group of characters. Examples include Courier, Helvetica, Times, Palatino, and so on. Typefaces are designed by artists, and the names of typefaces may be trademarked.

typefamily: A specific typeface and all its associated typestyles and fonts.

typestyle: An enhancement to a typeface, such as bold or italic typestyles.

widow: A line of type from the top of a paragraph left alone at the bottom of a column or page.

wrap: A section of text that runs around a graphic.

x-height: The height of lowercase characters, such as the x in a font, excluding ascenders and descenders.

INDEX